WESTERN WOMEN'S LIVES

A VOLUME IN THE
HISTORIANS OF THE
FRONTIER AND AMERICAN
WEST SERIES.

GENERAL EDITOR:
RICHARD W. ETULAIN

Gretchen Sammis, Chase Ranch, New Mexico.
© Barbara Van Cleve (c. 1997)

WESTERN WOMEN'S LIVES
continuity and change in the twentieth century

Edited by Sandra K. Schackel

University of New Mexico Press
Albuquerque

Library of Congress Cataloging-in-Publication Data

Western women's lives : continuity and change in the
twentieth century /
edited by Sandra K. Schackel.— 1st ed.
    p.   cm. — (Histories of the American frontier)
Includes bibliographical references.
ISBN 0-8263-2245-X (pbk. : alk. paper)
  1. Women—West (U.S.)—History—20th century.
  2. Women—West (U.S.)—Social conditions—20th century.
I. Schackel, Sandra. II. Series.
HQ1438.W45 W47 2003
305.4'0978'0904—dc21

2003010207

Printed and bound by Data Reproductions
Body text: Janson 10.5/13.6
Display text: Bank Gothic, Trade Gothic
Design and typography: Robyn Mundy

1   2   3   4   5

CONTENTS

CONTENTS (CONTINUED)

INTRODUCTION

Who is the twentieth-century western woman? She's not likely to be wearing a sunbonnet, walking behind a plow, or churning her own butter. Instead, you might find her in the cab of her air-conditioned John Deere, welding airplane parts together in a defense plant, or hawking merchandise on the streets of Los Angeles. These are some of the women whose stories you will find between the pages of this book. They are representative of the faces, and voices, of the twentieth-century American West and their stories are varied and rich. No single image, however, dominates the western story in the twentieth century as the "pioneer" woman did in the nineteenth century. Her image, of which the sunbonnet is deeply symbolic, is part of the powerful, gendered myth of the West embedded in American culture. Now, in the twenty-first century, we need to look beyond this familiar female image of the "old" West and recognize the women of the twentieth-century West, some of whom resemble their earlier sisters, some of whom are quite different. Their stories are both familiar and yet different as women have adapted to or resisted cultural and societal changes over the past one hundred years.

This anthology will introduce you to some of these western women and their experiences, many not readily recognized or acknowledged until recently. The collection includes sixteen articles, all previously published, that touch on some of the differences and continuities in western women's lives. Organized around five major themes—Politics and Power, Women and Mobility, Staying on the Land, Uncovering Women's Voices, and Reshaping Cultural Images and Ideas—*Western Women's Lives* illuminates the complexities of modern life that shape women's and men's beliefs, experiences, and expectations. The multi-discipline scholarship highlighted here is some of the most original and provocative work produced in the last decade. My only regret is that space would not permit a deeper examination into the vibrant research topics currently under way.

Two important anthologies on western women preceded this collection, both edited by Elizabeth Jameson and Susan Armitage.[1] In the fifteen years since *The Women's West* was published in 1987, historians of western women have worked hard to be more inclusive of the rich diversity of this region, "to see the western story from more than one perspective. . . ."[2] In their subsequent book, *Writing the Range*, published in 1997 by the University of Oklahoma Press, Armitage and Jameson have brought together an inspiring collection of materials that specifically focus on the lives of racial ethnic women whose histories are just beginning to find a wider audience. The editors acknowledge the difficulties inherent in this process of seeking to be inclusive; they urge us to look beyond the familiar paradigm of the white middle-class "pioneer" and remind us that the results are not only rewarding but important in the larger historical context. Uncovering and writing into history the stories of formerly unheard voices is an important process that can alter past beliefs and perceptions and require us to rethink and expand our understanding on many levels. I hope the book you are holding will trigger the same appreciation for the contributions included in this study of women's lives in the twentieth-century West.

The standard categories of gender, class, race, and ethnicity are only some of the lenses through which women's lives are revealed. Countless other categories and combinations can provide a deeper understanding of relations of power between groups as well, such as age, religion, sexual orientation, geography, and political preference, to name only a few. As Jameson and Armitage note, the boundless combinations of these and other perspectives on cultures, communities, and identities produce a richer but more complicated landscape.[3] In this light, the twentieth-century American West appears as a place of dynamic and diverse voices reflecting the progress and development of a once "nearly empty wilderness" into a teeming, progressive, and rich region.

Two major trends help explain the late development of research on the twentieth-century West. One is the tardy arrival of this region as a research field; the other is the recent growth of the field of women's history since the 1970s. In 1893, historian Frederick Jackson Turner defined the field and parameters of western history when he declared "the frontier closed."[4] His famous observation came to define western history well into the twentieth century. Understandably, scholars looked back at the eighteenth and nineteenth centuries for the subject matter of the western histories they were writing. Because of the emphasis on earlier centuries, the idea of a twentieth-century West as a field for research and publication did not take hold until well past the middle of the twentieth century. Then, as the twenty-first century loomed on the horizon, historians and others began to grapple with the changes wrought by World War II that continue to define the nation today, such as rapid technological change, postwar consumerism, awareness of environmental damage, increasing (again) immigration, continuing issues around racism, and the role of the larger global economy in western lives. As the chronological boundaries of western history have expanded, the twentieth century has become a valid and flourishing field for research and publication.

The second development grew out of the modern Civil Rights movement of the 1960s, a turbulent and conflicted decade. Many voices, including those of women and African Americans, Native Americans, Mexican Americans, Asian Americans, gay men, and lesbians began to protest their invisibility in the history and life of the dominant (white) culture. Seeking to learn about their past and to understand their "place" in the larger context of American life, female students on college and university campuses began to demand courses that included the study of gender and the contributions of women to the larger history of the world. Their activism led to the creation of women's studies departments at colleges and universities across the country. By the mid-1970s, hundreds of such departments had been established. At the same time, a virtual explosion of research and writing around women's issues triggered the publication of new journals, periodicals, and newsletters, and the proliferation of conferences and workshops on gender. In this exciting and invigorating period, the history of western women began to take shape.[5]

An important first step in this process was to construct a more inclusive western story, one that went beyond the narrow, mostly white male story of conquest and settlement to include the history of women, children, and families. Historians Joan Jensen and Darlis Miller were the first to ask researchers to "explore new possibilities for analysis" in an

important article in 1980.[6] They recognized that the lives of most
women were (and are) far more complex and multidimensional than
previous stereotypes allowed and far more ethnically diverse, as early
publications demonstrated. Overturning these limited images of women
brought together three main currents of scholarly tradition: women's
history, western history, and ethnic history.[7] Applying feminist perspectives and theories that use gender as a variable in understanding human
interactions, historians discovered new insights previously unnoticed,
unrecognized or unacknowledged in larger historical accounts.

American women's history, however, has been slow to include western women as part of the larger story, focusing instead on the Northeast
and national topics and only slowly branching out to include other
regions. This early "New England bias," based primarily on a white
middle-class construct, is now widely recognized although not always
acknowledged in current textbooks.[8] In addition, the story has been told
mostly in black and white terms, that is, the history of African American
women compared to white Euro-American women. Some of the richest work being done in the field now is about the rich mix of ethnic
women in the American West, one of the things that *Writing the Range*
does so well. Equally disappointing, eastern conference planners continue to ignore or minimize the history of their western sisters at the
largest United States conference on gender, the Berkshire Conference
on the History of Women, held every three years at a university east of
the Mississippi, indeed, often east of the Hudson!

So, not only historians in general but western historians as well
were slow in moving toward the inclusion of women in traditional western history. Reflecting the work of Turner, who saw the West in masculine terms, western historians did not concern themselves with
women's lives beyond the limited stereotypes of sunbonneted help-
mates, pioneer drudges, Indian princesses and squaws, and soiled
doves.[9] Since the 1980s, however, the "new western historians" have
expanded the field of inquiry, asking new questions, introducing new
topics, and generally broadening their accounts to include analyses of
gender, class, race, and ethnicity.[10] More directly, the New Western
History challenges how the West was—and is—viewed in terms of land,
space, people, culture, economic development, and political characteristics. Where once the West, even America, was seen as "exceptional,"
new western historians have challenged this view of exceptionalism to

ask what, if anything, makes the West unique?[11]

We might ask the same question about western women. How do we define a western woman? What makes her "western"? Is there some formula that creates a uniquely western woman (or man)? Must she be born in the West? Or does she have to live west of the Mississippi (or Missouri) a prescribed number of years to qualify as a western woman? Can she be a recent immigrant to the region? What about a migrant worker who, with her family, moves around the West following the agricultural seasons? Historian Glenda Riley suggests that the category western woman, which usually refers to white, middle-class, English-speaking women, has been subsumed under far more inclusive headings such as racial, ethnic, employed, lesbian, urban, rural, and twentieth-century western women, to suggest a few identifiers.[12] Perhaps the label "westerner" is more a matter of attitude than any one specific trait. Or perhaps it is something intangible, an identity with the West through some personal "alchemy" or "affinity to place and people. . . ."[13] The category of western woman best serves as shorthand for that most generalized of creatures, a female who lives in the western region of the United States.

We might ask as well, are the issues different for women who live in the American West? Like women elsewhere, the lives of western women revolved around family and work, much as they did in the nineteenth century. Because historians make it their business to look for patterns or themes over time, we can see that as the nation has become more urban, so have women living in the West. They often spend their days in wage labor in small communities or large cities. They face the double burden of balancing a job or career with family demands that surface when they return home. Issues around childcare consume their thoughts as well as their paychecks. These tasks are not unique to westerners but affect women in New England, the Midwest, or the deep South as well. The value of learning the western stories, however, provides a comparative approach that cannot be made until we know those stories. This anthology can help us reflect on the regional differences and/or similarities and point to the changes as well as the continuities that have shaped life for women in the West during the past century.[14]

The third stimulus to the growth of the field occurred in ethnic studies and the realization that the American West is one of the most diverse regions in the nation. Elizabeth Jameson has calculated that

between 1860 and 1900, one-fourth to one-third of the western population was foreign-born, a higher proportion than in any other region
of the United States.[15] The confluence of many cultures and races in
this region makes the West a rich field for studying diversity.[16] The
Euro-American presence is only one of many, though their history has
dominated "mainstream" history texts. In fact, Native Americans and
Spanish and Mexican settlers predate the appearance of Anglo peoples
by hundreds of years. By the nineteenth century, Chinese and Japanese
immigrants arrived and were joined by African Americans and an
increasingly complex mix of Euro-Americans. Also, to assume that this
latter group is homogeneous does an injustice to the ethnic diversity of
these peoples as well.[17] When race, ethnicity, class, gender, religion, age,
and countless other factors are added to the racial mix, the "face" of the
West becomes increasingly lined with complexity.

    This anthology touches on some of this richness. The collection is
arranged around themes that shaped the lives of women in the nineteenth century and continued to influence our lives in the twentieth
century. The three essays in the first section are reprinted from a special issue of the *Pacific Historical Review* of November 1992, "Western
Women's History Revisited." Twelve years after Jensen and Miller's call
in 1980 to develop a more inclusive or multicultural history, these essays
assess the progress historians have made toward that goal. One key
component has been to develop the theoretical base for the field, to
provide the scholarly and professional underpinnings of western
women's history. With that in mind, the authors in this section, Karen
Anderson, Antonia Castañeda, and Virginia Scharff, tackle some of the
most difficult issues in history, writing about power and politics within
the framework of multicultural history. As Jensen and Miller reaffirm
in their "Afterword," we need a theoretical framework that comes from
the experiences of racial and ethnic women themselves, not an Anglo-
centered theory imposed upon them.[18] Let them speak and let us read
the record in their words.

    The movement of women into and around the West is the theme
of the second section. The articles here focus on African American,
Chinese American, and Latina women as part of successive waves of
immigrants seeking to become wage laborers in the western United
States. Paul Spickard writes about the "overland" migration of thousands of African Americans to southern California during World War

II by bus, train, and automobile. They came alone and with families, their bags filled with hope for finding their share of the "California dream." Plentiful wartime jobs also drew Chinese American women into the labor market in the San Francisco Bay area, according to Xiaojian Zhao in the second article. She found that defense work marked a significant turning point for the Chinese American community, who finally began to feel accepted by the larger culture for the first time since their ancestors had begun to emigrate to this country a century earlier. And finally, Norma Chinchilla and Nora Hamilton address a current issue among immigrants, that of the many Latina women and their children who cope with, renegotiate, and redefine urban space, both public and private, in Los Angeles. Together, these articles remind us of the continuity of women's migration and immigration to the western region of America in both the nineteenth and twentieth centuries.

The third section is composed of articles that demonstrate some of the similarities as well as the changes in agricultural women's lives. Sherry Smith shows how the familiar nineteenth-century practice of homesteading spilled over into the twentieth century using the case of Elinore Pruitt Stewart, a single woman when she filed her homestead claim in April 1909. When Pruitt married her employer Clyde Stewart one week later, family cooperation and strategy trumped classic western individualism. In my article on ranch and farm women later in the century, I found that family cooperation was, and is, at a premium on an agricultural operation although in a different way. With the rapid growth of agribusiness in the post–World War II era, small- to medium-sized family farms cannot survive unless the wife, and sometimes both husband and wife, take off-farm jobs to supplement farm income. Finally, the last piece in this section takes a different form, one of very moving verse. Written by the grandmother of the contributor, Carol Wolfe Konek, Goldie Keltner Ford's story reaffirms the hardships, the endless repetition of worry and work, and the never-ending arrival of babies along with the seasons. A loving mother's biography of her husband and children, Ford's words reflect themes that permeate this section overall, the importance of the land and it's role in the growth and well being of western families.

The fourth section of the anthology focuses on an important and increasingly popular form of writing, the memoir and memory work. In "Uncovering Women's voices," the authors use oral history interviews to expand and deepen women's stories. In the first article, Emily Honig revisits and rereads oral histories she first collected in the late 1970s of women strikers at the Farah Manufacturing plant in El Paso, Texas. Returning to those histories in the 1990s, she hears the women give voice and power to their stories in ways that she hadn't recognized twenty years earlier. The second author, Dolores Delgado Bernal, uses oral history as an important source for recovering the stories of minority women, in this case the voices of Chicana women involved in the 1968 East Los Angeles School Blowouts. Previously reported from the male perspective, widening the gender lens to include women's stories revealed the roles that local women also played in community activism at the time. In the third piece in this section, sociologists Debra A. Castillo, María Gudelia Rangel Gómez, and Bonnie Delgado explore "border life," the intersections of class and race in the social construction of prostitution in Tijuana, Mexico. The trio has interviewed over two hundred sex workers at their workplaces over the past fifteen years, exploring "both its [prostitution's] dominant stereotypes and its unruly margins." Their intriguing article provides yet another demonstration of the value of memory work in writing women's histories.

In the fifth and final section, we explore the reshaping of cultural images and ideas that permeate western, and American, culture. The four authors here describe the ways in which western women create their identities, from creating public space in which to make and sell beer in Prohibition-era Butte, to the role a Navajo woman's weavings played in the construction of cross-cultural commerce in early twenti-eth-century New Mexico, to Japanese-American women torn between their parents' old-world culture and the siren songs of American pop-ular culture, to the role the Miss Chinatown U.S.A. Beauty Pageant plays in the reidentification of the Chinese American community in San Francisco. Using ethnically rich Butte as her research site, Mary Murphy discovered a certain irony in Prohibition's laws in which women discovered economic opportunities in liquor production, dis-tribution, and consumption. Visiting speakeasies and drinking in public places allowed women to redefine the boundaries of acceptable female behavior. In a second example of gender and cultural conflict, young, second-generation Japanese Americans, the Nisei, turn to popular advice columns to seek advice on love and marriage, American style. In this article, Valerie Matsumoto used the Japanese language press to examine the gender role and cultural shifts already in motion in prewar San Francisco. And finally, Judy Tzu-Chun Wu examines the development of ethnic and gender identity created through the yearly reenactment of the Miss Chinatown U.S.A. beauty pageants of the 1950s through the 1970s. More than a forum for the display of the female form and accompanying talent, the controversial pageants were important in creating idealized versions of womanhood that are reflective of broader issues around power and culture.

Western Women's Lives is intended to be representative of the gendered face of western history in the past century. In making my selections, I found a richness in the availability of published pieces not possible twenty years ago. The articles gathered here are a testament to the strength and vitality of the field, and still there is room for expansion and inclusion. Also notable is the broader disciplinary tone of recent research, across the fields of sociology, anthropology, criminal justice, political science, and geography as well as the arts and sciences in general. The most dramatic and important development, however, has been writers' commitment to using the variables of gender, class, race, etnicity, sexual orientation, political preferences, and other markers of individual and group experiences to provide a more inclusive regional history. In doing so, even this limited collection demonstrates that both continuity and change have marked women's twentieth-century lives; there is no reason to think the future will be any different. Twentieth-century western women have stories to tell; let us hear them here.

Notes

1. Susan Armitage and Elizabeth Jameson, eds., *The Women's West* (Norman: University of Oklahoma Press, 1987). The articles collected here are based on papers presented at the Women's West Conference held in Sun Valley, Idaho, in August 1983, the first national conference devoted to western women's history. The same editors published *Writing the Range: Race, Class, and Culture in the Women's West* (Norman: University of Oklahoma Press, 1987). This collection is one of the most exciting and inclusive collections of writings on western women to date. Armitage and Jameson have succeeded in moving beyond "the limited perspectives of the urban East, of public politics and power, of white Americans, and of men" (3). Their collection of twenty-nine articles and six selected bibliographies highlights the diverse cultures, genders, and races of the region.

2. See Charles Rankin's comments in "Historical Commentary: The History of Women in the West: A Search for Understanding Amid Diversity," in *Montana the Magazine of Western History* 41 (spring 1991): 57–73. This section contains four insightful essays by scholars of western women's history: Sarah Deutsch, Virginia Scharff, Glenda Riley, and John Mack Faragher.

3. See the editors' introduction to *Writing the Range*.

4. Frederick Jackson Turner, "The Significance of the Frontier in American History," *Proceedings of the Forty-First Annual Meeting of the State Historical Society of Wisconsin* (Madison, Wisc.: 1884): 79–112.

5. Sandra Schackel, "Becoming Visible: Women in American History," *Idaho Yesterdays* 41 (fall 1997): 4–9. Also see the Preface to the third edition of Nancy Woloch, *Women and the American Experience* (Boston: McGraw-Hill Companies, 2000).

6. Joan Jensen and Darlis Miller, "The Gentle Tamers Revisited: New Approaches to the History of Women in the American West," *Pacific Historical Review* 49 (May 1980): 173–213.

7. See Elizabeth Jameson, "Toward A Multicultural History of Women in the Western United States," *Signs: Journal of Women in Culture and Society* 13 (summer 1988): 761–91.

8. Glenda Riley, "Twentieth-Century Western Women: Research Issues and Possibilities," in *Researching Western History: Topics in the Twentieth Century*, eds. Gerald D. Nash and Richard W. Etulain (Albuquerque: University of New Mexico Press, 1997), 119–46.

9. Two of the earliest studies of western women focused on the degree to which frontier life increased or altered options for nineteenth-century Euro-American pioneers. See Sandra Myres, *Westering Women and the Frontier Experience, 1899–1915* (Albuquerque: University of New Mexico Press, 1982); and Julie Roy Jeffrey, *Frontier Women: The Trans-Mississippi West, 1840–1880* (New York: Hill & Wang, 1979). In 1998, Hill & Wang published a revised edition of Jeffrey's work entitled *Frontier Women: "Civilizing" the West? 1840–1880* in which she revised and expanded her earlier ideas and broadened her discussion of racial ethnic women.

10. For insights into the "new western history," see the following works: Patricia Nelson Limerick, *Legacy of Conquest: The Unbroken Past of the American West* (New York: W. W. Norton & Company, 1987); Richard White, *"It's Your Misfortune and None of My Own": A New History of the American West* (Norman: University of Oklahoma Press, 1991); Donald Worster, *Rivers of Empire: Water, Aridity, and the*

Growth of the American West (New York: Pantheon, 1986); and William Cronon, *Nature's Metropolis: Chicago and the Great West* (Chicago: W. W. Norton & Company, 1991).

11. For a well-reasoned discussion of exceptionalism, see David M. Wrobel, *The End of American Exceptionalism: Frontier Anxiety from the Old West to the New Deal* (Lawrence: University Press of Kansas, 1993).

12. Riley, "Twentieth-Century Western Women," 124. Riley's footnotes are a goldmine of possibilities for the twentieth-century researcher and suggest that historians have laid a solid foundation for building "the rest of the story[ies]."

13. Elizabeth Hampsten's words (in quote marks) from the introduction to Lillian Schlissel and Catherine Lavender, eds., *The Western Women's Reader* (New York: HarperPerennial, 2000), xvii.

14. For more insight on life in rural communities in the West, see Paula Nelson, "Rural Life and Social Change in the Modern West," in *The Rural West Since World War II*, ed. R. Douglas Hurt (Lawrence: University Press of Kansas, 1997), 38–57.

15. Jameson, "Toward a Multicultural History," 788.

16. Vicki L. Ruiz and Ellen Carol DuBois, eds., *Unequal Sisters: A Multicultural Reader in U.S. Women's History* 2d. ed. (New York: Routledge, 1994). See also Richard White, "Western History," in *The New American History*, ed. Eric Foner (Philadelphia: Temple University Press, 1997), 203–30.

17. See Frederick Luebke's remarks, "Whose West? Whose History?" in *Journal of the West* 37 (January 1998): 3–4, a special issue on women of the West. Although Luebke points out that "European immigrants are the forgotten people of the American West," the issue itself continues to focus on white Euro-American women with the exception of an article on Sacagawea.

18. Jensen and Miller, "Afterword," *Pacific Historical Review* 61 (November 1992): 598.

PART 1: POLITICS AND POWER
WRITING THEORY TO PRACTICE

INTRODUCTION

Politics and Power
Theorizing Western History

The field of western women's history is a young one, birthed by two wise "midwives," Joan Jensen and Darlis Miller, in 1980. Their article, "The Gentle Tamers Revisited: New Approaches to the History of Women in the American West," served notice to historians and others that the history of western women had yet to be written.[1] More importantly, their history had yet to be interpreted and incorporated into the larger historiographical context of the American West. Following the model used in the broader field of women's history, the authors suggested new possibilities of analysis, one of which was studies based on a comparative multicultural approach. Recognizing the West as a region rich in ethnic and racial diversity, the call to a more inclusive western history meant broadening the previous focus of settlement based on and seen through the eyes of Euro-American male settlers. The authors also called for oral histories, interdisciplinary approaches, and the case-study model to continue to provide valuable insights about western women. Their seminal piece has guided a generation of western scholars to search out and explore the richness so present in western American history.

Eight years later, Elizabeth Jameson, in "Toward a Multicultural History of Women in the Western United States," acknowledged the scholarship the Jensen/Miller article triggered in redefining the West as a multicultural region, a place where communities intersect. Jameson noted that this focus has expanded our understanding of the historical presence of people in the West across time and cultures. On the issue of theory and framework, she suggested "asking more complicated questions about role adaptation, change, and diversity" that promise "new frameworks yet to come."[2]

As scholars widened their historical nets, it became clear that the "standard approach," the study of the nineteenth-century Euro-American westward movement, would not do for either that era or the twentieth century. Difference, not uniformity, marked the lives of western women. Historians of women of color made clear their intention to move the experiences of multicultural women from "margin to center."[3] That they have made great strides in shifting the paradigm of the biracial model to one more inclusive of race and ethnicity is made clear in the 1997 publication of *Writing the Range*, a rich collection of articles edited by Susan Armitage and Elizabeth Jameson.[4] As they rightly note, the earlier white pioneer approach is insufficient to hold all the diversity, all the perspectives possible in western history. The editors call for a series of conversations rather than a monologue in order to hear these voices clearly and to do justice to the dynamic interplay of actions between westerners.[5] The search for theory needs to be inclusive yet able to recognize individual identities and the agency of those formerly on the margins as well.

Still another new approach has emerged in the field of immigration studies. Historians and sociologists have created a new paradigm that has moved away from the classical assimilation model, which assumes a linear progression from Old World traits toward the "melting pot" of assimilation.[6] Structural factors such as regional economies and occupational groupings appear to lend a clearer understanding of just how people connect and adapt to their locations. When we apply such a framework to the West—and look beyond the individual success stories of the mostly white males—we find a web of connections among groups. Instead of individuals assimilating or achieving, we find group strategies and networks. And in those groups, women are helping to build "bridges across the conceptual territories of race, class and gender."[7]

Three authors in the first section of this collection address such new frameworks. Karen Anderson reminds us that we need theory as an organizing concept to understand women's lives and change over time, especially in the field of women's labor history. She discusses several feminist theories, notes the tensions between them and reminds us that taken together, they enlarge our understanding of women's lives. Antonia Castañeda's article is a two-part essay that examines the historiography published both before and after the Jensen/Miller article and how the writing has been described, theorized, and interpreted in recent historical literature. She specifically urges historians to move beyond the white middle-class version of western history to create a more inclusive synthesis that incorporates women of color. And in the third essay, Virginia Scharff urges an expansion and redefinition of political history that would value women's activities, recognize differences among women, and include the experiences of all women. The multiracial character of the American West remains a rich site for the study and construction of a theory or theories sensitive to the variables of race, ethnicity, class, and gender. These authors have contributed important ideas toward the attainment of this goal.

NOTES

1. Joan M. Jensen and Darlis A. Miller, "The Gentle Tamers Revisited: New Approaches to the History of Women in the American West," *Pacific Historical Review* 49 (May 1980): 173–213.
2. Elizabeth Jameson, "Toward a Multicultural History of Women in the Western United States," *Signs* 13 (summer 1988): 761–91.
3. The phrase "from margin to center" is from bell hooks's work, *Feminist Theory: From Margin to Center* (Boston: South End Press, 1984). See Marian Perales's article in *Writing the Range* that builds on this theme by examining wider challenges to racial bias in U.S. women's history.
4. Elizabeth Jameson and Susan Armitage, eds., *Writing the Range: Race, Class, and Culture in the Women's West* (Norman: University of Oklahoma Press, 1997).
5. Ibid., 5.
6. See the introduction to Virginia Yans-McLaughlin, ed., *Immigration Reconsidered: History, Sociology, and Politics* (New York: Oxford University Press, 1990).
7. Vicki L. Ruiz and Ellen Carol DuBois, eds., *Unequal Sisters: A Multicultural Reader in U.S. Women's History*, 2nd. ed. (New York: Routledge, 1994).

WORK, GENDER, AND POWER IN THE AMERICAN WEST*

Karen Anderson

What do a Kansas farmwoman, a Chicana cannery worker, and a mining camp prostitute have in common? Among other things, they are all women workers in the area that historians have defined as the American West. Despite their apparent differences, they all worked in cultures that expected women to bear and care for children; to cook, keep house, and provide clothing for their families; and to provide sexual intimacy for men and emotional support for kin and community.

At the same time, their differences remind us that there are many histories to write about women workers in the U.S. West (or North or South or East), as Joan Jensen and Darlis Miller reminded us in their prize-winning essay.[1] How then do we go about telling their stories? How do we understand their commonalities and their differences?

As Miller and Jensen pointed out in 1980, "what is most needed is a picture of how women fit into the economic structure in the West through their labor."[2] In addition, it is important to examine women's roles in creating economic and cultural systems in order to suggest the ways in which western economic structures are different as a result of women's activities. Developing a framework for this picture entails three related tasks: 1) a consideration of those developments in feminist

---

*This chapter was previously published as: Anderson, Karen. "Work, Gender, and Power in the American West." In *Pacific Historical Review* 61 (November 1992): 481–99.

theory that might inform our understandings of this question, 2) entering into the discussions animating women's labor history, and 3) investigating the importance of region in constructing women's work experiences. This essay will focus primarily on the first of these tasks, while offering tentative observations regarding aspects of the others.

Feminist Theories and the History of Women and Work

In recent years, historians have begun to examine the utility of cross-disciplinary analytic frameworks for historical inquiry. The mere introduction of the issue of theory, however, can raise the hackles of historians. Joan Scott has suggested that there is a tension between history and theory: the former is dedicated to the study of specific events in the context of a particular time and place, the latter to large generalizations about social and cultural processes.[3]

At the same time, historical narratives and the very "facts" they invoke to support those narratives are theory-laden. They contain assumptions about historical significance, about the selection and interpretation of evidence and, more fundamentally, about how human societies and cultures operate. A theoretical approach enables those assumptions to be made more explicit so that readers may have guideposts and so that scholarly discussions about the connections among frameworks, methods, and interpretations in history may be advanced. The often-encoded debates regarding the "old" western versus the "new" western history make this a propitious time to begin a more open discussion of the assumptions that ground work in the field.

Within women's and labor history, discussions regarding the utility of various Marxist, feminist, and poststructuralist theories have become quite heated. The extensive discussion of theory that follows represents an attempt to make some sense of these discussions and to offer tentative suggestions for their use in the history of women and work. At a minimum, such theories would have to explain the connections between gender and other systems of inequality and to explore the ways in which gender inequality is constructed, reproduced, and undermined.

Many feminist theories have taken gender divisions of labor as a departure point for their analysis of the workings of gender in human societies. In the 1970s, commonalities in the assignment of tasks, authority, and prestige across cultures drew particular attention and prompted theoretical speculations regarding the origins and dynamics of gender systems. Scholars like Michelle Rosaldo, Sherry Ortner, and others focused on the virtually universal assignment of childrearing and domestic work to women and the equally common association of politics and war with men, concluding that such patterns reflected and reproduced deep structural dynamics.[4]

Moreover, they concluded that these dynamics entailed the derogation of women and their exclusion from formal authority in their cultures. According to Rosaldo, "Women may be important, powerful, and influential, but it seems that, relative to men of their age and social status, women everywhere lack generally recognized and culturally valued authority." Rosaldo concluded that this cultural and political subordination derived from the gender division of labor between women's domestic and men's public activities. In the economy, women's work is more private and particularistic, with the fruits of their labor intended for their kin groups or households. Men's work, by contrast, occurs in a public setting and requires an elaborate system "of norms, ideals, and standards of evaluation" that constitute the interfamilial social order.[5]

Nancy Chodorow contributed the most important theoretical framework for interpreting these patterns and understanding their relationship to the oppression of women. According to Chodorow, women's responsibility for mothering infants and small children has profound effects on personality formation in women and men. In order to establish a masculine identity in a world in which relations to fathers and to the world of masculine activities are distant, boys must deny their identification with and much of their emotional connection to their mothers. Throughout their lives, masculine identity is constructed negatively (as not feminine) and precariously. According to Chodorow, boys' need to individuate from their mothers necessarily entails fear of women's authority and the derogation of women and the tasks they perform.[6]

Women, by contrast, develop a more secure gender identity because they grow up in an environment where women's roles are integrated into their daily experiences and are therefore apprehensible to them and where their identification with their same gender parent is encouraged. Their socialization is characterized by continuity and by personalized and intimate connections to others. Because they have so little emotional (and cultural) support of individuation, women's primary developmental problem is the achievement of an autonomous identity. The gender division of childbearing labor, therefore, constructs and reproduces women's subordinate position in human societies.[7]

Subsequently, feminist scholars have questioned whether the gender division of labor and authority assumed by Chodorow and others is actually universal and have shifted the analytic attention to differences in gender systems across cultures, social groups, and time. Indeed, they have noted the degree to which the family pattern on which her analysis depends—one in which women give intense attention to a small number of children while men remain distant and relatively uninvolved in child socialization—characterizes middle-class families in mature industrial societies rather than all family systems. In addition, feminist scholars have offered different perspectives on the relationship between economic systems and women's status, roles, and power than that advanced by Rosaldo and others.[8]

In the process, they have shifted the emphasis from psychic structures to social structures and cultural processes. Within anthropology, scholars have examined the effects of different family structures on women's access to property and power, while others have contended that relationships between prestige systems and gender relations are more complex and varied than those posited by Chodorow, Sherry Ortner, and others. Scholars of racial/ethnic women have pointed to the multiplicities of women's experiences and the importance of class and race in constructing the meanings of womanhood. Taken together, these works bring into question the assumption that structuralist explanations positing one source for gender inequality adequately reflect the complexity of gender relations and their connections to other social and cultural dynamics.[9]

In recent years, scholars have questioned the utility of assuming that sharply separated public and private spheres organized men's and women's work roles or otherwise defined the relationship between economic arrangements and gender relations. Some have focused on the connections between women's unpaid work and economic structures; others have noted the various ways in which gender relations shaped everything from the dynamics of proletarianization to the ideologies and strategies of workers and managers.[10]

Although Jensen and Miller noted the absence of Marxist frameworks for interpreting western economic development, such works are
now beginning to appear in western history and have occupied a central place in Chicana history and women's labor history from the beginning. In the latter fields, they have offered some of the most important
interpretations of the connections between gender and class relations.
Moreover, Marxist scholarship has been especially important in
attempts to theorize the historical construction of racial inequalities in
the West and elsewhere.[11]

Few scholars, however, have attempted integrated analyses of the
connections among race, class, and gender hierarchies. Among the
exceptions is Karen Sacks. Using Marxist frameworks, she has offered
a "unified understanding . . . of how racial, class, and gender oppression are part of a single, specifiable, and historically created system."
According to Sacks, economic structures and the gender division of
labor in racial-ethnic cultures determine which workers are "expendable" and, thus, available for proletarianization. The dialectical relationship of this process with capital's search for cheap labor "has been
a major contributor to racial/ethnic segregation of working-class communities and racial/ethnic and sex segregation."[12]

One of the strengths of Sacks's analysis is that it reconceptualizes
class in the light of her thinking on race and gender. Rather than define
class status in terms of an individual's relationship to the mode of production, Sacks concludes that to be working class is to have "membership in a community that is dependent upon wage labor, but that is
unable to subsist or reproduce by such labor alone."[13]

Moreover, Sacks concludes that "not only is class experienced in
historically specific ways, but it is also experienced in racially specific,
gender-specific, and kinship-specific ways." These different experiences
in the working class produce various forms of political consciousness
and activism, all defined as forms of working-class consciousness.
Under her model, however, gender and race are, to a great extent, constructed and reproduced by capitalism. They have an independent
dynamic to the degree that their social construction promotes political
identities and struggles based on race and gender.[14]

Admittedly, class theories contain significant analytic advantages:
they are historical, and class relations often reveal and explain processes
of change and difference well. It is not that difficult to see them as

engines of history, especially in the history of race. Marxist scholars have also provided much of our insight regarding the dynamics of power, especially in examining the politics of cultural hegemony.[15]

Although Marxist frameworks are helpful in understanding historical struggles and material relations, they do not seem to offer the analytical range necessary for understanding sex/gender systems or the historical construction of race as a political and social category. In particular they often rely on functionalist arguments to explain gender and race oppression, viewing it solely in terms of the needs of capital. Specifically, they emphasize capitalism's need to divide the working class and secure cheap and tractable labor through discrimination.[16]

As Heidi Hartmann has cogently noted, this approach discounts or denies altogether gender as a social relationship between women and men. As articulated by Sacks and others, Marxist theories often rely on an unacknowledged consensus model of the family and examine only the family's economic functions (or some of them) in explaining, for example, who is "expendable" for wage labor. Moreover, it assumes that gender differences in access to wage labor offer a sufficient explanation for gender hierarchies. Such theories often miss the potent sexual-emotional dimensions of gender and race relations and see culture only as the creation of capitalism.[17] For Aihwa Ong, the general effect of such analyses is the "fetishization of capital accumulation and the valorization of women and men as commodities." Ong believes that purely economic frameworks ignore women and men as cultural beings, for whom the construction of value and meaning are more than economic in their origins or effects.[18]

The attempt to understand how culture operates in relation to economic processes has resulted in a variety of frameworks. Gayle Rubin has concluded that a "sex/gender system is not simply the reproductive moment of a 'mode of production.'" According to Rubin, the reproduction of labor involves biological human needs, environmental factors, and cultural traditions. Noting Marx's observation that the determination of the value of labor power contains "a historical and moral element," she further concludes that that element subsumes "the entire domain of sex, sexuality, and sex oppression." This "cultural" domain contains its own historically created dynamics, interacting with those of economic structures.[19]

Similarly, Belinda Bozzoli has offered a way to investigate economic relations, cultural processes, and the construction of race and gender. She states that it is essential to investigate the family and cultural (or racial/ethnic) groups as domains of conflict interacting with economic and political systems. Unlike Sacks, she does not assume that economic systems alone explain gender systems or family structures. Moreover, her approach restores women's agency to historical processes, requiring that we examine the sexual and economic politics of everyday life and their relationship to the gendered construction of the public order. In her framework, women (and men), therefore, find themselves engaged in multiple, interconnected struggles for power within families, racial/ethnic communities, and the institutions of the larger society. Bozzoli's framework, thus, draws historical attention to the "larger" significance of the dailiness and intimacy of gender politics.[20]

As Bozzoli and Ong have observed, gender relations are constituted at the intersections of various systems of power. These systems derive from political, economic, and cultural processes. The "patchwork of patriarchies" (to use Bozzoli's phrase) that results from these dynamics underscores the need to analyze race, class, gender, and other social systems as they interact.[21]

Such attempts to analyze the relationships between the material and the cultural have occasioned strong debates among labor historians and women's historians, who have examined the ways in which poststructuralist and linguistic theories can inform historical understandings of the relationships among experience, consciousness, and politics. Joan Scott and others have broadened those discussions to consider the implications of various theoretical frameworks for the place of women's history in labor and working-class history.[22]

According to Scott, only through the study of language can the significance of gender as a category of historical analysis be fully realized. Scott sees a necessary connection between language and gender because language constructs meaning through differentiation and gender serves as a central linguistic difference. Therefore, studying gender is essential to studying language, and linguistic approaches enable the analysis of gender in human societies.[23]

Because gender very often provides a vocabulary with which power is signified and authorized, it occupies a central role in discourses of dominance and resistance. Moreover, for Scott relations of class and gender are mutually constituted:

Gender certainly comes to be so implicated in concepts of class that there is no way to analyze one without the other. One cannot analyze politics separately from gender, sexuality, the family. These are not compartments of life, but integrally related systems; "language" makes possible the study of their interrelationships.[24]

Scott rejects a dichotomous view of the relationship between experience and perception, arguing that "there is no social experience apart from people's understanding of it." At the same time, her understanding of language as a non-referential (and capacious) category and her insistence that "language works to construct social identity [and] . . . ideas such as class become, through language, social realities" make her vulnerable to charges of linguistic determination. Indeed, the degree to which agency is attributed to discourses or signifying practices—rather than to individuals, institutions, or social groups—reveals the potential of such approaches to deflect attention from the structural relations that give political weight to particular discourses.[25]

As Linda Gordon has noted, Scott has not made her case that linguistic "theory is necessary to do proper feminist scholarship" or to resituate women's history at the center of historical inquiry. For Gordon, the materiality of domestic violence (from her own work) or of the attempts of a corporation like Sears to segregate and underpay women workers on the grounds of their "difference" from men (a subject treated by Scott) means that language alone cannot explain historical contest for power. Attention to difference in the abstract—the fundamental concern of many linguistic theorists—does not necessarily reveal what is at stake or how categorization operates within systems of social inequality.[26]

Gordon also remains skeptical that any particular analytic framework can guarantee that gender will be central to the analysis. According to Gordon, the appeal of feminist theories for scholars derives from their politics. Indeed, the vulnerability of poststructuralist scholarship to charges of androcentrism and racism would suggest that it does not automatically entail an understanding of the dynamics of gender and race in human societies. Ironically, linguistic theory itself suggests the contingent and multiple possibilities of language (as Scott herself clearly notes).[27]

Each party to this debate suggests the possibilities and pitfalls in

particular approaches. Linguistic theories provide a means to understand culture as a site and source of political struggle, while materialist
perspectives focus attention on inequalities of power and the institutional arrangements that buttress them. Ironically, though, some
Marxist analyses elide gender as a power relation or draw conclusions
about power inferred from institutional arrangements alone. Linguistic
frameworks remind us that the meanings of sexual difference for women
are more complex than the question of whether women contribute
essential labor to subsistence systems or participate in wage labor.
Although there are obvious tensions between material and cultural perspectives, taken together they can enlarge our understanding of the
relation between experience and perception, institutional practice and
cultural values, structures of domination and resistance.[28]

Gender, Class, and Labor History

These possibilities are evidenced not only in the works of the major
parties to the above debates, but also in those of historians who have
examined the workings of gender in the formation of working-class
identity and politics. They have given special attention to the taken-
for-granted quality of certain arrangements and ideologies: these
include the idea that women should not work outside the home; the
exemption of men from household work; and the ideology of masculine
privilege in family and economy deriving from men's position as wage
earners.[29]

Sonya Rose, for example, has pointed to the need to examine those
aspects of gender relations deemed to derive from "tradition" in order
to understand their meanings in periods of institutional change.
According to Rose, "The ideology of the family wage developed [in the
British working class] as part of an attempt to revitalize a traditional
notion of masculinity" in the face of proletarianization, not as a consequence of the ideological hegemony of the middle class. The "pride in
skill and in family headship" that defined masculinity in artisanal households required new ideological and institutional supports when men
entered wage work. In this new context, women's wage work outside
the household constituted a multiple threat: to men's jobs and wages,
to their gender identities, and to their control over labor and sexuality

in their families. As Sally Alexander has observed, the destruction of the household economy in the early nineteenth century occasioned "a language of grievance which embraced moral and sexual orders as well as economic discontents."[30]

Working-class men's "self-perceptions as workers" in the new order, thus, derived from their preindustrial gender identities and the patriarchal prerogatives they had justified. As they defined their class politics and goals in the industrial era, they stressed the need to secure a wage sufficient to support themselves and their dependents, revealing the connections between class consciousness and gender identity for men.[31]

Although Rose suggests that these men did not advocate "a family wage merely to dominate their wives and children," Wally Seccombe draws attention to the family power at stake for the men and to the deleterious effects this transformation had on women. According to Seccombe, the breadwinner ideology advantaged the husband in various ways: it legitimated his control of resources, his authority over the labor and sexuality of family members, and his refusal to do household work.[32]

These scholars have also drawn attention to the relationship between women's unpaid work and their labor force status. In the process, they have examined the ways in which women's socially essential household work comes to be culturally devalued. As Wally Seccombe noted, "What is concealed in the fully capitalist wage form is the private domestic labour of proletarian subsistence." That domestic labor, performed primarily by women, produces labor power, which is consumed at the point of production.[33]

Some feminist scholars have examined the unpaid work of women, whether performed in the family or in public institutions. They have explored the degree to which women's unpaid work is constructed by or essential to the operations of capitalism. Laura Balbo has analyzed the ways in which women "do the work of brokering between the family . . . and the market and public bureaucracies." This brokering work mediates the tensions between the needs of family members and "the external resources regulated by the logic of market profitability and state power." Although essential to the political economy, this labor often operates according to a set of values that resist those of capitalism. In a context of rising expectations for services and resources, women "most directly have to face the flaws, mystification, and failures in whatever the state and the market promise." In short, women's work and consciousness are critical to an analysis of the logic of economic structures.[34]

Western Women's History

These new lines of inquiry complement and inform work being done by historians of women in the West and provide analytical frameworks that will enable them to extend their already substantial contributions to western and women's history. As Virginia Scharff notes in this volume, whether anyone will notice is quite another matter. It is particularly unclear whether the "new" western histories will grasp the significance of gender for the construction of class and race/ethnicity in the American West.

Western women's historians have begun to reconceptualize feminist frameworks regarding public and private domains, their boundaries, and connections. Some of the most successful work in this area has examined the connections among public policy, economic structures, and family relations; the historical construction of race, class, and gender; sexuality and economics; and women's culture and work culture.[35] Scholars have given particular attention to the study of families as they allocate, control, and reward labor; organize sexuality and reproduction; and devise strategies for dealing with structural oppression. These studies necessarily focus on gender as a central mechanism for organizing property transfers, inculcating norms, signifying power relations, constructing visions of community, and defining work roles.[36]

Patricia Zavella, for example, has investigated why some Chicanas choose part-year work in the canneries in northern California. Family dynamics and values and access to a state wage subsidy (unemployment compensation) during periods of unemployment make this a culturally and practically acceptable work choice and also make these women available as cheap labor on a part-year basis. The gender division of labor and authority within Chicanas' families and in the canneries reflects an uneasy constellation of compromises: between women and men and among policy-makers, capitalists, and workers, explicable only when gender relations are taken into account.[37]

Sarah Deutsch, in *No Separate Refuge*, has attempted to understand the implications of economic transformations in New Mexico and southern Colorado for Hispanic women by placing gender and region at the center of her analysis. According to Deutsch, Hispanic village society afforded women power, dignity, and material security because their economic contributions to family and community were central and visible, their kin work was critical to the construction of community, and some property rights were secured for them by law and custom. The introduction of wage work destroyed village harmony and equality, rendering women economically and socially dependent.[38]

Deutsch's *No Separate Refuge* is strongest in its analysis of economic changes and the social relations of class and race/ethnicity. By contrast, the cultural construction of the gendered meanings of work, reproduction, the double standard in sexuality, and Catholicism in the lives of women and men receive superficial treatment. Most surprisingly, this work relies little on the words of women regarding their subjective experiences of gender differentiation.[39]

The author is, moreover, unaware of the ways in which she valorizes particular (and, I would argue, unequal) gender relations as essential to community and order. The fact that independent women (identified as divorcees or witches) were the ones ostracized by the villagers as threats to community she interprets as an expression of the inevitable disparity between the ideal and the real in egalitarian societies, rather than as a manifestation of gender conflict. In Deutsch's rendering of Hispanic women's lives, gender was neither a domain of struggle nor a source of cultural innovation. Instead, for Deutsch, continuity in gender relations was deemed essential to cultural preservation, and change occurred only in response to outside pressures. Her work suffers from the tendency in some social history, in the words of Richard White, "to reify culture and to see it as a shield magically holding back the malice of oppression."[40]

Despite its shortcomings, Deutsch's work suggests the rich analytical possibilities afforded by the multicultural nature of the West. The diversity in populations and economic structures facilitates the use of comparative approaches to analyze the relationship of gender inequality to economic structures, configurations of political power, and public policies (such as immigration, American Indian policies, development and employment policies, and education). Scholars can make multiple

comparisons and examine processes of economic stratification and cultural relations in various historical settings.[41]

Indeed, for women, work (paid and unpaid) was often the occasion
for cross-cultural interactions. In their work as reformers, field matrons,
missionaries, field nurses, anthropologists, social workers, and in other
fields, Anglo women often saw Hispanic and Native American women
as objects of their reforming efforts or, occasionally, models for emula-
tion. Whatever their preconceptions, these work experiences revealed
and constructed cultural relations. As Jensen and Miller pointed out,
Hispanic women's work as curanderas, traders, laundresses, and maids
involved them in cross-cultural relationships with other women.[42]

Peggy Pascoe has examined the ways in which intercultural relations in the West were constructed around relations among Anglo,
middle-class women reformers, and their women clients of different
racial/ethnic or class backgrounds. By analyzing the class, gender, and
racial politics that all parties brought to these interactions, she persua-
sively demonstrates the complexity of social relations and the centrality of gender to the politics of acculturation. That ethnic and class
identities and politics were defined in terms of gender relations reveals
the dense web of social relations being constructed in the American
West.[43]

For Indian women, the connections between the politics of gender
and those of class and race meant a vulnerability to systematic
acculturative efforts focused on redefining womanhood and often based
in a radical distrust of their maternal powers. The gender goals of white
officials were reflected in everything from the Dawes Act, which was
designed to create nuclear families under male provision, to the
boarding school system, which was intended to create a cultural chasm
between mothers and their children and to train girls in the frugal
domesticity and sacrificial womanhood deemed essential for the wives
of poor men. As Belinda Bozzoli's model of multiple struggles suggests,
it is essential to analyze the gender politics of Native American societies
in interaction with the gender-based acculturative strategies of whites
in order to understand the historical construction of race and gender
relations.[44]

The dialectical relationship between the gender politics of
everyday life and those of public institutions also informs women's
workplace experiences. Much recent work in women's labor history has

focused, in the words of Barbara Melosh, on "the ways in which gender informs work, and conversely, how work both reproduces and transforms existing relationships of power and inequality." One of the most fruitful lines of inquiry in this area entails examining the ways in which jobs come to be defined in gender-specific terms and the ways in which gender affects worker consciousness and political action. As Laura Balbo has noted, women are expected to bring "family" values, such as sacrifice for others (including employers), into paid employment.[45]

Those "family" values, however, have no given political meanings on the job, sometimes operating as an oppositional culture and sometimes complicitous with employer and patriarchal power. Patricia Zavella and Louise Lamphere have analyzed the ways in which managers and workers negotiate the meanings of gender identities and class relations in the cannery, garment, and electronics industries. In the process they have raised important questions. How does the organization of gender in the workplace interact with class politics? How do employers use gender as a mechanism for worker control? How do employers, unions, men, and women workers invoke gender as legitimation for their claims? In Lamphere's study, the values and rituals associated with women's culture sometimes provided a mechanism for women to identify across ethnic groups and work together in confronting employer power. By contrast, the Chicanas studied by Zavella created ethnically based support networks that enabled some to contest inequalities in their families.[46]

These and other similar works reveal the analytical potential of the study of women's work in the west. Realizing that potential requires that we recommit to doing history from the "bottom" up and that we move beyond "fear of theory" so that we can more precisely specify the questions that drive our work and their connections to our methodologies and interpretations. The work already begun by historians of women's work in the West illuminates the potential of this area of scholarship to reveal fundamental historical processes: the connections between family relations and economic processes; the historical construction of class, gender, race, and other social hierarchies; and the interrelated politics of the public and private domains.

Karen Anderson is a professor in the Women's Studies Program and the Department of History at the University of Arizona. She specializes in western and women's history. She is the author of *Wartime Women: Sex Roles, Family Relations, and the Status of Women during World War II* (1981) and *Changing Woman: A History of Racial Ethnic Women in Modern America* (1996).

NOTES

1. Joan M. Jensen and Darlis A. Miller, "The Gentle Tamers Revisited: New Approaches to the History of Women in the American West," *Pacific Historical Review* XLIX (1980), 173–213.
2. Ibid., 209.
3. Joan Scott, "Gender: A Useful Category of Historical Analysis," *American Historical Review* XCI (1986) 680–92.
4. Michelle Zimbalist Rosaldo, "Woman, Culture, and Society: A Theoretical Overview," in Michelle Zimbalist Rosaldo and Louise Lamphere, eds., *Woman, Culture, and Society* (Stanford, Calif.: Stanford University Press, 1974), 17–42.
5. Ibid.
6. Nancy Chodorow, "Family Structure and Feminine Personality," in Rosaldo and Lamphere, eds., *Woman, Culture, and Society*, 43–66.
7. Ibid.
8. Karen Sacks, *Sisters and Wives: The Past and Future of Sexual Equality* (Urbana: University of Illinois Press, 1982); Jane Fishburne Collier and Sylvia Junko Yanagisako, eds., *Gender and Kinship: Essays Toward a Unified Analysis* (Stanford, Calif.: Stanford University Press, 1987); Sherry B. Ortner and Harriett Whitehead, eds., *Sexual Meanings: The Cultural Construction of Gender and Sexuality* (Cambridge, Mass.: Cambridge University Press, 1981).
9. Sacks, *Sisters and Wives*; Rosaura Sánchez, "The History of Chicanas: Proposal for a Materialist Perspective," in Adelaida R. Del Castillo, ed., *Between Borders: Essays on Mexicana/Chicana History* (Encino, Calif.: Floricanto Press, 1990), 1–29.
10. Joan Wallach Scott, *Gender and the Politics of History* (New York: Columbia University Press, 1988); Linda K. Kerber, "Separate Spheres, Female Worlds, Woman's Place: The Rhetoric of Women's History," *Journal of American History* LXXV (1988): 9–39; Belinda Bozzoli, "Marxism, Feminism, and South African Studies," *Journal of South African Studies* IX (1983): 139–71; Sonya O. Rose, "'Gender at Work': Sex, Class and Industrial Capitalism," *History Workshop Journal* XXI (spring 1986): 113–31.
11. Natalie J. Sokoloff, *Between Money and Love: The Dialectics of Women's Home and Market Work* (New York: Praeger, 1980); Mario Barrera, *Race and Class in the Southwest: A Theory of Racial Inequality* (Notre Dame: University of Notre Dame Press, 1979); Richard White, *The Roots of Dependency: Subsistence, Environment, and Social Change among the Choctaws, Pawnees, and Navajos* (Lincoln: University of Nebraska Press, 1983); Rosalinda M. González, "Chicanas and Mexican Immigrant Families, 1920–1940: Women's Subordination and Family Exploitation," in Lois

Scharf and Joan M. Jensen, eds., *Decades of Discontent: The Women's Movement, 1920–1940* (Westport, Conn.: Greenwood Press, 1983), 59–84.

12. Karen Sacks, "Toward a Unified Theory of Class, Race, and Gender," *American Ethnologist* XVI (1989): 534–50; Teresa L. Amott and Julie A. Matthaei, *Race, Gender, and Work: A Multicultural Economic History of Women in the United States* (Boston: South End Press, 1991).

13. Sacks, "Toward a Unified Theory of Class, Race, and Gender," 534–50.

14. Ibid.

15. Anthony Giddens, *Central Problems in Social Theory: Action, Structure and Contradiction in Social Analysis* (London, 1979).

16. Richard White, "Race Relations in the American West," *American Quarterly* XXXVIII (1986): 396–416.

17. Heidi Hartmann, "The Unhappy Marriage of Marxism and Feminism," in Lydia Sargent, ed., *Women and Revolution: A Discussion of the Unhappy Marriage of Marxism and Feminism* (Boston: South End Press, 1981), 1–41; Bozzoli, "Marxism, Feminism, and South African Studies," 139–71. One suspects that in the analysis offered by Sacks, Marxism and feminism have become one again, although that "one" is a substantially altered Marxism. Jacqueline Dowd Hall and Ann Stoler have offered especially cogent analyses of the sexual/emotional dimensions of racial experience. Jacqueline Dowd Hall, "'The Mind That Burns In Each Body': Women, Rape, and Racial Violence," in Ann Snitow, Christine Stansell, and Sharon Thompson, eds., *Powers of Desire: The Politics of Sexuality* (New York: Monthly Review Press, 1983), 328–49; Ann L. Stoler, "Making Empire Respectable: The Politics of Race and Sexual Morality in 20th-Century Colonial Cultures," *American Ethnologist* XVI (1989): 634–60.

18. Aihwa Ong, "Colonialism and Modernity: Feminist Representations of Women In Non-Western Societies," *Inscriptions* (1988), 79–98.

19. Gayle Rubin, "The Traffic In Women: Notes on the 'Political Economy' of Sex," in Rayna R. Reiter, ed., *Toward an Anthropology of Women* (New York: Monthly Review Press, 1975), 157–210.

20. Bozzoli, "Marxism, Feminism, and South African Studies," 139–71. For a discussion of historians' tendency to trivialize the experiences of everyday life, see David Thelen, "An Afterthought on Scale and History," *Journal of American History* LXXVII (1990): 591–93.

21. Ong, "Gender and Power in Southeast Asia"; Bozzoli, "Marxism, Feminism, and South African Studies," 139–71; Susan Bordo, "Feminism, Postmodernism, and Gender-Scepticism," in Linda J. Nicholson, ed., *Feminism/Postmodernism* (New York: Routledge, 1990), 133–56; Jensen and Miller, "Gentle Tamers Revisited," 212.

22. Scott, *Gender and the Politics of History*; Joan W. Scott, "On Language, Gender, and Working-Class History," *International Labor and Working-Class History*, XXXI (1987), 1–13; Bryan D. Palmer, "Response to Joan Scott," ibid., 14–23; Christine Stansell, "Response to Joan Scott," ibid., 24–29; Anson Rabinbach, "Rationalism and Utopia as Languages of Nature: A Note," ibid., 30–36; Scott, "A Reply to Criticism," ibid., 39–45; "A Round Table: Labor, Historical Pessimism, and Hegemony," *Journal of American History* LXXV (1988): 115–61.

23. Scott, "A Reply to Criticism"; Scott, *Gender and the Politics of History*.

24. Scott, "A Reply to Criticism," 41.

25. Ibid., 40; Scott, "On Language, Gender, and Working-Class History," 5.

26. Joan W. Scott, "Heroes of Their Own Lives: The Politics and History of Family Violence," *Signs: Journal of Women in Culture and Society* XV (1990): 848–52; Linda Gordon, "Response to Scott," ibid., 852–53; Gordon, "Gender and the Politics of History," ibid., 853–58; Scott, "Response to Gordon," ibid., 859–60.

27. Ibid.; Barbara Christian, "The Race for Theory," *Feminist Studies* XIV (1988): 67–69; Frances E. Mascia-Lees, Patricia Sharpe, and Colleen Ballerino Cohen, "The Postmodernist Turn in Anthropology," *Signs: Journal of Women in Culture and Society* XV (1989): 7–33.

28. William Roseberry, *Anthropologies and Histories: Essays in Culture, History, and Political Economy* (New Brunswick, N.J.: Rutgers University Press, 1989); Hermann Rebel, "Cultural Hegemony and Class Experience: A Critical Reading of Recent Ethnological-Historical Approaches (Part One)," *American Ethnologist* XVI (1989): 117–36; Rebel, "Cultural Hegemony and Class Experience: A Critical Reading of Recent Ethnological-Historical Approaches (Part Two)," ibid., 350–65. For a good example of the strengths and shortcomings of institutional analysis, see Evelyn Nakano Glenn, "Split Household, Small Producer, and Dual Wage Earner: An Analysis of Chinese-American Family Strategies," *Journal of Marriage and the Family* XXXXV (1983): 35–46.

29. Rose, "Gender at Work," 113–31; Sally Alexander, "Women, Class and Sexual Differences in the 1830s and 1840s: Some Reflections on the Writing of a Feminist History," *History Workshop Journal* XVII (1984): 125–49; Wally Seccombe, "Patriarchy Stabilized: The Construction of the Male Breadwinner Wage Norm In Nineteenth-Century Britain," *Social History* XI (1986): 53–76; Scott, *Gender and the Politics of History*.

30. Rose, "Gender at Work," 113–31; Alexander, "Women, Class and Sexual Differences," 125–49.

31. Rose, "Gender at Work," 113–31.

32. Seccombe, "Patriarchy Stabilized," 53–76.

33. Ibid.

34. Laura Balbo, "The Servicing Work of Women and the Capitalist State," *Political Power and Social Theory* III (1982): 251–70. Other scholars have placed more emphasis on the power of capitalist consumer culture to co-opt women and shape their consciousness. Ruth Schwartz Cowan, *More Work for Mother: The Ironies of Household Technology from the Open Hearth to the Microwave* (New York: Basic Books, 1983); Susan Strasser, *Never Done: A History of American Housework* (New York: Pantheon Books, 1982); Glenna Matthews, *"Just a Housewife": The Rise and Fall of Domesticity in the United States* (New York: Oxford University Press, 1987). Heidi Hartmann pays more attention to men's interests (and success) in assigning housework to women. Heidi I. Hartmann, "The Family as Locus of Gender, Class, and Political Struggle: The Example of Housework," *Signs: Journal of Women in Culture and Society* VI (1981): 366–94.

35. Susan Armitage and Betsy Jameson, eds., *The Women's West* (Norman: University of Oklahoma Press, 1987); Lillian Schlissel, Vicki L. Ruiz, and Janice Monk, eds., *Western Women: Their Land, Their Lives* (Albuquerque: University of New Mexico Press, 1988); Joan M. Jensen and Darlis A. Miller, eds., *New Mexico Women: Intercultural Perspectives* (Albuquerque: University of New Mexico Press, 1986); Glenn, "The Dialectics of Wage Work," 432–71; Paula Petrik, *No Step Backward: Women and Family on the Rocky Mountain Mining Frontier, Helena, Montana, 1865–1900* (Helena: Montana Historical Society Press, 1987); Marion S.

Goldman, *Gold Diggers and Silver Miners: Prostitution and Social Life on the Comstock Lode* (Ann Arbor: University of Michigan Press, 1981); Patricia Zavella, "'Abnormal Intimacy': The Varying Work Networks of Chicana Cannery Workers," *Feminist Studies* XI (1985): 541–57; Louise Lamphere, "Bringing the Family to Work: Women's Culture on the Shop Floor," *Feminist Studies* XI (1985): 519–40; Rosalinda M. González, "Chicanas and Mexican Immigrant Families, 1920–1940: Women's Subordination and Family Exploitation," in Lois Scharf and Joan M. Jensen, eds., *Decades of Discontent: The Women's Movement, 1920–1940* (Westport, Conn.: Greenwood Press, 1983), 59–84.

36. Amott and Matthaei, eds., *Race, Gender, and Work;* Patricia C. Albers, "Autonomy and Dependency in the Lives of Dakota Women: A Study In Historical Change," *Review of Radical Political Economics* XVII (1985): 109–34; Vicki Ruiz, *Cannery Women, Cannery Lives: Mexican Women, Unionization, and the California Food Processing Industry, 1930–1950* (Albuquerque: University of New Mexico Press, 1987); Vicki L. Ruiz and Susan Tiano, eds., *Women on the U.S.-Mexico Border: Responses to Change* (Boston: Allen & Unwin, 1987), 61–76.

37. Patricia Zavella, *Women's Work and Chicano Families: Cannery Workers of the Santa Clara Valley* (Ithaca, N.Y.: Cornell University Press, 1987).

38. Sarah Deutsch, *No Separate Refuge: Culture, Class, and Gender on an Anglo-Hispanic Frontier in the American Southwest 1880–1940* (New York: Oxford University Press, 1987). Joan Jensen notes that married women could not manage or dispose of their property without their husband's consent. Joan M. Jensen, "'I've Worked, I'm Not Afraid of Work': Farm Women In New Mexico, 1900–1940," in Jensen and Miller, eds., *New Mexico Women*, 227–55.

39. Deutsch, *No Separate Refuge*. Published oral narratives are available. Nan Elsasser, Kyle MacKenzie, and Yvonne Tixier y Vigil, *Las Mujeres: Conversations from a Hispanic Community* (Old Westbury, N.Y.: Feminist Press, 1982); Fran Leeper Buss; *La Partera: Story of a Midwife* (Ann Arbor: University of Michigan Press, 1980).

40. Deutsch, *No Separate Refuge*, 60. Indeed, she argues that "At the *orderly* [emphasis mine] center of the village . . . lay a closely knit community of women." White, "Race Relations in the American West," 406.

41. Peggy Pascoe, "Gender, Race, and Intercultural Relations: New Vantage Points from the American West" (Paper presented at the Berkshire Conference on the History of Women, Douglass College, June, 1990); Betsy Jameson, "Toward a Multicultural History of Women in the Western United States," *Signs* XIII (1988): 761–91.

42. Jensen and Miller, "Gentle Tamers Revisited," 201–2; Peggy Pascoe, *Relations of Rescue: The Search for Female Moral Authority in the American West, 1874–1939* (New York: Oxford University Press, 1990); Leigh Pruneau, "'Drivin' Women': Field Nurses In the Indian Service, 1924–1955" (N.p., 1989); Deutsch, *No Separate Refuge*, 63–86; Barbara A. Babcock and Nancy J. Parezo, *Daughters of the Desert: Women Anthropologists and the Native American Southwest, 1880–1980: An Illustrated Catalogue* (Albuquerque: University of New Mexico Press, 1988). Domestic service particularly served as an important locus for the construction of gender, race, and class identities and relations. Evelyn Nakano Glenn, "The Dialectics of Wage Work: Japanese-American Women and Domestic Service, 1905–1940," *Feminist Studies* VI (1980): 432–71; Vicki L. Ruiz, "By The Day or the Week: Mexicana Domestic Workers in El Paso," in Ruiz and Tiano, eds., *Women on the U.S.-Mexico Border,* 61–76.

43. Pascoe, *Relations of Rescue*; Peggy Pascoe, "Gender Systems in Conflict: The Marriages of Mission-Educated Chinese American Women," in Ellen Carol DuBois and Vicki L. Ruiz, eds., *Unequal Sisters: A Multi-Cultural Reader in U.S. Women's History* (New York: Routledge, 1990), 123–40; Deutsch, *No Separate Refuge*, 63–86.

44. Robert A. Trennert, "Educating Indian Girls at Nonreservation Boarding Schools," in DuBois and Ruiz, eds., *Unequal Sisters*, 224–37; Christine Bolt, *American Indian Policy and American Reform: Case Studies of the Campaign to Assimilate the American Indians* (London: Allen & Unwin, 1987), 252–69. Joan Jensen and Carol Devens have offered especially cogent analyses of the ways in which Native American women and men were differently positioned with regard to issues of accommodation and resistance. Joan M. Jensen, "Native American Women and Agriculture: A Seneca Case Study," *Sex Roles* III (1977): 423–41; Carol Devens, "Separate Confrontations: Gender as a Factor in Indian Adaptation to European Colonization in New France," *American Quarterly* XXXVIII (1986): 461–80.

45. Barbara Melosh, *"The Physician's Hand": Work Culture and Conflict In American Nursing* (Philadelphia: Temple University Press, 1982), 7; Susan Porter Benson, "'The Customers Ain't God': The Work Culture of Department-Store Saleswomen, 1890–1940," in Michael H. Frisch and Daniel J. Walkowitz, eds., *Working-Class America: Essays on Labor, Community, and American Society* (Urbana: University of Illinois Press, 1983), 185–211; Micaela di Leonardo, "Women's Work, Work Culture, and Consciousness (an Introduction)," *Feminist Studies* XI (1985): 491–95; Balbo, "Servicing Work of Women and the Capitalist State," 255.

46. William Chafe, *Women and Equality: Changing Patterns in American Culture* (New York: Oxford University Press, 1977), 57–58; Ong, "Gender and Power in Southeast Asia"; Patricia Zavella, "Abnormal Intimacy," 541–57; Lamphere, "Bringing the Family to Work," 519–40; Sally Westwood, *All Day, Every Day: Factory and Family in the Making of Women's Lives* (Urbana: University of Illinois Press, 1984). Peggy Pascoe has discussed changes in scholarly understandings of culture in "Gender, Race, and Intercultural Relations."

WOMEN OF COLOR AND THE REWRITING OF WESTERN HISTORY

THE DISCOURSE, POLITICS, AND DECOLONIZATION OF HISTORY*

Antonia I. Castañeda

Historians have long struggled with the need to rewrite western history and to articulate a new, inclusive synthesis that fully incorporates the history of women of color.[1] In her concluding remarks at the Women's West Conference in Sun Valley, Idaho, in 1983, Susan Shown Harjo (identifying herself culturally as Cheyenne and Creek and politically as Cheyenne and Arapaho) charged that women of the West

> are still possessed of inaccurate information about who we are collectively, who we are individually, and who we have been. We view each other through layers of radical, ethnic, and class biases, perpetuated by the white, male ruling institutions, such as the educational system that teaches in the early years and controls later research in the history of women in the West.[2]

This critique of the reigning historiography has changed little since then or since Joan Jensen and Darlis Miller first called for a multicultural, or intercultural, approach in their essay, "The Gentle Tamers Revisited: New Approaches to the History of Women in the American West."[3] A decade of "multicultural" historiography has still not come

---

*This chapter was previously published as: Castañeda, Antonia. "Women of Color and the Rewriting of Western History: The Discourse, Politics, and Decolonization of History." In *Pacific Historical Review* 61 (November 1992): 501–33.

to terms with the historical, theoretical, political, and ideological issues raised by Harjo at Sun Valley.

This essay discusses the historiography that was written during the 1980s about women in the nineteenth-century West. It examines the issues, politics, concepts, methodologies, and language of the "multicultural" or intercultural approach first articulated by Jensen and Miller and the ways in which the intersection of gender, race, sexuality, ethnicity, class, and culture are described, theorized, and interpreted in the recent historical literature. The first section places in context the historiography of women of color in the decade before "The Gentle Tamers Revisited" was published, while the second places in context "The Gentle Tamers Revisited" itself.

The Historiography of Women of Color and the Politics of History

The academic discourse on the historiography of women in the West still does not accept that studying and writing the history of racial ethnic people as well as of women in the United States are avowedly political acts.[4] Yet the political and intellectual roots of the contemporary historical study of women in the West were sown in the political struggles of the late 1960s and 1970s—in the case of white women, in the women's liberation movements; in the case of women of color, in the national third-world liberation movement.[5] These movements were at times related, but their political and intellectual origins, commitments, and ideologies were markedly different.

The women's liberation movement in the United States focused specifically on gender oppression. Never of one mind or one ideology, the women's movement was nevertheless fundamentally rooted in a middle-class political liberalism that subscribed to including the excluded as long as they fit within the existing norms. Its origins, identification, and praxis sprang from the suffragist movement of the mid-nineteenth century—a movement that never reconciled its origins in abolitionism with an abiding belief in white racial superiority.

The study of women began with the political struggles of the women's movements of the 1960s and 1970s and with the feminist theories and scholarship that grew from them. The women's movement was a middle-class, white women's movement, and until very recently, the historians who have researched and written the history of women in the West have been principally white women. Many of them participated in the women's movement or are members of the generation of scholars who struggled to found women's studies programs and departments in western colleges and universities. Most feminist scholars write the history not of women, but of white women in the West.

In contrast, most women scholars of color who research and write the history of women of color look not to the women's liberation movement, but to third-world liberation movements. These movements focused on the race and class oppression of African Americans, Chicanos, Native Americans, Puerto Ricans, and Asian Americans in the U.S. and identified with global struggles of third-world peoples for economic and political freedom.[6] They found their historical and cultural origins in indigenous, native worlds that antedated European imperialism, and they began to reclaim those origins, which had been devalued and suppressed in Euro-American institutions and society.[7] These national movements interpreted the exploitation and oppression of third-world peoples in the United States as an extension of the historical, global colonial, and neocolonial relationships that tied Europe and subsequently the United States to third-world countries.[8] Drawing upon theories of dependency and, in some cases, interpreting their reality in the United States as internal colonialism, these movements had a transnational identification and praxis. Although different ideologies, including cultural nationalism, prevailed, most national liberation movements supported a Marxist or neo-Marxist perspective that focused on class and racial oppression but ignored issues of patriarchy and gender oppression, gay and lesbian oppression, and the intersection of gender, race, sexuality, and class.

Women scholars of color, however, also struggled against the internal gender oppression of their own families, organizations, and communities and against a historical sexual exploitation rooted in the intersection of their gender with their race and class. This consciousness distinguished their gender oppression markedly from that of white women and distinguished their racial and class oppression markedly from that of men of color. It also differentiated the feminist ideologies of women of color from those of white women.

Individually and collectively, in conferences, presentations, and published works, feminists of color challenged male-dominated ethnic studies departments that ignored gender and sexuality and women's studies departments that ignored race and class.[9] In the case of the latter, they were highly critical of the assumptions, the universalizing tendencies, and the lack of consciousness about the dynamics of power and privilege rooted in race and class that informed white feminist scholarship. Drawing upon contemporary writers and political activists, including Angela Davis, Dolores Huerta, Janice Mirikitani, and Janet McCloud, as well as upon their own experiences, these writers and scholars initiated a new body of creative as well as academic literature.[10] Although few in number, they began to recover the voices, histories, cultures, literatures, and experiences of women of color in the United States and to teach courses on women of color. In the decade of the 1980s they published several collections of creative and critical writings by women of color.[11] These collections, however, did not include historical studies on women of color in the nineteenth-century West. This was due to the abysmally small numbers of professionally trained women scholars of color who might have produced these studies. Statistics reveal that between 1975 and 1988 there were 192 doctoral degrees in history awarded to women of color: 8 to Native Americans, 42 to "Asians," 101 to African Americans, and 41 to "Hispanics."[12]

Multiculturalism and Its Discontents

With the publication of "The Gentle Tamers Revisited" in 1980, Jensen and Miller launched a new era in the field of women's history. Their essay provided Euro-American feminist and nonfeminist historians with a critical base from which to challenge the historiography in two subfields of U.S. history: the history of the American West and the history of women. For this group of scholars, Jensen and Miller's essay became the foundation on which to build a historiography of women in the West. It offered then a "new, multicultural" framework from which to contest both the East Coast focus of U.S. women's history and the biases of the male-centered frontier thesis.

Jensen and Miller called for a newer, ethnically broader, and more varied image of women in the West based on a multicultural approach that recognized and included the experiences of women from different races, ethnicities, cultures, and classes. They also stated that "a multi-cultural approach need not eliminate class or politics from western women's history" and that "women of the West were divided not only by culture but also by the conflicts among cultures."[13] Jensen and Miller's multicultural approach appeared to be the perfect base from which to include the excluded and thereby move women in the West from the periphery to the center of the history of both women and the American West. They did not, however, examine, analyze, discuss, or theorize about the conflicts and differences among cultures. Neither did they examine the applicability of the existing categories, concepts, and paradigms or redefine culture(s), politics, the parameters of cultural conflict, or sex-gender issues and women's roles within that cultural conflict. They also failed to analyze relations of power among women of different races, classes, and cultures.

Jensen and Miller's vague outlines for multicultural approaches to the history of women in the West have been uncritically appropriated, adopted, and applied, and in some cases extended or expanded, without question or analysis by feminist and nonfeminist historians alike. These scholars have begun to apply methods from numerous disciplines to research, write, discuss, anthologize, and publish a variety of works on gender, race, and class in the West.[14] Using a multicultural, intercultural, or, to a much lesser degree, comparative perspective, they have produced two principal types of work: descriptive studies and studies of the contact between white men or women and women of color.

The first type, principally journal articles and conference papers collected in anthologies, describes the experience of Euro-American, Spanish-Mexican, Indian, and, to a much lesser extent, African American women.[15] Asian and Asian American women—whether Chinese, Japanese, Korean, Filipino, South Asian, or Southeast Asian—appear in only one anthology, a multicultural reader published in 1990.[16] Although the early studies tend to focus on the nineteenth century—beginning with Euro-American westward expansion in the 1830s and ending with Frederick Jackson Turner's "closing of the frontier"—the study of women of color has of necessity pushed the time span back to the sixteenth and seventeenth centuries for Spanish-Mexican women and much earlier for Native American women.[17] Recent studies of workers from Asia and the Pacific Islands have also pushed it forward to the twentieth century and extended the geographic region to include

Hawaii and Alaska.[18] Moreover, interest in particular themes, such as widowhood and women in prisons, is beginning to result in thematic works, including the important anthology *On Their Own: Widows and Widowhood in the American Southwest, 1848–1939*. These works offer significant possibilities for the development of comparative studies across race, class, cultures, and region.[19]

The second type, which includes books as well as journal articles, focuses on Anglo perceptions of racial ethnic women or on the contact and relationships between Anglos and racial ethnic women, usually Native American and Mexican women.[20] Generally, studies on interracial contact in the nineteenth century do not examine interculturalism, interracial unions, or *mestizaje* (racial and cultural mixing) in Mexico's northern territories prior to the arrival of Euro-Americans in the 1820s and thus do not recognize these as core elements in the history of the West.[21] Research on intercultural contact has recently begun to focus on prostitution, a form of labor in which women of all races and cultures participated in the postwar nineteenth-century West; interracial marriage; and the moral reform movements of Euro-American women.[22] The study of interracial marriage and Anglo reform movements now embraces the twentieth century and has begun to examine relations between Anglos and Asian and Asian American women.[23] Despite the exceptions, few studies analyze the historical gender, "racial," political, economic, and cultural issues and conflicts inherent in interracial marriage, assimilation, and acculturation.

Diversity

The issue of diversity was, moreover, a reality for indigenous peoples in the Americas long before the arrival of Europeans. Although racial diversity in the West may be a relatively recent phenomenon (some two and four hundred years old in California and New Mexico, respectively), cultural diversity is not. Before the Spanish arrived in 1769, California was one of the most densely populated and culturally and linguistically diverse areas of the continent north of México.[24] Precontact indigenous societies throughout the Americas included a broad spectrum of social structures ranging from the matrilineal and matrilocal societies of the Navajo and Western Apache to egalitarian, foraging bands in California to highly stratified, hierarchically organized social orders in central Mexico and Peru.[25]

Recognizing and according significance to cultural diversity are important for two reasons. First, the recent emphasis placed on the nineteenth- and twentieth-century West as, according to Peggy Pascoe the "most racially and culturally diverse region of the nation" merely reconfigures and perpetuates, in another guise, the earlier myth of western America's uniqueness. Indigenous cultural diversity was not unique to the West, and its decline in other regions of the country, the South and Southeast for example, was due precisely to the impact of European and Euro-American expansion and colonization. Moreover, although the diversity among indigenous groups declined, the importation of Africans from different parts of the continent added new elements of cultural, as well as racial, diversity to nonwestern regions. Diversity in the American West, then, merely reflects a pattern in place long before the arrival of Europeans, and the change in the composition of diverse groups across time—the decline of some groups and the addition of others—is a function of the political and economic developments occurring in a particular region.

Second, women's gender experiences and definitions were as diverse as the cultures from which they came. Women apprehended knowledge and acted within their universe according to the culture and its particular economic and socio-politico-religious organization.[26] Understanding the nature of gender systems and experiences before contact is critical to understanding how those experiences changed with conquest and colonialism and why women responded and acted the way they did in intercultural settings and relationships. It is also critical to understanding how they maintained, adapted, and transformed their own cultural forms while resisting, adopting, adapting, and affecting those of other groups.

The Ideology of Race

Jensen and Miller should not be faulted for being merely suggestive or for how their call is applied by others. They should, however, be criticized for organizing their essay and discussion around concepts, issues, categories, and language that belong to the history of middle-class white women and for not addressing how these may differ for women of color. Although ostensibly centering *all* women as historical subjects, "The Gentle Tamers Revisited" fundamentally centered only Euro-American women. Jensen and Miller's brand of multiculturalism kept middle-class white women as the subject and the normative group for description, analysis, interpretation, and comparison. They neither challenged nor altered the standard Eurocentric focus, methodologies, or paradigms of women's history. The multicultural approach to the history of women in the West reflects the critical problem in American historiography, which, to quote Ann DuCille's recent review, "is the continued marginalization of those historically constituted as 'other.'"[27]

Jensen and Miller encoded their discussion and analysis with a range of images and stereotypes applied to and reserved exclusively for white women in the West, beginning with the term "gentle tamers."[28] None of the historical literature—neither the documents of the Euro-American conquest nor studies by historians or other writers—refers to any women of color as gentle tamers, meaning bearers of culture and "civilization."

Thus Euro-American individuals or groups, both male and female, remain the true subject of multicultural studies.[29] Based principally on Euro-American, English-language sources, these studies explore Anglo perceptions of women of color and the Anglo side of the cultural equation. While some of these works, particularly the most recent ones, recognize the poststructuralist debate about the meaning and definition of culture and seem to disavow the earlier paradigm of culture adopted by social historians, theoretical approaches that incorporate the historical realities of people of color, and their own interpretation of their realities, are still wanting.[30]

While feminist scholars are beginning to examine race and miscegenation within a multicultural framework, most continue to ignore the complexities of multiple racial and cultural mixtures in the United States and to avoid examining how the prevailing construction of race has been applied differently to different racial ethnic peoples across time and space.[31] Mexicans (both native and foreign born), for example, were included in the 1920 U.S. federal manuscript census as part of the white population. In 1930, however, the U.S. Bureau of the Census classified them as nonwhite and set up "Mexican" as a race unto itself. Since Mexicans have been officially classified both as white and nonwhite, antimiscegenation laws sometimes applied to them and sometimes did not.[32] Nevertheless, as one early study of the Mexican American community concluded, irrespective of the official racial classification, intermarriage with Mexicans was disparaged, and "the Anglo member of an intermarrying couple . . . is classified as a 'Mexican' by the American community."[33]

Theories about the social construction of race do not yet examine or account for these kinds of complexities. Nor does the significance of interracial marriage and mixing among peoples of color, or the *mestizaje* of the Mexican population, form part of how the social construction of race and studies of miscegenation are conceptualized for nineteenth- or twentieth-century North American society. Acutely aware that the new theories remain constructed and defined by the same "hegemonic voices," scholars of color have vigorously critiqued the "rush to theory" that ignores, excludes, or does not comprehend the realities of people of color and, in this case, women of color.[34]

Jensen and Miller examined the ideology of gender, but not the ideology and politics of race, culture, class, and expansionism that produced and maintained stereotypic images of white women and women of color. They acknowledged the existence of racial stereotypes and cultural conflicts without placing racial contact and cultural conflict in their historical or political or ideological context. They assumed that concepts, categories, terminology, methodology, and language are universally applicable. By doing so they remained squarely within both the Turnerian tradition of frontier history and the tradition established early in the field of women's history. White women remain, as Chandra Mohanty states, the authorial subject, "the yardstick by which to encode and represent cultural others."[35] Jensen and Miller merely substituted the experience of white males with that of white women and thus reproduced the same relationships of power and authority that male historians used when writing the canon of history. The discussions and analysis of multicultural contact and relations remain skewed, centered on, and interpreted from the Euro-American side of the relationship.

Generalizations about women of color perpetuate pernicious stereotypes. Native American, Chicana, African-American, and Asian American scholars have identified two dichotomous images of women of color in the literature—"good" and "bad." These images vary among racial ethnic groups but are in all cases totally unrelated to the notion of "gentle tamers."[36] Within this dichotomy, "good" women of color are light-skinned, civilized (Christian), and virgins. They are "good" because they give aid, or sacrifice themselves, so that white men may live; white men marry them. "Bad" women are dark-skinned, savage (non-Christian), and whores; white men do not marry them.

In the case of Native American and Mexican/Mexican American women, these dichotomies translate into contradictory images of the "noble princess/savage squaw" and the "Spanish señorita"/Mexican prostitute," respectively. The "noble princess" and the "Spanish señorita" are deracinated and converted into acceptable images of marriageable women. These "good" women are the "Indian princess" and the "Spanish" grandmother whom many white pioneer families proudly claim as ancestors. According to the mythology within which these stereotypes are steeped, such women reject their own kind, native men, in favor of their white saviors. Marriage to the blue-eyed strangers saves them from the oppression of their own men and thus from the savagery of their race, culture, group, and nation.

The negative stereotypes were applied to all Native American and Mexican women except those few belonging to what Euro-Americans considered the native ruling class, with whom they could form beneficial alliances, including marriage. They sexualize Indian and Mexican women, devaluing and dehumanizing them as women who give away or sell sexual intercourse. Within this stereotype, Indian women relate to "idle, shiftless, thieving, drunken" Indian men, while Mexican women are "fandango-dancing, *monte*-dealing consorts of Mexican bandits."

The historical literature presents stereotypic images of women that center on sexuality and the relationship that the particular women and their racial or national group, or both, have to the political economy. Moreover, the relation to the political economy informs the history of women of color and distinguishes the daughters of the country—Native American or Mexican women—from African American and Asian women.

During the first stages of contact and conquest, marriage to a Native American or a Mexican woman of a particular family or class had significant economic and political value. These marriages were often the vehicle by which Euro-American men gained access to land or other economic resources as well as to political and military alliances.[37] This was not the case with African American or Asian women in the nineteenth-century West. As enslaved or contract workers, African American and Asian women had neither economic nor political value as marriage partners. The miscegenation laws, which criminalized marriage to people of African descent, were later extended to Asians.[38]

Consequently, stereotypes of African and Asian women center almost exclusively on the pejorative "bad/whore." This image simultaneously sexualizes women and impugns their sexuality. The implicit sociopolitical message is clear: women of color are immoral because their peoples, races, and nations are immoral.[39] Whereas the pejorative stereotype of African American and Asian women is rooted in sexuality, the positive stereotype, when it appears at all, is rooted in work and servitude. "Good" African American and Asian women serve their owners, or former owners, well. They do not run away, join or lead revolts, learn to read or write, or cause trouble.

The Politics of Race and Power

Jensen and Miller did not analyze the relations of power among women of different races, classes, or cultures in the West. The devaluation of the sexuality of women of color, and by extension the devaluation of their people, was an important element in the rationale for war, conquest, exploitation, and subsequently exclusion.[40] It was—and remains—a central part of the racist argument that served the political and economic interests of an expansionist United States.

Anne Butler, for example, in her recent study of prostitution in the American West, paints Chinese and Mexican cultures as undifferentiated, static, and monolithic. She presents Mexican and Chinese women as unthinking, passive victims—entities with no agency. In this work, Mexican women come from a society and history of

> an unending cycle of victory and defeat, oppression and submission that comprise the history of the Southwest. . . . Oriental women carried with them to North America the societal hierarchy that they had lived with in China. . . . The emigrants . . . came from a life of control and rigidity, similar to the structure the Chinese merchants established. . . . These women simply moved from one controlling hierarchy to another without transformation in their own societal

roles. Brought from a preindustrial society and closeted in a minority subculture, Oriental prostitutes had little opportunity to develop changed self-concepts in their new environment.[41]

Butler judges Mexican and Chinese women and their cultures by traditional Euro-American norms of "progress" and ignores both the political economy of prostitution for women of color in the West and women's agency under extreme conditions of oppression and exploitation. Nor does she recognize, for example, that the "Chinese merchants who had a status in the U.S. they did not have in Chinese" society created the so-called minority subculture within a context of exclusion, racism, and inequality.[42]

Multicultural works about women written during the decade of the 1980s tend to emphasize harmonious, cooperative, mutually supportive relations between women of color and Anglo women in the American West.[43] Although they do not ignore the reality of racist attitudes among white women, their accounts are remarkably free of intercultural conflict in a land bloodied by three centuries of war and conquest.[44] Yet white women are "gentle tamers" because they are the female counterparts of white men who "tame the wild West." "Taming the West," gently in the case of white women and violently in the case of white men, is a metaphor for expansionism. Within their gender spheres and based upon the power and privilege of their race and class, Euro-American men and women expanded the geo-political-economic area of the United States and established Euro-American hegemony in the region. They did so by waging war, by displacing and removing the occupants, and by appropriating the land. By skirting the issue of conflict in expansionism, these studies perpetuate the myth of the "bloodless conquest" of California, the West, and the Southwest, one of the central tenants of the expansionist ideology that rationalized and justified war and conquest.

The multicultural approach also ignores the myriad roles—which sometimes include cultural, ideological, social, and physical violence—that women of the conquering group(s) assume in establishing hegemony over another group. It also ignores the economic and other privileges that women of the conquering group derive from the oppression of women and men of the group being oppressed. Ironically, by emphasizing the benign, conflict-free relationships between white

women and women of color in the American West, multicultural studies reaffirm the notion that white women are the "gentle tamers." This
harmonic view contrasts sharply with the reality. Rosalia Vallejo's rem-
iniscences of the Bear Flag Revolt in California, court records of cases
in which Mexican women were plaintiffs as well as defendants against
Anglos, including women, accounts of the wholesale sexual violence
against Indian women, the efforts of African-American women to free
themselves from bondage, and the sexual exploitation of Asian women
reveal the truth of those relations.[45]

The brutally violent conflicts engendered by expansionism and the
establishment of Euro-American hegemony—including conflicts
between white women and women of color—remain part of our daily
lives and are expressed in the contemporary writing of women of color.
According to Paula Gunn Allen, "like our sisters who resist in other
ways, we Indian women who write have articulated and rendered the
experience of being in a state of war for five hundred years."[46] Histories
of the West in which women of color are the subject, have agency, and
are located within their own culture are only now being researched,
written, and published.

The Empire Writes Back: The Decolonization of Western History

The literature by contemporary women writers of color in the United
States vividly depicts the conflicts, tensions, violence, and warfare—
physical, ideological, psychological, and cultural—that affect their own
lives and form part of the collective memories and lives of their female
kin and communities.[47] This new, immensely rich, powerful, and
growing body of literature—such as the autobiographical, biographical,
and fictionalized writings of Louise Erdrich, Gloria Anzaldúa, Amy Tan,
and Toni Morrison—helps to offset the dearth of historical studies about
women of color, at least for the twentieth century.[48] Women of color
are at the enter of these works, describing, analyzing, and expressing
their own historical and cultural subjectivities. Rooted in what theorist
Chela Sandoval terms oppositional consciousness, this literature offers
a critical base for new definitions, forms, expressions, and theories of
culture, that is, of what writers of color have, in their call for reimaging

America, termed cultures of collectivity and struggle.[49] These cultures are rooted in knowledge and experience that both antedate and supersede—just as much as they are shaped by, adapted to, resistant to, and coexistent with—European and Euro-American cultures of colonial domination. Collected in a wealth of new anthologies by and about women of color, this oppositional literature blurs academic disciplines and literary genres and crosses national boundaries. It expresses the complex, multiple subjectivities that women of color have lived, which Shirley Geok-Lin Lim describes as "the plural singularity" of Asian American women.[50]

This plural singularity refers to both the commonalities and the differences of gender, race, culture, class, and sexuality among women. It is present in the new historiography that examines women's history within the concepts and theories that frame the discourse of colonialism in historical studies, and discursive colonization in literary and cultural studies. Initially derived from the Marxist and neo-Marxist studies of Latin America, Africa, and India, this interdisciplinary approach draws upon methodologies and theories from cultural anthropology, ethnohistory, sociology, literature, and feminism to examine the conquest and colonization of the Americas. This approach, states Ramón Gutiérrez, views history as a "dialogue between cultures, each of which had many voices that often spoke in unison, but just as often were diverse and divisive."[51] Conceptualizing the historical process "as a story of contestation, mediation, and negotiation between cultures and between social groups," this approach clarifies the power dynamics of the European conquests and the contest of cultures that began in 1492 and remains very much with us.[52]

Especially important to historical scholarship on women of color in the United States, including the West, is the work of third-world feminists and other third-world scholars and writers who employ critical theory, postmodern anthropology, and poststructuralist literary criticism to analyze how the colonizer represented African, Native American, mestiza, and Asian women.[53] Analyzing woman and the female body as a metaphor for conquest, these scholars interpret the white colonizers' appropriation of the native woman—by representing her as sexually available to the colonizer and as oppressed within her own culture—to be pivotal to the ideology and the political agenda of colonialism. In analyzing colonialism, Malek Alloula, for example, interprets the colonizer's possession of the native woman by constructing false images of her and her society as "less of a conquest than a deformation of the social order."[54]

These scholars not only examine the centrality of sex-gender to the politics of colonialism but also focus on the relations of power both among cultures and within cultures. They view scholarship and the production of knowledge as a political and discursive practice—it has a purpose and is ideological. Within this broad framework, third-world feminists reexamine, reconstruct, and re-present native women within their own cultures as well as responding to colonialism. In doing so, they interrogate their own traditions from within. They call into question traditions, conventions, and contemporary relations of power and offer searching critiques of their own societies and historical conditioning.

This analysis, which examines both the historical and the contemporary writing on native African, Asian, and American women produced by Westerners, criticizes feminist writing on third-world women. Placing Western feminist writing within the context of a first/third world balance of power, Chandra Mohanty, for example, characterizes much of this work as rooted in "assumptions of privilege and ethnocentric universality, on the one hand, and inadequate self-consciousness about the effect of western scholarship on the 'third world' in the context of a world system dominated by the West, on the other."[55]

Rewriting the Nineteenth-Century West

For the nineteenth-century West, historical studies on comparative frontiers that begin to examine frontier expansion within a global context of European colonization and capitalist development employ the dialogic framework.[56] These historians define the frontier as a territory or zone of encounter, interchange, and conflict between distinct societies—one indigenous and one intrusive. Taking a macrotheoretical approach, they argue that the "history of frontier expansion in the Americas is the history of the expansion of European capitalism into non-European areas."[57] Americanist Patricia Limerick interprets the history of the American West as one chapter in the global and bloody story of Europe's expansion and centuries-long contest for property, profit, and cultural dominance.[58] Similarly, historian Rosalinda Méndez González argues that if we are to understand the experience of all women we must study "the larger, more fundamental political-economic forces in the development of the West."[59] Scholars who study Native Americans and Mexicans include the resistance to domination, and those who examine the pattern of global frontier expansion concentrate on the differences specific to each nation, region, and frontier.[60]

Work in ethnic and women's history has added gender, race, sexuality, and culture to class as categories of historical analysis in studies of global capitalist development. Placing these at the center of historical examination—that is, using them as organizing principles—provides the basis for reconceptualizing and reanalyzing all aspects of history and the historical process. Chicana/Latina historians who study Spanish-Mexican women in eighteenth-century California and nineteenth-century New Mexico reveal, for example, that sex-gender, race, and culture are central to the politics and policies of conquest and colonization and to the sociopolitical and economic development of these regions as they changed from Spanish to Mexican to Euro-American rule.[61] Gender, race, culture, and class are political designations as much as they are social constructions.

This approach enables us to examine the specific realities in which women of different races, cultures, and classes live in any society at any given time. It also allows us to examine gender systems and women's experiences within the sociopolitical and economic context of local, national, and international developments at any given historical moment and to compare similarities and differences among women within one society and across societies. Most particularly, doing so allows us to study gender experiences, which are rooted in an intersect with race, culture, and class, within distinct economies and societies—both precapitalist and capitalist. In brief, it allows us to be historically specific, to recognize women's agency, and to understand, in Mohanty's words, "the contradictions inherent in women's location within various structures."[62]

Anthropological studies, for example, examine women's relations of production in precontact societies and refute earlier interpretations of Native American women.[63] They reject principal tenets of Western feminism that had been applied to women worldwide, including the universality of male dominance and the dichotomy between public and private acts. These studies conclude that within egalitarian foraging band societies, women exercised control over their own lives and activities and operated formally and publicly in their own interest. Social and sexual reflections were reciprocal and complementary. Human sexuality, but most particularly women's sexuality, was not controlled by males, and a broad spectrum of sociosexual relations existed. Moreover, each society had its own customs for marriage, divorce, polygamy, polyandry, the berdache, and cross-gender dressing.

Historians are also reexamining various dimensions of the issue of sexuality within the context of colonization. Focusing on the response of native women to sexual and other violence, Albert Hurtado, among others, is detailing the historical resistance of Native American women.[64] Similarly, anthropologist Patricia Albers concludes that despite the structural and other changes wrought by capitalism, Dakota women and their communities did not dramatically change their basic values of reciprocity, collectivity, and complementarity.[65] These and other values were central to their resistance to and survival of colonialism and its attendant oppressions.

Moreover, while earlier studies dealt with Native American sexuality principally in terms of the "unspeakable things" done to white women captives, historical documents reveal that different practices of war prevailed in the Americas and that female captives fared according to the practices of the victorious group. Some of the native Californian groups, for example, practiced ritual but not physical warfare; some warred not at all; and some practiced warfare and captured women and children but never sexually molested female captives. Such was the case with the Yuma, who believed that intimate contact with enemy women caused sickness.[66]

Focusing on women of color changes the discourse and enables historians to examine how those women responded to changes in the economic and social order—including the changes wrought by violence—based on their own values, norms, and circumstances. Deena González, for example, examines interracial marriages as part of Spanish-Mexican patterns of racial and cultural contact. She focuses on the culture-specific gender strategies that Spanish-Mexican women in Santa Fe, New Mexico, used to resist and subvert structures of Euro-American colonialism in the nineteenth century.[67] Using Spanish-language sources, González weaves her analysis with the women's own language, imagery, and consciousness, which reveal the subjectivities, complexities, tensions, strategies, conflicts, and contradictions of their lives, as well as their sense of honor, propriety, justice, and right. Placing Chicana history in time, space, and social relationships prior to the arrival of Euro-Americans, González's work provides a critical new point of departure for studies of nineteenth- and twentieth-century Chicana/Latina history.

Likewise, Asian American historians, Sucheng Chan and Judy Yung, among others, use Chinese and other Asian-language sources to recover, reconstruct, and reinterpret the complex realities of Chinese, Japanese, Korean, Filipino, South Asian, and Southeast Asian women in the American West from the mid-nineteenth century to the present.[68] In addition to cultural and class differences, Asian-language sources, including oral history interviews, reveal that Chinese and Japanese women who consented to come to the United States as workers and subsequently as picture brides had their own individual motives for doing so. Some sought to contribute to the family economy; others wanted to be educated and to see the world.[69] Once in the United States, Asian women resisted marital and other conditions they did not like despite the difficulties and lack of recourse.

In her recent work on the Chinese in California, historian Chan studies gender issues imbedded in the Chinese Exclusion Laws of 1881–1882 and adds a vital new chapter to immigration history in general and to Asian American women's history in particular.[70] Shifting the focus of earlier studies on migration from "Chinese patriarchal culture and the sojourner mentality thesis" and centering on gender issues and U.S. immigration policy, Chan chronicles how different groups of Chinese women were targeted for exclusion and denied entry to the United States. Examining the legislation from the 1870s to 1943, Chan finds the sexuality of Chinese women to be a pivotal issue in legislative hearings, committee meetings, and statutes as well as in municipal ordinances. She concludes that

> contrary to the common belief that laborers were the target of the first exclusion act, the effort to bar another group of Chinese—prostitutes—preceded the prohibition against laborers. Given the widely held view that all Chinese females were prostitutes, laws against the

latter affected other groups of Chinese women who sought admission into the country as well.[71]

The stereotype that all Chinese women were prostitutes whose presence would corrupt the morals of the nation's youth can be traced to the 1850s and prevailed well into the twentieth century. The Page law, passed in 1875, was designed to end the threat of cheap Chinese labor and to prevent "immoral Chinese women" from landing in the United States. New laws passed in 1903, 1907, and 1917 were designed to deport alleged prostitutes, which included all Chinese women. According to Chan, "no Chinese woman, regardless of her social standing, was safe from harassment."[72]

Similarly, George Peffer argues that the government's targeted exclusion of Chinese women effectively prevented Chinese families from forming and thus kept a full-fledged Chinese/Chinese American society (or societies) from establishing itself in the United States during the nineteenth century.[73] Although Peffer's brief essay does not fully develop the relationship between sex-gender and economic issues, the links are certainly there to be examined and explored. That is, in Chinese contract labor, the expanding, postwar boom economy of the mid-nineteenth-century West found what it most needed: a large, mobile, exploitable, expendable source of cheap manual labor. Chinese laborers—both women and men—were brought in to do particular kinds of work in a segmented labor force that kept them mobile, transient, exploitable, and expendable.[74] Unlike men, Chinese women were also brought to perform sexual intercourse, and their sexuality could be and was impugned.

Moreover, the "sexuality/immorality" of Chinese prostitutes became the rationale for excluding not only all Chinese women, as Chan and Peffer demonstrate, but, with the beginning of the economic downturn of the 1870s, all Chinese.

The Chinese experience was not singular. Similar issues of sex-gender, contract labor, immigration policy, and exclusion prevail in the history of Japanese immigration to Hawaii and the mainland.[75] Hawaiian sugar planters began contracting Japanese laborers, both male and female, and importing Japanese women to Hawaii for purposes of prostitution beginning in the late 1860s. Agricultural interests in the West subsequently followed suit. In a pattern established earlier with the Chinese, the "sexuality/immorality" of Japanese women was a key element in the rationale for excluding the Japanese in the first decade of the twentieth century.[76]

The intersection of gender, race, and labor is also central in new studies of African-American women in the West. Historian Shirley Ann Moore examines these issues in her study reconstructing the experience of African-American women workers in Richmond, California, from 1910 to 1950.[77] Using extensive oral history interviews, family memoirs, documents, music, memorabilia, and other archival material, Moore explores the "development of strategies of economic empowerment of women who labored under the tripartite yoke of oppression and were compelled to develop resourceful, self-affirming strategies to carve out some measure of economic autonomy for themselves and their families."[78] This is the first study to examine the experience of the generation of African-American women who took part in the "great migration" in the prewar years of the early 1900s and who built and shaped African-American communities in the West.

Earlier studies of women and of African-Americans in the West discussed African-American women in general or focused on individual women such as Mary Ellen Pleasant and Biddy Mason; they did not use gender as a category of historical analysis or examine gender issues and women's experiences of slavery, freedom, or the boom-bust economy in the nineteenth-century West.[79] With the exception of Jack Forbes's work on Africans and Native Americans, no historians have focused on the nature of interracial marriage or other sociosexual and political relationships among people of color. The recovery of factual information and the interpretation of African-American women's lives in the nineteenth- and early twentieth-century West, like that of Native American and Asian American women and Chicanas, is only now being undertaken.

In focusing on women of color as historical subjects in the nineteenth-century Euro-American West, and employing gender, race, class, culture, and sexuality as categories of analysis within the context of colonization, newer studies, principally by women historians of color, are reexamining old sources, discovering new sources, using new methodologies, and challenging earlier interpretations of women in general. They are also refuting previous interpretations of women of color in particular. These scholars, states historian Deena González, have found it necessary first to "deconstruct the racialized and sexualized history of women of color in order to reconstruct it."[80]

Their examinations reveal important commonalities and differences based on historical presence and on gender and its intersection with race, sexuality, culture, and class. These new findings form a critical new basis for reconceptualizing and reinterpreting not only women's and racial ethnic history, but the labor, economic, political, immigration, cultural, and social history of the West as well.

They have sketched some of the broad themes that are of importance to women of color, including sexual and other physical, as well as psychological, violence within the context of the politics of expansionism; devaluation of their sexuality by Euro-American society; discrimination based on race, culture, and class; resistance to oppression; use as labor (enslaved, contract, and wage); the mestizaje within Mexican communities as well as intermarriage and racial-cultural mixing among people of color; settlement; family; religion; and community building. Other themes, such as accommodation and adaptation to the Euro-American presence in their homeland; intermarriage with Euro-Americans; immigration; deportation; and the experience of slavery and freedom from bondage in the West, are more specific to one group or another.

Drawing upon new, interdisciplinary methodologies and frameworks defined in the scholarly studies of third-world women, these studies examine and analyze women of color within their own cultures; in particular, they examine how these women responded to the alien, hostile, often violent society of the nineteenth-century American West. These studies focus on women's agency and on how women of color use their own culture and knowledge to sustain them, how they subvert and/or change the environment, and how they adopt or create new cultural forms. Further, these studies explore the multiple contradictions of women's lives in colonialism. They explore both the hegemonic and counterhegemonic strategies, roles, and activities that women, depending on their position in society, developed and employed in both the historical and contemporary period. Women of all races, classes, and cultures are active subjects, not passive objects or victims of the historical process.

Validating and drawing upon knowledge rooted in the experience of colonialism (but still manifest in their daily living), and drawing as well upon knowledge antedating colonialism, these historians are examining both the historical and the contemporary writing on African American, Asian American, Chicana, and Native American women and their communities on the land base we now call the American West. They are deconstructing, reconceptualizing, and reconstructing the histories of women and communities of color in this region. Thus they are equally critical of the early historical literature and of the recent historical studies, including those employing the multicultural approach to the history of women in the West and feminist writings on women of color.

Historians, including feminist historians and other feminist scholars, must examine their assumptions as well as their racial, class, and gender positions as they redefine historical and other categories of analysis. The structures of colonialism are the historical legacy of the United States and, as such, inform the profession of history and the production of historical scholarship as much as they do any other human relationship and endeavor. If western history is to be decolonized, historians must be conscious of their power and ideology within the structures of colonialism, and conscious as well of the ways in which historical scholarship has helped to sustain and reproduce those structures. The study of women of color requires us to reexamine, challenge, and change those structures. Only then will we decolonize western history.

Antonia I. Castañeda is a professor in the Department of History at St. Mary's University in San Antonio, Texas.

NOTES
I want to thank Deena González and Emma Pérez for reading and commenting on this essay, and Elizabeth Forsyth for editorial assistance.

   1. I use the term women of color to refer collectively to African American, Asian American, Mexican American/Chicana, and Native American women in the United States. I use the terms third world, third-world woman/women, and third-world movements with knowledge of the problems associated with the terms as discussed in Chandra Talpade Mohanty, Ann Russo, and Lourdes Torres, eds.,

Third World Women and the Politics of Feminism (Bloomington: Indiana University Press, 1991), ix–x. I use the terms raced ethnic and racial ethnic interchangeably with the term people of color to refer to the larger community that includes both men and women. For the term raced ethnic, see Norma Alarcón, "Chicana Feminism: In the Tracks of 'the' Native Woman," *Cultural Studies* IV (1990): 248–56; for the term racial ethnic, see Evelyn Nakano Glenn, "Racial Ethnic Women's Labor: The Intersection of Race, Gender, and Class Oppression," *Review of Radical Political Economics* XVII (fall 1985): 86–108.

For a brief synthesis of some of the central issues in the recent historical literature on women in the West, see "Historical Commentary: The Contributions and Challenges of Western Women's History—Four Essays by Sarah Deutsch, Virginia Scharff, Glenda Riley, and John Mack Faragher," *Montana, the Magazine of Western History* XLI (spring 1991): 57–73.

For scholarly discussion of the debates the historiography of frontier history/history of the West, generally exclusive of the issue of gender, see Patricia Limerick, *The Legacy of Conquest: The Unbroken Past of the American West* (New York: Norton, 1987); Roger L. Nichols, ed., *American Frontier and Western Issues: A Historiographical Review* (Westport, Conn.: Greenwood Press, 1986); Michael P. Malone, *Historians and the American West* (Lincoln: University of Nebraska Press, 1983); "Historical Commentary: Western History, Why the Past May be Changing—Four Essays by Patricia Nelson Limerick, Michael P. Malone, Gerald Thompson, and Elliot West," *Montana, the Magazine of Western History* XL (summer 1990): 60–77; Brian Dippie, "The Winning of the West Reconsidered," *Wilson Quarterly* XIV (summer 1990): 70–85; Sandra Myres, "What Kind of Animal Be This?" *Western Historical Quarterly* XX (1989): 5–17; Charles S. Peterson, "The Look of the Elephant: On Seeing Western History," *Montana, the Magazine of Western History* XXXIX (spring 1989): 69–73; Arnoldo De Leon, "Whither Borderlands History? A Review Essay," *New Mexico Historical Review* LXIV (1989): 349–60; William G. Robbins, "Western History: A Dialectic on the Modern Condition," *Western Historical Quarterly* XX (1989): 429–49; Martin Ridge, "The American West: From Frontier to Region," *New Mexico Historical Review* LXIV (1989): 125–42; Gerald E. Poyo and Gilberto M. Hinojosa, "Spanish Texas and Borderlands Historiography in Transition: Implications for United States History," *Journal of American History* LXXV (1988): 393–416; Donald Worster, "New West, True West: Interpreting the Region's History," *Western Historical Quarterly* XVIII (1987), 141–56; David J. Weber, "John Francis Bannon and the Historiography of the Spanish Borderlands: Retrospect and Prospect," *Journal of the Southwest* XXIX (1987): 331–63; Gerald D. Nash, "Where's the West?" *Historian* IL (1986): 1–9; Richard White, "Race Relations in the American West," *American Quarterly* XXXVIII (1986): 396–416; Gene M. Gressley, "The West: Past, Present, and Future," *Western Historical Quarterly* XVII (1986): 5–23; Walter Nugent, "Western History: Stocktaking and New Crops," *Reviews in American History* XIII (1985): 319–29; Rodman W. Paul and Michael P. Malone, "Tradition and Challenge in Western Historiography," *Western Historical Quarterly* XVI (1985): 26–53; David Weber, "Turner, the Boltonians, and the Borderlands," *American Historical Review* XCI (1986): 66–81; Gene M. Gressley, "Whither Western American History? Speculations on a Direction," *Pacific Historical Review* LIII (1984): 493–501; John W. Caughey, "The Insignificance of the Frontier in American History," *Western Historical Quarterly* V (1974): 6–15; W. N. Davis, Jr.,

"Will the West Survive as a Field in American History?" *Mississippi Valley Historical Review* L (1964): 672–85; Jack Forbes, "Frontiers in American History," *Journal of the West* I (1962): 63–73.

2. Susan Shown Harjo, "Western Women's History: A Challenge for the Future," in Susan Armitage and Elizabeth Jameson, eds., *The Women's West* (Norman: University of Oklahoma Press, 1987), 307. After the first conference at Sun Valley in 1983, three additional conferences were held during the 1980s and one, entitled "Suspect Terrain: Surveying the Women's West," is being planned for 1992 at Lincoln, Nebraska. Issues of race and class bias surfaced at each of the conferences both in discussions of the new historiography of women in the West as well as in the conceptualization and organization of the conferences themselves. These same issues will inform the 1992 conference.

   The conferences of the 1980s were "Western Women: Their Land, Their Lives," Tucson, Ariz., January 12–15, 1984; "The Women's West, 1984," Park City, Utah, July 11–14, 1984; "The Women's West: Race, Class, and Social Change," San Francisco, Calif., August 13–15, 1987. Two edited anthologies of works presented at the first two conferences have been published: Armitage and Jameson, eds., *Women's West*, and Lillian Schlissel, Vicki Ruiz, and Janice Monk, eds., *Western Women: Their Land, Their Lives* (Albuquerque: University of New Mexico Press, 1988).

3. Joan M. Jensen and Darlis A. Miller, "The Gentle Tamers Revisited: New Approaches to the History of Women in the American West," *Pacific Historical Review* XL (1980): 173–214.

4. Rodolfo Acuña, *Occupied America: A History of Chicanos* (3d ed., New York: Harper & Row, 1988), 307–62; Joan Wallach Scott, *Gender and the Politics of History* (New York: Columbia University Press, 1988); Gary T. Okihiro, ed., *In Resistance: Studies in African, Caribbean and Afro-American History* (Amherst: University of Massachusetts Press, 1986); Gary T. Okihiro, "Education for Hegemony, Education for Liberation," in Gary Y. Okihiro, ed., *Ethnic Studies* (2 vols., New York: M. Wiener Pub., 1989), I, 3–10.

5. Adela de la Torre and Beatriz Pesquera, "Introduction," in Adela de la Torre and Beatriz Pesquera, eds., *Building with Our Hands: New Directions in Chicana Studies* (Berkeley: University of California Press, 1993); Cheryl Johnson-Odim, "Common Themes, Different Contexts: Third World Women and Feminism," in Mohanty, Russo, and Torres, eds., *Third World Women and the Politics of Feminism*, 314–27; Alarcón, "Chicana Feminism," 249–56; Alma Garcia, "The Development of Chicana Feminist Discourse, 1970–1980," in Ellen Carol DuBois and Vicki L. Ruiz, eds., *Unequal Sisters: A Multicultural Reader in U.S. Women's History* (New York: Routledge, 1990), 419–31; Esther Ngan-Ling Chow, "The Feminist Movement: Where Are All the Asian American Women?" in Asian Women United of California, ed., *Making Waves: An Anthology of Writings by and about Asian Women* (Boston: Beacon Press, 1989), 362–76; Nancy Diao, "From Homemaker to Housing Advocate: An Interview with Mrs. Chang Jok Lee," ibid., 377–87; Teresa de Lauretis, "Feminist Studies/Critical Studies: Issues, Terms, and Contexts," in Teresa de Lauretis, ed., *Feminist Studies/Critical Studies* (Bloomington: Indiana University Press, 1986), 1–19; Linda Gordon, "What's New in Women's History," ibid., 20–30; Marilyn J. Boxer, "For and about Women: The Theory and Practice of Women's Studies in the United States," in Nannerl O. Keohane, Michelle Z. Rosaldo, and Barbara C. Gelpi, eds., *Feminist Theory: A Critique of Ideology* (Chicago:

University of Chicago Press, 1982), 237–72; Patricia Hernández, "Lives of Chicana Activists: The Chicano Student Movement (A Case Study)," in Magdalena Mora and Adelaida R. Del Castillo, eds., *Mexican Women in the United States: Struggles Past and Present* (Los Angeles: Chicano Studies Research Center Publications, University of California, 1980), 7–16; Roxanne Dunbar Ortiz, "Toward a Democratic Women's Movement in the United States," ibid., 29–36.

6. For representative descriptions and discussions of the various national liberation movements, see *The Struggle for Chicano Liberation* (New York, 1972); Armando B. Rendón, *Chicano Manifesto* (New York: Macmillan, 1971); Alvin M. Josephy, Jr., ed., *Red Power: The American Indians' Fight for Freedom* (New York: American Heritage Press, 1971); Vine Deloria, *Custer Died for Your Sins: An Indian Manifesto* (New York: Macmillan, 1969); Julius Lester, *Revolutionary Notes* (New York: R. W. Baron, 1969); Stokley Carmichael, *Black Power: The Politics of Liberation in America* (New York: Random House, 1967).

7. I use the terms native and indigenous to mean belonging to a particular place by birth. For an examination of the problems associated with the use of these terms, see Trinh T. Minh-ha, *Woman, Native, Other: Writing Postcoloniality and Feminism* (Bloomington: Indiana University Press, 1989).

8. Daniel A. Offiong, *Imperialism and Dependency: Obstacles to African Development* (Washington, D.C.: Howard University Press, 1982); Ronald H. Chilcote and Joel C. Edelstein, eds., *Latin America: The Struggle with Dependency and Beyond* (Cambridge, Mass: Schenkman Pub. Co., 1974); Ronald H. Chilcote, *Dependency and Marxism: Towards a Resolution of the Debate* (Boulder, Colo.: Westview Press, 1982).

9. For early critiques by women of color of the biases of feminist theories and the politics of what Chandra Talpade Mohanty has termed "imperial feminism," as well as for unexamined philosophical positions in feminist and other scholarship, see Chandra Mohanty, "Under Western Eyes: Feminist Scholarship and Colonial Discourses," *Boundary 2: A Journal of Post-Modern Literature and Culture* (spring/fall 1984): 333–58; Adaljiza Sosa Riddell, "Chicanas en el Movimiento," *Aztlán* V (1974): 155–65; Cherríe Moraga and Gloria Anzaldúa, eds., *This Bridge Called My Back: Writings by Radical Women of Color* (Watertown, Mass.: Persephone Press, 1981) xxii–xxvi; Barbara Smith, "Racism in Women's Studies," in Gloria T. Hull, Patricia Bell Scott, and Barbara Smith, eds., *But Some of Us Are Brave* (New York: Feminist Press, 1982), 48–56; Hazel V. Carby, "White Woman Listen: Black Feminism and the Boundaries of Sisterhood," in Center for Contemporary Cultural Studies, *The Empire Strikes Back: Race and Racism in Seventies Britain* (London: Hutchinson in association with the Centre for Contemporary Cultural Studies, University of Birmingham, 1982), 212–35; Bonnie Thorton Dill, "Race, Class and Gender: Perspectives for an All-Inclusive Sisterhood," *Feminist Studies* IX (1983): 131–50; Mujeres en Marcha, *Chicanas in the 80s: Unsettled Issues* (Berkeley: Chicano Studies Library Publications Unit, UC Berkeley, 1983), 130–50; bell hooks, *Feminist Theory: From Margin to Center* (Boston: South End Press, 1984); Alice Y. Chai, "Toward a Holistic Paradigm for Asian American Women's Studies: A Synthesis of Feminist Scholarship and Women of Color's Feminist Politics," *Women's Studies International Forum* VIII (1985): 59–66; Cynthia Orozco, "Sexism in Chicano Studies and the Community," in Teresa Córdova, Norma Cantú, Gilberto Cárdenas, Juan Garcia, and Christine M. Sierra, eds., *Chicana Voices: Intersections of Class, Race, and Gender* (Austin: Center for Mexican

American Studies, University of Texas, 1986), 11–18; Alma Garcia, "Studying Chicanas: Bringing Women into the Frame of Chicano Studies," ibid., 19–29; Barbara Christian, "The Race for Theory," *Feminist Studies* XIV (1988): 67–70; Jonella Butler, "Difficult Dialogues," *Women's Review of Books* VI (February 1989): 16; bell hooks, *Talking Back: Thinking Feminist, Thinking Black* (Boston: South End Press, 1989).

For the critiques of the 1990s, see "Editor's Note," and "Speaking for Ourselves: From the Woman of Color Association," *Woman's Review of Books* VIII (February 1990): 27–29; Gloria Anzaldúa, "Introduction" and "Section 7: 'Doing' Theory in Other Modes of Consciousness," in Gloria Anzaldúa, ed., *Making Face, Making Soul: Haciendo Caras* (San Francisco: Aunt Lute Foundation Books, 1990), xv–xxviii and 335–402; Emma Pérez, "Sexuality and Discourse: Notes from a Chicana Survivor," in Carla Trujillo, ed., *Chicana Lesbians: The Girls our Mothers Warned Us About* (Berkeley: Third Woman Press, 1991), 159–84.

10. For a discussion of gender in the historiography of colonial and nineteenth-century California, including early studies in Chicano history, see Antonia I. Castañeda, "Gender, Race, and Culture: Spanish-Mexican Women in the Historiography of Frontier California," *Frontiers: A Journal of Women's Studies* [a special issue on Chicanas] XI (1990): 8–20. For feminist activist-scholar-philosopher Angela Davis, see Angela Davis, *With my Mind on Freedom: An Autobiography* (New York: Random House, 1974); for Dolores Huerta, vice-president of the United Farm Workers Union, see the UFW newspaper *El Malcriado* (published at Delano and Keene, California, from the mid-1960s to the 1970s); for Janet McCloud, a Tulalip woman who was one of the founders and leaders of the Survival of American Indians Association, Inc., and a leader in the struggle for Native American fishing rights in Washington state, see Laura McCloud, "Is the Trend Changing," in Alvin M. Josephy, Jr., ed., *Red Power: The American Indians' Fight for Freedom* (New York: American Heritage Press, 1971), 99–104; for activist-poet Janice Mirikitani, see Janice Mirikitani, *Awake in the River: poetry, prose* (San Francisco: Isthmus Press, 1978) and Mirikitani, *Shedding Silence* (Berkeley, 1987).

11. Moraga and Anzaldúa, eds., *This Bridge Called My Back*; Hull, Scott, and Smith, eds., *But Some of Us Are Brave*; Gretchen M. Bataille and Kathleen Mullen Sands, eds., *American Indian Women: Telling Their Lives* (Lincoln: University of Nebraska Press, 1984); Shirley Geok-lin Lim, Mayumi Tsutakawa, Margarita Donnelly, eds., *The Forbidden Stitch: An Asian American Women's Anthology* (Corvallis, Ore.: Calyx Books, 1989); Asian Women United, ed., *Making Waves*; Anzaldúa, ed., *Making Face, Making Soul*.

12. American Historical Association, *Guidelines on Hiring Women Historians in Academia* (3rd ed., Washington, D.C., 1990). The guidelines homogenize distinct populations into broad "Asian" and "Hispanic" categories. See also, Joan M. Jensen, "Committee on Women Historians, 1970–1990: A Twenty-Year Report," *Perspectives: American Historical Association News-letter* XXIX (March 1991): 8–9; Deena J. González, "Commentary: The Rose Report, the Twenty-Year Report of the Committee on Women Historians, and National Ethnic Minority Women in the Professions" (Comments prepared for the American Historical Association Roundtable, Washington, D.C., Dec. 1990).

13. Jensen and Miller, "The Gentle Tamers Revisited," 212–13.

14. Peggy Pascoe, "At the Crossroads of Culture," *Women's Review of Books* VII (February 1990): 22–23, raises critical questions about feminist theory, ideology,

and politics. Although Pascoe argues for multiculturalism and inclusion of women of color in the women's history curriculum, she neither questions nor analyzes the concepts and assumptions of multiculturalism. Pascoe, in "Gender, Race, and Intercultural Relations: The Case of Interracial Marriage," *Frontiers: A Journal of Women's Studies* XII (1991): 5–18, argues for the social construction of race and raises critical questions about historical scholarship and paradigms of culture but accepts uncritically Euro-centered notions of multiculturalism. Elizabeth Jameson, in "Toward a Multicultural History of Women in the Western United States," *Signs: Journal of Women in Culture and Society* XIII (1988): 761–91, expands and updates the categories of a multicultural approach but does not analyze the concepts or theories and thus reaffirms Euro-centered definitions of multiculturalism. Sarah Deutsch, in "Women and Intercultural Relations: The Case of Hispanic New Mexico and Colorado," *Signs: Journal of Women in Culture and Society* XII (1987): 719–39, and in her subsequent book (cited below) conceptualizes "intercultural" and issues of assimilation, acculturation, and resistance for Nuevo Mexicanas as originating with the arrival of Euro-Americans and ignores the historical reality of Mexican/Native American interculturalism as well as the significance of this history in the subsequent relations with Euro-Americans. For troublesome generalizations about women of color rooted in unexamined concepts and assumptions about culture and people of color, see Deutsch, *No Separate Refuge: Culture, Class, and Gender on an Anglo-Hispanic Frontier in the American Southwest, 1880–1940* (New York: Oxford University Press, 1987); and Anne M. Butler, *Daughters of Joy, Sisters of Misery: Prostitutes in the American West, 1865–90* (Urbana: University of Illinois Press, 1987). For a similar critique of Deutsch's *No Separate Refuge*, see Rodolfo Acuña, "The Struggles of Class and Gender: Current Research in Chicano Studies," *Journal of American Ethnic History* VIII (spring 1989): 134–35. Marion Goldman, *Gold Diggers and Silver Miners: Prostitution and Social Life on the Comstock Lode* (Ann Arbor: University of Michigan Press, 1981), examines prostitution within the boom-bust economy of the Comstock Lode and discusses racial and class hierarchies in prostitution within an economic, not a cultural or multicultural, framework.

15. Schlissel, Ruiz, and Monk, eds., *Western Women: Their Land, Their Lives*; Armitage and Jameson, eds., *Women's West*; Joan M. Jensen and Darlis A. Miller, eds., *New Mexico Women: Intercultural Perspectives* (Albuquerque: University of New Mexico Press, 1986); Cathy Luchetti in collaboration with Carol Olwell, *Women of the West* (St. George, Utah: Antelope Island Press, 1982), a pictorial history with a section on "Minority Women" and photographs of African-American, Chinese, and Native American women—but no Mexican women; Janet Lecompte, "The Independent Women of Hispanic New Mexico, 1821–1846," *Western Historical Quarterly* XII (1981): 17–35.

16. DuBois and Ruiz, eds., *Unequal Sisters*. Much of the periodical literature on Asian women has been collected in anthologies by and about Asian American women that are not conceptualized within the framework of the multicultural approach examined here.

17. Rosalind Z. Rock, "'Pido y Suplico': Women and the Law in Spanish New Mexico," *New Mexico Historical Review* LXV (1991): 145–60; Jameson, "Toward a Multicultural History"; Cheryl J. Foote and Sandra K. Schackel. "Indian Women of New Mexico, 1535–1680," *New Mexico Historical Review* LXV (1991): 1–16; Salomé Hernández, "Nueva Mexicanas as Refugees and Reconquest Settlers,

1680–1696," *New Mexico Historical Review* LXV (1991): 17–40; Sylvia Van Kirk, *Many Tender Ties: Women in Fur-Trade Society, 1670–1870* (Norman: University of Oklahoma Press, 1980).

18. Mary Paik Lee, *Quiet Odyssey: A Pioneer Korean Woman in America*, edited by Sucheng Chan (Seattle: University of Washington Press, 1990); Ronald Takaki, *Strangers from a Different Shore: A History of Asian Americans* (New York: Penguin Books, 1989); Yuji Ichioka, *The Issei: The World of the First Generation Japanese Immigrants, 1885–1924* (New York: Free Press, 1988); Evelyn Nakano Glenn, *Issei, Nisei, War Bride: Three Generations of Japanese American Women in Domestic Service* (Philadelphia: Temple University Press, 1986); Akeme Kikumura, *Through Harsh Winters: The Life of a Japanese Immigrant Woman* (Novato, Calif.: Chandler & Sharp, 1981); Judy Yung, "The Social Awakening of Chinese American Women as Reported in Chung Sai Yat Po, 1900–1911," DuBois and Ruiz, eds., 195–207. See the following essays, all of which are contained in Asian Women United of California, ed., *Making Waves:* Dorothy Córdova, "Voices from the Past: Why They Came," 42–49; Sun Bin Yum, "Korean Immigrant Women in Early Twentieth-Century America," 50–61; Marcelle Williams, "Ladies on the Line: Punjabi Cannery Workers in Central California," 148–58; Barbara Posadas, "Mestiza Girlhood: Interracial Families in Chicago's Filipino Community since 1925," 273–82. See also David Beesley, "From Chinese to Chinese American: Chinese Women and Families in a Sierra Nevada Town," *California History* LXVII (1988): 168–79; Joan Hori, "Japanese Prostitution in Hawaii during the Immigration Period," Nobuya Tsuchida, ed., *Asian and Pacific American Experiences: Women's Perspectives* (Minneapolis: Asian/Pacific American Learning Resource Center and General College, University of Minnesota, 1982), 75–87; Alice Y. Chai, "Korean Women in Hawaii, 1903–1945," ibid., 56–65; Yuji Ichioka, "Amerika Nadeshiko: Japanese Immigrant Women in the United States, 1900–1924," *Pacific Historical Review* XL (1980): 339–57.

19. Arlene Scadron, ed., *On Their Own: Widows and Widowhood in the American Southwest, 1848–1939* (Chicago: University of Illinois Press, 1988); Anne M. Butler, "Still in Chains: Black Women in Western Prisons, 1865–1910," *Western Historical Quarterly* XX (1989): 19–36.

20. Sherry L. Smith, "A Window on Themselves: Perceptions of Indians by Military Officers and Their Wives," *New Mexico Historical Review* LXIV (1989): 447–62; Sherry L. Smith, "Beyond Princess and Squaw: Army Officers' Perceptions of Indian Women," Armitage and Jameson, eds., *Women's West*, 68–75; Lisa Emmerich, "Civilization and Transculturation: Field Matrons and Native American Women, 1891–1938" (Paper presented at the conference, "The Women's West: Race, Class, and Social Change," San Francisco, Calif., Aug. 13–15, 1987); Glenda Riley, *Women and Indians on the Frontier, 1825–1915* (Albuquerque: University of New Mexico Press, 1984); Annette Kolodny, *The Land before Her: Fantasy and Experience of the American Frontiers, 1630–1860* (Chapel Hill: University of North Carolina Press, 1984); Darlis A. Miller, "Cross-Cultural Marriages in the Southwest: The New Mexico Experience, 1846–1900," *New Mexico Historical Review* LVII (1982): 335–59; Sandra L. Myres, "Mexican Americans and Westering Anglos: A Feminine Perspective," *New Mexico Historical Review* LVII (1982): 414–30; Rebecca McDowell Craver, *The Impact of Intimacy: Mexican-Anglo Intermarriage in New Mexico, 1821–1846* (El Paso: Texas Western Press, University of Texas at El Paso, 1982).

21. Susan L. Johnson's "Sharing Bed and Board: Cohabitation and Cultural Difference in Central Arizona Mining Towns, 1863–1873," Armitage and Jameson, eds., *Women's West*, 77–92, addresses the specific Mexican history of informal unions in its discussion of cohabitation among Mexican women and Anglo men as well as their conflicting values concerning informal unions. Johnson, however, generalizes about Mexican culture, Mexican women, and Mexican communities in Arizona mining towns without any gender-centered primary research on the issue of informal unions in Mexican culture and without any substantive evidence upon which to base her generalizations.

22. Butler, *Daughters of Joy;* Goldman, *Gold Diggers and Silver Miners;* Darlis A. Miller, "Foragers, Army Women, and Prostitutes," *New Mexico Historical Review* LXV (1991): 141–68.

23. Peggy Pascoe, *Relations of Rescue: The Search for Female Moral Authority in the American West, 1874–1939* (New York: Oxford University Press, 1990); Pascoe, "Gender, Race, and Intercultural Relations"; Posadas, "Mestiza Girlhood," 273–82.

24. Joseph L. Chartkoff and Kerry Kona Chartkoff, *Archaeology of California* (Stanford: Stanford University Press, 1984); Robert F. Heizer and Albert B. Elsasser, *The Natural World of the California Indian* (Berkeley: University of California Press, 1980); Sherburne F. Cook and Woodrow Borah, *Essays in Population History: Mexico and the Caribbean* (3 vols., Berkeley: University of California Press, 1971–1979); Sherburne F. Cook, *The Population of the California Indians, 1769–1970* (Berkeley: University of California Press, 1976).

25. Irene Silverblatt, *Moon, Sun, and Witches: Gender Ideologies and Class in Inca and Colonial Peru* (Princeton, N.J.: Princeton University Press, 1987); June Nash, "Aztec Women: The Transition from Status to Class in Empire and Colony," Mona Etienne and Eleanor Leacock, eds., *Women and Colonization: Anthropological Perspectives* (New York: Praeger, 1980).

26. Ramón A. Gutiérrez, *When Jesus Came, the Corn Mothers Went Away: Marriage, Sexuality, and Power in New Mexico, 1500–1846* (Stanford: Stanford University Press, 1991), xvii–36; Sara M. Nelson, "Widowhood and Autonomy in the Native American Southwest," in Scadron, ed., *On Their Own,* 22–41; Alice Schlegel, "Hopi Family Structure and the Experience of Widowhood," ibid., 42–64; see the following essays in Eleanor Leacock and Richard Lee, eds., *Politics and History in Band Societies* (Cambridge, Mass.: Cambridge University Press, 1982): Eleanor Leacock and Richard Lee, "Introduction," 1–20; Lee, "Politics, Sexual and Non-sexual, in an Egalitarian Society," 23–36; and Leacock, "Relations of Production in Band Society," 159–170. See also June Nash, "A Decade of Research on Women in Latin America," June Nash and Helen I. Safa, eds., *Women and Change in Latin America* (South Hadley, Mass.: Bergin & Garvey Publishers, 1986), 3–21; Etienne and Leacock, eds., *Women and Colonization,* 1–24; Eleanor Burke Leacock, *Myths of Male Dominance: Collected Articles on Women Cross-Culturally* (New York: Monthly Review Press, 1981); Eleanor Leacock, "Women, Development, and Anthropological Facts and Fictions," *Latin American Perspectives* IV (winter-spring 1977): 8–17; Eleanor Leacock, "Women in Egalitarian Societies," Renate Bridenthal and Claudia Koonz, eds., *Becoming Visible: Women in European History* (Boston: Houghton Mifflin, 1977), 11–35.

27. Ann DuCille, "Othered Matters: Reconceptualizing Dominance and Difference in the History of Sexuality in America," *Journal of the History of Sexuality* I (1990): 102–27 (quote is from page 103).

28. Dee Brown, *The Gentle Tamers: Women of the Old Wild West* (New York: Bantam Books, 1974). Although Brown may have coined and been the first to use the term "gentle tamers," the concept of Euro-American women as the gentle, genteel bearers of "civilization" across successive frontiers is standard fare in the historical literature.

29. For an earlier, succinct critique of this approach, see Deena González, "Commentary [on a paper by John Mack Faragher, 'The Custom of the Country: Cross-Cultural Marriage in the Far Western Fur Trade']" *Western Women*, 217–22.

30. Rayna Green, ed., *Native American Women: A Contextual Bibliography* (Bloomington: Indiana University Press, 1983), 1–19; Green, "Native American Women," *Signs: Journal of Women in Culture and Society* VI (1980): 248–67; and Green, "The Pocahontas Perplex: The Image of Indian Women in American Culture," *Massachusetts Review* XVI (1975): 698–714; Antonia I. Castañeda, "The Political Economy of Nineteenth Century Stereotypes of Californianas," in Adelaida del Castillo, ed., *Between Borders: Essays in Mexicana/Chicana History* (Los Angeles: Floricanto Press, 1990), 213–36; Castañeda, "Gender, Race, and Culture: Spanish-Mexican Women in the Historiography of Frontier California."

31. For a discussion of the new approaches to culture in literature and history, see Lynn Hunt, ed., *The New Cultural History* (Berkeley: University of California Press, 1989). For a discussion of the issues in anthropology, see James Clifford, *The Predicament of Culture: Twentieth-Century Ethnography, Literature, and Art* (Cambridge, Mass.: Harvard University Press, 1988); for the earlier approaches in social history, see Peter N. Stearns, "Social History and History: A Progress Report," *Journal of Social History* XIX (1985): 319–34.

32. Richard Griswold del Castillo, *The Los Angeles Barrio, 1850–1890: A Social History* (Berkeley: University of California Press, 1979), app. A, 180–81; Leo Grebler, Joan W. Moore, and Ralph C. Guzmán, *The Mexican-American People: The Nation's Second Minority* (New York: Free Press, 1970); José Hernández, Leo Estrada, and David Alvírez, "Census Data and the Problem of Conceptually Defining the Mexican American Population," *Social Science Quarterly* LIII (1973): 671–87. See also Ricardo Romo, "Southern California and the Origins of Latino Civil-Rights Activism," *Western Legal History* III (1990): 379–406; Ramón A. Gutiérrez, "Ethnic and Class Boundaries in America's Hispanic Past," in Sucheng Chan, ed., *Social and Gender Boundaries in the United States* (Lewiston, N.Y.: E. Mellen Press, 1989), 37–53; Gloria A. Miranda, "Racial and Cultural Dimensions of Gente de Razón Status in Spanish and Mexican California," *Southern California Quarterly* LXX (1988): 265–78.

33. Grebler, Moore, and Guzmán, *Mexican-American People*, 322.

34. Alarcón, "Chicana Feminism"; Christian, "The Race for Theory"; Henry Louis Gates, Jr., ed., *Race, Writing, and Difference* (Chicago: University of Chicago Press, 1986); Mohanty, "Under Western Eyes"; Cornel West, "Minority Discourse and the Pitfalls of Canon Formation," *Yale Journal of Criticism* I (fall 1987): 173–200.

35. Mohanty, "Under Western Eyes," 336.

36. Deena J. González, "La Tules Image and Reality: Euro-American Attitudes and Legend Formation on a Spanish Mexican Frontier," in De la Torre and Pesquera, eds., *Building with Our Hands;* Patricia Albers and William James, "Illusion and Illumination: Visual Images of American Indian Women in the West," in Armitage and Jameson, eds., *Women's West*, pp. 35–50 examine the unrealistic images of American Indians produced for postcards for the tourist trade; Green, ed., *Native*

American Women, 1–19; Green, "Native American Women," 248–67; Green, "Pocahontas Perplex," 698–714; Maryann Oshana, "Native American Women in Westerns: Reality and Myth," *Frontiers: A Journal of Women Studies* VI (fall 1981): 46–50; Castañeda, "Political Economy of Nineteenth Century Stereotypes," 213–36; Castañeda, "Gender, Race, and Culture"; Renee E. Tajima, "Lotus Blossoms Don't Bleed: Images of Asian Women," Asian Women of California, ed., *Making Waves*, 308–17; Paula Giddings, *When and Where I Enter: The Impact of Black Women on Race and Sex in America* (Toronto: Bantam Books, 1984), 31.

37. Castañeda, "The Political Economy of Stereotypes"; Green, "The Pocahontas Perplex."

38. Megumi Dick Osumi, "Asians and California's Anti-Miscegenation Laws," in Tsuchida, ed., *Asian and Pacific American Experiences*, 1–37; Akemi Kikumura and Harry H. L. Kitano, "Interracial Marriage: A Picture of the Japanese Americans," ibid., 193–205. The Kikumura and Kitano essay was first published in 1973. Although California was a "free" state, slave owners still brought slaves to it and other western territories, and Euro-Americans still tried to enslave Indians. The fact that enslaved black people were able to win their freedom in California if they could get their case heard does not obviate the reality of enslavement in the West nor the need to examine it.

39. Castañeda, "The Political Economy of Stereotypes."

40. For a discussion of the devaluation of the sexuality of women of color as central to imperialism, with a specific focus on Native American women in California, see Antonia I. Castañeda, "Sexual Violence in the Politics and Policies of Conquest," in De la Torre and Pesquera, eds., *Building with Our Hands.*

41. Butler, *Daughters of Joy*, 11–12.

42. Ibid., 12.

43. Armitage, "Through Women's Eyes," in Armitage and Jameson, eds., *Women's West*, 9–19; Kolodny, *The Land before Her*; Riley, *Women and Indians on the Frontier*; Myres, "Mexican Americans and Westering Anglos."

44. For discussion of sexual and other violence toward women of color in frontier California, see Albert Hurtado, *Indian Survival on the California Frontier* (New Haven, Conn.: Yale University Press, 1989), 169–92; Castañeda, "Sexual Violence in the Politics and Policies of Conquest" and "The Political Economy of Nineteenth-Century Stereotypes"; Giddings, *When and Where I Enter*; Lucie Cheng Hirata, "Chinese Immigrant Women in Nineteenth-Century California," in Tsuchida, ed., *Asian and Pacific American Experiences*, 38–55; and Hirata, "Free, Indentured, Enslaved: Chinese Prostitutes in Nineteenth-Century America," *Signs: Journal of Women in Culture and Society* V (1979): 3–29.

45. Rosalia Vallejo de Leese, "History of the Bear Flag Party," Manuscript Collection, Bancroft Library, University of California, Berkeley; Hurtado, *Indian Survival in California*; Giddings, *When and Where I Enter*; Hirata, "Chinese Immigrant Women," 1.

46. Paula Gunn Allen, ed., *Spider Woman's Granddaughters: Traditional Tales and Contemporary Writing by Native American Women* (Boston: Beacon Press, 1989), 2.

47. The first part of this subtitle is derived from Bill Ashcroft, Gareth Griffiths, and Helen Tiffin, eds., *The Empire Writes Back: Theory and Practice in Post-Colonial Literatures* (New York: Routledge, 1989).

48. For representative works, see Gloria Anzaldúa, *Borderlands-La Frontera: The New Mestiza* (San Francisco: Spinsters/Aunt Lute, 1987); Amy Tan, *The Joy Luck Club*

(New York: Putnam's, 1989); Toni Morrison, *Beloved* (New York: Knopf, 1987); Louise Erdrich, *Love Medicine* (New York: Holt, Rinehart, and Winston, 1984).

49. Chela Sandoval, "U.S. Third World Feminism: The Theory and Method of Oppositional Consciousness in the Postmodern World," *Genders* X (spring 1991): 1–24; Bernice Johnson Reagan, "Forward: Nurturing Resistance," in Mark O'Brien and Craig Little, eds., *Reimaging America: The Arts of Social Change* (Philadelphia: New Society Publishers, 1990), 1–8.

50. Shirley Geok-lin Lim, "Introduction: A Dazzling Quilt," in Lim, Tsutakawa, Donnelly, eds., *Forbidden Stitch*, 12; Alarcón, "Chicana Feminism."

51. Gutiérrez, *When Jesus Came*, xvii–xviii.

52. Ibid.

53. See the excellent collection of essays in Mohanty, Russo, and Torres, eds., *Third World Women*; Kumkum Sangari Sudesh Vaid, eds., *Recasting Women: Essays in Indian Colonial History* (New Brunswick, N.J.: Rutgers University Press, 1990); Minh-ha, *Woman, Native, Other*; Malek Alloula, *The Colonial Harem*, translated by Myrna Godzich and Wlad Godzich (Minneapolis: University of Minnesota Press, 1986).

54. Alloula, *Colonial Harem*, xiv.

55. Mohanty, "Under Western Eyes," 335.

56. Howard Lamar and Leonard Thompson, eds., *The Frontier in History: North America and Southern Africa Compared* (New Haven, Conn.: Yale University Press, 1981).

57. Ibid., 7.

58. Limerick, *Legacy of Conquest*, 26–27.

59. Rosalinda Méndez Gonzalez, "Distinctions in Western Women's Experience: Ethnicity, Class, and Social Change," in Armitage and Jameson, eds., *Women's West*, 237–52.

60. Deena J. González, *Refusing the Favor: The Spanish-Mexican Women of Santa Fe, 1820–1880* (New York: Oxford University Press, 1999); Hurtado, *Indian Survival*; Victoria Brady, Sarah Crome, and Lyn Reese, "Resist! Survival Tactics of Indian Women," *California History* LXIII (1984): 140–49; Lamar and Thompson, *Frontier in History*; George Harwood Phillips, *Chiefs and Challengers: Indian Resistance and Cooperation in Southern California* (Berkeley: University of California Press, 1975); Jack Forbes, *Apache, Navaho, and Spaniard* (Norman: University of Oklahoma Press, 1960).

61. Helen Lara-Cea, "Notes on the Use of Parish Registers in the Reconstruction of Chicana History in California Prior to 1850," in Del Castillo, ed., *Between Borders*, 131–60; González, *Refusing the Favor*; Angelina Veyna, "A View of the Past: Women in Colonial New Mexico, 1744–1767," in De la Torre and Pesquera, eds., *Building with Our Hands*; Antonia I. Castañeda, "Presidarias y Pobladoras: Spanish Mexican Women in Frontier Monterey, California, 1770–1821" (Ph.D. dissertation, Stanford University, 1990).

62. Mohanty, "Under Western Eyes," 346; Chandra P. Mohanty and Saya P. Mohanty, "Review: Contradictions of Colonialism," *Women's Review of Books* VIII (March 1990): 19–21.

63. Etienne and Leacock, *Women and Colonization*; Leacock and Lee, *Politics and History in Band Societies*; Evelyn Blackwood, "Sexuality and Gender in Certain Native American Tribes: The Case of Cross-Gender Females," *Signs: Journal of Women in Society and Culture* X (1984): 27–42.

64. Hurtado, *Indian Survival in California*; Brady, Crome, and Reese, "Resist!"
65. Lois Risling, "Native Women in California" (Paper presented at the Huntington Library Seminar in Women's Studies, San Marino, Calif., Jan. 20, 1991); Patricia Albers, "Autonomy and Dependency in the Lives of Dakota Women: A Study in Historical Change," *Review of Radical Political Economics* XVII (fall 1985): 109–34; Patricia Albers and Beatrice Medicine, eds., *The Hidden Half: Studies of Plains Indian Women* (Washington, D.C.: University Press of America, 1983); see Gutiérrez, *When Jesus Came*, for a discussion of socio-sexual reciprocity among the Pueblos of New Mexico.
66. On the Yuma, see Hugo Reid, "Letters on the Los Angeles County Indians," Susana Dakin, ed., *A Scotch Paisano: Hugo Reid's Life in California, 1832–1852* (Berkeley: University of California Press, 1939), app. B, 215–16, 240; see also Castañeda, "Presidarias y Pobladoras," 63–113.
67. González, *Refusing the Favor*. For a discussion of Nuevo Mexicanas and widow-hood in the postwar period, see Deena J. González, "The Widowed Women of Santa Fe: Assessments on the Lives of an Unmarried Population, 1850–80," in Scadron, ed., *On Their Own*, 65–90.
68. Sucheng Chan, "The Exclusion of Chinese Women, 1870–1943," in Sucheng Chan, ed., *Entry Denied: Exclusion and the Chinese Community in America, 1882–1943* (Philadelphia: Temple University Press, 1991), 94–146; Ichioka, *The Issei*; Marlon K. Hom, *Songs of Gold Mountain: Cantonese Rhymes from San Francisco Chinatown* (Berkeley: University of California Press, 1987); Judy Yung, *Chinese Women of America: A Pictorial History* (Seattle: Published for the Chinese Culture Foundation of San Francisco by University of Washington Press, 1986); Judy Yung, "The Social Awakening of Chinese American Women," in DuBois and Ruiz, eds., *Unequal Sisters*, 195–207; the following articles appear in Tsuchida, ed., *Asian and Pacific American Experiences*; Hirata, "Chinese Immigrant Women in Nineteenth-Century California," 53–55; Hirata, "Free, Indentured, Enslaved," 3–29; Hori, "Japanese Prostitution in Hawaii," 56–65; and Emma Gee, "Issei Women," 66–74.
69. Gail M. Nomura, "Issei Working Women in Hawaii," in Asian Women United of California, ed., *Making Waves*, 135–47; Ichioka, *Issei*, 164–75; Glenn, *Issei, Nisei, War Bride*, 42–66.
70. Chan, "Exclusion of Chinese women," 94–146.
71. Ibid., 95.
72. Ibid., 132.
73. George Anthony Peffer, "Forbidden Families: Emigration Experiences of Chinese Women under the Page Law, 1875–1882," *Journal of American Ethnic History* VI (fall 1986): 28–46.
74. Lucie Cheng and Edna Bonacich, eds., *Labor Immigration under Capitalism: Asian Workers in the United States before World War II* (Berkeley: University of California Press, 1984); Mario Barrera, *Race and Class in the Southwest: A Theory of Racial Inequality* (Notre Dame, Ind.: University of Notre Dame Press, 1979).
75. Nomura, "Issei Working Women in Hawaii," 135–47; Ichioka, *Issei*, 28–90; Ichioka, "Amerika Nadeshiko," 339–57; Ichioka, "Ameyuki-san: Japanese Prostitutes in Nineteenth Century America," *Amerasia Journal* IV (1977): 1–21; Glenn, *Issei, Nisei, War Bride*, 3–20; Hori, "Japanese Prostitution in Hawaii," 56–65.
76. Ichioka, *Issei*, 20–39.
77. Shirley Ann Moore, "Not in Somebody's Kitchen: African-American Women

Workers in Richmond, California, 1910–1950" (Paper presented at the Huntington Library Seminar in Women's Studies, San Marino, Calif., Jan. 19, 1991); Shirley Ann Moore, *To Place Our Deeds: The Black Community in Richmond, California, 1910–1963* (Berkeley: University of California Press, 2000).

78. Moore, "Not in Somebody's Kitchen."

79. Joan Jensen and Gloria Ricci Lothrop, *California Women: A History* (San Francisco, 1987), 32, 37; Rudolph M. Lapp, *Afro-Americans in California* (2d ed., San Francisco, 1987); William Loren Katz, *The Black West: A Pictorial History* (3d ed., Seattle: Open Hand Pub., 1987); Lawrence B. de Graaf, "Race, Sex, and Region: Black Women in the American West, 1850–1920," *Pacific Historical Review* XL (1980): 285–313; Delilah L. Beasley, *The Negro Trail Blazers of California* (1919; New York: Negro Universities Press, 1969).

80. Deena J. González, "The Spanish-Mexican Women of Santa Fe: Mocking the Conquerors" (Paper presented at the Writing on the Border Conference, Claremont Colleges, Oct. 27, 1989).

ELSE SURELY WE SHALL ALL HANG SEPARATELY

THE POLITICS OF WESTERN WOMEN'S HISTORY*

Virginia Scharff

In 1980, Joan Jensen and Darlis Miller, in "'Gentle Tamers' Revisited," called for "a broader approach to women and politics in the West."[1] They questioned in particular the narrowness of the existing literature on what they called "the politics of middle-class women in the West," chiefly studies of the woman suffrage movement. The energy devoted to research on suffrage, they believed, diverted scholarly attention from other political events, organizations, and processes in which women participated. The focus on middle-class woman suffragists, they said, further ignored politically active women usually left out of suffrage studies, including African American, Hispanic, and Native American women. Jensen and Miller also called for attention to working-class women's political participation, specifically in labor politics.[2]

Jensen and Miller proposed a substantial expansion of the topic of "western women and politics." They nevertheless retained a traditional view of politics itself, using the word to refer generally to the formal operations of public institutions, and the public activities of particularly powerful individuals. Defined thus narrowly, politics has always been the sanctioned subject of written history, along with warfare, which has sometimes been considered an extreme form of politics. Those who

*This chapter was previously published as: Scharff, Virginia. "Else Surely We Shall All Hang Separately: The Politics of Western Women's History." In *Pacific Historical Review* 61 (November 1992): 535–55.

wrote about history, wrote about politics. In the past twenty years, historians of women have sought a place at the center of the historical profession. Therefore, if for no other reason than the very practical one of attracting the attention of those who define what history is, and write it according to conventional precepts, exploring women's political role must be among the first tasks of women's history.

The institutional question—gaining access to what one used to call "the establishment" of the historical profession—is one justification for advocating research on women's political history. However, in recent years, traditional political history has lost its central place in the canon. Most of those who call themselves political historians today have embraced an expanded view of politics encompassing what the historian Thomas Bender has called "public culture."[3] Such a concept is valuable to women's historians in particular, because American women have, as a group, been barred from exercising legitimate economic and governmental power for most of the nation's history. The desire to write a history that values women's activities, recognizes differences among women, and includes the experiences of all women therefore requires not only claiming the realm of politics as women's domain, but also rethinking the very notion of politics.[4]

Nearly a decade after "'Gentle Tamers' Revisited," Joan Wallach Scott, borrowing from the work of Michel Foucault, argued for moving beyond the notion that politics is limited to the "formal operations of government" and for embracing a definition of the term that would encompass all "contests that involve power"—"power not only as a relationship of repression or domination but also as a set of relationships or processes that produce positive effects."[5] The study of politics may therefore mean examining all relations of power, including those involved with the professional practice of history.

Using Scott's wider definition, I want to look specifically at what is presently called "western women's history" as a political enterprise. Scott has written that we need to see history *not* as "what happened, what 'truth' there is 'out there' to be discovered and transmitted," but instead as a set of practices for producing knowledge and as a political exercise that "both reflects and creates relations of power."[6] In other words, there is no self-evidently important body of data, obviously identifiable as "history," waiting around to be discovered like a starlet on a stool at Schwab's Hollywood drugstore. Instead, we need to conceptualize the data of history as an infinite set of past happenings, none of which are *necessarily* more important than others. Events derive their importance as "history" when persons charged with conserving and interpreting the past (in our culture, they include novelists, television producers, movie stars, and persons who identify themselves as *historians*) relate them to other sets of events, constructing what we recognize as historical narratives. Since these past happenings can be linked to one another in any number of ways, the data of history are subject to a huge variety of sometimes conflicting interpretations. *History*, then, is one word commonly and confusingly used to refer to two things: what happened, and what we say happened.

Given the unlimited possible combinations of past events and proliferating narratives, students of history rely on common wisdom, on some kind of agreement among thinking people, to tell us what history is and what parts of the past matter. Yet common wisdom is, and probably always was, unreliable. As an academic discipline, history has become more and more a fragmented domain in which practitioners of different specialties know less and less about what other people are doing. Whatever fragile agreements remain are unstable products of continuing conflict. The question of which interpretations dominate discussions among historians at any given time is very much affected by contests within the profession over *who* gets to define the past. Such contests for power have shaped the process of building a body of work called "western women's history."

With trepidation, then, and in an effort to provoke discussion about the customs and conflicts inherent in academic practices, I want to focus on one dimension of western women's history, its incarnation as a contemporary scholarly enterprise dedicated to unearthing and interpreting the stories of women who have lived in the area we call the West. This professional endeavor involves numerous people engaged in at least three sets of interlocking struggles, recognized a decade ago in "'Gentle Tamers' Revisited," that are at once pragmatic and intellectual. Jensen and Miller called for "an evaluation of the experiences of all ethnic groups of women," an enterprise that would "necessitate the rewriting of western history, a task which should be undertaken with an eye to other work now being done in women's history."[7] They charged historians of western women, then, with three tasks: writing a multicultural history of western women, finding a place for western women's history in the larger history of women, and transforming western regional history by their efforts. Investigators have undertaken each of these tasks, and in each case have faced political conflicts and choices.

First, a growing number of scholars have taken up Jensen and Miller's challenge "to evaluate the experiences of all ethnic groups of women" and have begun to build a multicultural history of their subjects. This process has as often produced antagonism as agreement, and has imperiled the assumptions upon which the field is constituted.[8] The more western women's historians confront the challenge of constructing an ethnically inclusive account of the past, the more problematic their status either as United States regionalists, or as people who work within women's history.

"Western women"? The last ten years of research vindicate Jensen and Miller's prescience in seeing this compound term as ethnocentric.[9] The name we have given the field bespeaks historical power configurations and demands explanation. For millennia before Europeans defined the reaches of the North American continent as the West, it was home to Native Americans. For the heirs of Spanish conquerors and the native peoples with whom they intermarried, the United States West was and is a North. For immigrants from Asia, it is the East. For those who come now from all over the world, air travel has diminished the significance of compass directions.[10]

To speak of the West is to assume the importance of national borders fixed in the middle of the nineteenth century, boundaries established through conquest and still in force, and to ignore multidirectional, overlapping patterns of inhabitation that reach back thousands of years and forward into an uncertain future. Thus, obviously, the term "western history" is historical and political and ultimately reductive. Replacing it requires finding a term or set of terms that transcend the limitations of time and space in describing human activity, a difficult if not impossible task.

To speak of "women" as a group is to forget that notions of womanhood vary from time to time, place to place, group to group. In search of women in the multicultural West, historians must first sort out their own understandings about gender, and then move to the task of establishing the ways in which their subjects constructed masculinity and femininity. Just as nineteenth-century ideas about geography and nationality have shaped the ways in which we think about what we do,

Victorian ideas about men and women have influenced, and continue to influence, many western historians, including those who work on women's history.[11] Amid the legacies of the past and present clashes of people and interests, historians grope to find words to describe both bygone power relations and the never-to-be-finished process of occupying the terrain we persist in calling the West.

Many western women's historians have taken seriously the necessity to describe and analyze the West in multicultural as well as gender-conscious terms. Yet meeting this challenge has turned out to be more complicated than it at first appeared. Throughout the 1980s and into the 1990s, American feminists have grappled with racism. Euro-American scholars have been called upon to recognize and dispense with the ways racist assumptions and practices shape the research they do, the works they read and credit, and the professional activities they undertake.[12] Since at least 1984, women (and some men) of color have repeatedly voiced their feelings of marginalization at conferences on western women's history, insisting that they be involved from the earliest stages, that their work be treated as central rather than supplementary, that their perspectives structure the "common wisdom" of western history, rather than entering this scholarly discourse as objections. As historian Deena González wrote to organizers of a 1992 conference sponsored by the Coalition for Western Women's History and the Center for Great Plains Studies, "If we are not involved from the outset, before the ideas themselves coalesce around a conference, then we are excluded. . . . [T]he act is not only unconscionable, but exclusionary and racist."[13] Clearly, the process of reorienting the production of knowledge about western women, shot through as it is with questions of power, is difficult and cannot help producing conflict.[14]

Historians of women began by placing the notion of *difference* at the center of their work, by insisting that traditional history is male-centered and that there is a need to examine women's history, a history overlapping with, yet often divergent from, that of men, in its own right. Having founded this enterprise on that intellectual distinction, women's historians face the task of reconciling the desire to see common patterns in women's past, with the recognition that differences—and conflicts—among women exist and are historically significant.

One way out of this dilemma is to recall that divergences between men's and women's experiences have more to do with *gender* (or historically specific ideas and practices elaborated around biological categories) than with *sex* (purportedly essential and transhistorical biological differences). If the connotations of gender, of masculinity and femininity, vary from one culture to another and change with the passage of time, then gender must itself, as a system of explanations about the world, interact with other mutable systems of meanings and relationships. No individual, in short, is only one thing—a woman, a European American, a citizen of the United States, an inhabitant of New Mexico, a historian. It makes sense, then, to see race, ethnicity, class, and locale as variables not simply affecting women's experience in important ways, but as central and mutually contingent components of the gendered identities of historical persons.[15]

Historians of western women are mostly female and share a concern with womanhood. But these commonalities obscure as much as they reveal. Products of history themselves, western women's historians are working through real problems. Conflicts among scholars are rooted in the long-standing ethnocentricity of the Euro-American historical tradition, both as a profession dominated by middle- and upper-class Euro-Americans and as a body of knowledge concerned chiefly with Euro-Americans (and in both cases, until recently, Euro-American men). Antonia Castañeda has written that recent works by Euro-American feminist and social historians "mirror the larger problems of the earlier historiography. That is, the new scholarship lacks a clear framework to examine the historical experience of women whose race and culture at not Anglo North American. Moreover, it often reflects the underlying assumptions and race and class biases of the earlier historiography."[16] In pointing to the coexistence of feminism and racism in western women's history, Castañeda's critique raises fundamental questions about who should define this field of inquiry, and how that definition will be carried out in practice. How can Euro-American women, who are privileged by virtue of race if marginalized by dint of sex, justify the failure to research the history of racial ethnic women? Or, conversely, for the growing number of Euro-American scholars who have begun to study the history of women of color, by what authority do they investigate women unlike themselves? Does scholarship on women of color by persons of the dominant ethnic group inevitably constitute an illegitimate appropriation, a recolonization, of some women's past?[17]

Women historians of color, who are acutely aware of the political nature of scholarship, confront dilemmas of their own. The growing body of historical research on people who have come to this country from Latin America, Asia, Africa, and the Middle East implies continuing struggles that extend again to naming the subject. Evelyn Nakano Glenn has argued for the use of the term racial ethnic, rather than third world or people of color, "to refer collectively to blacks, latinos and Asian Americans, groups that share a legacy of labor exploitation and special forms of oppression."[18] What are the politics of different terms for this vast array of historical actors and how do they reflect shifting power arrangements, strategies, and alignments? What is the relation between current politics and past events? How, indeed, do we define "groups" as historical entities?[19]

The legacy of colonialism historians have described provides grounding for mistrust among women currently in the profession. Scholars of color today are debating the merits of attempting to integrate their work into a politically suspect field, or building a separate body of knowledge. "Dwelling on 'diversity' and multiculturalism (a euphemism for the emperializing and now defunct 'melting pot') is a way of avoiding seriously dismantling Racism—by both white women and women-of-color," writes Gloria Anzaldúa."[20] At a session on Chicana history at the 1990 Berkshire Conference on the History of Women, several Chicana scholars argued powerfully against multicultural work, and for devoting their efforts to Chicana history. But is there any guarantee that either further research or future contests for power will reinforce, rather than undermine, today's seemingly straightforward political lineations? Philosopher Maria Lugones has written that "One cannot really answer questions like 'What is a Hispanic?' . . . What it means to be a 'Hispanic' in the varied so-called Hispanic communities is also up in the air."[21] Historians, who study the past, are on shaky ground when we practice crystal-gazing. Can we assume that our current attempts to eradicate intellectual bias and ensure academic democracy carry us toward some endpoint of truth, destined to withstand future scrutiny?

These questions have arisen in response to forthright, and sometimes angry criticism of Euro-American women's historians by women of color in the profession. One rather obvious reason for anger is that Euro-American women's historians like me (who work mostly on the history of Euro-American women) are reluctant to give up racial enti-tlement. For "white" women, says Karen Anderson, it is often easier to reinforce the system than to change it.[22] To the extent that Euro-American women have been able to legitimate themselves as academ-ics, they have benefited from possessing identities that pose no peril to the idea of white privilege. Speaking for myself, I have had to be con-fronted repeatedly with the partiality of my accounts before I "got" the significance of ethnicity and race and began to admit that Euro-American women's experiences do not constitute a deracinated or class-free standard for women as a group, but are instead also products of race and class relations. In 1978, Adrienne Rich referred to this kind of thinking as "white solipsism."[23] Fourteen years later, I think I under-stand what she meant.

Euro-American women's responses to challenges by women of color—at conferences, in print, over coffee, over the long distance tele-phone lines—have been as various as the individuals on all sides who have entered these debates as combatants, peacemakers, creative thinkers, and interested bystanders. Speaking personally again, I have vowed patience and exchanged warm reassurances, but have also expe-rienced rage, depression, guilt, hurt feelings, a determination to think harder and do better. I find confrontations debilitating, but they have forced me to change the way I teach and think about women. I have moved away from seeking a narrative line for women's history, to trying to learn about, describe, and compare various women's experiences in different times and places. I would like to become, in Lugones's term, a "'world'-traveller."[24]

I am learning the painful lesson that the assumptions with which I approach history, and indeed my own good faith, remain open to ques-tion. Grounds for struggle remain. But I can see no recourse except to stumble on in hopes of establishing a lasting basis of trust that breaches color and class lines. That is my own utopian, and urgent, objective. Our common goal, as historians of women, is to render as fairly and fully as possible an account of the lives of women who have been and continue to be as often divided against one another as united. We must find a way to develop the often troubling histories we seek to write, and still keep talking to one another.

I have begun by describing a group of conflicts that seem at first glance to be internal to western women's history but soon reveal them-

selves to be about global issues. The second set of struggles, also potentially global in scope, arises from the realm of United States women's
history. Certainly, western women's historians have done their work
"with an eye to other work now being done in women's history," as
Jensen and Miller suggested. Other historians of American women have
not always returned the favor. Just as eastern-trained male historians
have regarded western and frontier history as professional backwaters,
many of the most prominent historians of American women continue
to regard research on western women as narrow, derivative, and
insignificant. In some regards, one might see parallels between the position of scholars of color working on western women's history topics vis-
à-vis Euro-American women in that subfield, and the status of western
women's history relative to eastern-dominated U.S. women's history.

Parochialism has impeded the task of building good explanations
of U.S. women's history. Marginality has perpetuated a public view of
western women as gentle tamers, naughty madams, Calamity Janes.
Good work on Mexican American union organizers and Silicon Valley
working women, for example, deserves both a wide audience and serious treatment as integral to the history of western women in particular
and American women in general.[25] Paradoxically, in the quest for legitimacy, western women's historians may also have ignored precisely
those aspects of their subject that raise the question of the significance
of region. Could we imagine Calamity Jane in, say, Boston? Why ever
not? Surely a city of that magnitude must have seen its share of hard-
drinking, cross-dressing prostitutes. Why should such a violator of feminine decorum be more visible, and be taken as more typical, in South
Dakota than in Massachusetts?

Parochialism has also cost eastern women's history the chance to
learn from the West. The biracial model of women's experience, so
often implicit in the works of eastern women's historians, made no sense
in the West.[26] Western women's history likewise has scrambled the
periodization of American women's history, offering historians the
opportunity to view, for example, the arrival of the *Mayflower* from the
perspective of Santa Fe or, for that matter, Gran Quivira.[27] Western
women's history, moreover, has introduced to American women's
history the need to account for the physical environment, the landscape
and all it bears, as a critical factor in women's experience.[28]

In the years since "'Gentle Tamers' Revisited," the ranks of west-

ern women's historians have swelled. The best work in the field is
beginning to attract the notice of others in U.S. women's history, a
development attributable in no small measure to the accomplishments
of young historians, including Valerie Matsumoto, Peggy Pascoe, and
Vicki Ruiz, to name but a few.[29] A recent anthology in women's history,
Unequal Sisters: A Multicultural Reader in U.S. Women's History, edited
by Ellen DuBois and Vicki Ruiz, represents an attempt to recognize and
correct earlier regional biases in the canon of U.S. women's history.
Works-in-progress by Matsumoto, Mary Odem, Fran Leeper Buss,
Antonia Castañeda, Deena González, and others promise to unveil new
material, raise fresh questions, and offer original interpretations.

It is also time to recall the remarkable record of Joan Jensen, who
above all other scholars has mapped out a path toward new methods
and concepts that will enable us to create an exquisitely detailed, inclusive women's history. As essayist, monograph writer, and editor, Jensen
has turned her attention to women's experience in numerous locales
including California, New Mexico, the Midwest, and the Middle
Atlantic. In 1981, just as the new wave of women's history was coming
into its own, she challenged understanding of the time frames and borders of women's lives by collecting documents on women's agricultural
work, from Native American oral traditions to speeches by the Populist
agitator Mary Lease to the recollections of United Farm Workers'
activist Dolores Huerta. Her recently published work on Asian Indian
immigrants to North America reminds us of the need to keep our definitions of American pluralism open-ended and dynamic. Her new collection of essays on rural American women demonstrates unequivocally
the promise of the multicultural perspective for opening up new possibilities in women's history. Not simply prolific, Jensen has also provided
a model for other historians because of her wisdom, her meticulous
care, and her practice of treating her subjects, as well as her students
and colleagues, with respect.[30]

While Joan Jensen and others have made western women's history
more visible to U.S. women's historians, work on western women has
also achieved more and more recognition among mainstream western
historians. Still, western women's historians sometimes feel that they
are not quite fully either "women's" or "western" historians. While several of us have joked that "We Mae West; then again we may not," we
find ourselves puzzled and sometimes resentful at somehow slipping

between the cracks. Numerous men in the western history field have been helpful and sympathetic (the jobs some of us hold bear ample witness to that help and sympathy). Yet we remain conscious of our status as a "special interest group" sharing the position of the insider/outsider so eloquently described by filmmaker and theorist Trinh T. Minh-ha: "Not quite the same, not quite the other, she stands in that threshold place where she constantly drifts in and out."[31] This brings me to the third part of Jensen and Miller's visionary agenda. I do no think any of us believe that we have yet succeeded in "rewriting western history."[32]

Here again, I want to raise the issue of *difference*, or what we might call the multiple subject of western history, to speculate about who does what kind of history and why. Many historians of the United States West have avoided dealing with issues of gender, race, or class. Those who do study these relations of power are often themselves still considered deviant from the white, male, middle-class norm—that is, women of all ethnicities, and all people of color. If some Euro-American women feel like interlopers in the field, men and women of color have felt their difference from the majority of western historians to an acute degree.

Western historians as a group traditionally have affirmed one difference, that is, the distinction between western history and other history. That affirmation is partly defensive. Western historians have long been derided by practitioners of other histories as cowpoke scholars, as workers in a field dominated by popularizers and buffs who assemble together in "corrals." The best western historians have produced sophisticated and significant work equal to any in American history, but have nevertheless been unable to escape this redneck stereotype. The persistence of this contrasting identity has sometimes led western historians seeking mutual recognition and legitimization to minimize differences among themselves, to fit in, to be good ol' boys. This socialization process, which makes "western historians" out of perfectly ordinary people, is often reinforced by academic training, which may include work on and by women, but still assumes the centrality of men's experiences to western history.

The field of western history is, however, changing. Difference has begun to make a difference. Racial and ethnic conflict and contact have become not only categories of historical analysis, but in some accounts, have become central themes.[33] The first reason for the change is demographic and sociological; there are more people of color, and more women of several ethnicities, studying the history of the region, identifying themselves as "western historians," and seeking admission to the professional community.

The consciousness of the multiplicity of historical experiences in the American West, so eloquently set forth in "The 'Gentle Tamers' Revisited," has spread from subfields often treated as marginal to western history at large (ethnic, women's, Indian, Chicano history), to the field as a whole. This consciousness has sometimes been described as a challenge on the part of "new" western historians to such hegemonic concepts as the westward march of progress, from frontier to frontier. Yet I wonder precisely who fits in these camps. What sets the so-called "new" western historians apart from those styled "old" is not the tendency to see the history of the West as evil and exploitative instead of progressive and glorious, but instead a willingness to deal with new persons and groups in a new way. What is so exciting in the work of William Cronon and Richard White, for example, is that their thoughtful accounts of western history begin by assuming that the Native American experience is neither more nor less legitimate (or, for that matter, neither more nor less problematic) than the Anglo-American experience.

At this point, I would like to return to the subject of redefining "politics." The expanded definition of politics, embracing all contests for power taking place in a given place (the West, in this case) and time (a period still yet to be defined) has already begun to shift the focus of western history from the dominant group to relations among various contenders for power, individual and collective.[34] Such western history is necessarily multicultural and includes dealing with gender as a category of historical analysis. But research and writing aside, the historical texts we produce also require other kinds of concrete actions on the part of people engaged in detailing and defining western history.

This is a troubled time for all historians, who, after all, do not do their work in isolation. Our efforts today take place amid diatribes against a purported leftist insistence on "political correctness," as well as in the face of the left's seeming inability to avoid the fragmenting, particularizing tendencies of a scholarship based on a recognition of human variety. Political controversy within western women's history overlaps with and reflects these larger quarrels; the "new" western history's quarrel with the "old" echoes controversies in the historical profession at large.[35] Demanding that many voices be heard, we shout one another down. We need to act now to restore the possibility of discussion. I would like to make four proposals for action.

First, historians of western women, like all historians, must look again at the contributions of some of our predecessors, keeping in mind the open-endedness of the process of historical revision and the incompleteness of our own visions. There are clear intellectual reasons for doing so. We have learned, as Jensen and Miller suggested a decade ago, that a multicultural history may hold the key to certain puzzles in western women's history still unsolved, including the much-debated yet still bewildering question of why women in the American West got the vote before those in the East. Yet even such seemingly overworked issues as the suffrage question may not be fully illuminated by accounting for the variables of race, ethnicity, and culture. The "old" western history was assuredly marred by racism, sexism, and romanticism, but history has always been a discussion rather than a monologue. Even the western woman suffrage question was once bold and new, as when T. A. Larson first pursued it seriously in the 1960s. We need to be prepared to retrace our steps, as Jensen and Miller did, and reclaim as well as critique some of what "old" western historians like Larson taught us about "old" questions like suffrage as we inquire anew.[36]

There are ethical and political as well as intellectual justifications for grounding multiculturalism in the historical tradition. It has recently become the fashion in academic and journalistic writing to mischaracterize all pleas for attention to the past and present of subordinated people as a monolithic, nihilistic movement for "political correctness." According to writers who use this buzz phrase, the foundations of American civilization are presently threatened by the ascendancy of thought police representing "special interest groups," persons whose goals and interests are narrow at best, totalitarian at worst. In the name of free speech, respect for tradition, and scholarly objectivity, crusaders against political correctness have assailed work by and on people of color and women of all ethnicities.

The campaign to eradicate political correctness has been remarkably successful in attracting public support, but its attacks on the new scholarship demand the very narrowing of inquiry and suppression of dissent that campaigners supposedly deplore. We need to defuse this criticism, which threatens to mire us all in pointless and mean-spirited name-calling. One way to do so is to disassemble the categories of new and old history, to recognize contradictions among seeming allies as well as commonalities among apparent adversaries. The historical tradition is full of such revisionist reconfigurations and reconciliations, including one recent masterful effort by the intellectual historian John Toews.[37]

Second, western women's historians must practice a professional politics of inclusiveness. Since Euro-Americans hold most of the power in the profession, this means affirmative action for people of color, recruiting women and men of color for positions of responsibility, including scholars of color in conference planning and on organizational boards and committees, seeking out collaborations of all kinds. This process is under way in professional organizations, including the American Historical Association, the Organization of American Historians, and indeed the Western History Association. Of course, not all purported efforts at engagement and dialogue are well-intentioned, as both feminists and scholars of color drawn unwittingly into shouting matches have discovered. Still, good faith efforts at representativeness require engagement on the part of women and men, of people of color as well as Euro-Americans, from the moment projects are initiated to the point of completion.

Professional inclusiveness also means that Euro-American scholars must read, cite, and teach work on and by women of color. Anthologies like Gloria Anzaldúa and Cherríe Moraga's *This Bridge Called My Back* and Anzaldúa's *Making Face, Making Soul: Haciendo Caras* are good places to begin. Films like *Salt of the Earth*, *El Norte*, and *Bagdad Café* belong in western women's history classrooms. The lives of Maya Angelou and Anita Hill are part of this history too. If, as I have suggested, we are to look seriously at the Calamity Jane-style "hell-raisers" who have occupied so prominent a place in the popular image of western womanhood, we can learn much from Deena González's study of Gertrude Barceló, the nineteenth-century gambling house operator better known as Doña Tules.[38]

My third proposal is a rhetorical and intellectual challenge to come up with some new ways of discussing the past. The rhetoric of professional history writing proceeds through contradiction, through pointing out the errors in one's predecessors' and colleagues' assumptions, analyses, and accounts. The literature of western women's history includes important critiques of the ways in which history written by outsiders (notably, white men) has trivialized and marginalized the experiences of all women, and women of color in particular, beginning, of course, with "'The Gentle Tamers' Revisited," which took as its point of departure Dee Brown's romantic book of essays on predominately Euro-American western women.[39]

We cannot get along without this kind of criticism, to be sure, but we also need to ask whether this rhetorical method, and the consequent creation of a community based on opposition, is sufficient for the history we hope to create. Our discussions have, at times, become downright vicious. The past provides ample evidence of the burden of hatred and suspicion among women of different ethnic groups, or for that matter, between any people of different races, or between women and men. Conflict and confrontation help us refine our ideas, but in the absence of alternatives to antagonism, the whole process of communication threatens to break down. We need some more equipment in our rhetorical and intellectual tool chest.

Fourth, in an effort to establish western women's history as an enterprise grounded in mutuality as well as criticism, I want to affirm Maria Lugones's call for a pluralist feminism, and to extend to all western women's historians a critical challenge in the name of community. The time has come to reaffirm the simultaneity of similarity and difference, of both common and divergent interests. There can be no doubt that separatism based on gender, race, ethnicity, class, age, region, or sexual/affectional preference can be an instrument of empowerment for people of all kinds. We all require spaces of reflection, regeneration, and acceptance, as well as bases from which to organize on behalf of specific interests and goals. Historically, separatist networks have indeed been critical to the enhancement of women's status and opportunities.[40] Such spaces, including women studies and ethnic studies programs, remain important as intellectual and political entities. Yet those who look for tranquility, permanent consensus, or even transhistorical stability in separatism pursue an impossible dream. Schism begets schism; grounds for separation are truly endless.

I thus hold out a fervent hope that historians of western women will not give up on each other, or on other western historians, or on other women's historians. I hope all of us can resist the impulse to permanent separatism, to what Trinh T. Minh-ha has called "the apartheid type of difference," whether among male, middle-class, heterosexual, or Euro-American scholars weary of being accused of manifold political sins, or female, racial ethnic, homosexual, or working-class scholars who are sick of having to educate those who possess privileged social status.[41] We must find ways to disagree and continue to talk, to differ without hating each other. Our attacks on one another give those who would silence all of us the ammunition they need in the crusade to mobilize public opinion against "political correctness": Who would want to be a member of a movement that devours its young?

In answering Gloria Anzaldúa's charge that multiculturalism may be simply another colonialist version of cultural pluralism, Valerie Matsumoto has written that multiculturalism has been "a means to increase our students' and colleagues' awareness of racial dynamics, as well as an entering wedge for restructuring the curriculum. This is too valuable a tool to relinquish."[42] We may drive each other crazy at times, but only by struggling together can we reaffirm the power of the human imagination to span social distances and find some way to create trust.

The past decade of western women's history has been fruitful, if sometimes difficult. The time has come for historians of women in the region to reaffirm a politics of inclusiveness. Without a mutual rededication to one another, we court defeat at the hands of those who denounce us as the avatars of political correctness. Following Maria Lugones, Matsumoto has written that it "becomes imperative that we understand each other's histories, that we develop the loving perception that will enable us to work together."[43]

The word "love" uttered in the context of a discussion of the politics of history may seem frivolous or sentimental, but it has yet to be proven that good ideas need to be cold to be serious. There is nothing new about American utopianism, and perhaps there is something to be reclaimed from Frances Wright's Nashoba, from the Provincetown Players, from the early days of the Student Nonviolent Coordinating Committee, from Woodstock even. In the 1960s counterculture critique of American society, the recognition of race, ethnicity, age, and sex as bases for different historical experiences and claims— "Different strokes for different folks," in Sly Stone's catchy phrase— also carried an injunction to compassion and common struggle. To quote Sly again, "We got to live together." Lugones writes, "Travelling to each other's 'worlds' enables us to *be* through *loving* each other."[44] The American revolutionary Benjamin Franklin, seeking strength in coalition, put it somewhat differently. We must all hang together, he said. Else surely we shall all hang separately.

Virginia Scharff is a professor in the history department at the University of New Mexico. She is the author of *Taking the Wheel: Women and the Coming of the Motor Age* (1991) and *Twenty Thousand Roads: Women, Movement, and the West* (2003).

NOTES

I would like to thank those who read and commented on this article in its various phases of development: Susan Armitage, Larry Durwood Ball, Richard Etulain, Elizabeth Jameson, Jane Slaughter, and anonymous readers for the *Pacific Historical Review*. And as always, I would like to thank Karen Anderson for the wise and honest comments and encouragement.

1. Joan M. Jensen and Darlis A. Miller, "'The Gentle Tamers' Revisited: New Approaches to the History of Women in the American West," *Pacific Historical Review* XLIX (1980): 205–6.
2. Ibid., 204–8.
3. Thomas Bender, "Wholes and Parts: The Need for Synthesis in American History," *Journal of American History* LXXIII (1986): 127–32.
4. For studies of western women that employ expanded definitions of politics and political activism, see Mary Pardo, "Mexican American Women Grassroots Community Activists: 'Mothers of East Los Angeles,'" *Frontiers* (November 1990): 1; Virginia Scharff, "Of Parking Spaces and Women's Places: The Los Angeles Parking Ban of 1920," *National Women's Studies Association Journal* I (1988): 37–51.
5. Michel Foucault, "Truth and Power," in Paul Rabinow, ed., *The Foucault Reader* (New York: Pantheon Books, 1984), 61; Joan Wallach Scott, "History in Crisis? The Others' Side of the Story," *American Historical Review* XCIV (1989): 680–81.
6. Scott, "History in Crisis," 680.
7. Jensen and Miller, "'Gentle Tamers' Revisited," 186.
8. Ibid., 174; see also Peggy Pascoe, "Western Women at the Cultural Crossroads," in Patricia Nelson Limerick, Clyde A. Milner II, and Charles E. Rankin, eds., *Trails: Toward a New Western History* (Lawrence: University Press of Kansas, 1991), 40–58; Peggy Pascoe, "Introduction: The Challenge of Writing Multicultural History," *Frontier* XII (1991): 3.
9. Jensen and Miller, "'Gentle Tamers' Revisited," 186.
10. Lillian Schlissel, Vicki L. Ruiz, and Janice Monk, eds., *Western Women: Their Land,*

Their Lives (Albuquerque: University of New Mexico Press, 1988), 1; Ellen Carol DuBois and Vicki L. Ruiz, eds., *Unequal Sisters: A Multi-cultural Reader in U.S. Women's History* (New York: Routledge, 1990), xii.

11. Virginia Scharff, "Gender and Western History: Is Anyone Home on the Range?" *Montana, the Magazine of Western History* XLI (1991): 62–65.

12. Landmark texts in this ongoing conversation include Gloria T. Hull, Patricia B. Scott, and Barbara Smith, eds., *All the Women Are White, All the Blacks Are Men, But Some of Us Are Brave* (Westbury, N.Y.: Feminist Press, 1982); Cherríe Moraga and Gloria Anzaldúa, eds., *This Bridge Called My Back: Writings by Radical Women of Color* (Watertown, Mass.: Persephone Press, 1981); and Gloria Anzaldúa, ed., *Making Face, Making Soul, Haciendo Caras: Creative and Critical Perspectives by Women of Color* (San Francisco: Aunt Lute Foundation Books, 1990).

13. Deena González to Paula Petrik, Kathleen Underwood et al., February 22, 1991 (in author's files).

14. Three important anthologies arising from conferences and informal contacts among western women's historians are Joan Jensen and Darlis Miller, eds., *New Mexico Women: Intercultural Perspectives* (Albuquerque: University of New Mexico Press, 1986); Susan Armitage and Elizabeth Jameson, eds., *The Women's West* (Norman: University of Oklahoma Press, 1987); and Schlissel, Ruiz, and Monk, eds., *Western Women*. For a bibliographic guide, see Elizabeth Jameson, "Toward a Multicultural History of Women in the Western United States," *Signs: Journal of Women in Culture and Society* XIII (1988): 761–91.

15. Evelyn Nakano Glenn, "Racial Ethnic Women's Labor: The Intersection of Race, Gender, and Class Oppression," *Review of Radical Political Economics* XVII (1985): 86–108; DuBois and Ruiz, eds., *Unequal Sisters*, xi–xvi; Jane Flax, "Postmodernism and Gender Relations in Feminist Theory," *Signs: Journal of Women in Culture and Society* XII (1987): 624.

16. Antonia Castañeda, "Gender, Race, and Culture: Spanish-Mexican Women in the Historiography of Frontier California," *Frontiers* XI (1990): 14.

17. See, for example, Karen Anderson, *Changing Woman. A History of Racial Ethnic Women in Modern America* (New York: Oxford University Press, 1996); Fran Leeper Buss, *La Partera: Story of a Midwife* (Ann Arbor: University of Michigan Press, 1980); Sarah Deutsch, *No Separate Refuge: Culture, Class, and Gender on an Anglo-Hispanic Frontier in the American Southwest, 1880–1940* (New York: Oxford University Press, 1987); Joan M. Jensen, "Crossing Ethnic Barriers in the Southwest: Women's Agricultural Extension Education, 1914–1940," *Agricultural History* LX (1986): 169–81; Susan Johnson, "Sharing Bed and Board: Cohabitation and Cultural Difference in Central Arizona Mining Towns," *Frontiers* VII (1984): 36–42.

18. Glenn, "Racial Ethnic Women's Labor," 105n.

19. James Clifford, "On Collecting Art and Culture," in James Clifford, *The Predicament of Culture: Twentieth-Century Ethnography, Literature, and Art* (Cambridge, Mass.: Harvard University Press, 1988), 215–51; Richard White, *The Middle Ground: Indians, Empires, and Republics in the Great Lakes Region, 1650–1815* (Cambridge, Eng.: Cambridge University Press, 1991); Tessie P. Liu, "Race and Gender in the Politics of Group Formation: A Comment on Notions of Multiculturalism," *Frontiers* XII (1991): 155–65.

20. Anzaldúa, *Making Face, Making Soul*, xxii.

21. Maria Lugones, "Playfulness, 'World'-Traveling, and Loving Perception," in

Anzaldúa, ed., *Making Face, Making Soul*, 395.

22. Karen Anderson, personal communication, August 1991.

23. Adrienne Rich, "Disloyal to Civilization: Feminism, Racism, Gynephobia," in Adrienne Rich, *On Lies, Secrets, and Silence: Selected Prose, 1966–1978* (New York: Norton, 1979), 306. See also DuBois and Ruiz, eds., *Unequal Sisters*, xi.

24. Lugones, "Playfulness," 390.

25. Vicki Ruiz, *Cannery Women, Cannery Lives: Mexican Women, Unionization, and the California Food Processing Industry* (Albuquerque: University of New Mexico Press, 1987); Patricia Zavella, *Women's Work and Chicano Families: Cannery Workers of the Santa Clara Valley* (Ithaca, N.Y.: Cornell University Press, 1987); Judith Stacey, *Brave New Families: Stories of Domestic Upheaval in Late Twentieth Century America* (New York: Basic Books, 1990). For selected bibliographies on African American, Asian American, Latina, and Native American women, see DuBois and Ruiz, eds., *Unequal Sisters*, 447–62.

26. See DuBois and Ruiz, eds., *Unequal Sisters*, xii.

27. See Deena González, "The Spanish-Mexican Women of Santa Fe: Patterns of Their Resistance and Accommodation, 1820–1880" (Ph.D. dissertation, University of California, Berkeley, 1985); Ramón Gutiérrez, *When Jesus Came, the Corn Mothers Went Away: Marriage, Sexuality and Power in New Mexico, 1500–1846* (Stanford, Calif.: Stanford University Press, 1991); Joan M. Jensen, "Southwest Monuments of the Salinas," in Joan M. Jensen ed., *Promise to the Land: Essays on Rural Women* (Albuquerque: University of New Mexico Press, 1991), 110–29.

28. Landscape, and women's responses to it, has been a continuous theme of western women's history. For an early attempt to come to grips with this question, see Johnny Faragher and Christine Stansell, "Women and Their Families on the Overland Trail to California and Oregon, 1842–1867," *Feminist Studies* II (1975): 150–66. See also essays in Vera Norwood and Janice Monk, eds., *The Desert is No Lady: Southwestern Landscapes in Women's Writing and Art* (New Haven, Conn.: Yale University Press, 1987); and Scharff, "Of Parking Spaces and Women's Places."

29. Valerie Matsumoto, "Japanese American Women during World War II," in DuBois and Ruiz, eds., *Unequal Sisters*, 373–86; Matsumoto, "Desperately Seeking 'Deirdre': Gender Roles, Multicultural Relations, and Nisei Women Writers of the 1930s," *Frontiers* XII (1991): 19–32; Peggy Pascoe, *Relations of Rescue: The Search for Female Moral Authority in the American West, 1874-1939* (New York: Oxford University Press, 1990); Pascoe, "Race, Gender, and Intercultural Relations: The Case of Interracial Marriage," *Frontiers* XII (1991): 5–18; Ruiz, *Cannery Workers, Cannery Lives*; Ruiz, "Dead Ends or Gold Mines? Using Missionary Records in Mexican-American Women's History," *Frontiers* XII (1991): 33–56.

30. Joan M. Jensen, ed., *With These Hands: Women Working on the Land* (Old Westbury, N.Y.: Feminist Press, 1981); Jensen and Miller, eds., *New Mexico Women: Intercultural Perspectives*; Joan M. Jensen, *Loosening the Bonds: Mid-Atlantic Farm Women, 1750–1850* (New Haven, Conn.: Yale University Press, 1986); Joan M. Jensen and Gloria Ricci Lothrop, *California Women: A History* (San Francisco, 1987); Joan M. Jensen, *Passage from India: Asian Indian Immigrants in North America* (New Haven, Conn.: Yale University Press, 1988); Jensen, *Promise to the Land*.

31. Trinh T. Minh-Ha, "Not You/Like You: Post-Colonial Women and the Interlocking Questions of Identity and Difference," in Anzaldúa, ed., *Making Face, Making Soul*, 374.

32. Jensen and Miller, "'Gentle Tamers' Revisited," 174.

33. See, for example, William Cronon, *Changes in the Land: Indians, Colonists, and the Ecology of New England* (New York: Hill and Wang, 1983); Deutsch, *No Separate Refuge*; Gutiérrez, *When Jesus Came, the Corn Mothers Went Away*; Pascoe, *Relations of Rescue*; Patricia Nelson Limerick, *Legacy of Conquest: The Unbroken Past of the American West* (New York: Norton, 1987); Douglas Monroy, *Thrown among Strangers: The Making of Mexican Culture in Frontier California* (Berkeley: University of California Press, 1990); Richard White, *The Roots of Dependency: Subsistence, Environment, and Social Change among the Choctaws, Pawnees, and Navajos* (Lincoln: University of Nebraska Press, 1983); White, *The Middle Ground*; White, *"It's Your Misfortune and None of My Own": A History of the American West* (Norman: University of Oklahoma Press, 1991). For the most complete bibliographic information on works taking racial and ethnic, as well as gender differences into account, see the series-in-progress of bibliographies published by the Center for the American West, University of New Mexico, Albuquerque, New Mexico (Richard W. Etulain, Director).

34. For an early example of this approach, see Richard White, "The Winning of the West: The Expansion of the Western Sioux in the Eighteenth and Nineteenth Centuries," *Journal of American History* LXV (1978): 319–43. See also Limerick, *Legacy of Conquest*, 25–27; Pascoe, *Relations of Rescue*.

35. See "AHR Forum: The Old History and the New," *American Historical Review* XCIV (1989): 654–98.

36. T. A. Larson, "Woman Suffrage in Wyoming," *Pacific Northwest Quarterly* XLI (1965): 57–66; Larson, "Woman Suffrage in Western America," *Utah Historical Quarterly* XXXVIII (1970): 7–19; Larson, "Dolls, Vassals, and Drudges—Pioneer Women in the West," *Western Historical Quarterly* III (1972): 5–16; Larson, "The Women's Rights Movement in Idaho," *Idaho Yesterdays* XVI (1972): 2–15, 18–19; Larson, "Montana Women and the Battle for the Ballot," *Montana, the Magazine of Western History* XXIII (1973): 24–41; Larson, "The Woman Suffrage Movement in Washington," *Pacific Northwest Quarterly* LXVII (1976): 49–62.

37. John Toews, "Perspectives on 'The Old History and the New': A Comment," *American Historical Review* XCIV (1989): 693–98.

38. González, "The Spanish-Mexican Women of Santa Fe"; and González, "Sexuality and the Gendered Economy of Colonization in New Mexico" (Paper presented to the Western History Association, Austin, Tex., October 1991).

39. See Dee Brown, *The Gentle Tamers: Women of the Old Wild West* (New York: Putnam, 1976); Jensen and Miller, "'The Gentle Tamers' Revisited"; Rayna Green, "The Pocahontas Perplex: The Image of Indian Women in American Culture," *The Massachusetts Review* XVI (1975); Castañeda, "Gender, Race, and Culture."

40. Estelle Freedman, "Separatism as Strategy: Female Institution Building and American Feminism, 1870–1930," *Feminist Studies* V (1979): 512–29.

41. Minh-Ha, "Not You/Like You," 372.

42. Valerie Matsumoto, "From Silence to Resistance," review of Anzaldúa, ed., *Making Face, Making Soul*, in *Women's Review of Books* VIII (1990): 4.

43. Ibid.

44. Lugones, "Playfulness," 394.

Women and Mobility
Immigration/Migration

Americans are a mobile population. The earliest peoples were nomadic populations joined in the seventeenth century by immigrants from Europe. We call them settlers but once settled, many packed up and moved again. Women, no less than men, have been part of this stream of migration. Native American women were among the earliest migrants within and throughout North America, many with babies strapped to their backs and trailed by a travois stacked with the family's belongings. Mexican and Hispanic women migrated with their men and children north into what would, by the nineteenth century, become the American Southwest. In that same century, immigrants from Asia, primarily men, arrived on the west coast and migrated to mining and railroad centers in the western region. Their numbers, including women, have increased in the twentieth century, along with Spanish-speakers from Mexico and Latin America. Now, early in the twenty-first century, the movement of peoples into and within the region continues to shape the face, and color, of the American West.

One of the ongoing patterns of western development continues to be the high rate of immigration to this country. Between 1890 and 1920, America experienced the highest rates of immigration to date; nearly 6.3 million newcomers arrived in the decade of 1900–1910 alone.[1] A key feature of immigration in this period was the shift in place of origin from earlier northern and western Europeans (90 percent prior to 1890) to peoples immigrating from southern and eastern Europe (70 percent between 1900 and 1914). Several decades later, in the 1970s and 1980s, immigration rates soared again, and once more the source of origin shifted, from Europe to Asia, Latin America, and Mexico.[2] Both historical immigration movements triggered social concerns, fear of economic competition, and the passage of laws and statutes to attempt to contain or reduce "undesirable" immigration. Presently, western states both encourage and decry such immigration, much of it consisting of undocumented workers who are caught in the double bind of serving as much-needed laborers in the American economy yet forced to enter this country illegally.

As Elizabeth Jameson has noted, between 1860 and 1900, the American West had a higher proportion of foreign-born peoples than any other region in the country.[3] The increase continued into the twentieth-century and, now in the twenty-first century, this region is still the most diverse part of the nation.[4] The 1990 census found that "more than any other factor, the flood of immigrants has redefined the nation, especially in urban areas such as Los Angeles, Miami, Chicago and the District of Columbia."[5] Demographers predict that by 2060, minorities will outnumber whites and, among minority groups, Hispanics will outnumber blacks within the next twenty years. In 1990, African Americans made up 12 percent of the population with Hispanics at 9 percent and Asians at 4 percent.[6] A decade later, the prophecy is on its way to becoming true, albeit at a slight margin: the black population numbers 12.3 percent while the Hispanic population is 12.5 percent or nearly 650,000 more citizens.[7]

In the 1990 census, figures showed that Los Angeles County was the most populous county in America. Among minority groups there, the Asian population doubled to 10.8 percent and Hispanics rose 10 percentage points to nearly 37.8 percent while the black population declined to 10.5 percent.[8] But during World War II, it was the black population that outnumbered all ethnic groups. According to Paul J. Spickard in the first article in this section, the explosive growth of war industries drew migrants of every class, color, and region to southern California in the early forties. Blacks comprised one hundred thousand of the migrants, over half of them women. African women were more likely than other minority women to migrate on their own, or with their children, to seek work in cities and towns. Bypassing domestic work, they went to work in the shipyards, steel plants, and aircraft factories, which brought relatively high pay and high status. It was a short-lived reality, however, as the author explains how "red-baiting" in the 1950s dashed their hopes for a chance to live the California Dream.

The thriving war-related industries in the San Francisco Bay area also allowed Chinese American women opportunities for work not present before the war. Because of immigration restrictions prior to World War II, these workers were mostly second-generation Chinese American women. Their wage-earning mothers were essentially isolated in ethnic communities primarily as wives, mothers, and workers in family-run businesses. Xiaojian Zhao, in the second article, found that despite discrimination and prejudice long visited upon the Chinese in America, defense work provided Chinese American women and men an entry into the larger American society, a goal their ancestors had long struggled toward.

Norma Chinchilla and Nora Hamilton tell a different kind of migration story in the last article in this section. As noted above, the decade of the 1980s was one of high immigration of Latino peoples to California. Although Mexicans comprised the majority of Spanish speakers, 62 percent, the fastest-growing groups consisted of Central and South Americans. With the exception of Mexicans, women were a majority among many immigrant groups and often came alone to the United States to work as domestics.[9] As the economic situation worsened in the 1990s, jobs dried up and the numbers of women on the streets of Los Angeles as street vendors increased.[10] The authors provide a fascinating account of the ways in which these undocumented arrivals, often with their children, navigated and renegotiated public spaces, including public sidewalks and streets and LA's extensive urban transportation system.

One question around the issue of women's, and men's, migration is: What has changed most, the country to which they have immigrated or the women themselves? Do they fully assimilate to a fundamentally Anglo culture or has that culture become as heterogeneous and cosmopolitan as the many peoples from all over the world who have immigrated here? Some suggest that women cope with the dilemma or conundrum by finding a middle ground, in which they bring parts of their heritage with them and meld or insert them into the larger culture, a situation that allows them to be in the country if not of the county.[11] More research on women's migration experiences will help us further understand the complex processes such women undergo. The three pieces included here contribute to the colorful if conflicted mosaic of immigration/migration stories of the American West.

Notes

1. Irwin Unger and Debi Unger, *Twentieth Century America* (New York: St. Martin's Press, 1990), 36.
2. U.S. Department of Justice, Immigration and Naturalization Service, "Immigration to the United States since 1820," *Statistical Yearbook of the Immigration and Naturalization Service*, (Washington, D.C.: The Service, 1996).
3. Elizabeth Jameson, "Toward a Multicultural History of Women in the Western United States," *Signs* 14 (summer 1988): 788.
4. "Immigration changes face of U.S. as minorities become the majority," *The Idaho Statesman*, April 27, 1997.
5. "Many Nations, Under God, With Liberty and Justice for Some," *The Washington Post National Weekly Edition*, June 8–14, 1992.
6. "Fighting for a Piece of the Political Pie," *The Washington Post National Weekly Edition*, September 23–29, 1991.
7. "Overview of Race and Hispanic Origin," in *Census 2000 Brief*, March 2001, Table 1, p. 3, at www.census.gov.
8. *The Washington Post Weekly Edition*, September 23–29, 1991.
9. Virginia Yans-McLaughlin, ed., *Immigration Reconsidered: History, Sociology, and Politics* (New York: Oxford University Press, 1990), 15.
10. In LA's sister city on the east coast, a similar situation takes place on the streets of New York City. *The New York Times* reported that ten thousand immigrants had "created an illegal but profitable 'makeshift marketplace' of sidewalk stands from which they hawk video and audio tapes, sunglasses and women's lingerie." *The Washington Spectator* 19 (August 15, 1993): 3.
11. "The Immigrant's Dilemma," *The Washington Post National Weekly Edition*, March 27, 2000. This article reviews a collection of essays edited by Meri Nana-Ama Danquah, *Becoming American: Personal Essays by First Generation Immigrant Women* (New York: Hyperion, 2000).

WORK AND HOPE

AFRICAN AMERICAN WOMEN IN SOUTHERN
CALIFORNIA DURING WORLD WAR II*

Paul R. Spickard

Southern California during World War II was a magnet for hundreds of thousands of people from all over the United States. Drawn by the explosive growth of war industries, migrants from every region, of every class and color, made their way to greater Los Angeles. Among them were more than one hundred thousand African Americans. More than half of those were women. They transformed the Southern California African American community. They came seeking opportunity: they found hard work and, for a time, they found hope.

Before World War II, African American women and their families lived in an old black neighborhood just southeast of downtown Los Angeles near the corner of Central and Pico within earshot of the tracks of the Southern Pacific Railway. Many of the early African American men worked as porters or laborers on this line. Their wives and children stayed in Los Angeles while the men worked lines all over the Southwest. Around them grew a modest-sized community of tens of thousands of African Americans in the 1920s and 1930s. They were surrounded by a welter of other people: Russians and other European immigrants in Boyle Heights to the east, Mexicans in East Los Angeles a little farther east, Japanese in Little Tokyo to the north, Chinatown

---

*This chapter was previously published as: Spickard, Paul R. "Work and Hope: African American Women in Southern California during World War II." In *Journal of the West* 32 (July 1993): 70–79.

just beyond that. There were small clusters of African Americans in other parts of Southern California—in San Diego, Calexico, Long Beach, Pasadena, and elsewhere—but the Los Angeles black community was the largest, and the hub around which the others turned.

By 1940, the Los Angeles African American community had reached sixty thousand in number and stretched in all directions from this central zone south along Central Avenue, the main thoroughfare of black culture in the West. It was quite a wonderful place, as any old-time resident is eager to recount. As one drove slowly down Central Avenue in 1941, the decaying southern fringes of downtown were left behind for a black city teeming with street life. The Avenue's many stores, humble and grand, all boasted shoppers. And families with small children as well as the unemployed—the fruit of the Depression— "hung out" and were shooting dice. There were moviegoers at the Lincoln Theater, earnest black dentists, and secretaries from the offices of Golden State Mutual Insurance. And there were also prostitutes and drug pushers, Garveyites and disciples of Father Divine, as well as newcomers, just walking the streets and gawking.

At the corner of 41st Street, about a mile and a half south of Pico, stood the Dunbar Hotel, the jewel of Central Avenue. Built in 1928 as the Somerville, this luxury hotel was where notable African Americans came to stay. Mary White Ovington, W. E. B. DuBois, and Jack Johnson stayed at the Dunbar. Billie Holiday, Lionel Hampton, and Bessie Smith stayed there, too, and played in the Big Apple, the Club Alabam, and the Savoy nearby. Hollywood actresses Louise Beavers and Ethel Waters came down from their swank homes on Sugar Hill to see and be seen. Central Avenue was also the center of West Coast jazz. It was the most exciting street west of Chicago.

Central Avenue was part of the glamour that African Americans in the South associated with Los Angeles, part of what drew them to Southern California. Times were hard for Southern black women in the 1930s and early 1940s, as they were for many other Americans. Prices for cotton and other crops were low. Lots of families who had owned farms became tenants, and tenants became laborers. Men thrown out of work went looking for jobs and did not always come back. Women were often left to support families in the midst of hard times. Throughout the 1930s, large numbers of black women left the rural South, sometimes with husbands but often without, frequently with

children in tow, and headed for nearby towns and cities in search of
work. Some went farther. For Mississippians who left the South, the
natural place to go by virtue of habit, proximity, and ease of transport,
was Chicago. For Carolinians it was New York. For those from the
Southwest—Texas and Oklahoma—and the Southeast—Louisiana and
Arkansas—the West Coast was a possibility. Nearly half of the African
Americans who came to Los Angeles came from those four states. Texas
was the largest contributor; there was a regular pipeline of black people
from Houston to Los Angeles from the 1920s on.

Yet it was more than proximity that drew them. For blacks as for
whites, California was not just a place but an idea. In California, the
world was made new every day. It was a place where the living was easy,
where people could pick fruit right from the trees, where they could
own their own homes, where they could find work and hope to retire
someday. Those economic dreams seemed especially promising in the
early 1940s when the impending Second World War brought new
industries to Los Angeles. Shipyards, steel plants, and aircraft factories
meant jobs with relatively high pay and high status. African American
women and men left their homes in the South and headed for California.

Tina Hill was typical. Hard times in the 1930s had forced her and
her sister to drop out of high school in Prairie View, Texas. She related
in 1938,

> [W]e finally decided to break up housekeeping and go to the city. I
> decided I wanted to make more money, and I went to a little small
> town—Tyler, Texas. . . . [But] the only thing I could do there for a
> living was domestic work and it didn't pay very much. . . . So I decided
> I'd better get out of this town. I didn't like Dallas because that was
> too rough. Then someone told me, "Well, why don't you try
> California?" So then I got Los Angeles in my mind.[1]

In 1940, she invested her savings in a train ticket and headed for
California.

Black women came on their own, or with their children, or sometimes following their husbands. Frequently they already had a relative
living in California who offered to help them make a start. Some came
via the Southern Pacific Railway, but trains were expensive. More came
by bus or by car, across the hot dusty stretches of U.S. Highways 66,

80, and 60. Texas, Arizona, and New Mexico were segregated states in those days, with no hotel rooms for black people, so they camped out along the way or, if they were lucky, stayed in the homes of the few African Americans who lived in Amarillo and Santa Fe, Albuquerque and Flagstaff, Phoenix and Barstow.

The inflow of African Americans during World War II was large and sudden. The state officials who counted migrants at the border noted only about 100 blacks per month bound for Los Angeles in the period 1940 to 1942. But toward the end of 1942, some aircraft plants, as well as the Southern Pacific Railway and other major employers, were driven by labor shortages, black protests, and federal government pressure to begin to employ African American workers. Word spread quickly that there was good money to be made in Southern California. In short order, thousands of blacks poured in—as many as 10,000 to 12,000 per month during the summer of 1943. In those months, blacks constituted two-thirds to three-quarters of the total migration to Los Angeles. Altogether, over 140,000 African Americans were added to the population of Los Angeles County in the decade of the 1940s.

The African American women who came to California found their situation was not so pleasant as they had imagined. They did find work, but more often it was in somebody's kitchen at moderate pay rather than in a war plant at high pay. When World War II began, very few African Americans held jobs in the industrial sector of Los Angeles. Eighty-five percent of the black women before the war (and half of the men) were engaged as domestic servants. Early any morning, one could see them on street corners along Central Avenue, waiting for the buses that would take them to Bel Air and Santa Monica and Glendale to their day's work. Tina Hill described her experience as a domestic:

> In less than ten days I had found a job living on the place doing domestic work. I started there from some time in August until Christmas. I was making thirty-five dollars a month. That was so much better than what I was making at home, which was twelve dollars a month. I saved my money and I bought everybody a Christmas present and sent it. Oh, I was the happiest thing in the world!
>
> The family I worked for lived in Westwood. I had to cook breakfast, serve. They had a man and a wife and four kids. The smallest ones was twins and they wasn't too old. They had a nurse that took

care of the twins. So I had to wash and iron, clean the house, cook.
That was my job. So it was all day or practically, and I had very little
time for myself. I had every Thursday off and every other Sunday.
That just killed me to have to work on a Sunday, but I told myself I
wasn't going to cry because I was coming out to do better and I would
do better sooner or later.[2]

She quit that job soon enough and tried several others, but was not
able to crack the industrial work force until 1943.

Much of the reason for the small number of black women and men
in aircraft, steel, shipbuilding, and the other industrial enterprises can
be laid at the door of white discrimination. Both management and labor
did their part. For example, the manager of industrial relations at
Consolidated-Vultee, an aircraft manufacturer, told representatives of
the National Negro Congress, "I regret to say that it is not the policy
of this company to employ people other than the Caucasian race, consequently we are not in a position to offer your people employment at
this time."[3] The president of North American Aviation (later Rockwell
International) echoed those sentiments: "Regardless of their training as
aircraft workers we will not employ Negroes in the North American
Plant. It is against company policy."[4] But labor, if anything, outdid management in discriminating against African American workers. The
AFL-affiliated International Association of Machinists first refused
black applicants for membership, then segregated them into a separate
unit, the Jim Crow auxiliary local that lacked full voting rights or an
independent voice. At the beginning of the war, despite a racially open
national policy, Los Angeles CIO union organizers were only margin-
ally more receptive to black membership. African Americans were shut
out of the aircraft industry until the spring and summer of 1943, when
it became apparent that the war-induced labor shortage would not go
away. Then management at Lockheed and North American led the way
in hiring and training black industrial workers and bulldozed the unions
into accepting them.

Because of the convoluted logic of racism and sexism at that time,
it was easier for black women than for black men to get the higher
paying industrial jobs. At North American, it was hard for an African
American man to get a production line job, because men, black or white,
were viewed as permanent employees. To put a black man on the line

was, in white eyes, to overturn the prewar racial system: so African American men had a hard time laying down the broom and picking up the rivet gun. But to hire an African American woman for an industrial job was not seen as such a threat to the prevailing racial hierarchy. Women of whatever race were viewed as only temporary employees, because the prevailing ideology said they would go back to being housewives at the war's end (never mind that most had been wage workers before the war). So, even though factory managers' sexism kept them from regarding women as fully competent workers, they still could see their way clear to hiring black women for industrial jobs. Tina Hill went to a school on Figueroa Street for four weeks. She took psychological tests, then learned to drill and rivet and file pieces of metal, all the while earning 60 cents an hour. Margaret Wright did the same thing, and then took her place on the line at Lockheed:

> I worked an eight-hour shift. If they asked me to work overtime I got paid for overtime. . . . It was a bit boring at times, but all in all I was doing the same work that other people were doing. If things didn't work right, I could always go to the union. . . . I could either quit, pack up and leave, or whatever, but I did have some say so and a job in the factory. There was another difference, too. Instead of working alone all the time like they do in domestic work, somewhere in the kitchen or wherever you were at by yourself, I was always with a bunch of other women.[5]

Even when they got jobs, however, African American workers generally were denied positions commensurate with their skill level, and they frequently received lower pay than white workers for the same work. They also found themselves on segregated work teams, often with white foremen. Tina Hill recalled, "They did everything they could to keep you separated. They just did not like for a Negro and a white person to get together and talk."[6] Segregation diminished as the years went by, and some blacks did manage to ascend to team leader positions, but usually only supervising other African Americans.

Sometimes racial tensions flared on the job. Lyn Childs, a woman who worked in a San Francisco ship repair yard, described a scene perhaps more vivid than, but not fundamentally unlike, many that occurred in Los Angeles:

I was working down in the hold of the ship and there were about six Filipino men and over these men was a nineteen-year-old officer of the ship, and this big White guy went over and started to kick this poor Filipino and none of the Black men that was working down there in the hold with him said one word to this guy. And I sat there and was getting madder and madder by the minute. I sprang to my feet, turned on my torch, and I had a flame about six to seven feet out in front of me, and I walked up to him and I said (you want me to say the real language?) I said to him "You so-and-so. If you go lift one more foot, I'll cut your guts out." That was my exact words. I was so mad with him.

Then he started to tell me that he had been trained in boot camp that any national group who was dark-skinned was beneath all White people. So he started to cry. I felt sorry for him, because he was crying, really crying. He was frightened, and I was frightened. I didn't know what I was doing, so in the end I turned my torch off and I sat down on the steps with him.

About that time the intercom on board the ship started to announce, "Lyn Childs, report to Colonel Hickman immediately." So I said, "I guess this is it." So I went up to Colonel Hickman's office, and behind me came all these men, and they lined up behind me, and I said, "Where are you guys going?" They said, "We're going with you." He said (Colonel Hickman), "I just wanted to see Lyn Childs," and they said, "You'll see all of us, because we were all down there. We all did not have guts enough to do what she did, and we're with her."

Colonel Hickman said, "Come into this office." He had one of the guards take me into the office real fast and close the door real fast and keep them out, and he said, "What kind of communist activity are you carrying on down there?" [I said], "A communist! What is that?" He said, "You know what I am talking about. You're a communist." [I said], "A communist! Forget you!" I said, "The kind of treatment that man was putting on the Filipinos, and to come their rescue. Then I am the biggest communist you ever seen in your life. That is great. I am a communist." He said, "Don't say that so loud." I said, "Well, you asked me was I a communist. You're saying I am. I'm saying I'm a. . . ." [He said], "Shh! Shh! Shh! Hush! Don't say that so loud." He said, "I think you ought to get out of here and get

back to work." [I said], "Well, you called me. Why did you call me?"
He said, "Never mind what I called you for. Go back to work."[7]

Those opportunities that did open up for African American women
were not simply a product of the forces or the labor market. They were
also the result of a series of campaigns for jobs by African American
organizations. A black woman, Charlotta Bass, was a central figure in
the drive to compel businesses to hire blacks. Bass was the crusading
editor of the *California Eagle*, the state's largest African American newspaper. Since the 1910s she had covered strikes, lynchings, the Ku Klux
Klan, race riots in Houston, housing discrimination in Los Angeles, the
case of the Scottsboro Boys, and other stories both topical and dangerous. The *Eagle* was also the daily monitor of activities and achievements among African Americans in Southern California.

During the war, the *Eagle* kept up a constant barrage of front-page
stories and editorials aimed at getting jobs and housing for African
Americans and at ending harassment. Teaming with the Reverend
Clayton Russell of the Negro Victory Committee and other black leaders, Bass daily hammered on city, state, and federal officials to do something about discrimination against African American workers in war
industries. Bass, Russell, and their allies petitioned national and local
officials for redress. They marched and picketed. They shamed the War
Manpower Commission (WMC) and the U.S. Fair Employment
Practices Committee into taking action against local companies that
refused to hire African Americans.

An example will illustrate their tactics and general success. In July
1942, an official of the U.S. Employment Service (USES) expressed the
opinion that black women were not interested in jobs in war industries,
that they were better fitted for domestic work. Russell got into the *Eagle*
and on the radio and gathered several hundred followers, together with
representatives of the NAACP (National Association for the
Advancement of Colored People) and the Urban League. They
marched on the USES office. Women filled the lines downstairs applying for jobs, while members of the Victory Committee were upstairs
negotiating with USES officials. The government agreed to have the
WMC investigate; and after several months of continuing pressure,
African American women began to find jobs building aircraft and ships.
Charlotta Bass kept her *Eagle*-eye out for cases of discrimination—in

the municipal railway system, the boilermaker's union, the post office, and elsewhere—and trumpeted the names and details in the pages of her newspaper. By 1944, the combination of worker shortage and militant activism by this fiery woman and her colleagues had achieved black integration into the work force in all major industrial enterprises.

By the war's end, significant numbers of African Americans, women and men, were working in skilled positions in each of the heavy industries that the war had brought to Southern California. Precisely how many is not clear, because the only figures available are from the U.S. Census. The war ended in 1945, but numbers are available only for 1940 and 1950. As the war-spurred industrial boom wound down in 1945 and collapsed in 1946, black women, even more than black men and white women, lost the jobs they had found in industry. As Lyn Childs described it: "The women were laid off first, and then the less senior Black men were laid off next, and last, but as time went on, finally many of the White workers were laid off. But originally the first number that were laid off were women."[8] Margaret Wright recalled: "I knew how to rivet. I knew how to weld. I knew how to work on assembly lines. I knew how to run a dolly—you know [what] the good jobs are. I thought I had several skills that, you know, [were] very good, and I wouldn't have any problems getting a job anywhere else." But she was laid off by Lockheed, and "I had to fall back on the only other thing that I knew, and that was doing domestic work."[9] Tina Hill also worked cleaning people's homes, then in a garment factory reweaving damaged clothing.

Women's income plummeted, but not their independence and self-esteem. The war had permanently changed the job scene for African American women. As Tina Hill put it: "The war made me live better, it really did. . . . Hitler was the one that got us out of the white folks' kitchen."[10] Contrary to most people's expectations, the Depression did not return at the war's end. Manufacturing picked up again, and the companies started calling back their workers. By 1950, half of the black working women were in domestic service, but the other half were back in the skilled industrial, white collar, or professional positions that they had occupied during the war. In this they were unlike their white sisters; more of the whites remained out of the work force. Tina Hill remembered,

When North American called me back, was I a happy soul! I dropped
that job [in the garment factory] and went back. That was a dollar an
hour. So, from sixty cents an hour, when I first hired in there, up to
one dollar. That wasn't traveling fast, but it was better than anything
else because you had hours to work by and you had benefits and you
come home at night with your family. So it was a good deal.[11]

She worked for North American Aviation for almost forty years.

Loss of jobs was not the only problem black women faced. Once
the color bar in employment had been broken, the biggest problem for
Los Angeles African Americans was housing. Los Angeles was a segregated metropolis. African Americans were not barred by law from white
towns and neighborhoods, but white antagonism kept them near the
city's core nonetheless. More than one black family felt the necessity to
display a shotgun prominently and keep it near at hand when they
moved out of the central black district and into a white area. As the
African American population increased and inched southward during
the war, residents of some all-white, working-class suburbs adopted
racially restrictive covenants (some had used such covenants since the
1920s) that made it illegal for anyone to sell a house to a black family.
These kept the African American population bottled up in Watts and
Willowbrook, for instance, and out of such neighboring communities
as Southgate and Huntington Park. One woman described her experience in trying to buy a house just outside the black zone:

> My husband and I, who worked very hard during World War II in
> order to save enough to buy a decent house for our family, were con-
> fronted by hostile White realtors who tried to discourage us from
> wanting to move into an area recently integrated by Blacks in a sur-
> rounding community. They refused to take our deposit on a house.
> The realtors told us that the house was already sold and that there
> were no other houses in that area for sale.[12]

Sometimes the resistance in white areas was less subtle. In late 1945,
Helen Short, her husband, and two small children bought five acres in
Fontana, a working-class suburb east of Los Angeles, and started to
build a house. After a string of threats from local whites, the Shorts'
burned bodies were found in the ashes of their oil-soaked home. No

one was prosecuted. Just after the war, in 1946, Klansmen visited ten African American families who had moved into white neighborhoods and burned crosses on their lawns.

Such opposition from whites left African Americans confined to a central ghetto that expanded only very gradually, never enough to accommodate their growing numbers. Most housing in black areas was substandard and overcrowded even before the war; by the war's end, conditions were far worse. In 1940, Little Tokyo had thirty thousand Japanese American residents. Four years later, it had been renamed Bronzeville and held eighty thousand (mostly African American) inhabitants. Dorothy Baruch described Little Tokyo storefronts that had been converted into housing:

> In place after place children lived in windowless rooms, amid peeling plaster, rats, and the flies that gathered thick around food that stood on open shelves or kitchen-bedroom tables. Ordinarily there was no bathtub; never more than a single washroom or lavatory. Sometimes as many as forty people shared one toilet. Families were separated only by sheets strung up between beds. Many of the beds were "hot," with people taking turns sleeping in them.[13]

Willowbrook and Watts, along with some previously white working-class suburbs, swelled with African American migrants. They housed their inhabitants somewhat more graciously—typically, in one-story, two-bedroom bungalows of cheap construction. Such structures by war's end frequently housed two or three black families, with another put up in a makeshift structure out back. Chicken coops and garages became houses. People showered at work and went next door to use the toilet or outhouse. They cooked on open firepits and wood stoves.

Not all African Americans were poor renters in need of public housing. Over a third were home owners. Most owned the small, cheaply constructed bungalows that filled the corridor around Central Avenue as it made its way south to Watts. But there were middle-class blacks, too. Many old-time residents and a few newcomers who had a little cash moved west after the war into the Crenshaw and West Adams districts. There they bought or built more substantial single-family homes with wide lawns and gardens along quiet streets. Previously, these had been all-white districts, and both white residents and public authorities resisted the black incursion. A series of cases challenging the racially restricted covenants made their way through state courts. Pauletta Fears and her parents did time in jail for contempt when they refused to vacate their home on 92nd Street in 1945, despite protests from the *Eagle* and a picket line of sympathizers. But in 1948 a Michigan case reached the U.S. Supreme Court, and the restrictive covenants were overturned. African Americans in larger numbers began to move west and south into previously all-white areas, but these did not become completely black neighborhoods. In Crenshaw especially, African Americans mixed with Japanese Americans returning from wartime concentration camps and with others to form a polyethnic, middle-class neighborhood that endures to this day.

Related to the housing problem was the difficulty of transport. Public war housing—flimsy, temporary buildings and trailers—was built by the state, county, and federal governments to house war industry workers. But only 1,510 units were built in the Central, Vernon, and Watts black districts. Over 5,800 units were built in Wilmington and San Pedro, where the shipbuilding jobs were: almost all of these were segregated units designated for whites. There was little public housing—and none at all for African Americans—in places like Long Beach, Inglewood, and Fontana, where most steel and aircraft manufacturing took place. The concentration of black housing in south central Los Angeles, combined with the scattering of industrial plants far to the south, west, north, and east, meant that African Americans had to travel long distances to work. Typically, a woman from Watts or Central Avenue would spend an hour and a half each way in a car pool or riding the Los Angeles Railway's Red Car. Pauletta Fears recalls getting up at 4:00 in the morning, walking from Florence down to Watts, catching the Red Car for San Pedro, riding for over an hour, then walking the last mile to her job at California Shipbuilding.

All this commuting, together with long hours in the factory, kept black women away from their homes and children for long hours, some-times days. Lyn Childs recalled:

> While I came to . . . work in the shipyard, I had a little child that I had
> to leave behind. I had to leave her with my mother because up here I
> didn't think I would have any place for her to stay, and I was going into
> a new community and a new town, and I didn't want to bring my child

with me. I left her with my mother, and that's one of the most awful
things that I did to anybody, because even today that child hurts
because I promised her that, "Give me one year and I will come back
for you." That one year stretched into two years and finally into three
years, and ended up almost five years before I could go back and get
her. That's one of the things that is very sad. If there had been any kind
of conditions under which I could have brought her with me, I certainly would have brought her.[14]

Margaret Wright did not have to leave her children. Her challenge
was to manage them and her job at the same time: "My kids were little,
and so I worked at nights so I would get home in the morning. I didn't
have a washing machine, and so I washed by hand, hung the clothes on
the line. Then I would have to clean the house, bathe the babies. Then
I would have to go shopping."[15]

These difficulties were compounded by the fact that many men
were off in the war. Women were left to handle their jobs, children,
finances, housing, and other matters on their own. Even when men
were present, they were not always helpful. Margaret Wright complained that "[Y]our husband [would] come home, you know, prop his
feet up, get his can of beer while you fixed dinner. Or even if we weren't
working the same shift, you fixed dinner and left it where it would be
convenient for him to get."[16] There was a lot for a woman to do.

As the war went on and more African Americans secured defense
jobs, they managed to integrate some of the housing projects in the
Long Beach Harbor industrial area. Mixing black and white, Latino and
Asian in these projects proved inflammatory in several instances. But
the conflict was not bad enough to dissuade public housing authorities
from continuing the experiment in social engineering after the war.
Between 1945 and 1952, most of the wartime "temporary" housing
projects were converted to permanent status. A dozen other larger and
better constructed housing projects were built, from Little Tokyo down
to Watts, and more were planned. They bore names like Avalon
Gardens, Aliso Village, William Mead Homes, and Nickerson Gardens
that bespoke their sylvan aspirations. At first these were pretty spartan
places, but soon they began to live up to the illusory term "gardens"
that was often part of their names. Those that survive do not look much
like gardens now. But that was the ideal—to create a cheaper, smaller,

but recognizably similar version of the bungalows that were going up for middle-class whites out in Orange County and the San Fernando Valley for poor, inner-city African Americans.

The 1940s were not an easy time for African American women in Southern California, but they were a time of hope, and the number of black women grew. They had to work hard, often at menial tasks. They had difficulty finding good jobs, housing, and transportation, managing families with men absent, making stable lives for themselves and their children. They endured discrimination, both subtle and overt, sometimes extending to violence. But they fought back, worked hard, and won places for themselves. They found good jobs and better pay than they had ever dreamed was possible. Their children received better education than could be had in the South; many were graduating from high school, and some were going on to college. Housing, though crowded, was better—even the slums had plumbing and electricity, and the housing projects seemed like gardens. By the end of World War II, blacks and whites went to the same beaches and sometimes shared the same municipal pools. Social relations between the races were not close, but there was little of the domination and hostility many had known in the South. This was a hopeful era for most Angeleno African Americans.

Then in the 1950s, the hope began to recede. The destruction of the war-era dreams of Los Angeles African Americans is the subject of another paper, but a few summary comments here will mark the way of the future. In the late 1940s and early 1950s, the Los Angeles African American community was ripped apart by allegations of communist involvement in the NAACP. Charges and countercharges flew around the community and were inflated in the *Los Angeles Times* and other organs of white opinion. Charlotta Bass and other community leaders were called to testify before witch-hunting Congressional committees. The *Times*, realtors' organizations, Chief of Police William H. Parker, and others mounted a campaign to prevent the housing authority from building any more public housing projects, and to cut the funding for maintenance at existing ones. With black leadership immobilized, with the dream of good housing gone bust, and with other looming disasters in jobs, education, and relations with the police, Los Angeles blacks began to lose the faith in their future that the war years had created. For Southern California African Americans, women and men, hard work continued, but hope had begun to ebb. By the mid-1960s, the tide was out, and the African American community exploded in the Watts riot of 1965. The story of black women in that disaster has yet to be told.

Paul R. Spickard is a professor of history at Brigham Young University-Hawaii. His previous books include *Mixed Blood: Intermarriage and Ethnic Identity in Twentieth-Century America* (1989) and *Japanese Americans: The Formation and Transformations of an Ethnic Group* (1996).

NOTES

1. Sherna Berger Gluck, *Rosie the Riveter Revisited: Women, the War, and Social Change.* (New York: New American Library, 1988), 31–32.
2. Ibid., 33.
3. National Negro Congress, *Jim Crow in National Defense* (Los Angeles, Calif.: National Negro Congress, 1940).
4. James R. Wilburn, "Social and Economic Aspects of the Aircraft Industry in Metropolitan Los Angeles During World War II," Ph.D. diss., University of California at Los Angeles, 1971, 165–66.
5. Connie Field, "The Life and Times of Rosie the Riveter" (Emeryville, Calif.: Rosie the Riveter Film Project, 1980).
6. Gluck, *Rosie the Riveter Revisited*, 43.
7. Field, "The Life and Times of Rosie the Riveter."
8. Ibid.
9. Ibid.
10. Gluck, *Rosie the Riveter Revisited*, 23.
11. Ibid., 41–42.
12. Keith E. Collins, *Black Los Angeles: The Maturing of the Ghetto, 1940–1950* (Saratoga, Calif.: Century Twenty One Publishing, 1980), 72–74.
13. Dorothy W. Baruch, "Sleep Comes Hard," *Nation* 160 (Jan. 27, 1945): 96–96.
14. Field, "The Life and Times of Rosie the Riveter."
15. Ibid.
16. Ibid.

CHINESE AMERICAN WOMEN DEFENSE WORKERS IN WORLD WAR II*

Xiaojian Zhao

In February 1945, *Fortune Magazine* published an article on the Kaiser shipyards in Richmond, California, including eight photos of the shipyards workers. One of the captions for the photos says, "Chinese Woman: she hasn't missed a day's work in two years."[1] This woman was Ah Yoke Gee, welder in Kaiser Richmond Shipyard Number Two.** The weekly magazine of the Kaiser Richmond shipyards, *Fore 'N' Aft*, described her as one of the oldest crew members of Richmond shipyards. From July 31, 1942, when she started to work in the shipyard, to April 20, 1945, Ah Yoke Gee had missed only one day of work to spend time with her oldest son, a serviceman who was passing through San Francisco on his way to the Pacific front.[2] At a time when there was a shortage of labor, Ah Yoke Gee's story was apparently useful for the Kaiser company's public relations. Here, a middle-aged Chinese American woman was being recognized as a patriotic, hard-working defense worker, who was doing her best to contribute to the nation's war effort.

---

*This chapter was originally published as: Zhao, Xiaojian. "Chinese American Women Defense Workers in World War II." In *California History* 75 (summer 1996): 139–53.

**The real names of some of my informants are not given in this essay upon their request. I use the pinyin system in transliterations, except for names of well-known persons. If a person's name has been printed in English sources before, I follow the way it was in print to avoid confusion.

Ironically, this model shipyard worker had been deprived of citizenship by her own government. Born in 1895 on the Monterey Peninsula in California, Ah Yoke Gee was a second-generation Chinese American for whom U.S. citizenship was a birthright. Her legal status changed, however, after she married a Chinese immigrant from Hong Kong. During the period of Chinese exclusion from 1882 to 1943, Ah Yoke Gee's husband, an alien from China, was racially ineligible for naturalization.[3] Moreover, the Cable Act of September 22, 1922, stipulated that women citizens who married aliens ineligible for citizenship could no longer be citizens themselves.[4] Though Ah Yoke Gee worked for the nation's defense industry, she could not vote as a citizen. Her daughters recalled that she had been very upset about losing her citizenship because she always considered herself an American. At age forty-six, she finally had the opportunity to work in a defense industry to demonstrate her patriotism to her country. It was also during the war that Congress repealed the Chinese exclusion laws and made it possible later for Ah Yoke Gee to regain her citizenship through naturalization. Unfortunately, her husband, who died before the war, did not live to see the happy day.[5] Ah Yoke passed away in 1973.

World War II marked a turning point in the lives of Chinese Americans. For the first time, Chinese Americans began to be accepted by the larger American society. Chinese American women not only had a chance to work at jobs traditionally held by men, but were also allowed to show their loyalty to their country. Although scholars have long recognized the importance of World War II in the lives of American women, and there has been increasing popular interest in the topic since the release in the late 1970s of a documentary—"The Life and Times of Rosie the Riveter"—the existing literature has overlooked the profound impact of the war on Chinese American women. Partly because of a scarcity of English-language sources on this topic, some scholars simply have assumed that Chinese American women did not share the experience of "Rosie the Riveter."[6]

Based on sources from Chinese-language newspapers and reports, company documents, and oral history interviews, this essay focuses on the unique experience of Chinese American female defense workers in the San Francisco Bay area. It examines the racial discrimination and prejudice that had forced Chinese Americans to isolate themselves in their ethnic communities, and explores how second-generation Chinese

American women, together with men of their communities, grasped the wartime opportunity to enter the larger American society. I chose the San Francisco Bay area as the setting of this study because the area had both the largest concentration of defense industries and the largest concentration of Chinese American women during the war.

The war created a favorable climate for Chinese Americans to be accepted by American society, but looking back, many Chinese Americans have mixed feelings about the war. The bombing of Pearl Harbor was one of the most tragic incidents in the history of the United States. Without it, however, Chinese Americans would not have been able to enter defense industries or the armed services. Since the United States and China were allies against common enemies during the war, American images of Chinese began to change from negative to positive ones. Whereas, once, negative stereotypes of the Chinese had dominated popular culture, the American mass media now described the Chinese as polite, moderate, and hard-working. On December 22, 1941, *Time* magazine, for example, published a short article to help the American public differentiate their Chinese "friends" from the Japanese. The facial expressions of the Chinese, according to the article, were more "placid, kindly, open," while those of the Japanese were more "positive, dogmatic, arrogant."[7] Also, because World War II was considered by the American public as a "good war" against fascists who had launched a racist war, it was important for the United States itself to improve its domestic race relations. Chinese Americans, too, recognized the racial dimension of this war. "It is fortunate," said an editorial in the *Jinshan shibao (Chinese Times)*, a San Francisco-based Chinese-language daily newspaper, "that this war has the white race and the yellow race on both sides and therefore will not turn into a war between the two."[8]

Moreover, Chinese Americans were needed for the nation's armed forces and defense industries. In May 1942, Bay Area defense establishments began to advertise jobs in local Chinese newspapers. Richmond shipyards, in particular, announced that they would hire Chinese Americans regardless of their citizenship status or their English skills. In a recruitment speech, Henry Kaiser, president of Kaiser Industries, which operated four shipyards in Richmond, called upon Bay Area Chinese Americans to work in his shipyards to support the war effort. The Moore Dry Dock Company hired Chinese-speaking instructors in their Oakland welding school and started a special bus service between the shipyard and Chinatown for Chinese American trainees.[9]

After decades of isolation imposed by the larger American society, the Bay Area Chinese American communities lost no time in seizing this opportunity. In various meetings and social gatherings, community leaders and organizations urged Chinese American residents to participate in the war efforts. Because military service would qualify immigrants for U.S. citizenship and some Chinese immigrants had been granted citizenship while in the Army, it was considered a breakthrough in challenging the exclusion acts. *Jinshan shibao* published a number of articles regarding the advantages of defense jobs. First, defense jobs were well paid. Second, these jobs could be used for draft deferment. Third, defense employees could apply for government-subsidized housing, which provided a great opportunity for Chinese Americans to move out of their isolated ethnic ghettos.[10]

Because few companies recorded the number of their Chinese American employees, the existing literature tends either to overlook them or give inaccurate estimates of them. In *The Chinese Experience in America*, Shih-shan Henry Tsai estimated that in 1943, Chinese Americans "made up some 15 percent of the shipyard work force in the San Francisco Bay area."[11] Since in 1943, the Bay Area had about 100,000 shipyard workers, Tsai's estimate suggests that 15,000 were Chinese Americans.[12] However, given the fact that the Bay Area's entire Chinese American population, including all age groups, was only about 22,000 in 1940, and only a small number of Chinese Americans migrated to the West Coast during the war, it was very unlikely that 15,000 of them (over 68 percent) were defense workers.[13] On August 21, 1942, the *Chinese Press*, a San Francisco Chinatown-based English-language newspaper, reported that 1,600 Chinese Americans worked in Bay Area defense industries.[14] This was one year before the peak of the war, before several of the Bay Area's major wartime shipbuilding establishments, including Richmond Shipyard Number Three and Marinship in Sausalito, began production. The number of Chinese American defense workers would increase significantly a few months later, after major defense establishments ran their ads in Chinese community newspapers. Marinship alone, according to *Jinshan shibao*, employed 400 Chinese Americans in March 1943. At the launching ceremony of *Sun Yat-sen*, a Liberty Ship named after the leader of the Chinese Revolution of 1911, Marinship invited all the yard's Chinese American employees and members of their families. The ship was christened by Mrs. Tao-ming Wei, wife of the Chinese ambassador to the U.S., and Madam Chiang Kai-shek was the guest of honor.[15] Based on these scattered pieces of information and interviews with old timers of local Chinese communities, a reasonable estimate is that by 1943, about 5,000 Chinese Americans were working (or had worked) for defense-related industries in the Bay Area, and between 500 to 600 of them were women.[16]

For a number of reasons, there were fewer female than male Chinese Americans in defense industries. The Chinese population in the United States historically has had an unbalanced sex ratio. Most of the early Chinese immigrants were male, and the Exclusion Act of 1882 also forced male Chinese immigrants who had married women in their native provinces to leave their wives and children in China. Only registered merchants and their families, students, teachers, diplomats, and travelers could be exempted from the exclusion. In order to bring their wives to the United States, many Chinese laborers were eager to change their status to merchants. Some of them accomplished this by saving a small amount of money and then raising capital through a *hui* to start their own businesses.[17] Others listed their names as partners in businesses of relatives and friends. In exchange for such privileges, they sometimes offered years of free labor. The 1906 earthquake in San Francisco to some extent facilitated the immigration of Chinese. Since birth records of the city were destroyed during the earthquake and fire, many Chinese grasped the opportunity to claim U.S. citizenship and used their new status to send for their sons and daughters.[18] Not until after 1910 did family-oriented life begin gradually to replace the old bachelor society. By 1940, Chinese American citizens finally outnumbered alien residents in Chinese American communities.[19] Nevertheless, that year there were still 285 Chinese American men for every 100 Chinese American women.[20]

The precarious economic situation of immigrant Chinese families compelled the majority of Chinese American women to help earn an income, no matter whether they were wives of business owners, wives of laborers, or daughters of immigrants.[21] Women's work in Chinese communities was often integrated with family life and family businesses.

In small shops, women worked alongside their husbands, between their household chores. Children of shop-owners often worked from an early age, beginning by folding socks in laundry shops or cleaning vegetables in restaurants and moving on to more difficult tasks as they got older. While women and children did not earn wages, their work was indispensable to the family business since few businesses could afford to hire extra hands.[22]

Women whose families were not wealthy enough to own businesses found employment mostly as cannery workers, shrimp cleaners, or garment workers. Cleaning shrimp was a common job for women with young children. During the shrimp season, some women would bring shrimp home and sit with their children shelling the shrimp from morning till night, sometimes under candlelight. Wages were based on the weight of the shrimp that they shelled daily. The most common employment for Chinese American women was in the garment industry, which made up 58 percent of all industrial employment in San Francisco's Chinatown in the late 1930s. In the early 1940s, there were more than seventy garment shops, most of which had fewer than fifty employees. At a time when unionized garment workers received $19 to $30 a week, workers in Chinatown's garment shops received only $4 to $16. A typical garment shop was located at the owner's home, where family members of the shop-owner and employees often worked together.[23]

During the war, in contrast to Chinese American men, who were more likely to be encouraged to join the military or defense work, women's primary duties still consisted of being wives and mothers. Throughout the war years, there were no articles or editorials in Chinese newspapers specifically calling on Chinese women to enter defense industries. "It is the servicemen who will do the fighting for us," Madame C. T. Feng, chairman of the American Women's Voluntary Service (an overseas Chinese organization) told Chinese American women. "We must show our fighting men that we are . . . absolutely behind them."[24] As part of its war effort, the Chinatown branch YWCA in San Francisco started a special weekly class for women to learn time-saving ways for preparing nutritious food. In a speech delivered to a YWCA open house meeting, the Y's administrator, Jane Kwong Lee, called upon Chinese American women to support the country by giving their families "the right nutritional food."[25] What open support existed for defense employment for women came mostly from the American-educated second generation. As a matter of fact, only the English-language *Chinese Press* occasionally reported activities of Chinese American women defense workers. In contrast, *Jinshan shibao*, a major local Chinese-language newspaper that had a larger circulation, paid little attention to the subject. On April 16, 1943, Jade Snow Wong, a San Francisco–born young Chinese American woman, christened a Liberty Ship at a Richmond shipyard and made the news in the *San Francisco Chronicle*, but there was no coverage of the event in *Jinshan shibao*. Not until three days later, after friends and relatives of the Wong family made complaints, did the newspaper print Wong's story and offer a public apology.[26]

It was difficult for many Chinese American women to go outside their communities to work, even when they wanted to. Jobs in ethnic factories were low paying. Nevertheless, the piece-work system and the flexible working hours made it possible for women to combine wage-earning with their family obligations. Before the war, 80 percent of the women who worked in San Francisco's Chinatown were married and 75 percent of them had children. Married garment shop workers could take time off to cook meals, shop, and pick up children from school. Garment shops also allowed women to bring their small children with them to work. It was very common to see babies sleeping in little cribs next to their mothers' sewing machines and toddlers crawling around on the floor.[27] Jobs outside the ethnic community, however, did not allow such practices.

The ethnically exclusive working environment, moreover, provided a place where immigrant Chinese women could socialize. A married Chinese woman with children did not have much time for social life. At work, however, she could chat with friends. Since everyone at work spoke Chinese, women found the working environment agreeable, and intimacy in sharing experiences of life in the United States developed naturally. The relationship between shop-owners and workers, if often economically exploitative, was nonetheless friendly. Family members of the shop-owners often worked side-by-side with the workers. Their children were told to respect the employees, often addressing older workers as "Auntie" or "Uncle." Garment factory jobs, therefore, were in great demand in Chinese American communities. Even the wives of bankers or small merchants sometimes sought employment there.[28]

Thus, although most Chinese American women were compelled to earn money to supplement their family income, they did it while taking care of their husbands and children. Since the exclusion acts made it difficult for Chinese women to immigrate to the United States and those who made it often did so after years of separation from their husbands, it was extremely hard for them to take jobs that conflicted with their household duties. Childcare was one of the major problems. Nursery schools were not available in San Francisco's Chinatown until the early 1940s, and Chinese American women were not accustomed to the idea of leaving their children at childcare facilities. Since very few Chinese immigrated to the United State with their parents, they usually did not have their parents helping out with childcare.[29]

The decades-long isolation had also limited the ability of immigrant Chinese working women to communicate with the outside world. Since they often worked between household chores, they had no time to participate in mainstream cultural activities and little chance to speak English. After years of working at Chinatown jobs, they found the outside world too remote from their daily experience. They did not have any non-Chinese friends and did not know whom to trust outside their ethnic communities. For wives of shop-owners, their departure for outside jobs would harm the family businesses that depended on the free labor of family members. Transportation was also an almost insurmountable problem. Since very few Chinese families had cars at the time (4 percent in the late 1930s in San Francisco), the majority of Chinese immigrant working women were familiar only with the area within walking distance from their homes. To these women, commuting from one city in the Bay Area to another was no different from traveling from one state to another.[30]

Given the social isolation of the immigrant generation, it is not surprising that the Chinese American women who worked in defense industries were mostly the second-generation daughters of immigrant women.[31] Among the eighty-two Chinese American women about whom I found information in various sources, and the twenty-seven women whom I was able to locate to conduct oral history interviews, only four were over the age of forty at the time they worked.[32] Few of them were married with children. Most of these women had gone to California's public schools; they had at least a high school education, and quite a few of them had attended college. With relatively few household responsibilities, in contrast to their mothers, they had the freedom and independence to work outside the home.

Since most of them were already living in the Bay Area before the war, these younger Chinese American women were among the first American women to join the Bay Area's defense labor force. As early as May 1942, the *Chinese Press* reported that young Chinese American girls were working in most of the defense establishments in the region. At the Engineer Supply Depot, Pier 90, eighteen-year-old Ruth Law was the youngest office staff member in the company. Her co-worker, Anita Lee, was an assistant to the company's chief clerk. Fannie Yee, a high school senior at the time, won top secretarial honors for her efficiency at work at Bethlehem Steel Corporation in San Francisco. She worked with two other young women, Rosalind Woo and Jessie Wong. The major defense employers in San Francisco for Chinese American women at the time, according to the *Press*, were the Army Department and Fort Mason. In Oakland, the Army Supply Base recognized Stella Quan as a very capable clerk. The first two Chinese American women who worked at Moore Dry Dock Company were Maryland Pong and Edna Wong. The State Employment Bureau also had Chinese American women on its staff. Before Kaiser's Richmond shipyards and Marinship began production work, many young Chinese American girls worked at Mare Island Navy Shipyard. Among them were Anita Chew, Mildred Lew, and Evelyn Lee of Oakland. Both Jenny Sui of San Francisco and Betty Choy of Vallejo started as messenger girls in the yard, but they were soon promoted to clerk-typists.[33]

Some women even left their professional training or occupations for defense-related work. Miaolan Ye, an Oakland-born Chinese American girl, was a college student majoring in agriculture at the time. She left school during the war to work as an inspector in a defense establishment in San Leandro.[34] Honolulu-born Betty Lum had been a nurse before the war. She, however, thought "shipbuilding is the present must industry of America" and resigned from her nursing job to learn acetylene burning at a Richmond shipyard. According to *Fore 'N' Aft*, there were three reasons for Betty to support the war effort: she was an American citizen, she was Chinese, and she had a nephew who was killed during the attack on Pearl Harbor. It is unclear when Betty Lum moved to the Bay Area, but the Kaiser company used her voice to urge other Chinese women to participate in defense work. Betty also had two sisters working in defense industries, one of them at Richmond Shipyard Number Three. Her brother, a dentist at the time, was prepared to join the Army.[35]

Unlike single young women, it was much more difficult for married Chinese American women to take defense jobs unless they did not have small children at home. After she married, Ah Yoke Gee spent most of her time at home taking care of her six children. She kept her sewing machine running whenever she was free from household chores. One of her daughters remembered that sometimes she woke up at two o'clock in the morning and could still hear her mother sewing. By the time the war started, Ah Yoke was widowed. Two of her older children had left home and the rest of them were in either high school or college. Although she still cooked for her family, her children had their own routines and did not expect to be served in a formal way. Every morning before leaving for her swing shift job in the shipyard, Ah Yoke would cook enough food for the whole family for the day. On weekends she shopped, washed, and cleaned.[36]

A few married Chinese American women managed to find defense work alongside their husbands. In late 1942, the Mare Island Navy Shipyard decided to select a Chinese female employee to christen a Liberty Ship. Among the eight Chinese American nominees, two were married. The honor went to Mrs. Yam, a Shop 51 electrician's helper. Mrs. Yam had just graduated from San Jose High School. Her newly-wed husband, Fred Yam, was the yard's pipe-fitter. Having joined the shipyard in June 1942, the young couple took the bus to work together from San Francisco's Chinatown to Vallejo. On December 18, 1942, Mrs. Yam, accompanied by six young Chinese American girls, smashed a bottle of champagne at HMS *Foley's* launching ceremony and became the first Chinese American woman in California shipyards to receive this highest wartime honor. She said she felt like "the proudest and happiest girl in the world."[37]

Other married Chinese American women joined defense work while their husbands were away from home. Jane Jeong, a burner at Richmond Shipyard Number Two, started her job in the shipyard only four months after her wedding. Before the war, Jane Jeong had been a dancer and a nightclub manager. She had also accumulated two hundred flying hours and dreamed of being a pilot fighting against the Japanese in China.[38] After the United States officially entered the war, however, she realized that she could support the war effort both in China and in the U.S. by building ships. Since her husband was a merchant seaman who was away from home most of the time, Jane Jeong took a job at a Richmond shipyard.[39]

Coming from a farming community in Fresno, Mannie Lee moved to Richmond along with her husband and children. At a Kaiser ship-yard, her husband Henry Lee was a graveyard-shift welder, while Mannie worked with her two daughters, Henrietta Lee and Hilda Fong, and a daughter-in-law, Lena Lee, in the yard's electric shop. In addition to the five shipyard workers of the family, Mannie Lee's two sons and her son-in-law were all in the Army. Although born in America, it was a big change for Mannie to move from her vegetable farm to Richmond. But at least the family still worked and lived together. The difference was that everyone worked fewer hours and made more money. More-over, they enjoyed the publicity from the company. Mannie and her family had never received any recognition as hard-working farmers.[40]

Although the majority of the Chinese American defense workers had grown up in the United States, racial discrimination and prejudice before the war had prevented their participation in many areas of American society. Since sons in Chinese American families usually had priority over daughters in receiving family support for higher education, Chinese American girls had to work harder than other students to save money or win scholarships to go to college. And despite the fact that these women were educated in the United States and had a good com-mand of English, Chinese American children in racially integrated public schools in San Francisco were excluded from most of the extracurricular activities. They could not dance with white children and few were invited to parties organized by people other than Chinese. The way they were treated in the job market was even worse: engineering graduates of Chinese descent from the University of California, Berkeley, were frequently rejected by American firms. While white women with college degrees and special training worked as teachers, nurses, secretaries, and social workers, similarly educated Chinese American women could only find service jobs as elevator operators, wait-resses, dancers, and maids. Outside Chinese communities their profes-sional degrees were meaningless, for few people wanted their services.[41]

It was the war that opened the door to better-paying jobs for Chinese American women. Aimei Chen, who came to the United States shortly after she was born, had grown up in a small Chinese community in Stockton. Before the war, she had worked as a waitress in a Chinese café while attending junior college. Some Caucasian girls her age got jobs in local dime stores, ice cream parlors, and department stores. Aimei, however, had never applied for those jobs because she knew no Chinese would be hired. While in college taking business classes, Aimei was very pessimistic about her future. As a Chinese American woman, it was unlikely that she could find a job outside Chinatown. Moreover, Stockton's Chinatown was very small and could not provide full-time employment for most of the women in the community. But, shortly after Pearl Harbor, Aimei learned from friends that defense industries were hiring, regardless of the applicants' ethnic backgrounds. She went with a friend to the Stockton Army Depot and was hired on the spot as a secretary.[42]

Yulan Liu, an Oakland-born Chinese American girl, had just graduated from high school in the summer of 1942. Her father, who had come to the United States as a "paper son" in 1915, worked seven days a week in a grocery store in Oakland's Chinatown.[43] Yulan's mother worked in a laundry shop, where her four children spent most of their childhood. Yulan also started to work in a laundry shop at age twelve. She did not have time to play with other children, and she did not recall ever being invited to a Caucasian's house. After she graduated from high school, Yulan began to work full time. She did not like the laundry shop job, but there were few other alternatives. Most of the girls in Chinatown were waitresses and garment workers. Some of her friends worked as maids in private homes. One day, her brother got a job at Moore Dry Dock Company in Oakland and told Yulan that there were many women shipbuilders there. Yulan went to the yard the next day and got a job as a welder.[44]

Being employed in a defense industry gave some Chinese American women a sense of belonging—of finally being accepted by American society. At Marinship in Sausalito, Jade Snow Wong was happy that she was employed by an "American" company. A San Francisco–born Chinese American girl, Jade Snow was the fifth daughter of a garment shop owner. She started to work in the shop when she was ten, helping her parents load garments on pick-up days. At eleven, she learned to sew and worked next to her mother. Although living in an ethnic community, she was quite aware of the differences between white Americans and people from her own ethnic group and was eager to venture into the outside world. Because of the financial difficulties of her family and her parents' belief that it was unnecessary for girls to obtain a college education, she could not get family support to go to college as her brother had. With determination, however, Jade Snow studied very hard and finally went to Mills College on a scholarship. In the summer of 1942, she graduated from Mills College. As she stopped at the college placement office seeking advice for her job search, she was told not to expect any opportunities in "American business houses," and to look only for places within her ethnic community. Jade Snow was stunned; an honor student, she felt "as if she had been struck on both cheeks." She was, however, determined to get a job in a non-Chinese company. Her younger sister at the time worked at Marinship in Sausalito. Jade Snow wanted to support the war effort as a citizen, so she went with her sister to Marinship. Twenty-four hours after she submitted an application, she was hired.[45]

Maggie Gee, Ah Yoke Gee's daughter, was born in Berkeley. In a community where Chinese American families were relatively few, Maggie grew up among children from various ethnic backgrounds. As a teenager, Maggie delivered newspapers and helped Caucasian women with their babies and cooking. She thought the people whom she worked for were nice to her. Nevertheless, as a Chinese, she was not allowed to join white students' clubs and she could not swim in community pools. After she graduated from high school, Maggie entered the University of California, Berkeley. She paid the $28 tuition each semester out of her own earnings and bought books and clothes with her own money. Her mother had supported Maggie's older brother in college and had no money left for Maggie's education. But Maggie did live and eat at home while in college. Maggie was a good student in school, but she did not know what she could do with a college degree. She heard that many Chinese American male college graduates, let alone Chinese American women, had difficulties finding jobs in the field in which they had been trained.

Pearl Harbor finally brought Chinese Americans and white Americans together on new common ground. On December 7, 1941, Maggie was spending the afternoon studying in the campus library. She found many students there talking very emotionally. Maggie sensed that something unusual had happened. To Chinese Americans, World War II had begun on September 18, 1931, when the Japanese invaded Manchuria in northeastern China. Maggie had been in the fourth grade at the time. Her mother had planned to send her and her sister to China to study, and they had to cancel the trip after the Japanese occupied Chinese territory. After July 7, 1937, when the Japanese attacked Chinese troops at Lugou Bridge near Beijing, the war against Japan became a nationwide effort in China. Overseas Chinese were actively involved in supporting their fellow countrymen. Maggie often went with her mother to San Francisco's Chinatown to attend rallies and fundraising activities. She remembered how badly she felt when she learned about the outrageous atrocities during the 1937 Nanjing Massacre, but she was surprised to notice that her American classmates knew very little about what had happened in China. Not until Pearl Harbor did everyone seem involved in the war effort. The Berkeley campus offered classes for defense employment, in which Maggie and many other students received training. While still a full-time student at Berkeley, she got a graveyard-shift job at Richmond Shipyard Number Two.

Wartime employment provided tangible benefits to many Chinese Americans. "For people who used to have very little money," recalled Aimei Chen, "the war was a time of great economic opportunity." She started to buy things for her family—food, kitchenware, and other household items. Aimei's mother also got a job in a cannery in Stockton, where many former employees had left for defense jobs. Yulan Liu, meanwhile, made $65 a week, four times more than she had made before the war. She gave some money to her mother and saved the rest for herself. On her day off, she went to the movies and bought herself candies and pastries. As for Ah Yoke Gee, her family endured great difficulties for many years after she lost her husband. During the war, with both her and her daughters working in the shipyard and her son in the service, the living standard of the family improved significantly. Jade Snow Wong, for her part, contributed part of her income to her parents and saved money for her future education.

The ethnically diverse working environment provided an opportunity for women such as Ah Yoke Gee to meet people about whom
they had known little before the war. For over forty years, ever since
her birth, Ah Yoke had lived in the United State, but as she moved from
the Monterey Peninsula to San Francisco and then to Berkeley, she had
little contact with people other than Chinese. It was at work that she
met all kinds of people and gained respect as one of the oldest crew
members of the yard.[46] Yulan Liu was also very popular among her
teammates. A small figure weighing only eighty pounds at the time, she
not only worked hard but was also the only one of the team who could
handle welding jobs in narrow areas of the ships. Her teammates liked
to hear her stories about people living in Chinese American communities. Upon their request, she led a tour of the group to San Francisco's
Chinatown.[47]

Defense industries provided an opportunity for Chinese women to
put to good use their knowledge of the world beyond school. After
months of research, Jade Snow Wong produced a paper on the absen-
teeism of shipyard workers. The paper won first prize in an essay contest sponsored by the *San Francisco Chronicle* and Bay Area defense
industries. In addition to a fifty-dollar war bond, she was offered the
privilege of christening a Liberty Ship at a Kaiser shipyard. When her
pictured appeared in both English and Chinese newspapers, she gained
respect from members of her family and from people in the community. Many people in Chinatown came to congratulate her parents for
their daughter's success in the "American world."[48]

Although some women were doing traditionally male jobs, compared to what they had done before the war, most of them did not think
defense work was that hard. Joy Yee, a San Francisco–born high school
graduate, was the second daughter of a garment shop owner in Oakland.
Although Joy had tried to sew with her mother and sisters in the shop,
her mother thought that Joy was not good at sewing and that she would
never make it as a seamstress. During the war, however, Joy got a job
as a mechanic at Alameda Naval Air Station. Excited at having "a real
job" in a defense industry, she learned to use different tools and became
very efficient at work.[49] Before the war, Yulan Liu had worked ten hours
a day, seven days a week, at a laundry. "There was nothing heavier than
the iron," she said. "Sometimes my arm was so sore at night that I could
not hold my chopsticks." On the other hand, "the welding torch," as

she remembered, "was lighter," mainly because she did not have to hold it for hours. Even on an assembly line, she was able to work in different parts of the ships and she always had a chance to chat with people between assignments. In the laundry shop, no matter how fast she worked, there was always more to be washed, ironed, and folded, and she could hardly find any time to rest.[50] The big change for Ah Yoke Gee was that she did not have to sew late at night any more. She worked eight hours a day for most of the days and had Sundays off.[51]

For some women, however, a defense job was not easy. Maggie Gee, for example, found working at night in the shipyard to be tiring. Welding itself was not bad, but at night she did not have people around to talk to. It was difficult to stay awake at work, since she was still attending school during the day and could not get much sleep. When the job was slow, she sometimes fell asleep, but it was so cold at night in the shipyard that she could never sleep well. A year later, when she graduated from college, Maggie decided to do something different for a change. She got a new job at Mare Island Navy Shipyard as a draftswoman.

It was the job at Mare Island that led Maggie to the most exciting adventure of her life. Working in a big office with over thirty people, she and two young women, one a Caucasian and one a Filipina, quickly became close friends. At lunch time, the three of them would meet in the rest area adjoining the ladies' room. They would chat, eat their lunches, and drink coffee. They all liked the idea of helping the country fight the war, but at the same time, they all wanted to do something more exciting. The Filipina had taken some flying lessons before the war, and the three of them decided to save money for aviation training. When Maggie finally saved enough money for a training program, she was so overjoyed that she tossed the money into the air. Although as a child Maggie had enjoyed watching airplanes at the Oakland Airport, she had never dreamed of flying an airplane herself. After she graduated from an aviation school in Nevada, she interviewed with the Women's Airforce Service Pilots (WASPs). When she returned to her drafting job at Mare Island, waiting for a call from the Army, Maggie realized that her life had changed. Everyone—mostly men—in her work area was interested in what she and her friends had done. Some people were envious. A few months later, Maggie was called by the Army and became one of only two Chinese American women in the WASPs. Her mother saw her off at the train station. Ah Yoke Gee was proud of her daughter. She wished that she herself were twenty years younger because she would have liked to fly too. Maggie remained a WASP until the unit was disbanded in late 1944. While in the service, she transported military supplies throughout the country.[52]

Although Chinese Americans were accepted in defense industries, they had little chance to be promoted to supervisory positions. Many companies simply assumed that white employees would not follow orders given by Chinese. For those who had upgraded their skills over the years (usually male workers), this could be very frustrating. One male Chinese American worker at a Richmond shipyard had years of working experience with an excellent performance record. But he, too, saw several less qualified white workers promoted to foreman positions with no chance being given to him. Although he complained, no one listened. Finally he got so angry that he quit his job.[53]

Because women were not expected to work in defense industries after the war, they were not in a position to compete with male employees for supervisory positions. Therefore, unlike the Chinese American men, very few Chinese American women had direct conflict with other workers or their supervisors. Some women recalled that better jobs usually went to Caucasian women. On the other hand, except for the few immigrants who did not speak English, most of the Chinese American women had at least a high school education, and therefore did not work as janitors.[54] They were mostly employed as office clerks, draftswomen, welders, burners, and in other semi-skilled positions. Since not many defense establishments employed large groups of Chinese American women, it was hard for these women to socialize exclusively among themselves. This, in fact, gave Chinese American women opportunities to meet people from different ethnic backgrounds.[55] Other workers also showed a great deal of curiosity about Chinese American women, for few of them had met Chinese American women before the war. Leong Bo San, a middle-aged Chinese American woman from San Francisco, was described in *Fore 'N' Aft* as "a tiny, doll-like figure" who "walks with the dainty, mincing gait of the upper class Chinese lady whose feet once were bound" in her "flat rubber-soled shoes of the shipyard." According to the report, Leong Bo San had drawn attention from "everyone" who rode "the graveyard ferry boat." At Assembly Line 11, the report went on, Leong Bo San was "everybody's favorite," for she often came to the yard with Chinese shrimp, fruit, and cake to share with other workers. Although she looked tiny and delicate, she worked with "an energy that amazes people twice her size." Her boss, James G. Zeck, reportedly said that "I wish I had a whole crew of people like her."[56]

Nevertheless, some women did find themselves trapped in a place where the future was dismal. For example, Jade Snow Wong's talent and ability were recognized by her boss at Marinship. Every time the boss got promoted to a higher position, he would take her with him to his new office. But Jade Snow noticed that while many clerks, secretaries, and other office workers in Marinship were women, their bosses, those who read the reports prepared by their secretaries and made decisions, were all men.[57] Asked later whether she would like to stay at Marinship when the war ended if she had the choice, she answered "no" without any hesitation. "I decided to leave before they started to lay people off," she said. "There was no future for me, no future for women in the ship-yard." At Mills College, Jade Snow had found a few female role models—her professors, the dean for whom she had worked, and the college president. She wanted to be a professional woman like them. But "in defense industry," she said, "a woman could only be someone's secretary. The bosses were all men." Before the war ended, she started searching for a career in which she did not have to be treated differently because she was a Chinese American and a woman.[58]

Toward the end of the war, defense industries gradually reduced the volume of their production, and their workers were free to leave their jobs. Some Chinese American women had waited for this day to come. Jade Snow Wong was happy that she had done her part to support the war effort of her country, but she quit her job right after V-J day. With the money that she had saved, she started a business of her own in San Francisco's Chinatown and began writing books.[59] Alameda Naval Air Station was one of the few defense establishments in the Bay Area that was able to keep some of its female employees after the war. Some women in the station, nevertheless, decided to leave. Lanfang Wong, a metalsmith in the yard for over three years, quit her job for two reasons. First, she found it tiring to commute two hours a day from San Francisco's Chinatown to Alameda to work. Second, she did not think her work was skilled work. After a while, she realized that it was not much different from making clothes except that metal instead of cloth was used. As soon as she learned that the war was over, she found a new job working for an insurance company in San Francisco. She later married a war veteran and moved with him to Napa Valley to work on a small farm.[60]

Only a few Chinese American women continued to work in defense industries after the war. Yuqin Fu worked as an office clerk at Alameda Naval Air Station until 1947, when she got married. After a few years at home taking care of her children, she found a job at Pacific Telephone and Telegraph.[61] Born and schooled in Oakland, Elizabeth Lew Anderson worked as a metalsmith at the Alameda Naval Air Station during the war. She later married a Caucasian merchant seaman. Although her husband had to move from one place to another all over the country (and sometimes outside the country) and Elizabeth followed him most of the time, she was called back to work by the Naval Air Station during the Korean War (and later again, during the Vietnam War), when her family moved back to the Bay Area.[62] Joy Yee continued to work at the Naval Station until 1955, when she was about to have her first child. But when she stayed at home, she missed her job and her friends at work. In 1968, she went back to work and kept her job for another seventeen years until her retirement. To celebrate the fiftieth anniversary of the war, Joy Yee helped organize a reunion of Chinese American women who had worked at the Alameda Naval Air Station during the war.[63]

A few others, however, were reluctant to leave their defense jobs. Ah Yoke Gee loved her job in the shipyard so much that she would not leave it for anything else. She knew that other jobs would not pay as well. Aimei Chen also wanted to stay at her defense job. Since so many white women were then also job-hunting, the chances for her to find a good job were slim. By late 1945, however, most of the Bay Area's defense establishments were about to shut down, and large-scale lay-offs began. With limited training and skills, these women could not find jobs in other industries; they had to look for jobs that were traditionally held by women.

These Chinese American women's wartime work nevertheless had important consequences: their lives were no longer restricted within their ethnic communities. Most of them found jobs outside Chinatowns as race relations and the economy improved in the postwar years. Ah Yoke Gee took a job at a post office in Berkeley, where she worked until her retirement. Meanwhile, she became actively involved in Berkeley's Chinese American community.[64] Aimei Chen married and moved with her husband to Berkeley. Under the GI Bill, her husband became an engineering student at the University of California. Aimei found a job as an office clerk in a small firm, where she worked until her first child was born.[65] Yulan Liu married her former shipyard foreman, a white man. The young couple bought a house in Vallejo, where Yulan's husband worked in the Navy Shipyard at Mare Island. Yulan worked as a nursing aide on and off for over thirty years. Lili Wong, daughter of a San Francisco restaurant waiter, left her job at a Richmond shipyard and went to medical school. She later moved to Washington, D.C., and practiced medicine with her husband.[66]

Their wartime experience gave Chinese American women confidence and maturity. They found that they could do the things that men could. Maggie Gee left the WASPs and went to graduate school in Berkeley. She was not a shy Chinese American girl anymore and was soon elected president of the Chinese Students Association on the Berkeley campus. Thereafter, she became active in local communities. She also decided to become a physicist, although most graduate students in physics were men. She later worked at the Lawrence Livermore National Laboratory and was the only woman physicist there for many years.[67] Jade Snow Wong, however, was no longer eager to work outside her ethnic community. After she left Marinship, she went back to San Francisco's Chinatown looking for her own identity. Her first book was about herself; she wanted the outside world to know what the life of a Chinese American was like, especially a Chinese American woman. It was at that time that she decided to give up her English name "Constance," a name that she had been known by in school and at Marinship. The girl in her autobiography was "Jade Snow," translated originally from her Chinese name.[68]

While acknowledging that World War II brought significant changes to their lives, many Chinese American women noticed that racial discrimination and prejudice did not disappear after the war. They continued in subtle ways. When Maggie Gee and her sister tried to find an apartment in Berkeley in the early 1950s, they knew that some people would not rent their properties to Chinese Americans. So they told people their ethnic identity when they first inquired over the telephone. At least in one case, a landlady refused to show the sisters the apartment when she learned that they were Chinese.[69] Limin Wong, a defense worker during the war, remembered calling a business firm in Berkeley for an advertised office position after the war. The person who answered the phone at first told her that the job was available. When he realized that she was Chinese, however, he changed his statement and said the position had been filled. Limin later found a job at the State Employment Office. She worked there for thirty years and was the manager of the office before she retired.[70]

The young Chinese American women who participated in defense work had had fresh memories of discriminatory practices in American society before the war, and they were fully aware of the political implications of taking defense jobs. Although very few of them were able to keep their jobs after the war, and some of them might not necessarily have cared about the limited skills that they acquired, what they had accomplished was far more significant than the jobs themselves. They were accepted, for the first time, as Americans, even though most of them were born in the U.S. and had been Americans since birth. To a large extent, the war provided an entry for Chinese American women into the larger American society, something for which their ancestors had struggled a hundred years.

Xiaojian Zhao is a professor of Asian American studies and history at the University of California, Santa Barbara. She is the author of *Remaking Chinese America: Immigration, Family, and Community, 1940–1965* (2002).

NOTES

1. "Richmond Took a Beating," *Fortune Magazine*, February 1945, 267. This essay is adapted from part of the author's Ph.D. dissertation, "Women and Defense Industries in World War II" (University of California, Berkeley, 1993). I would like to thank Paula Fass, Leon Litwack, and Aihwa Ong for their encouragement and generous support for the project. Special thanks to Sucheng Chan, Paula Fass, Bryna Goodman, Him Mark Lai, and Nancy Quam-Wickam for their comments on earlier drafts of the paper, and to Maggie Gee, Perter Lew, Jade Snow Wong, and many other individuals who shared their life stories and who helped with my research.

2. *Fore 'N' Aft*, April 20, 1945. Marion Gee was the name used for Ah Yoke Gee in this source.

3. The Naturalization Act of 1790 limited naturalization to "free white persons" who had resided in the United States for at least two years. The Naturalization Act of 1870 extended this privilege to aliens of African descent. Chinese as well as other Asians, however, were excluded in these acts. The Circuit Court for California ruled in 1878 that Chinese, who were classified racially as Mongolians, were neither white nor African and thus ineligible for naturalization. This ruling was officially adopted by the U.S. government in the Chinese Exclusion Act of 1882. For details on legal restrictions against Chinese immigrants and their court-tested implications, see Charles J. McClain, *In Search of Equality: The Chinese Struggle Against Discrimination in Nineteenth-Century America* (Berkeley: University of California Press, 1994), 70–73; Sucheng Chan, "The Exclusion of Chinese Women, 1870–1943," in *Entry Denied: Exclusion and the Chinese Community in America, 1882–1943*, ed. Sucheng Chan (Philadelphia: Temple University Press, 1991), 94–146; Jeff H. Lesser, "Always 'Outsiders': Asians, Naturalization, and the Supreme Court," *Amerasia* 12 (1985–86); 83–100; and Jack Chen, *The Chinese of America* (San Francisco: Harper & Row, Publishers, 1980), 147–48.

4. Act of September 22, 1922, 42 *United States Statutes at Large* (First Part) 1021; Chan, "The Exclusion of Chinese Women," 109.

5. Interview with Maggie Gee, February 20, 1994, and March 27, 1994; interview with Florence Gee Tom, August 23, 1994. Although the Chinese exclusion acts were repealed in 1943, it was not until 1952 that racially based denial of naturalization was abolished in the McCarran-Walter Act. According to her daughters, Ah Yoke was not aware of the changes in the naturalization laws until the late 1950s.

6. On women workers in World War II, see Ruth Milkman, *Gender at Work: The Dynamics of Job Segregation by Sex during World War II* (Urbana: University of Illinois Press, 1987); Sherna Berger Gluck, *Rosie the Riveter Revisited: Women, the War, and Social Change* (Boston: Twayne Publishers, 1987); Sheila Tropp Lichtman, "Women at Work, 1941–1945: Wartime Employment in the San Francisco Bay Area" (Unpublished Ph.D. dissertation, University of California, Davis, 1981); and Miriam Frank, Marilyn Ziebarth, and Connie Field, *The Life and Times of Rosie the Riveter: The Story of Three Million Working Women During World War Two* (California: Clarity Educational Productions, 1982). Although these works include information on some minority women, none of them discusses the experience of Chinese American women. In her dissertation on wartime women shipyard workers, Deborah Ann Hirshfield concluded that not many Asians worked in the shipyards because Japanese Americans were interned during the war and "restrictions on the aliens' access to confidential Navy or Army plans discouraged most shipyards from hiring" Chinese Americans "in significant numbers." See Deborah Ann Hirshfield, "Rosie Also Welded: Women and Technology in Shipbuilding During World War II" (Unpublished Ph.D. dissertation, University of California, Irvine, 1987), 127. Historian Charles Wollenberg, in his book on Marinship, pointed out that many Marinship workers came from local Chinese American communities. However, since very little could be found in English-language sources about Chinese American workers, his discussion on Chinese American women was limited. See Charles Wollenberg, *Marinship at War: Shipbuilding and Social Change in Wartime Sausalito* (Berkeley: Western Heritage Press, 1990).

7. *Time*, December 22, 1941.

8. *Jinshan shibao*, July 4, 5, 1942.

9. Ibid., April 22, May 11, 20, 24, 30, June 20, 23, 24, August 12, 22 and November 16, 1942; March 1, 2, 17, April 13, 19, August 12, November 16, 1943.

10. In his survey of the African American population in San Francisco conducted in 1943, sociologist Charles S. Johnson found that before and up to 1943, "no rigidly segregated Negro community existed in the city." The Chinese population in the city, however, "represents a counterpart of the distinctly Negro district of New York's Harlem, Chicago's Southside Area, and Detroit's Paradise Valley." See Charles S. Johnson, *The Negro War Workers in San Francisco, A Local Self-Survey* (San Francisco, 1944), 3; *Jinshan shibao*, April 28, 1942 and March 17, 1943; *Chinese Press*, August 21, 1942.

11. See Shih-shan Henry Tsai, *The Chinese Experience in America* (Bloomington and Indianapolis: Indiana University Press, 1986), 116.

12. Marshall Maslin, ed., *Western Shipbuilders in World War II, A Detailed Review of Wartime Activities of Leading Maritime and Navy Contractors* (Oakland, 1954), 59.

13. I found only one woman reportedly working on Kaiser Richmond shipyards who arrived in the United States from China during the war. Lena Chiang, a Yard Three plate-shop swing-shift shipfitter, according to a report in *Fore 'N' Aft*, was a second cousin of Generalissimo Chiang Kai-shek, the leader of the Chinese Nationalist Party. Having graduated from a Chinese university, Lena left China in 1941 with her husband, Major Pei Lun Chiang. The major was injured during a Japanese air raid in Chongqing, China, and came to the United States to receive medical treatment. He then stayed for training at an American military school. Meanwhile, Lena, together with her brother Paul, joined the nation's defense work. See *Fore 'N' Aft*, July 1943.

14. *Chinese Press*, August 21, 1942.

15. Although Marinship's first Liberty Ship was launched in late June of 1942, large-scale production work began only toward the end of the year, when major construction of the facility was completed. See Wollenberg, *Marinship at War*, 3–4; *Jinshan shibao*, March 21, 1943.

16. Some of the workers, especially men, were employed by the defense industries for only a short period of time before they joined the Army.

17. Stanford M. Lyman, *Chinese Americans* (New York: Random House, 1974), 59; Victor G. and Brett de Bary Nee, *Longtime Californ': A Documentary Study of An American Chinatown* (New York: Pantheon Books, 1973), 148–49. Early Chinese immigrants often raised their capital among themselves when they decided to start a business. For example, a group of ten men with twenty dollars apiece would form a *hui*. Each would then write on a piece of paper secretly the amount of interest he was willing to pay to have the first use of the $200 available in the hui. The highest bidder got the money, which he could use to start a small business. When he gave the money back a month later, the next highest bidder got his turn. See Renqiu Yu, *To Save China, to Save Ourselves: The Chinese Hand Laundry Alliance of New York* (Philadelphia: Temple University Press, 1992), 10–11; Chen, *The Chinese of America*, 197–98.

18. Nee and Nee, *Longtime Californ'*, 63; Roger Daniels, *Asian America: Chinese and Japanese in the United States since 1850* (Seattle and London: University of Washington Press, 1988), 94–95; interview with Ben Fee by Ben Tong and Kathleen Chin, Oral History Project, Bancroft Library, University of California, Berkeley, 3.

19. According to the 1940 census, 52 percent of the Chinese American population in the United States and 58 percent in the state of California were American-born.

20. *Sixteenth Census of the United States*, 1940, Population: Characteristics of the Nonwhite Population by Race, 5–6.

21. This, however, is not apparent in the published U.S. census. The census of 1940 shows that only 25.7 percent of Chinese women fourteen years and older were in the labor force in San Francisco and Oakland, lower than the proportions of both white and black working women (32.4 and 41.3 percent, respectively). This is because there were not many Chinese American women employed steadily as factory hands. For those who took piecework home and those who worked in their family-owned small shops—a phenomenon that could be found everywhere in the streets of both San Francisco's and Oakland's Chinatowns—their work was not counted in the census.

22. Jade Snow Wong, *Fifth Chinese Daughter* (Seattle: University of Washington Press, 1989), 6; interview with Jade Snow Wong, November 25, 1991. Also see Evelyn Nakano Glenn, "Split Household, Small Producer, and Dual Earner: An Analysis of Chinese-American Family Strategies," *Journal of Marriage and the Family* (Feb. 1983): 39–41.

23. Ginger Chih, "Immigration of Chinese Women to the U.S.A., 1900–1940" (Unpublished M.A. thesis, Sarah Lawrence College, 1977), 27–28. In the late 1930s, there were eighty-four small factories in San Francisco's Chinatown, including forty-nine garment shops, seven shrimp-shelling shops, three cigar shops, and twenty-six others. See *Sanfanshi nugong shehui diaocha zhi shiquing* (Survey of Social Work Needs of the Chinese Population of San Francisco), California SERA Project 2F 2-256, 1936, Bancroft Library, University of California, Berkeley, 1–2. On Chinatown workers, see Lyman, *Chinese Americans*, 154–55; Tsai, *The Chinese Experience in America*, 109–10; Judy Yung, "Unbinding the Feet, Unbinding their Lives: Social Change for Chinese Women in San Francisco 1902–1945" (Unpublished Ph.D. dissertation, University of California, Berkley, 1990), 223. Judy Yung's dissertation has been revised and published as *Unbound Feet: A Social History of Chinese Women in San Francisco* (Berkeley and Los Angeles: University of California Press, 1995). According to a survey made by the California State Employment Service in June 1938, the average monthly wage of the Chinese in San Francisco was $70 or less per month. The women's income was much lower than men's. See Ruth Hall Whitefield, "Public Opinion and the Chinese Question in San Francisco, 1900–1947" (Unpublished M.A. thesis, University of California, Berkeley, 1947).

24. *Chinese Press*, October 9, 1942.

25. *Jinshan shibao*, February 9, 22, April 1, 1942; *Chinese Press*, January 30, 1942.

26. *San Francisco Chronicle*, April 17, 1943; *Jinshan shibao*, April 19, 20, 1943.

27. *Sanfanshi nugong shehui diaocha zhi shiqing*, 1:35–36; Nee and Nee, *Longtime Californ'*, 289; Wong, *Fifth Chinese Daughter*, 165.

28. Wong, *Fifth Chinese Daughter*, 165; *Sanfanshi nugong shehui diaocha zhi shiqing*, 3; interview with Mrs. F. J. Chin by Sharlene Chinn, 1977, in "Combined Asian American Recourse Oral History Project," Bancroft Library, University of California, Berkeley, 1–9.

29. Lucy Jen Huang, "The Chinese American Family," in *Ethnic Families in America: Patterns and Variations*, ed. Charles H. Mindel and Robert W. Habenstein (New York: Elsevier North Holland, 1981), 124. In the early 1940s the idea of using

public daycare facilities was new to the majority of working women. Although many female defense workers had difficulties in coping with their work and childcare, few used childcare facilities at the time. In fact, many childcare centers in Richmond, California, could not get full enrollment for that reason. In addition to avoiding the cost of childcare, women in general felt more comfortable having their relatives or someone they knew take care of their children. See *Fore 'N' Aft*, Sept. 3, 1943.

30. *Sanfanshi nugong shehui diaocha zhi shiqing*, 38.
31. I use the term "second-generation" in this essay to refer to children of Chinese immigrants who either came to the U.S. with their parents at a young age or were born in the United States.
32. Four of the twenty-seven women, for various reasons, were not available for interviews, and I learned their stories from members of their families.
33. *Chinese Press*, May 29, 1942.
34. *Jinshan shibao*, Nov. 29, 1942.
35. *Fore 'N' Aft*, Nov. 19, 1942.
36. Interview with Maggie Gee, November 24, 1992.
37. *Chinese Press*, Dec. 18, 1942.
38. Private aviation classes were available for women during the war. One such training program, provided by the American Women's Volunteering Service, advertised in Chinese-language newspapers. The program offered classes on aviation, operation, radio, and geography. Women with training in basic arithmetic were qualified to take classes. See *Jinshan shibao*, June 7, 1942.
39. *Fore 'N' Aft*, Dec. 31, 1942.
40. *Fore 'N' Aft*, April 16, 1943, and April 14, 1944.
41. Richard Kock Dare, "The Economic and Social Adjustment of the San Francisco Chinese for the Past Fifty Years" (Unpublished M.A. thesis, University of California, Berkeley, 1959), 20; interview with Jane F. Lee by Ben Tong and Kathleen Chin; interview with Maggie Gee, June 1991; Wong, *Fifth Chinese Daughter*, 189.
42. Interview with Aimei Chen, July 11, 1994.
43. A "paper son" was an individual who claimed he or she was a child of a Chinese born in the U.S. Such claims became common after the 1906 San Francisco earthquake and fire destroyed birth records of the city.
44. Interview with Yulan Liu, January 8, 1993.
45. Interview with Jade Snow Wong; Wong, *Fifth Chinese Daughter*, 4–5, 12–15, 18, 29, 33, 52–55, 71, 73, 90, 92, 95, 109, 188–99.
46. *Fore 'N' Aft*, April 20, 1945.
47. Interview with Yulan Liu.
48. Wong, *Fifth Chinese Daughter*, 92–93, 189–91, 194–98.
49. Interview with Joy Yee, August 18, 23, 1994.
50. Interview with Yulan Liu, January 8, 1993.
51. Interviews with Maggie Gee and Florence Gee.
52. Interview with Maggie Gee; for information on Maggie Gee in WASPs, also see Vera S. Williams, *WASPs, Women Airforce Service Pilots of World War II* (Osceola, Wisc.: Motorbooks International Publishers & Wholesalers, 1994), 24, 31, 54, 69, 76, 77, 115, 126, 129, 140, 144.
53. *Chinese Press*, September 29, 1943. Also see *Jinshan shibao*, September 9, 1943.
54. Constance Wong, "Marinship Chinese Workers Are Building Ships to Free Their

Home Land," *Mariner* (June 26, 1943): 3. One of my male informants, who worked briefly in a Richmond shipyard during the war, also remembered seeing a couple of Chinese American women laborers in Richmond shipyards. Although he never talked to these women, he believed that they were immigrants with limited English skills; interview with Peter Lew, August 23, 1994.

55. At Alameda Naval Air Station, however, there were more than a dozen Chinese American girls from Oakland, and they often got together after work; interview with Joy Yee.

56. Interview with Aimei Chen; *Fore 'N' Aft*, April 7, 1944.

57. Wong, *Fifth Chinese Daughter*, 94, 233–34, 237.

58. Interview with Jade Snow Wong, November 23, 1991; Wong, *Fifth Chinese Daughter*, 236.

59. Wong, *Fifth Chinese Daughter*, 237.

60. Interview with Lanfang Wong, August 20, 1994.

61. Interview with Yuqin Fu, August 19, 1994.

62. Interview with Peter Lew.

63. Interview with Joy Yee.

64. Interview with Maggie Gee; *Looking Back at Berkeley: A Pictorial History of a Diverse City* (Berkeley: Berkeley Book Committee of the Berkeley Historical Society, 1984), 28.

65. Interview with Aimei Chen.

66. Ibid.; interview with Lili Wong, August 10, 1994.

67. Interview with Maggie Gee.

68. Interview with Jade Snow Wong.

69. Interview with Maggie Gee.

70. Interview with Limin Wong, July 19, 1994.

NEGOTIATING URBAN SPACE

LATINA WORKERS IN DOMESTIC WORK AND STREET VENDING IN LOS ANGELES*

Norma Chinchilla and Nora Hamilton

The Latino population in Southern California experienced dramatic growth during the 1980s, much of it fueled by immigration. The number of Mexican immigrants (traditionally the largest group) increased as a result of economic recession and widespread unemployment in Mexico, and an unprecedented number of Central Americans, primarily Salvadorans and Guatemalans came to Southern California escaping war, political crises, and deteriorating economic conditions in their respective countries. According to the 1990 census, the U.S. Latino population grew at seven times the rate of the non-Latino population between 1980 and 1990, with Mexicans comprising the largest group, 62 percent of all Latinos, while the fastest-growing groups consist of Central and South Americans (Brownstein-Santiago, 1992). One-third of all Latinos live in California, where the Latino population represents one-fourth of the total. The city of Los Angeles is nearly 40 percent Latino, and the Latino populations of the Southern California cities of El Monte and Santa Ana represent 72.5 percent and 75.2 percent of the respective totals (Southwest Voter Research Notes, 1991).

Although little acknowledged by researchers, policy makers, and community activists until recently, women were an important part of

*This chapter was originally published as: Chinchilla, Norma and Nora Hamilton. "Latina Workers in Domestic Work and Street Vending in Los Angeles." In *Humboldt Journal of Social Relations* 22, no. 1 (1996): 25-35.

this immigrant influx and constitute a majority among many immigrant groups. Mexican immigrants are an exception; in 1990, only 45 percent of the foreign-born Mexicans in Greater Los Angeles were female, undoubtedly reflecting a traditional pattern of cyclical male labor migration generally from western rural areas of Mexico to jobs in California agriculture (and, more recently, manufacturing and services as well). As migration from Mexico becomes less cyclical and includes a greater proportion of urban migrants from a variety of social classes and other regions of the country, the proportion of women migrating from Mexico may increase and several studies have indicated that the undocumented Mexican settler population of the 1980s, as opposed to temporary migrants, was roughly equally divided between men and women (Hondagneu-Sotelo, 1994A:2). In contrast to the pattern of Mexican immigration, women are often the pioneers in migration streams, and many Central American women came alone to the United States in the 1960s and 1970s to work as domestics (Hondagneu-Sotelo, 1994B). In 1990, women accounted for the majority of foreign-born Salvadorans and Central Americans generally and nearly half of Guatemalans in the Greater Los Angeles area.

Foreign-Born Hispanic Immigrants according to Gender, 1990

Greater Los Angeles

	Mexican	Salvadoran	Guatemalan	Other CenAm	Other Hisp.
Male	54.95	49.07	50.93	44.47	48.29
Female	45.05	50.93	49.07	55.53	51.71

Source: Zentgraf, 1995.

The new immigrants to Los Angeles found themselves in a rapidly changing urban environment and became an important element in that change. In contrast to other parts of the United States, the Los Angeles economy was expanding during the 1980s, resulting in an increase in well-paid, highly skilled jobs related to technology production and research, much of it defense related, and a boom in construction and real estate. Low-income jobs in low-skill services and labor-intensive manufacturing also expanded, resulting in a net job gain of 50 percent, from approximately 3 million in 1972–73 to approximately 4.5 million in 1990 (Wolff, 1992). Immigrants filled many of these low-income jobs as janitors in new high-rise office buildings, dishwashers, bus boys, and maids in the booming hotel and restaurant business, domestic servants, nurses, or gardeners in suburban homes, and workers in low-paying manufacturing jobs in the garment, furniture, and food-processing industries. As the boom of the 1980s gave way to the recession of the 1990s, however, formal jobs were eliminated at all levels, swelling the ranks of the unemployed as well as the number of informal areas such as street vending.

The following analysis focuses on the spatial dimensions of the lives and work of Latina immigrants in Los Angeles. It draws upon a study by the authors of 173 Central American and Mexican workers, personal interviews with Latina workers, and reports from informants in the Central American and Mexican communities, as well as other studies, to examine how immigrant Latinas, particularly domestics and street vendors, cope with, negotiate, and redefine urban space in public and private spheres.

Gender and the Concept of Social/Geographical Space

Traditional studies of women's labor tend to isolate their experiences in the workplace from those in the public (social) and domestic spheres, reifying a sense of fragmentation and discontinuity rather than uncovering relationships of mutual determination and dependence. Urban theory, while offering the potentially more fluid, interdisciplinary, and holistic concept of "urban space," i.e., a spatial-temporal dimension through which the movement of individuals and groups can be traced, traditionally took for granted gender-related distinctions between public and private, work and home, and production and reproduction, privileging those more closely identified as "male" as objects of study (McDowell, 1983; Pratt and Hanson, 1988).

"New" urban theory, pioneered by sociologist Castells (1987), and feminist urban theorists such as Dolores Hayden (1980, 1984) and others (Spain, 1992; Wilson, 1991; McDowell, 1983; Pratt and Hanson, 1988; Gillian Rose, 1993; Damaris Rose, 1989; Wekerle and Rutherford, 1989) has attempted to remedy this oversight by analyzing the processes and sites of reproduction, that is, the myriad of activities that contribute to the daily and generational reproduction of the labor force through the provision of food, shelter, clothing, recreation, sex, physical reproduction, socialization, and health and mental health. While such activities may be carried out collectively in the public sphere ("eating out," for example), under capitalism the tendency has been to associate such activities with the domestic sphere where women tend to predominate. This focus on the "private sphere of women's lives," while making women more visible, tends to take for granted the segregation of male and female roles and women's isolation in the family rather than explaining how these characteristics emerged historically and the contemporary context that reinforces or undermines them (McDowell 1993).

Explaining the context for domestic sphere roles and the ways in which they are reproduced, symbolically and actually in public sphere activities, particularly in paid work, is important in understanding the lives and spatial mobility of Latina immigrants in a metropolitan center like Los Angeles. In the case of Salvadorans and Guatemalans, for example, domestic roles are often carried out in the context of geographically separated families, and households' probabilities of reunification depend greatly on economic and political factors at the societal and global level.

This new conceptualization of women's work in an urban context suggests several premises underlying our analysis. First, gender divisions are an important structuring element of urban space and urban processes. Second, the structure of urban social relations frequently contributes to the exploitation and subordination of women; at the same time, women attempt to resist, modify, and subvert that subordination. Third, production and reproduction constitute a single inseparable process that varies across space and over time, and according to marital status, type of work, class, ethnicity, immigrant-native, and legal status.

Domestic Workers: Navigating Public and Private Space

Immigrant women who work in private homes as cleaners, child-care workers, or health-care workers negotiate three qualitatively different kinds of space that are shaped by and in turn help to shape their employment: 1) the public sphere through which they obtain information about jobs, move to and from jobs, socialize, study, go to church, and obtain necessary goods and services; 2) the private sphere of the household or family unit that serves as their workplace, i.e., their "public" work space; and 3) their own domestic space.

Navigating Through Public Space

Given the marked segregation of housing according to income in the greater Los Angeles area, few private domestic workers live near their work. The geographical areas where the greatest demand for their labor is generated are removed in space and travel time from the areas of greatest recent immigrant concentration. Even when domestic workers "live in" they may have an apartment or room to return to on days off that they share with others or occupy alone. In addition, very few have cars, although some of the men manage to obtain trucks for gardening and maintenance work.

Getting to the worksite by public transportation in a region where it is assumed workers have cars can be a time-consuming and frustration-filled experience, often involving transfers between two or more buses. Routes that might take twenty to forty minutes by car may take up to two hours by bus (*Los Angeles Times*, July 16, 1995). Julia, who was living in Inglewood and cleaned for several different employers, took three buses to several of her jobs on the Westside, a trip of an hour or an hour and a half. Mila, who lived in Pasadena, cleaned a different house each day of the week and traveled by bus to Long Beach to clean the house of the mother of one of her longtime employers because she felt the job was more secure than one she might obtain nearby. Maria, a live-in domestic in Redondo Beach, took two hours each way to visit her friends in Echo Park on weekends. Although she felt isolated caring for an infant alone during the day and had only her English classes in an adult school at night as a place to consolidate and extend her social networks, she often sacrificed the trip to see her friends in favor of resting on weekends.

Learning to move around in any metropolitan area is a challenge, but this is particularly true for those who come from the rural areas of third world countries or countries in which the largest urban center is small by the standards of Southern California. Language difficulties and lack of literacy often add to the problem. Nevertheless, according to trainers at Listo, an employment cooperative for Latina workers described in more detail below, most of the members are surprisingly adept at getting to a worksite on their own. Many have learned to use the Thomas Guide, a book of maps for Los Angeles and Orange counties. Those who can't read or read well rely on memorizing landmarks. Of some fifty to fifty-five new jobs to which workers were sent weekly in 1990, Listo reported receiving only one to three calls on the average related to lost employees.

Latinos constitute the single largest ethnic group of bus riders, 47 percent of the total according to a 1995 Metropolitan Transit survey, and it is safe to assume that a significant proportion of bus riders are immigrant Latinas. The dependence of immigrant workers on buses for transportation involves certain risks as well as opportunities. Immigration and Naturalization Service agents have been known to use bus stops to make arrests, and bus stops may also be the site of interethnic tensions, robbery, or attacks on women (especially when they get off work at night or have to leave early in the morning).

At the same time, buses and bus stops serve as sites for networking and information exchange. Immigrants learn about jobs, legal rights, social services, and housing through social networks formed with other immigrants and/or from representatives of service agencies who use the bus as a means to approach potential clientele. Since a large number of Latina immigrant domestics depend on buses to transport them to areas of the city where their labor is in demand, bus stops and bus rides often become crucial components of their urban networks/infrastructure.

In addition to opportunities for networking, bus riding undoubtedly provides a sense of the city and its different communities lacking to those who depend on their cars and the freeways. Using public transportation to move between predominantly Latino or multicultural communities to largely Anglo West-side communities, Latina domestic workers inevitably come into contact with diverse aspects of urban life to a much greater degree than many who have lived in Los Angeles for decades.

The urban institutional environment, including church, schools (for those with children), and service agencies, provide further opportunities and challenges for Latina immigrants, particularly those who are live-in domestics. One of the most important institutions is adult school where English is taught—an attraction for many immigrants who perceive it to be an avenue to better job opportunities and reduced vulnerability to exploitation. Adult schools serve many purposes, including socializing and networking with other immigrants and learning about customs, laws, and policies in the United States. Most important of all, for some immigrants, is the opportunity to get an education that they were denied or did not value at home. Maria, a Guatemalan Indian woman whose father wanted her educated just enough to read his documents and do basic math, said that she resisted even the two years of primary school that he wanted her to have. She is now determined to finish her English classes and study to be a dental assistant. She is presently working as a babysitter, but has changed jobs several times in order to guarantee her right to attend night classes. When transportation to night classes became a problem, Maria saved money to take a private driving school course, got her license and eventually bought an old car, which she uses to negotiate the streets of Los Angeles, to the amazement of herself and her friends.

Working in the Private Space of Others

Private paid work in homes is largely unregulated and thus open to great variability and possible exploitation (Hondagneu-Sotelo, 1994B). Cultural differences, immigrant (and often undocumented) status, and language barriers add to the problem of working in an environment that is so characterized by intimacy, emotion, and lack of distance. While some employers may be genuinely concerned about the welfare of the domestic (e.g., a former employer of Julia who accompanied her to the hospital and stayed with her during labor when her child was born), others take advantage of the vulnerable situation of undocumented immigrants, paying low wages for long hours of work, jobs are often ill-defined, and immigrants may find themselves called upon to do work they had not initially agreed upon (Smith and Kraul, 1993).

Cultural differences can be an important source of discomfort or misunderstanding. Different expectations about the nature, quantity, and timing of meals offered as part of the wage may generate tensions between employers and domestic workers. Perhaps in no sphere are these differences more profound than in child-rearing. Smith and Kraul cite an example of the differences between Latina women, who feel that a baby should be held, and U.S. mothers who want their child to move around and explore. Other tensions emerge around employers' desires that their young girls be dressed in "unisex" comfortable play clothes and that children not be given candy as a reward. Brought up in a relatively structured environment in which children, especially girls, were expected to take on responsibilities such as caring for younger siblings at an early age, many Latina domestics and child-care workers are astonished at what they consider to be the liberal child-rearing practices of many middle- or upper-middle-class U.S. families.

Women who live in are often unable to relieve their sense of cultural isolation and alienation through daily contact with family and friends, unless they manage to plug into networks of nannies and house cleaners who meet on the sidewalks and in the neighborhood parks. But plugging into such networks requires having the freedom to leave the house with children or elder being cared for in tow, talk on the telephone, or receive visitors, which are privileges that not all domestics enjoy. Isolation from other adults with whom to share problems is particularly difficult for mothers who must leave their own children in the care of relatives or neighbors while they care for the children of someone else. In at least one case, a live-in domestic hired someone to live in to care for her own children in her absence (communication with Hondagneu-Sotelo, 1995).

Occasionally, domestic workers come into contact with social service, mutual aid, or community organizing projects sponsored by church or immigrants' rights groups (such as the Coalition for Humane Immigrant's Rights) who can provide advice, resources, and serve as intermediaries. The Coalition's Domestic Worker Outreach Project sends organizers to bus stops, parks, and buses to inform domestic workers of their rights and disseminates information through *fotonovelas* (literally, photo-novels, booklets using captioned photos to tell a story) (Hondagneu-Sotelo, 1994B). Educational projects focusing specifically on domestic workers such as these are relatively recent and the methods of reaching and retaining members from this dispersed and mobile population of workers are still in the experimental stage. The long-term success of such efforts remains to be seen.

Listo, an employment cooperative for Mexican and Central American immigrant women, is one of the few organizations with experience acting as an intermediary between immigrant workers and employers. Established in 1986 with the help of religious groups, and sponsored by St. Vincent's Social Service Center, *Listo* provides minimum training for domestic workers and screens them for employers, seeking to increase their bargaining power in the marketplace and protect them from the more blatant forms of discrimination. Workers placed in jobs through *Listo* have some protection through a contract that specifies hours and days of work, wages, duties, and accountability. The organization can mediate problems between employers and employees. Through the cooperative framework, *Listo* also seeks to develop members' leadership and organizing skills.

Potential members enter the cooperative by applying during open enrollment periods or through referral by another member (especially if the individual can fill a job for which there is no qualified available member). Workers must pass a week-long training course in which they learn basic skills and practices, including domestic cleaning, basic home repair, emergency procedures, child-care and health-care practices, etc., as well as work-related vocabulary and phrases. Members in good standing must observe certain work rules (e.g., notifying employers in case of illness), attend meetings regularly, pay dues, and participate in the self-governance of the cooperative.

Since 1990, *Listo* has had a membership of 150 individuals (though not necessarily the same ones throughout), made up most of Mexican, Salvadoran, Guatemalan, and Honduran immigrants. The demand for its workers has also remained at a relatively stable level. Some employers, however, are now asking the organization to verify a worker's legal status, which the cooperative agreed from the beginning not to do. While other employers, often alerted to *Listo* through announcement in church newspapers and newsletters, have sent messages of sympathy and support in response to the passage of Proposition 187, pressures from sponsors to drop the explicitly immigrant and Latino focus of the project threaten to change its original character and function. In response, organizers are exploring the possibility of facilitating the formation of self-employment entrepreneurial groups among their members, especially for house painting and gardening, to whom jobs can be referred. The anti-immigrant climate, therefore, presents a serious challenge to even the most long-standing church-sponsored projects such as *Listo*.

The Domestic Sphere of Domestic Workers

Live-in domestics typically have a "private" space at their work site but the conditions of the space and the degree to which it offers privacy vary greatly. Sleeping spaces range from sofas in a sitting room, rooms shared with children, or converted closets (with bathrooms shared with the employers or their children) to relatively well-endowed guest houses or backyard apartments clearly separated from the main site of their work. The lack of separation between the work site and "private" living quarters of many live-in domestics accentuate the often fluid temporal boundaries between work and leisure. Such fluid boundaries often include being "on call" during the night, for parties and social events, and working full time when employers are out of town.

Most women who work in private homes negotiate the relationship, the boundaries, and conditions of their work as individuals without clear guidelines, making inexperienced workers vulnerable to abuse. In other cases, employment agencies serve as temporary intermediaries in the early stages of employment or as contractor with the employer, making them in effect the employer of the domestic in a subcontracting arrangement. In the latter case, domestics have little opportunity to negotiate directly with the homeowners, apartment dwellers, or parents for whom they work indirectly and may be unaware of the conditions negotiated by their intermediaries.

Although non-live-in domestics have a clearer separation between their "private" domestic and "public" work sites, the fact that they enter the private world of another household means that they share with live-in domestics the ambiguities and contradictions of being present in and witness to another family's private sphere. They also share with live-in domestics the problem of finding child care for their own children, if they have them, and have the extra burden of their own housework to do when they return home at the end of the day. Living conditions for immigrants typically tend to be crowded, unstable, and sometimes unsafe, which complicates the lives of women who have to leave their children while they work, even if they are not live-ins.

Street-Vending: Redefining Urban Space

In Los Angeles, the presence of a large number of undocumented immigrants has been one factor in the growth of a large informal economy, including a significant number of people selling or providing services out of their home, ranging from shoe repair, tailoring, catering, auto repair service, to medical and dental services. The economic recession of the 1990s as well as the effects of the Immigration Reform and Control Act (IRCA) making it illegal to employ undocumented workers have expanded the number of people involved in informal sector activities.

Street vending represents the most visible part of the informal sector. It has been estimated that there are two thousand to three thousand street vendors selling in Los Angeles at any one time, but since many people vend on a part-time basis the total number of vendors is probably much larger. Latinos constitute the main group of street vendors; a 1992 study found that among Latino vendors, approximately two-thirds are Mexican while most of the remaining are Central American, especially Salvadoran. Estimates put the proportion of women at approximately 60 percent of the total; the above-mentioned study suggested that Mexican vendors are roughly equally divided between men and women but 75 percent (or more) of Salvadoran vendors are estimated to be women (Sirola, 1992; 1994:7).

Vendors sell a wide range of products, including clothing, jewelry, tape cassettes, household goods; mangos and other fresh fruit and juices; and cooked food, such as corn and tamales. Much of the fresh fruit is bought at central markets; cooked food is prepared at home; and other merchandise purchased from downtown wholesalers. Street vending responds to a need among a relatively low-income segment of the population in a declining economy by providing food, clothing, household items, and other goods at a reduced price.

Interviews with street vendors suggest that many have worked previously at other jobs and went into vending when the factory closed down or they lost their jobs due to lack of documents or insufficient work, or left due to low wages and poor working conditions. For others, vending in the evenings and/or on weekends is a way to supplement income earned from other jobs (Sirola, 1994:10). For some women, street vending has several advantages over other types of available

employment, such as garment factory jobs, for those without documents and/or having limited language ability, in terms of type of work,
freedom of working for oneself, and even in some cases for monetary
reasons. In contrast to a formal job, where children would often not be
allowed and there is no control over the location or timing of work,
vendors, especially women, often work in their own neighborhood,
have some choice over hours, and can take time off if there is an
emergency.

Reclaiming Public Space

Informal activities often break down traditional divisions between work
and domestic spheres (McDowell, 1983), and as a particular form of
informal activity, street vending may break down real or apparent distinctions between public and private spheres, work and home, production and reproduction. The growth in street vending in recent decades
has had an important role in redefining and, in effect, reclaiming urban
space in Los Angeles. With some exceptions, street life is limited in the
Los Angeles area; people ride rather than walk, and travel in their own
private space rather than through public transportation; thus opportunities for public interaction are limited.

Historians remind us that during the nineteenth century, street
vending was an important part of the Los Angeles urban scene, particularly in Mexican areas of the city and downtown. This changed as the
city became increasingly Europeanized and new downtown business
entrepreneurs and city authorities began to restrict and eventually eliminate vending except in very limited circumstances. The current
renewal has been traced to the early 1980s when vendors began to sell
on Broadway, a major shopping street in downtown Los Angeles; from
there vending has expanded west and northwest to Westlake, Echo
Park, and parts of Hollywood and parts of the San Fernando valley,
south to South Central, and east to East Los Angeles (Martinez,
1991:19–20).

Street vending is a public activity in a double sense; not only does it
constitute work outside of the home, but (in contrast to most formal activities) it also takes place in an open, public space—streets and street corners, parks, shopping centers, freeway entrances and exits. It redefines

public space in the important sense of creating areas for public interaction that didn't exist before.

There are different uses of urban space by men and women vendors, although families may also sell together, especially on weekends.
Men are more likely to sell alone and are more likely to sell in places
far from home (although some women do this as well—especially if they
move to a new home they may return to their old vending spots).
Freeway vendors are often, though not always, men, as are vendors with
ice cream carts. (These are usually entry-level jobs for new immigrants
who work for a contractor, who may also arrange for housing, generally rented rooms shared with other workers.) Women are much more
likely to work in groups, and to work in their own community or other
Latino communities. Aside from mutual protection, there is a certain
amount of socializing, not only of women working together but also
interaction with buyers, often friends or long-term acquaintances.

Street vending represents a way of combining work at home, or
non-remunerated domestic work, and work outside the home, or remu-
nerated non-domestic work. First, for many women vending is an
extension of domestic work, since they prepare food at home to sell on
the street. Second, they can bring their young children to the work spot,
and women often share in child care—another reason for selling in
groups. Street vending may also incorporate socialization and training.
Many women selling on the streets of Los Angeles began as small children working with their mothers on the streets or in the rural areas of
El Salvador, Guatemala, or Mexico. Some went out on their own at the
age of ten, or even six or seven.

Vendors, including women, have been very adept at navigating
urban space in the sense of finding out which wholesalers offer the best
prices, which areas are good for selling, what products sell well and
where. In part this learning process is through informal research based
on networking with other vendors. In some cases, vendors may be able
to take advantage of contacts resulting from previous jobs, e.g., in the
garment industry, for access to wares at wholesale prices.

Similar to domestic workers, vendors have received help from nontraditional institutions such as the Coalition for Women's Economic
Development (CWED). Modeled on organizations in Latin America
and Asia, the CWED provides credit and technical training to low-
income, self-employed women (and also men as of 1992) in "micro-

enterprises"—small business managed by single person or family. The loan program operates through Solidarity Circles—support groups of five "micro-entrepreneurs" in which a loan received by one member is collectively guaranteed repayment. Loans go to women producing clothing, to enable them to buy sewing machines and material, to small retailers, to buy merchandise, and to vendors of food so they can buy carts, rent kitchen space, or obtain health licenses.

Nevertheless, vendors in Los Angeles work in very difficult circumstances. Vendors have been subject to harassment and arrest; in many cases their merchandise has been confiscated, and they can be fined up to $1,000. There have been frequent complaints of police abuse. These risks prevent vendors from selling efficiently, and cut into profits they can make. Health regulations are very stringent for food vending, and there are numerous restrictions on where and how food can be prepared, what kinds of carts may be used for vending, and even how food carts should be stored.

In addition, there is often strong resistance by merchants in formal stores and shops who claim that vendors, who don't have to pay rent, taxes, or insurance, have an unfair advantage in competing with them. More recently, with the growth of crime in many neighborhoods such as Westlake and South Central Los Angeles, vendors are often vulnerable to robbers and gangs. Gangs have demanded protection payment from a number of vendors, taking advantage of the fact that vending is illegal and many of the vendors are undocumented and thus they are not likely to protest such extortion schemes. Several vendors have been robbed and/or wounded, and some vendors have been killed (Millican, 1991; Sengupta, 1992).

Contesting Public Space: The Street Vendors' Association

The Street Vendors' Association was formed at the end of 1987 to address some of these issues, and has carried out negotiations with a range of city agencies, including meetings with the Health Department regarding regulations on food vending and the Police Department regarding complaints of police abuse. Its major emphasis, however, has been on efforts to legalize street vending. It had an active role in the Task Force on Street Vending, formed by City Councilman Michael

Woo in 1989, which brought together vendors, downtown merchants, representatives of city agencies, lawyers, and activists to propose legislation permitting street vending in Los Angeles. The task force held regular meetings over a period of about eighteen months, which culminated with a report released by Woo in December 1990, recommending legalization and registration of street vending, including the formation of special districts in which vending would be permitted, as well as city-wide vending under more restricted conditions. After extensive lobbying efforts by the street vendors and their supporters, the city council voted to draft legislation to permit vending in special districts, especially Latino neighborhoods, in 1992.

The council, however, did not approve city-wide vending, which both the association and task force had wanted, and it was not until January 1994 that legislation was finally passed allowing the creation of eight special districts, potentially including 20 percent of current vendors (Lopez, 1993). In addition, the procedures for establishing a special district are so onerous[2] that a year later only two of the projected eight districts were near approval (Berenstein et al. 1995). Because of the costs for vending permits (approximately $1,500 annually for an official permit) and the restriction on vending outside the special districts, the legislation threatens to create a two-tier system of legalized vs. non-legalized vendors.[3]

In addition, differences over strategy and tactics led to a split in the Street Vendors' Association into two organizations in July 1994, with one group choosing to continue working through established channels while the other advocated more militant tactics including protests in front of police stations over harassment of vendors.[4]

In short, the effects of the seven-year struggle to legalize street vending are mixed. The length of the process, the restricted nature of the legislation that resulted, the excessively bureaucratic procedures for establishing special districts, and the costs of obtaining vending licenses indicate that the legislation will benefit only a minority of those by whom it is needed. While the vendors and their advocates had originally hoped that more inclusive legislation could be enacted over time, this appears unlikely in the present climate of hostility toward immigrants, especially undocumented immigrants.

At the same time the vendors have gained political experience, and several women have taken an active leadership role. The first board of the association was composed of men with the exception of one woman who came to meetings but rarely spoke out. The second board, however, was all women, and subsequent boards have included both women and men. For several years, the association was led by Dora Alicia Alarcon, a mango vendor who was involved in a similar organization in El Salvador, and is now a leader in the Pico Union group, which has taken the name AVALA (Association of Street Vendors of Los Angeles). With all its frustrations, the campaign to legalize street vending has enabled the vendors, and particularly women, to gain experience in navigating the public sphere of city politics.

Conclusions

Latina immigrant workers have had to cope with the numerous problems of living and working in Los Angeles, often as undocumented immigrants with limited English language ability. In the process they have intentionally and inadvertently redefined urban space and the relationship between the public and private spheres. In contrast to many Angelinos who never use public transportation and rarely leave their suburban enclaves, Latina domestic workers often travel to all parts of the city, using public space for networking. Street vendors have transformed public space and created new spaces for personal interaction in a city notorious for its restricted opportunities for such interaction. Working with existing institutions, and in some cases helping to create new ones, Latinas have increased their skills, improved their work opportunities, and gained political experience.

These political and coping skills will be important in confronting the political backlash resulting in part from passage of Proposition 187 in California and increased immigrant bashing at the local, state, and national levels. Some will return home, but given lack of economic opportunities in their countries of origin most will remain. Among those who remain, an increased stratification by legal status will overlay other status and class differences. Those Mexicans and Central Americans who were permanent residents or received amnesty through the IRCA are applying for citizenship in unexpected numbers, catalyzed by threats of attacks against the privileges of non-citizen permanent residents. Those not eligible for amnesty or permanent residency, including a large number of Central American immigrants, will face increased obstacles in the way of social mobility, economic well-being, and integration into the mainstream of urban life.

The authors would like to express their appreciation to Allison Becker, Suzanna Brenner, Pierette Hondagneu-Sotelo, Noemi Perez, Lissette Perez, Mari Riddle, and Paula Sirola for information and suggestions.

Norma Chinchilla is a professor in the Department of Sociology at California State University, Long Beach. Nora Hamilton is a professor in the Department of Political Science at the University of Southern California in Los Angeles. Both have written extensively on Central America, women, and Central American immigrants in southern California.

NOTES

1. Because a "snowball" sampling method was used, the findings of our survey cannot be generalized to the immigrant community as a whole, which, given the undocumented status of a large proportion of immigrants, is difficult if not impossible to survey through a random sample. Over 50 percent of the respondents in our survey came after 1986, much larger than in the population as a whole. Partly because some interviews were conducted at predominantly male work sites, such as areas where day laborers look for jobs, it underrepresents women. It nonetheless provides useful insight into the range of experience of Latin American immigrants, including women.

2. A petition to Board of Public Works, with final approval granted by the city council, must include 1) a design of the special vending district to be established; 2) signatures from 20 percent of the businesses proving that there is support for vending in the area; 3) an administrative plan; 4) a merchandising plan; 5) a vending cart design; 6) a kitchen and commissary facility; 7) bathroom facilities; and 8) a district community advisory committee to oversee the plans.

3. Efforts of vendors in the border cities of El Paso and Ciudad Juárez to contest the uses of public space had strikingly similar results in terms of the restrictiveness of legislation and the high costs of licenses and fees, which in the case of El Paso add up to approximately $3,000.

4. See Weber (1995), for a discussion of the tensions leading to the eventual split between the two groups.

BIBLIOGRAPHY

Berenstein, L., et al. 1995. "Wheeling and Dealing," *Los Angeles Times:* Westside (February 2).

Brownstein-Santiago, C. 1992. "Census Data Track Status of Latinos." *Nuestro Tiempo* (bilingual section of the *Los Angeles Times*) (September 10), p. 1, 9.

Castells, M. 1987. *City, Class and Power.* London: Macmillan.

Fujimoto, M. and M. Janis. 1990. *Report of the Task Force on Street Vending in Los Angeles.*

Gross, J. 1995. "Getting There the Hard Way, Every Day." *Los Angeles Times* (July 16), p. A1, 18, 19.

Hayden, D. 1984. *Redesigning the American Dream: The Future of Housing, Work and Family Life.* New York: W. W. Norton.

———. 1980. "What would a Non-Sexist City Look Like?" in Stimpson, C. et al., eds., *Women and the American City,* Cambridge: MIT Press, 167–84.

Hondagneu-Sotel, P. 1994A. *Gendered Transitions: Mexican Experiences of Immigration.* Berkeley: University of California Press.

———. 1994B. "Latina Immigrant Women and Paid Domestic Work: Upgrading the Occupation," in *Clinical Sociology Review,* 12:257–70.

Lopez, R. J. 1993. "Pushcart Power." *Los Angeles Times,* July 25, p. 1, 16.

Martinez, R. 1991. "Sidewalk Wars: Why LA's Street Vendors Won't Be Swept Away," *LA Weekly* (December 6–12): 18–28.

McDowell, L. 1983. "Towards an Understanding of the Gender Division of Urban Space," *Environment and Planning D: Society and Space,* Vol. 1:59–72.

Millican, A. 1992. "For Pico-Union Vendors, It's Marked Turf." *Los Angeles Times* (December 20): A1, A36–7.

Pratt, G. and Hanson, S. 1988. "Gender, Class and Space." *Environment and Planning D: Society and Space,* Vol. 6:15–35.

Rose, G. 1993. *Feminism and Geography: The Limits of Geographical Knowledge.* Minneapolis, Minn.: University of Minnesota Press.

Rose, D. 1989. "A Feminist Perspective of Employment Restructuring and Gentrification: The Case of Montreal," pp. 118–38 in J. Wolch and M. Dear, eds., *The Power of Geography: How Territory Shapes Social Life.* Boston: Unwin Hyman.

Sengupta, S. 1992. "Criminals Prey on Vendors," *Los Angeles Times* (September 28): B1–8.

Sirola, P. 1992. "Beyond Survival: Latino Immigrants in the Los Angeles Informal Sector." Paper presented at the LASA Conference, Los Angeles, 24–27 September.

———. 1994. "Immigrant Latinos in the Los Angeles Economy." Paper presented at the *XIII Congreso Internacional de Ciencias Antropologicas y Etnologicas,* Mexico City, August 1993. Updated August 1994.

Smith, L. and C. Kraul. 1993. "Together in the Shadows of the Law," *Los Angeles Times* (Jan. 28): A-1.

Southwest Voter Research Notes. 1991. Southwest Voter Research Institute. V, I (July).

Spain, D. 1992. *Gendered Spaces.* Chapel Hill: University of North Carolina Press.

Staudt, K. 1994. "Struggles in Urban Space: Street Vendors in El Paso and Ciudad Juarez," paper presented at the Latin American Studies Association conference, Atlanta (March).

Weber, C. M. 1995. "Latino Street Vendors in Los Angeles: Heterogeneous Alliances, Community-Based Activism, and the Dynamics of Ethnicity, Class and the State." Unpublished masters paper, University of California Irvine.

Wilson, E. 1991. *The Sphinx in the City: Urban Life, the Control of Disorder, and Women.* Berkeley: University of California Press.

Wolch, J. and M. Dear. 1989. *The Power of Geography: How Territory Shapes Social Life.* Boston: Unwin Hyman.

Wolff, G. 1992. "The Making of a Third World City? Latino Labor and the Reconstructing of the Los Angeles Economy." Paper presented at the LASA Conference, Los Angeles, 24–27 September.

Staying on the Land
Rural Issues

For thousands of years, humans have scratched, dug, raked and plowed the face of the earth in order to plant, grow, and harvest food for themselves and others. In many locations around the globe today, this primitive process continues. Women, sometimes women alone, are a natural and integral part of the agricultural process. This has been true in America as well, although women's part in the nation's agricultural history has not been well-documented until recently.[1] For both men and women, the changes wrought in agriculture during the past one hundred years have altered life on the farm in ways our great-grandparents would not recognize. Machines have replaced animals; bioengineering has brought the increased use of fertilizers, pesticides, and hybrid seeds and grains; the henhouse has evolved into a vast multistoried warehouse where the chickens never come in contact with the earth; and cattle are "plugged into" automatic milking machines twice a day.[2] Corporate domination, government policies, and global developments determine the economic well being of farmers and ranchers to a degree never before experienced. A nation founded on agrarian principles three hundred years ago has undergone a steep decline in the number of farms that produce America's foodstuffs today. At the beginning of the twentieth century, less than 3 percent of the population counted themselves as farmers or ranchers (3 million); one hundred years later that figure is 2 percent or 1.9 million.[3]

The face of agriculture has always been male, at least the face that counted in U.S. census reports. Despite this historical view of agriculture as a patriarchal endeavor, scholars are beginning to acknowledge that the business of agriculture is far more than a male-only enterprise. Since the 1980s, historians, sociologists, anthropologists, and others have begun to explore the gender division of labor on American ranches and farms. Most studies have concentrated on the Midwest, South, and Atlantic coastal regions of the country leaving the American West unexamined. Yet on the vast ranches, the family farms, and in sparsely populated rural areas, women's labor has contributed to the process of bringing food to the nation's dinner tables. Often this is unseen or invisible labor, such as raising a garden and canning or freezing the harvest, running to town for parts for a broken plow, or more recently, managing farm or ranch records on the computer. Because such activities often occur in the "private" or domestic sphere, women's efforts largely go unacknowledged. More recently, the pressures of modernization and urbanization have weighed heavily on both sexes as they increasingly and with difficulty attempt to maintain an agricultural lifestyle, one that continues to bring great satisfaction as a "way of life" to many.[4]

Since the end of WWII, both men and women have had to make adjustments to new technological developments that have drastically changed the way agriculture is practiced, produced and marketed. Beginning in the 1980s, researchers began to examine some of these changes to see how, or if, they have altered traditional gender roles on farms and ranches. One development is clear: to be able to continue to stay on the farm, one of the partners almost always must take a job off-farm. Most often this is the woman but men, too, have worked full or part-time jobs for wages in order to sustain the family farm lifestyle. Frequently, gender lines become blurred with the demands required of agriculturalists and each does what must be done to survive. And in the doing, women shoulder much of the burden.[5]

The theme of this next section demonstrates some of the ways that women's labor is crucial to the farm family's economic condition. Sherry L. Smith, writing about the "perplexing" case of Elinore Pruitt Stewart as a homesteader, demonstrates the continuity between the nineteenth and twentieth centuries in matters of land ownership. Although Stewart proudly proclaimed the independence that came with staking a claim to the 160 acres she was legally entitled to, she quickly found that the pride and pleasure of her independence also required the cooperation and labor of family members. Homesteading required a family effort. Similarly, in examining the changes in ranch and farm women's lives in the last half of the twentieth century, Sandra Schackel notes that as technology improved and family farms gave way to the growth of agribusiness, farm families became even more hard-pressed to maintain their role as producers of the nation's and the world's food supply. Many women took jobs in small rural towns nearby or joined their husbands on the tractor and in the fields, leaving the domestic tasks to be done in the margins of their workdays and weekends. Nowhere is this more poetically recalled than in the verse of Goldie Keltner Ford, farm wife and mother of eleven. A loving and clear-eyed biography of her children, Ford's words depart from the typical interpretative style of the anthology to show us the commitment to both land and family that kept her on the Kansas prairie long after the children left for city lives. Granddaughter Carol Wolfe Konek came to understand and love her grandmother while seeking her mother's voice.

Late in the twentieth century, when it seems that a highly technological and urbanized nation sees no future in family farming, thousands of Americans defiantly stand their ground on long-held family land. Will the next generation be satisfied with genetically engineered foodstuffs and imported grains and meats from other nations? Global agriculture is determining the future of America's agrarian families. Ranch and farm women, as well as men, decry a future that denies them the chance to stay on the land where they have labored for centuries.

NOTES

1. See Joan Jensen, *With these Hands: Women Working on the Land* (Old Westbury, N.Y.: Feminist Press, 1981).
2. Katherine Jellison, *Entitled to Power: Farm Women and Technology, 1913–1963* (Chapel Hill: University of North Carolina Press, 1993).
3. U.S. Bureau of Labor Statistics, 1997 Census of Agriculture, Summary, and State Data, vol. 1, Geographic Area Series Part 51 (Washington, D.C.: U.S. Department of Agriculture, 1998), 418.
4. This somewhat romantic-sounding theme is one I have encountered repeatedly from the farm and ranch women I have interviewed over the past five years.
5. Corlann G. Bush, "'The Barn is His, the House is Mine': Agricultural Technology and Sex Roles," in *Energy and Transport: Historical Perspectives on Policy Issues*, ed. George H. Daniels and Mark H. Rose (Beverly Hills, Calif.: Sage, 1982).

SINGLE WOMEN HOMESTEADERS

THE PERPLEXING CASE OF ELINORE PRUITT STEWART*

Sherry L. Smith

"When I read of the hard times among the Denver poor," Elinore Pruitt Stewart wrote in 1913, "I feel like urging them every one to get out and file on land." This washerwoman-turned-Wyoming-homesteader was especially enthusiastic about women homesteading. "It really requires less strength and labor to raise plenty to satisfy a large family," she claimed, "than it does to go out to wash, with the added satisfaction of knowing that their job will not be lost to them if they care to keep it."[1]

Stewart understood that the original Homestead Act of 1862 allowed women to apply for land under the same conditions as men, requiring only that they be at least twenty-one years old, single, widowed, divorced, or head of a household. Until recently, however, historians overlooked many aspects of women's experiences, in part, because their sphere seemed largely domestic and private. Yet, women homesteaders' activities were also part of the public record. The story of their land transactions was, consequently, as accessible as that of men. Apparently no one thought to ask about them until the last decade or so. The record of these women's efforts simply awaited scholarly scrutiny.[2]

---

*This chapter was originally published as: Smith, Sherry L. "Single Women Homesteaders: The Perplexing Case of Elinore Pruitt Stewart." In *Western Historical Quarterly* 22 (May 1991): 163–83.

Historians, then, have begun to ask and answer the following questions about the women who took up the government's offer. How many filed and proved-up on homesteads? What motivated them? Did they file with the intention of securing independently earned and managed homesteads for themselves, or were they operating in the context of family interest? Did the women's motivations and experiences, in the end, differ from those of men who also attempted homesteading? Finally, does the information about women homesteaders alter our view of the entire homesteading experience?

The first question is relatively easy to answer. The General Land Office kept tract books, ledgers that documented activity on the public lands and recorded all entries and actions, successful and unsuccessful. Relying upon these and other legal records, several scholars have provided precise data on the numbers of women who made homestead entries in specific regions of the West. One study of forty-three townships in North Dakota, for example, revealed that between the 1870s and 1910, the number of women land recipients ranged from 1 to 22 percent, with the average coming to 10 percent. Another study showed that before 1900 women made up 12 percent of the entrants in Logan (and 10 percent in Washington) County, Colorado. After that date, the percentages reached nearly 18 in both counties. A third study revealed that nearly 12 percent of homestead patents issued in five Wyoming counties between 1888 and 1943 went to women.[3] These numbers are significant, if not overwhelming. They represent women who merit investigation, particularly regarding the matter of motivation—since taking up homesteads, at least in the popular perception, remains an activity associated with men.

Answers concerning women's motivations, however, are elusive. Public documents do not reveal private purposes. Therefore, sociologist H. Elaine Lindgren concludes that case studies provide the best, and often the only, source for this kind of information. With that in mind, this article examines the case of Elinore Pruitt Stewart, author of *Letters of a Woman Homesteader*, subject of the film "Heartland," and perhaps the best-known woman homesteader. She provides insight into the matter of motivation and suggests ways that consideration of women's experiences should change the way historians look at all homesteaders.

Stewart's is an intriguing and perplexing case. While she left a public record of her reasons for filing on a homestead, research into her efforts to secure government land suggest different motives. Her book presents a classic case, familiar to historians, of an individual who says one thing and does another. Stewart's case also demonstrates the difficulties one can expect to find in attempting to understand even one woman's motivations for homesteading and the necessity, in some cases, of going beyond the individual to examine an entire family's land activities.

In the book, Stewart undoubtedly intends her experiences as a *woman* homesteader to be a central theme. Her work appeals to some modern readers precisely because it offers a feminist perspective (although Elinore might resist that label) on the prospects of home-steading for single women. It could be argued that Stewart's book presents an idealized image of independent western women. Certainly, the book offers an antidote to the tired stereotypes of western women who were supposedly weepy, reluctant, depressed pioneers. In fact, she offers homesteading as a panacea to the problems of wage-working, urban women, and she suggests that her own example should serve as encouragement to these unfortunates. Stewart maintains "homesteading is the solution of all poverty's problems."[4]

Stewart also presents homesteading as the solution to her personal problems, making it clear that one of her goals is proving-up, on her own. To succeed at homesteading meant paying the requisite fees ($15.51 for Elinore in 1909), residing on the land for five consecutive years, and making some improvements. In addition, the applicant for land had to swear the homestead was for her exclusive use and benefit. In the book, Stewart eventually confesses her marriage, but insists her husband promised *not* to help her meet the homestead requirements. In this way, she establishes her own rather narrowly defined criterion for "independence": doing it alone. For Mrs. Stewart "proving up" meant more than meeting the legal requirements to claim the land as her own. She was, according to one analysis, "responding to a profound inner need to 'prove out' . . . on herself, on her desire for an identity of her own—and, beyond that, as a woman showing the way to other women."[5] As Elinore put it, "any woman who can stand her own company, can see the beauty of the sunset, loves growing things, and is willing to put in as much time and careful labor as she does over the washtub, will certainly succeed; will have independence, plenty to eat all the time, and a home of her own in the end."[6]

As a result of these kinds of statements, Stewart is often presented in historical literature as an independent (if not literally single) and successful woman homesteader. Is this image warranted? Was she successful in the terms she defined: to acquire a homestead on her own, with help from no one? Did she ever "prove up"? What do the facts of her land transactions with the federal government reveal about her motivations in homesteading and about the "real" Mrs. Stewart? And what does her case suggest about other women—and men—who homesteaded in the early twentieth-century West?

Elinore Pruitt Rupert, a widowed laundress from Denver, arrived in Wyoming in the spring of 1909 to work as a housekeeper for rancher Clyde Stewart. Up to that point, poverty, hardship, deprivation, and insecurity characterized her life. She was born 3 June 1876, in Fort Smith, Arkansas, to Elizabeth Courtney Pruitt. Her father died when Elinore was young and her mother married Thomas Isaac Pruitt, Elinore's uncle. Elinore's parents had died, and she took on responsibility for eight younger brothers and sisters. To make matters worse, the Pruitts were landless. A grandmother cared for the three younger children while the rest went to work in Indian Territory, preparing meals and laundering for railroad crews. In this manner, Elinore entered the working class.[7]

Around 1902, she married a civil engineer named Harry Cramer Rupert in Grand, Oklahoma, where the couple also filed on a homestead. The future must have looked promising compared to her earlier life. Her husband was better educated than she was, and he may have urged Elinore toward self-education. Encouraged, she began writing.

She gave birth to their daughter, Jerrine, in 1906. Although Elinore later claimed Rupert was killed in an accident one month after Jerrine's birth, evidence suggests they actually divorced.[8] Whatever the case, Elinore was again on her own. She began nurse's training and found time to write some pieces for the *Kansas City Star*. In fact, it was this newspaper's offer to write an article on the cliff dwellings of the Southwest that brought Elinore Rupert to the West. Poor health interfered with these plans, however, and she ended up in Denver, laundering for a living.[9]

Elinore eventually became a housekeeper and nurse for Mrs. Juliet Coney, a well-to-do and widowed schoolteacher from Boston. Elinore labored seven days a week and earned two dollars or her efforts. Yet,

she held greater aspirations. Rupert continued writing, studied for a
civil service examination and, in 1909, answered Clyde Stewart's advertisement for a housekeeper on his ranch near Burnt Fork, Wyoming.[10]
It is difficult to discern, with certainty, her intention in taking this job
and moving farther west. She was dissatisfied with her prospects in
Denver. In her letters to her former employer, Mrs. Coney (the letters
that were eventually published in book form), Rupert offered only bits
and pieces of information about her own motivations and actions.
Evidently, she moved to Wyoming with the intention of filing on a
homestead. Elinore was already familiar with the process from her
Oklahoma experience. More important, it is likely that she saw in land
ownership the economic security that had previously eluded her.

Five weeks after she arrived in Wyoming, on 23 April 1909, Elinore
traveled to Green River and applied for a 147-acre homestead. Soon
after, she reported this event in a letter to Mrs. Coney, mentioning in
passing that her land adjoined Mr. Stewart's. What Mrs. Rupert did not
report, however, was her marriage. On 30 April 1909—one week after
applying for her homestead as a single woman—Elinore and Clyde
applied for a marriage license.[11] Elinore Rupert's days as a single woman
homesteader were clearly limited.

In September, Elinore informed her correspondent that Mr.
Stewart was building her house, part of the requirements for obtaining
the homestead patent, in exchange for extra work. In this way she continued the deception, admitting neither her marriage nor the fact that
Clyde was simply adding onto his own homestead cabin. This sequence
of events suggests that Rupert and Stewart intended to take advantage
of homestead laws that allowed single, divorced, or widowed women to
file on homesteads but prohibited married women from doing so if their
husbands also applied. By filing for land one week and applying for a
marriage license the next, Elinore was able to increase the newly formed
family's landholdings. While this kind of arrangement violated the spirit
and intention of the homestead laws, it did not appear to violate the
letter of the law. Congress intended the Homestead Act to provide one
homestead per family. Nevertheless, many families (particularly in the
arid West) found ways around Congress's miserly intentions in order to
make a living.[12]

One year passed before Elinore revealed more about her situation
to Mrs. Coney. She explained she selected property adjoining Mr.

Stewart's in order to keep both the land and her job. At first, she wrote, she did not want to do this, but added, somewhat mysteriously, that now she saw the wisdom of it. Finally, in a June 1910 letter, Elinore admitted her 1909 marriage to Clyde—an act she described as "inconsistent." Another two years passed before she disclosed the details of the wedding day and indicated some shame for the haste with which she had married—six weeks after her arrival in Wyoming. "The engagement was powerfully short," she wrote, "because both agreed that the trend of events and ranch work seemed to require that we be married first and do our 'sparking' afterwards." Although Elinore says nothing about the land issue, it apparently was more a marriage of convenience than romance. To acknowledge this is not to say it was a match devoid of love. Elinore described Clyde affectionately as "really the kindest person." She also wrote, "Although I married in haste, I have no cause to repent . . . ," adding, "[t]hat is very fortunate because I have never had one bit of leisure to repent in."[13]

But what about the homestead and Mrs. Stewart's own desire to "prove up," not only to acquire property, but also to demonstrate to herself and to other working-class women the possibilities that awaited them in the West? Mrs. Coney apparently wondered the same thing for, in an October 1911 letter, later printed as a chapter entitled "Proving Up," Elinore responded to some of her friend's queries. She explained that she would not lose her land even though she had married. Clyde had proved up on his own homestead years before (1905) and held his deed. Consequently, she was allowed her own homestead since she had *filed* as a single woman.[14]

Even if her actions proved legal (which, as explained below, is questionable), what about her personal goals of independence? Of this Mrs. Stewart repeated her determination to achieve ownership on her own. "I should not have married if Clyde had not promised I should meet all my land difficulties unaided. I wanted the fun and the experience. For that reason I want to earn every cent that goes into my own land and improvements myself. . . . I know I shall succeed; other women have succeeded." And in a January 1913 letter, later published under the title "The Joys of Homesteading," Mrs. Stewart offered her treatise on women homesteaders, pitching her appeal to wage-earning, urban women, suggesting they could do it and implying that her own example should give them heart.[15]

Ironically, when Elinore Stewart penned these words she had already relinquished her homestead. On 24 June 1912, she completed the relinquishment paper and signed it "Elinore Rupert." Clyde and Elinore's mother-in-law, Ruth C. Stewart, served as witnesses. Then, swearing that she was a widow, Ruth Stewart took up the homestead that Elinore relinquished. In 1912, Ruth was seventy-three years old and had been a widow for twenty-two years. Her husband, James C. Stewart, died in 1891. Ruth never remarried. Although she made Boulder, Colorado, her home, Ruth claimed Burnt Fork her residence for purposes of making the homestead entry.[16]

Why did Elinore relinquish her homestead and, presumably, her dream of an independently earned landholding? Of this transaction she makes no mention in her publications. She never admits the relinquishment. Presumably, the Stewarts believed it was either legally necessary, or at least prudent, for Elinore to relinquish her homestead and for Ruth to take it up, in order to insure the land would remain in the family's control.

An analysis of similar—although not identical—cases that came before the General Land Office and Department of Interior in the early twentieth century suggests further explanation for the Stewarts' actions. By 1909, the General Land Office had clearly established that a woman who filed on a homestead and subsequently married could keep her homestead as long as her husband did not also have an unperfected homestead entry. She could take her claim, providing she performed the requirements concerning both residence and cultivation.[17] If at the time of the marriage, however, the husband also had an unperfected homestead entry, then one of the two claims had to be relinquished, for a "husband and wife, during the marital relation, can not [sic] maintain contemporaneous residences upon different tracts under the homestead law."[18]

Now, by 1909, Clyde Stewart had already obtained title to his homestead, so Elinore's marriage to Clyde alone did not automatically eliminate her legal right to her own homestead. To put it another way, Clyde did not have an unperfected homestead entry when she filed her claim. The problem for the Stewarts, however, seemed to be a blend of marriage and residency. Cases brought before the Department of Interior made it quite clear that it was not legal for a couple to share a residence while homesteading adjacent properties. Even though Clyde was no longer perfecting his homestead patent, Elinore was living in his cabin and on his land. She could not, then, legally meet the residency requirement for her own homestead. Further, the law assumed a wife took up her husband's residency, so the Stewarts, if challenged, would have had to prove, beyond doubt, that they had left Clyde's residence and built another on Elinore's homestead. The Stewarts, of course, did not do this. Therefore, it seems plausible that the Stewart family decided Elinore would relinquish her homestead claim. Ruth Stewart would immediately take it up, and in that manner, they could rest assured that the property would remain theirs. While Ruth lived with the Stewarts, the law would not automatically assume that was the case, since she was not Clyde's wife. In this way, they could avoid the potentially troublesome legal issues of marriage and residency.

In 1912, Congress lowered the residency requirements for homesteaders from five years to three years. Further, this new law permitted the homesteader an absence of five months per year. Ruth Stewart filed under these more liberal conditions.[19] Taking advantage of the law's allowance for an absence from the homestead, Mrs. Ruth Stewart left 1 December 1913 (presumably to winter in Boulder) and returned the following May. On 29 October 1914, Ruth applied for final proof of the homestead and it was patented on 26 August 1915. In her testimony she indicated the tract's cultivable land was planted with flax, hay, and some vegetables. The remainder of the claim was good for grazing only, being too rocky for planting. Forty head of cattle and ten head of horses, owned by her and her son, grazed there. Clyde was present as one of the witnesses and swore he had no interest in the claim. Ruth Stewart maintained legal ownership of the property for four years. In August 1920, she sold the land to Clyde for one hundred dollars.[20]

Elinore Pruitt Stewart evidently abandoned her dreams of proving up on her homestead. But she neither related such discouraging news in her *Letters*, nor did she relinquish her interest in owning property. By 1920, her original homestead entry was secured through the efforts of her mother-in-law. This tract was added to the lands Clyde had already obtained: his 1905 homestead along with an additional 80 acres that he acquired in 1911 under the provisions of the Desert Land Act.[21] In 1922, Elinore applied for a Desert Land entry as well. No legal impediments concerning marriage and residency existed here, as they had with the homestead. The land she hoped to acquire had been part of a homestead entry made in 1921 by Mrs. Marion Hortense Langley. Mrs. Stewart claimed Langley had not resided on the land for one year. In fact, she had not been heard of, or from, since leaving the area in July 1921. Further, Elinore testified that Mrs. Langley had indicated upon her departure from the Burnt Fork area that she did not intend to return. Contending the 160-acre tract under consideration was too rocky for cultivation, but potentially useful for grazing if water was conveyed to it and it was sown with grass seed, the forty-six-year-old ranch woman paid her forty-dollar fee.[22] Under this act, the claimant paid twenty-five cents down per acre and swore to try to irrigate any amount up to one section (640 acres) within three years. After that time had lapsed, if the claimant provided proof that he or she had sufficiently irrigated the area, the payment of an additional dollar an acre completed the deal.

Elinore Stewart's contest of the Langley homestead entry was originally rejected because of a technicality. She neglected to state Langley's absence was not due to military or naval service. Such a statement was necessary, even though in the case of women military service was not a reality. This, of course, reflects the law's implicit assumption that homesteading was a man's activity. Elinore did return the contest document with the statement attached.

However, the General Land Office eventually dismissed Stewart's challenge because the defendant Langley was not served notice of the contest against her. According to the "Rules of Practice," Langley had to be personally informed of such action against her homestead claim. If that was not possible, notice could be published in a local newspaper. Only then could the contest proceed.[23] The records indicate Langley did not receive "personal" notice concerning Stewart's charges. Nor did Elinore advertise her intentions in the newspaper. The contest action was therefore closed.[24]

Elinore's failure to pursue the contest she initiated against Mrs. Langley is linked to Clyde's frustrated efforts to confirm his right to property he had purchased at a public auction in 1917 at $2.50 an acre. The Stewarts' neighbor, John Hutton, had fenced in twenty-two acres Clyde believed belonged to him, by virtue of this purchase at public auction. Eventually, Stewart brought an ejection suit against Hutton in the Third Judicial District Court. He lost the case. Confusion resulting from a resurvey of the area apparently caused the problem. In 1919,

Stewart asked the commissioner of the General Land Office to investigate the resurvey, but his request was denied. Finally, by 1922, Stewart resigned himself to the loss of this land, but still hoped, at least, to regain the $55.00 he paid the federal government for this property. He was unsuccessful on the reimbursement issue as well.[25] By the fall of 1922, the Stewarts experienced serious financial problems.[26] They could no longer afford the cost of proving up on another Desert Land Entry. Even contesting the issue was too expensive. So, they suspended the effort.

What can we conclude from all these complicated land purchases and legal actions? What we have here is a family working in concert to acquire sufficient property under the government's land laws to make a living at ranching. Husband, wife, mother-in-law—all did what they could to enhance the family's landholdings and possibilities for success in an environment that was not conducive to agriculture. What Elinore did made abundant sense in the arid West. What she *wrote* appealed to urban, and perhaps especially women, readers. To accept Mrs. Stewart's "literary creation" as literal history, however, is a mistake.

Intriguing questions remain, about the gap between land office records and Stewart's own rendition of her transactions. How would she explain the discrepancies? Was she conscious of the difference between what she did and what she wrote? If so, then by what processes did she reshape her experiences into her published works? On these matters, unfortunately, Stewart remained silent. In none of her published or unpublished letters did she acknowledge this gap or reflect on the way in which she transformed the raw material of her experiences into the finished product of her pen. The best one can do is speculate on possible answers to these questions.

On one level, it seems apparent that Elinore was simply a good storyteller. She intended her writing to be optimistic, hopeful, somewhat inspiring; and once she realized it would be published, even commercially appealing.[27] She chose homesteading as her literary theme and focused on its supposed opportunities as a vehicle for her optimism. However, since she claimed she wanted to encourage urban, working-class women to consider homesteading as an alternative to the limitations and drudgery of wage earning, a totally accurate rendition of her own experience would not have served that purpose. So, she engaged in literary license.[28]

In the process, what she offered, of course, was a feminine version of the popular safety-valve myth. This theory maintained, in historian Clarence H. Danhof's words, "that the western lands drew off eastern labor whenever eastern industrial conditions were unsatisfactory, and in this way western land performed the function of a safety valve for socio-economic conflicts."[29] It rested on a number of assumptions, including the idea that depression, unemployment, horrible working conditions, and poor wages encouraged laborers to take up cheap western lands; that they could do so with relative ease; and that significant numbers did file on homesteads. But Danhof and others have proved this theory a myth. Urban workers had neither the skills nor the capital to succeed in the harsh West.

Why should we assume that women could succeed where their male counterparts had failed? Further, the high arid plains of Wyoming posed particular problems for homesteaders. One hundred sixty acres proved far from sufficient for successful ranching. Moreover, it was a life fraught with perils, and if one reads *Letters of a Woman Homesteader* carefully, the difficulties of that existence are apparent. The cheery tone of the book does not completely mask the harsh realities.

If working-class women in Denver and elsewhere had read her book, filed on homesteads, and consequently failed in droves, Stewart could be charged not only with deception, but worse. On this score, she is certainly less culpable than railroad companies and town promoters, who lured thousands of unsuspecting homesteaders out to the arid West. The fact is, it is highly unlikely *Letters* inspired poor women to attempt homesteading.[30] Her initial audience, of course, was Mrs. Coney, a well-to-do, retired woman. Once *The Atlantic Monthly* published her letters, Stewart's readership consisted primarily of middle- and upper-class urban men and women who read that magazine. Elinore's work was neither intended, nor read, as a manual for women homesteaders. Rather, it was written and received as a collection of charming, entertaining tales and vignettes of western homesteading life. Most of her readers would not fault Stewart for her tendency, as her son put it, to "never let the truth get in the way of a good story!"[31]

At the same time, it is not appropriate to conclude *Letters From a Woman Homesteader* is total fabrication. Beyond serving as an engaging group of tales, the work should be viewed as an experientially accurate account of how Stewart perceived her life and what she thought was important. We have two perspectives on Stewart's homesteading activities—her own narrative, and the version that emerges from land office documents. The latter presents the legal dimension to Stewart's life; the former, the ideational dimension. *Letters* signifies the human part of her historical experience, albeit the more subjectively rendered part, for it offers only the things she chose to reveal. Her account serves as the form and structure through which she channels her experiences. In this sense, the fact that its details do not coincide with the land office's version does not make it any less "true." Reality consists of a constant dialogue between a person's perceptions of experience, "the pictures inside" one's head, and the objective world.[32] Likewise, the reality of Elinore Pruitt Stewart's experience is *both* the one revealed in the legal documents and the "pictures" she presents in her book. *Letters* depicts how Stewart construed the events of her life, how she made sense of them. The General Land Office records ordered these events one way, Elinore another.

With this in mind, Mrs. Stewart's case is instructive on several levels. First, the legal version demonstrates the way *some* homesteaders, though by no means all, used the land laws to their own advantage. Success required a good deal of back-breaking work not only from a husband and wife, but from children, other relatives, and helpful neighbors. In most cases, it was a not a life for a single person, male or female. It suggests that many operated in the context of family, and that the land transactions of the entire family (husband, wife, even mother-in-law in this case; perhaps parents and siblings, in other cases) need to be considered in order to better understand any individual's, female or male, motivations and actions.

To acknowledge this possibility is not to dismiss women's actions as merely the result of men's decisions. It is difficult to discern families' decision-making processes, because evidence is scant. No family corollary to *The Congressional Record* exists to indicate the nature of debate or the final vote on important issues. Yet, it is unreasonable to assume women had no voice in certain types of family economic decisions. Elinore's daughter, Jerrine, for instance, remembers her parents made decisions together, although Clyde publicly headed the household. On several occasions in her book, Elinore insists Clyde did not "boss" her.[33]

Further, although Elinore did not prove up on her own homestead, the property did remain in the family's hands, and that was the important goal for the Stewarts. Elinore was clearly a successful ranch woman, operating in the framework of her family. True, she did not succeed as an "independent woman homesteader," in Elinore's own narrowly defined sense of that term. However, to the extent that "independent" means more than "alone," to the extent it also means individualistic and self-reliant, the term certainly applies to Mrs. Stewart. She was a free-spirited, forceful personality, working along-side, rather than under the domination of, her husband.

The Stewart case, then, underscores the necessity of including family considerations in any analysis of homesteaders. Some historians have begun to acknowledge this factor in their work on women home-steaders. Paula Nelson indicated that women rarely homesteaded alone on the northern plains, opting instead to come with family or friends from their hometowns, although the majority of the 220 women in her western South Dakota sample were single. Further, Nelson divided these homesteaders into two types: absentee and bona fide settlers. Only eight of the 220 worked as full-time farmers, leaving the vast majority to be the absentee variety: people who approached homesteading with the goal of acquiring property as an investment, but who did not intend to settle. Erikka Hansen, a schoolteacher from eastern South Dakota, was one of these. She filed a claim adjoining her brother's. Eventually, another brother filed on another adjoining claim and the three siblings helped one another. In time, Hansen, who made her actual living by teaching, proved up and sold her homestead for $500. She is significant because she succeeded with the help of family members. The same could be said of her brothers.[34] As for bona fide settlers of both sexes, turning grasslands into productive farmland, according to Nelson, "involved all family members. While some tasks were divided by gender, many others including field work and barnyard chores, were performed by anyone able to do them."[35]

Barbara Allen, in her book on eastern Oregon homesteaders of the 1905–1915 era, also recognized the importance of family and offered an example more akin to the Stewart's case than that of Erikka Hansen. In a 1908 letter to his father-in-law, Henry Morgenstern proposed the following: "You can take 160 Desert yet Mother can take 320. Frank can take Homestead Desert all 320. Roe can do the same when he gets of age. I can take 320. If we all could get together it would be a bunch of 1440 acres."[36] One hundred sixty acres of Oregon desert proved no more sufficient for a family enterprise than it did in southwest Wyoming. "It became, in fact," Allen contends, "common practice for family members—husbands and wives, brothers and sisters, cousins— to take up blocks of land in adjoining claims." She concludes, "The General Land Office tract books . . . are strewn with family names shared by four, five or six different individuals."[37] Not unlike the Stewarts, some of these enterprising homestead families engaged in activities that could be called fraudulent. They did so not because they were speculators but because they were simply "people . . . trying to make homes for their families."[38]

The challenge for historians now is to transcend anecdotal evidence and examine those tract books more carefully. Identical surnames can certainly suggest family connections and possible cooperation. Analyzing these records with an eye toward similar names will provide a more precise picture—albeit not a perfectly precise one—of the role of family and kinship ties among homesteaders. To be sure, identical surnames do not assure relationship or cooperation. Cooperating relatives do not always share the same name. Nevertheless, a preliminary study of the Roosevelt County, New Mexico, plat book indicates that of seventeen women who homesteaded in Uxer township, only two had no apparent family ties there.[39] Careful scrutiny of other plat books might reveal similar patterns and results. Such data, enhanced with anecdotal evidence as well as information gleaned from marriage, divorce, and death records, and probate, tax, and land transactions could lead to an enhanced understanding of both male and female homesteaders' motivations.

A more accurate assessment of family connections, cooperation, and maybe even collusion, does not mean the whole issue of motivation will be reduced to numbers and percentages. It can lead to a more precise explanation than the common and not very satisfying: "the reasons were as varied as the individuals." It may lend more credence to the argument that most homesteaders of both sexes wished to acquire property in order to provide additional economic security for their families. Undoubtedly, the importance of family considerations in analyzing women homesteaders' motives, must be applied to a consideration of men's motives, as well. It may also mean that the number of single men and women attracted to homesteading by a sense of adventure and desire for independence was less than Elinore Pruitt

Stewart's book implies. Or, perhaps, it suggests the ways people and their purposes can change over time. An individual might stride forth onto the public domain inspired by notions of single-spirited independence and slide into a greater appreciation for family strategies out of necessity, economics, loneliness, or even love. Possibly, Stewart passed through this range of motivations. In presenting the public version of her life, however, she simply emphasized those motives she thought Mrs. Coney and other readers would find most compelling.

The other way Stewart's case is instructive relates to her pictures of homesteading, to her own, perhaps quite consciously constructed, myth of the frontier. In the book, Stewart offers ideas about, and symbols of, her experiences. In this respect, the account stands as a cultural record of her circumstances, time, and place. The editors of the *Atlantic Monthly* recognized her talent for expressing the perceptions, hopes, and aspirations of an American type: a woman homesteader. So, they published her letters. The meaning she found in that life revolved around certain cultural issues of her day, most notably: feminism, individualism, the back-to-the-land movement, and the crucial link between these ideas and the powerful American dream of land ownership. These served as the major components of Stewart's own frontier myth.

Elinore's remarks about independence, for instance, certainly reflect what Glenda Riley has called "a slowly liberalizing attitude toward women during the last two decades of the nineteenth century and the opening decades of the twentieth century," an attitude, Riley adds, that freed women homesteaders "from much criticism from their peers."[40] That non-westerners also made the connection between emerging feminism and women homesteaders is apparent in Edith Kohl's tale of a newspaperman covering the Rosebud Land Lottery. He asked a woman landseeker if she was a suffragette. She looked at him "wonderingly" before the throng pushed her on and she disappeared.[41] Kohl's point was that for homesteaders seeking a secure stake in a place where aridity posed monstrous problems, the issue of woman suffrage did not weigh heavily. Nevertheless, it *was* important to newspapermen, the editors of *Atlantic Monthly*, Elinore Pruitt Stewart's readership, and to the woman homesteader herself.

Of course, Elinore's ideas about independence seem contradicted by the actions revealed in the paper trail of her land transactions. Yet, this apparent contradiction may actually demonstrate a point historian

Robert Griswold recently made about many western women. An individual, he wrote, "might exhibit behavior and attitudes that simultaneously confirmed and seemingly contradicted the ideology of domesticity. The staunch believer in a single woman's ability to homestead . . . might also insist that wifehood and motherhood were women's ultimate callings. Her ideology might incorporate both traditional and proto-feminist assumptions."[42] This is a useful way to understand Stewart and even reconcile her rhetoric with her actions. Elinore's published work promoted a "proto-feminist" view. Yet, like most American women, she operated on a daily basis in the cultural context of domestic ideology. Further, for all her talk of accomplishing goals without Clyde's aid, the importance of husband, children, and family remains a dominant theme in Stewart's book.

At times, Stewart seems to set individualism at odds with marriage and family. Actually, she blended them quite effectively in her own life. Others no doubt did the same. New research on western women reveals that family units, providing all kinds of crucial "support services," proved critical in the trek and settlement of the West. "Was individualism in fact, nurtured by intense cooperative effort," several historians ask, with the family acting as the "central building piece of westward (or northward) settlement"?[43] Stewart's example is pertinent here for, publicly, she unquestionably perpetuated the nineteenth-century "sacred ideas of individualism and self-reliance."[44] Yet, her private actions reveal the importance of family and cooperation. That she emphasized a perhaps mythological individualism is a reflection of her time. That we now see the role of families acting "as a subculture [weaving] the binding cords of mutual support and cooperation," is a reflection of ours.[45] In the end, her case represents the importance of both individualist ideology and family strategy. Here again, Stewart is representative of many men and women who blended this ideology with this strategy in the course of homesteading.

Finally, Stewart's work incorporates some of the ideas of the popular "back-to-the-land" movement. This crusade was based on the assumption that rural life proved more healthful than city life. It was, according to one historian, "a rhetorical binge about the virtues of life on the land as the American public struggled to adjust to the closing of a three-hundred-year-old frontier."[46] This national infatuation with rural life partially explains Congress's passage of the Enlarged

Homestead Act and the fact that "more land was homesteaded between 1898 and 1917 than in the preceding thirty years."[47] The back-to-the-land movement probably does not explain Elinore's motives in leaving Denver for Burnt Fork, Wyoming. It *does* help explain why her stories appeared in the *Atlantic Monthly*. A number of popular magazines, such as *Colliers, Outlook*, and one called *Country Life in America*, regularly ran pieces like Stewart's. In fact, these periodicals became the medium through which the back-to-the-land movement gained its widest exposure. These articles ran from the practical to the promotional, and emphasized the physical, spiritual, and financial rewards of rural life— all significant themes in Stewart's work. She was just one of several women homesteaders who contributed articles of this nature. She was just one of many spokeswomen for these popular ideas.[48]

Not long after her letters were first serialized in *Atlantic Monthly*, Elinore wrote to the editor of that magazine about the many cards and letters she had received from appreciative readers. "One dear old lady eighty-four years old wrote me that she had always wanted to live the life I am living, but could not, and that the Letters satisfied her every wish. She said she had only to shut her eyes to see it all, to smell the pines and the sage, and she said many more nice things that I wish were true of me."[49] This must have been very satisfying to Elinore Pruitt Stewart for it validated her primary purpose in writing. If she did not succeed at acquiring a homestead as a literally single, independent woman, she certainly succeeded as a popular writer. Stewart's perceptual world of homesteading struck a responsive chord and found an enthusiastic readership. It still does.

When Elinore Pruitt Stewart died in 1933, the *Rock Springs Rocket* noted her passing with a short obituary on the bottom of page two: "Rites for Novelist Who Died Here to Be Held Tomorrow." In the story, she is identified as "the author of 'The Woman Homesteader,' western *fiction* [author's emphasis] book."[50] Such notice was appropriate. Stewart's literary creations and the semi-fictional individuals who people her stories undoubtedly contribute to our understanding of how homesteaders perceived their experiences. She provides insight into homesteaders' mythical worlds.

The other version of Stewart's experience, the one revealed in the legal documents, is equally important. It demonstrates how Elinore and the entire Stewart family managed to make a stake—and survive—in that world. It affords insight into the complex strategies western men and women devised in the process of homesteading. Husband, wife, mother-in-law all did their part. They used various versions of the Homestead Act and the Desert Land Act. They tried to reconcile family needs with legal requirements and sometimes violated the letter and spirit of those laws in the process. In this respect, Elinore Pruitt Stewart epitomizes much more than a single case study. She is that rare person who left enough information to raise significant questions about all homesteaders' motives. Her writings and her life lead to a greater appreciation of the important roles women and families played in the American homesteading experience.

Sherry L. Smith is a professor of history at Southern Methodist University. Her previous books include *Reimagining Indians: Native Americans through Anglo Eyes, 1880–1940* (2000), *The View from Officers' Row: Army Perceptions of Western Indians* (1990), and *Sagebrush Soldier: Private William Earl Smith's View of the Sioux War of 1876* (1989).

NOTES

1. Elinore Pruitt Stewart, *Letters of a Woman Homesteader* (1914; Boston: Houghton Mifflin, 1982), 214–15.
2. The major studies of women homesteaders include Mary Hargreaves, "Women in the Agricultural Settlement of the Northern Plains," *Agricultural History* 50 (January 1976): 179–89; Sheryll Patterson-Black, "Women Homesteaders on the Great Plains Frontier," *Frontiers* 1 (spring 1976): 67–88; Paula Nelson, "No Place for Clinging Vines: Women Homesteaders on the South Dakota Frontier, 1900–1915" (master's thesis, University of South Dakota, 1978); Kathryn Llewellyn Harris, "Women and Families on Northwestern Colorado Homesteads, 1873–1920" (doctoral dissertation, University of Colorado, 1983); Jill Thorley Warnick, "Women Homesteaders in Utah, 1869–1934" (master's thesis, Brigham Young University, 1985); Paula Bauman, "Single Women Homesteaders in Wyoming, 1880–1930," *Annals of Wyoming* 58 (spring 1986): 39–53; Paula Nelson, *After the West Was Won: Homesteaders and Town-Builders in Western South Dakota, 1900–1917* (Iowa City: University of Iowa Press, 1986); Barbara Allen, *Homesteading the High Desert* (Salt Lake City: University of Utah Press, 1987); and H. Elaine Lindgren, "Ethnic Women Homesteading on the Plains of North Dakota," *Great Plains Quarterly* 9 (summer 1989): 157–73. Glenda Riley's *The Female Frontier: A Comparative View of Women on the Prairie and the Plains* (Lawrence: University Press of Kansas, 1988); and Riley's introduction to Edith

Eudora Kohl's *Land of the Burnt Thigh* (St. Paul: Minnesota Historical Society Press, 1986) also contain information on women homesteaders.

3. Lindgren, "Ethnic Women Homesteading," 159–61; Harris, "Women and Families," 32; and Bauman, "Single Women Homesteaders," 48. For other examples of similar statistics see Patterson-Black, "Women Homesteaders on the Great Plains Frontier," 68; and Warnick, "Women Homesteaders in Utah, 1869–1934," 47–54, 78–79.

4. Stewart, *Letters*, 215.

5. Elinor Lenz, "Homestead Home," in *Women, Women Writers, and the West*, ed. L. L. Lee and Merrill Lewis (Troy, N.Y.: Whitston Pub. Co., 1979), 50.

6. Stewart, *Letters*, 215.

7. Susanne Kathryn Lindau, "My Blue and Gold Wyoming: The Life and Letters of Elinore Pruitt Stewart" (doctoral dissertation, University of Nebraska, 1988), 1–11; Elizabeth Fuller Ferris, "Foreword," in *Letters*, by Stewart, vi–viii; and Eleanore Purett [*sic*] Stewart Death Record, Vital Records Services, Division of Health and Medical Services, Cheyenne, Wyoming.

8. Lindau, "My Blue and Gold Wyoming," 11–12.

9. Ferris, "Foreword," viii–ix.

10. Lindau, "My Blue and Gold Wyoming," 12–28; transcript of interview with Jerrine Wire by Dorothy Garceau, Croyden, Pennsylvania, 23 March 1986.

11. Unpatented Serial Application File 01631, Evanston Land Office, Branch of Records Management, Bureau of Land Management, U.S. Department of Interior, Washington, D.C.; Clyde Stewart and Elinore Pruitt Rupert, Statement of Applicant for a Marriage License, 30 April 1909, copy on file at County Clerk and Ex-Officio Register of Deeds, Sweetwater County Courthouse, Green River, Wyoming. Elinore and Clyde were actually married on 5 May 1909 at the Stewart ranch. For Elinore's account of filing for a homestead see Stewart, *Letters*, 7.

12. Stewart, *Letters*, 22. Legally, Clyde Stewart could have filed under the recently passed Enlarged Homestead Act and thus expanded his own landholdings in that way. However, he did not do so. Perhaps the Stewarts were not aware of this option.

13. Stewart, *Letters*, 78, 79, 75, 185, 184, 187.

14. Ibid., 134. Clyde completed his homestead application on 14 November 1898 in Evanston, Wyoming, and his final proof was taken at Green River on 3 July 1905. One of the witnesses claimed that Stewart had lived on the property since July 1898 and that his improvements included a house, stables, sheds, a granary, other out-buildings, and fencing valued at $500.00. Clyde testified that he built the house in 1898 and that his family consisted of a wife. The couple had no children. Cynthia Hurst Stewart died in 1907 leaving Clyde a widower when Elinore Rupert came to Wyoming in 1909. Serial Patent 1117, Evanston Land Office, RG 49, Bureau of Land Management, National Archives.

15. Stewart, *Letters*, 134, 215.

16. A copy of Elinore Stewart's relinquishment paper is contained in Unpatented Serial Application File 01631, Evanston Land Office, Branch of Records Management, Bureau of Land Management, Washington, D.C. For more information on Ruth Stewart's homestead application and final proof see Serial Patent Case File 488179, Evanston Land Office, RG 49 Records of Bureau of Land Management, National Archives, Washington, D.C.

17. "Maria Good (22 October 1886)," Department of the Interior, *Decisions of the Department of the Interior and the General Land Office in Cases Relating to the Public*

Lands From July 1, 1886 to June 30, 1887, ed. S. V. Proudfit (hereafter, for all dates, cited as *Decisions*), vol. 5 (Washington, 1887), 196–98. I am indebted to James Muhn, BLM Historian, Denver Federal Center, Denver, Colorado, for his help on these legal issues.

18. Quoted in "Thompson v. Talbot (22 November 1895)," *Decisions*, vol. 21 (1896), 430–31. For similar decisions see "Hattie E. Walker (15 October 1892)," *Decisions*, vol. 15 (1893), 377–79; "Jane Mann (12 February 1894)," *Decisions*, vol. 18 (1894), 116–17; and "Leonora H. Fores (12 February 1898)," *Decisions*, vol. 26 (1898), 194–95.

19. According to one study of women homesteaders in Wyoming, the majority of women who filed claims did so after the residency requirement was dropped to three years. Bauman, "Single Women Homesteaders," 41. For information on the 1912 act see Benjamin Horace Hibbard, *A History of the Public Land Policies* (Madison: University of Wisconsin Press, 1965), 394–96; and Roy Robbins, *Our Landed Heritage: The Public Domain, 1776–1970* (Lincoln: University of Nebraska Press, 1976), 375.

20. See Serial Patent Case File 488179. A copy of the Warranty Deed transferring the property from Ruth C. Stewart to Henry Clyde Stewart, 9 August 1920, is filed at the Office of the County Clerk and Ex-Officio Register of Deeds, Sweetwater County Courthouse, Green River, Wyoming. This coincides with Harris's contention that women who did prove up on land to increase the family's holdings retained the right to that property and received compensation for it when they sold it. Harris, "Women and Families," 32–33.

21. Lindau states that at its height the Stewart ranch consisted of 1100 acres. They ran about one hundred cattle, a medium-size operation. See Lindau, "My Blue and Gold Wyoming," 33. For information on Clyde's homestead transactions see Homestead Final Certificate 1117, Evanston Land Office, RG 49, Records of the BLM, National Archives; and on his Desert Land Act transactions, Serial Patent File 525300, Evanston Land Office, RG 49, Records o the BLM, National Archives.

22. Elinore's "Application to Contest," can be found in Evanston Serial File 08378, Branch of Records Management, BLM, Washington, D.C.; Elinore Stewart's "Desert-Land Entry Declaration of Applicant," Serial Application 09049, can be found in the same office. More than ten years before this action, Elinore told Mrs. Coney she intended to file a desert land entry "some day when I have sufficient money of my own earning." Stewart, *Letters*, 134.

23. "Rules of Practice," in *Decisions of the Department of the Interior in Cases Relating to the Public Lands*, ed. Daniel M. Greene, vol. 48, 1 February 1921–30 April 1922 (Washington, D.C., 1923), 247–49.

24. Evanston Serial 08378, BLM, Washington, D.C. Langley's entry was also contested by two men in 1923 and 1924. John Briggs, Jr.'s contest successfully cancelled Langley's homestead entry.

25. Serial Patent File 642950, Evanston Land Office, RG 49, Records of the BLM, National Archives.

26. Lindau, "My Blue and Gold Wyoming," 137.

27. The letters that comprise the book were actual letters Stewart wrote to her former employer, Mrs. Juliet Coney. On a visit back to Boston, Coney showed the letters to Ellery Sedgwick, editor of the *Atlantic Monthly*, who agreed they should be published. For more on Stewart's publishing career see Lindau, "My Blue and Gold

Wyoming," 41–69. Presumably, the letters were edited for publication.

28. To dwell on the pessimistic and discouraging was simply not part of her character or personality. On one rare occasion, Stewart confessed to Coney, "If you only knew how far short I fall of my own hopes you would know I could *never* boast." Stewart, *Letters*, 63. Ironically, had she admitted failure more often, Stewart might have been an even more appropriate spokeswoman for her generation's actual experiences. Several historians stress failure as a major theme in the lives of twentieth-century homesteaders. Many of those who migrated to western South Dakota, according to Paula Nelson, failed, and "their failure added a bitter twist to the frontier dream." Barbara Allen concluded that the story of eastern Oregon homesteaders was also largely one of failure. Stewart, however, spoke to aspirations more than about actual experiences. See Nelson, *After the West*, xiv; and Allen, *Homesteading*, xviii.

29. Clarence H. Danhof, "Farm-Making Costs and the 'Safety Valve': 1850–1960," in *The Public Lands: Studies in the History of the Public Domain*, ed. Vernon Carstensen (Madison: University of Wisconsin Press, 1968), 253–54. See also Fred A. Shannon, "The Homestead Act and the Labor Surplus," in *The Public Lands*, ed. Carstensen, 297–314. Edith Kohl also presents the safety valve theory in her first-hand account of homesteading. See Kohl, *Land of the Burnt Thigh*, 47–49.

30. Bauman's sample concerns only women who had patented their homesteads, rather than those who tried and failed. However, she indicates no poor women tried homesteading. Most of the single women homesteading in Wyoming had skill and jobs (teaching, nursing, etc.) that served as their primary source of income. See Bauman, "Single Women Homesteaders."

31. Clyde Stewart, Jr. to author, telephone interview, 13 May 1988.

32. This discussion is based, in part, on observations historian Gene Wise has made. "It may be," he wrote, "that reality in history lies on more than one plane, and that what is objectively real from a detached position may not jibe with what is perceptually real in the experience of involved people." "Experience—or at least the human part of experience," he continues, "lies along the plane of transactions between men's pictures of the world and what the world throws up to them." Gene Wise, *American Historical Explanations: A Strategy for Grounded Inquiry* (1973; Minneapolis: University of Minnesota, 1980), 32, 44.

33. Garceau interview with Jerrine Wire, 1986; Stewart, *Letters*, 24, 74.

34. Nelson, "No Place," 3–6; and Nelson, *After the West*, 43–47, 50–60.

35. Nelson, *After the West*, 50; see also Riley, *The Female Frontier*, 47, 80, 135.

36. Allen, *Homesteading*, 33.

37. Ibid., 32, 36. See also Warnick, "Women Homesteaders in Utah," 56–58, 65–75, and 87, on the repeated occurrence of surnames in tract books. Her sample is complicated by the Mormon practice of polygamy. Warnick also concludes that in most cases, success in proving up reflected family effort rather than individual achievement.

38. Quoted in Allen, *Homesteading*, 31. See also Patterson-Black, "Women Homesteaders on the Great Plains Frontier," 78–79.

39. Coreta Justus, "Single Women and Homesteading Patterns in Southeastern New Mexico, 1900–1920," paper in author's possession, 4–5.

40. Riley, *Female Frontier*, 134.

41. Kohl, *Land of the Burnt Thigh*, 155.

42. Robert Griswold, "Anglo Women and Domestic Ideology in the American West in the Nineteenth and Early Twentieth Century," in *Western Women: Their Land,*

Their Lives, ed. Lillian Schlissel, Vicki L. Ruiz, and Janice Monk (Albuquerque: University of New Mexico Press, 1988), 16.

43. Schlissel, Ruiz, and Monk, "Introduction," in *Western Women*, 4, 6.

44. Ibid., 4.

45. Ibid.

46. Stanford J. Layton, *To No Privileged Class: The Rationalization of Homesteading and Rural Life in the Early Twentieth-Century American West* (Provo, Utah: Brigham Young University, Charles Redd Center for Western Studies, 1988), 2.

47. Allen, *Homesteading*, 136.

48. Layton, *To No Privileged Class*, 41–47. For an interesting analysis of Stewart's cultural context and the literary tradition into which her work fits see Peter C. Rollins, "The Film *Heartland*: Faithful Adaptation or Independent Vision," unpublished TS in author's possession.

49. Elinore Rupert Stewart to editor, 23 January 1914, published in the *Atlantic Monthly* 113 (April 1914): 532. For notices of *Letters* see "The Joys of Homesteading," *Dial* 57 (1 July 1914): 21–22; and *The Nation* 99 (16 July 1914): 75. The book was reviewed in several other periodicals including *New York Times*, 7 June 1914, 259; *Outlook* 107 (1 August 1914): 820–21; and the *Wisconsin Library Bulletin* 10 (July 1914): 191. Stewart's other publications include "The Return of the Woman Homesteader," *Atlantic Monthly* 123 (May 1919): 590–96; and "Snow: An Adventure of the Woman Homesteader," *Atlantic Monthly* 132 (December 1923): 780–85. See Lindau for an interesting discussion of Stewart's unpublished manuscript, *Sand and Sage*, which *Atlantic* and Houghton Mifflin rejected. Lindau, "My Blue and Gold Wyoming," 136–41.

50. *Rock Springs Rocket*, 5 October 1933, 2.

RANCH AND FARM WOMEN IN THE CONTEMPORARY AMERICAN WEST*

Sandra Schackel

In 1981, historian Joan Jensen made the point that women have been "active participants in every stage of agricultural production and in every period of agricultural history." In a society that views farming as a male occupation, however, farm women's lives often have been ignored or misunderstood. As the agrarian economy of the seventeenth century has evolved into the present urban industrial economy, major changes have occurred in the agricultural production system. Over time, women's productive roles have changed, causing a shift in the sexual division of labor. As a result, the workday roles of women and men have altered life on the family farm.[1]

Historians have been slow to acknowledge the significance of farm women's lives. Since the 1920s, rural sociologists have looked at the part of culture that agricultural historians have not—the families and communities within which rural people lived out their lives. In the 1980s, when a few historians began to study rural women, they drew on the work of sociologists, anthropologists, folklorists, and others. As the field has grown, historians have begun to uncover a rich and varied tapestry that demonstrates the significance of women's work on farms and ranches. To date, much of this work has focused on America in the eighteenth and nineteenth centuries.

---

*This chapter was originally published as: Schackel, Sandra. "Ranch and Farm Women in the Contemporary American West," in *The Rural West since World War II*, ed. R. Douglas Hurt (Lawrence: University Press of Kansas, 1998).

The past fifty years represent a period of rapid agricultural change in the United States characterized by, among other factors, a steady decline in farm population, the disappearance of small-scale family farms, and the identification of large-scale operations with agribusiness. How have farm women fared in this new agricultural age? How have the structural changes in agriculture altered their lives, most particularly the patriarchal nature of farming? How have women adapted to the new technology that has shaped agriculture in the twentieth century? Historian Katherine Jellison, in her recent study of midwestern farm women, pointed out: "Farm women as well as men have played a role in modernizing farm life and changing forever the face of rural society and the character of its relationship to urban America." Jellison's work can be extended to the American West, using the voices of farm women in Idaho and New Mexico as a model for further study. Oral history interviews can help show the effect of technology on women's role as consumers and the link between such consumerism and the pattern of their off-farm work.[2]

At the close of World War II, farmwives throughout the nation were poised to become consumers in a new era of prosperity. In 1946, for example, a Nebraska farm mother and her daughter wrote to the editors of *Wallaces' Farmer* regarding postwar home improvements that were beginning to alter lifestyles for some farm families. "When Dad got the new manure scoop, the elevator and other modern farm tools, daughter and I approved, feeling that one of these days it would be our turn to enjoy electricity and a few modern conveniences. Just when we thought we had him convinced, what does he do? Orders another new tractor for the boys!" This farm wife obviously had looked forward to sharing in the postwar technological bounty awaiting war-weary consumers after four years of sacrifice and rationing. When the war ended, women began to discuss what they wanted to purchase "now that the war [was] over . . . and there [would] be all kinds of new equipment on the market." Such expectations were typical of farmwives in a period of rising prosperity and technological change that would alter life on the farm in postwar America.[3]

Much is known about the consumer habits of postwar urban families. Nationwide, American families were growing and spending; that is, family size increased dramatically as the soldiers returned home, and consumer spending rose to accommodate both the larger families and the bigger appetites that postwar affluence encouraged. Significant increases in discretionary spending power marked the postwar years. Between 1947 and 1961, the number of families rose 28 percent, national income increased over 60 percent, and the group with discretionary income (those with money for non-necessities) doubled. Rather than spending for personal luxury items, Americans bought for the home. In the five years after World War II, consumer spending increased 60 percent, but the amount spent on household furnishings and appliances rose 240 percent. Between 1946 and 1950, consumers purchased 21.4 million automobiles, more than 20 million refrigerators, 5.5 million electric stoves, and 11.6 million television sets, a trend that continued into the 1950s.[4]

Many of these new items could be found in fast-growing suburban cities. Here, in a crabgrass-free, three-bedroom, two-bathroom ranch home, young families could raise children in a nice neighborhood complete with cars, washing machines, refrigerators, television sets, and other appliances associated with the good life. Yet farm families also desired to, and in fact did, purchase many of these same commodities, assuming, of course, they had electricity. By 1954, 91.4 percent of rural families in the Mountain West (Montana, Idaho, Wyoming, Colorado, New Mexico, Arizona, Utah, and Nevada) and 96.7 percent in the Pacific West (Washington, Oregon, and California) had electric power. Farm families were not without many of the new consumer items their city counterparts were enjoying.[5]

Still, U.S. Department of Agriculture (USDA) officials estimated in 1946 that only middle- to high-income farm families would benefit from increased farm incomes. In the corn and wheat belts, which led all other areas of the country in increased farm incomes and wartime savings, only "farm families with the largest savings look[ed] forward to having the conveniences that [were] generally available in cities— central heat, automatic hot water, telephone, electricity, and an all-weather road to the door." One study listed the appliances now expected by middle-class rural families in this order: refrigerators, washing machines, irons, radios, deep-freeze units, brooders, and churns. As it did for their urban counterparts, increased income gave farm women "the opportunity," as one woman put it, "to get some of the things we've always wanted."[6]

How widespread was this pattern of consumerism in the West?

Limited sources suggest at least some farms and ranches shared in the bounty. Martha Ascuena, who in the 1950s lived on a sixty-acre ranch south of Mountain Home, Idaho, felt very content with her refrigerator and conventional washing machine. However, she lacked a dining room set, so her husband determined that they should have one, went to town, and purchased a set that Martha has loved ever since. When asked if she ever thought women in town had more or better things than she, Martha replied: "I never in my life wanted things anybody else had; that never bothered me one bit. They definitely lived better, there's no doubt about that. They dressed better, they went more, they did things that way but that didn't bother me because I didn't miss it. And I think farm women of my time didn't miss it."[7]

Perhaps farm women did not miss those things because many of them already had at least the basic comforts prior to World War II. In her article "How're You Gonna Keep 'Em Down on the Farm?" historian Cynthia Sturgis notes that by 1931 in Utah, 96 percent of homes had electricity, more than three-fourths of the families had electrical equipment, and more than two-thirds of the homes had running water. In addition, 94 percent of the homes had sewing machines, 80.4 percent had electric washing machines, and 43 percent had vacuum cleaners. This is not to suggest that rural living was easy, compared with urban standards, but that life on Utah farms and ranches had greatly improved by World War II.[8]

Yet this standard was not met in all western states. On the Great Plains, for instance, as late as 1940, only 15.7 percent of Kansas farm homes had running water and 27.3 percent had electricity. The situation was even more dismal in the Dakotas, where just 6 percent of homes in North Dakota had running water and 27.3 percent had electricity; the corresponding numbers for South Dakota were 11.8 percent and 17.9 percent. In the 1930s, however, the creation of the New Deal's Rural Electrification Administration (REA) provided a major breakthrough for rural people. Speaking directly to farm women in 1936, Secretary of Agriculture Henry A. Wallace promised that "rural electrification [would ease] the burden of the farm wife more and more." According to one North Dakota woman, the coming of the REA "really changed [housekeeping], because then we got electric stove, electric refrigerator, electric iron and electric lights. It was just wonderful. [Especially the] electric stove. Push that button and there you had heat.

Didn't have to chop wood or carry coal to get some heat to cook on."[9]

For an Arizona widow, the REA provided a lifeline for her general store. Violet Irving led an extensive campaign in the 1940s to bring electricity to her remote rural area in Skull Valley. When the local power company declined to extend power lines to the area, Irving and others solicited subscribers at five dollars apiece and built a powerful coalition. "[I was the leader in the electrification movement from] let's call it necessity. I had the one business there that really [needed it]. By that time there were frozen foods and that meant a lot to my business. It was a necessity as far as I was concerned. . . . I was the one who was going to benefit the most." For Irving, determination and effort toward a public cause brought not only personal power but economic power as well.[10]

Government efforts to make life easier on America's farms began early in the twentieth century when Progressive Era reformers initiated the Country Life Movement, an attempt to stem the flow of population from farms to cities. Overall, the Country Life Movement failed to keep people "down on the farm," not because farm life could not be made more appealing through modernization but because the movement's supporters failed to recognize the strong pull of economic opportunity in the city. Embedded in this early reform movement were two goals that ultimately proved contradictory—"to preserve traditional agrarian ideals in the face of industrialism and to adapt agriculture to the modern age." Another less overt force was at work, however, in the form of reformers' attempts to prop up the patriarchal farm family by encouraging women to become modern homemakers. Over the next several decades, the message to farm women was intended to reinforce their traditional role as homemakers, one they persistently resisted. In time, many women would in fact leave the farm to take jobs in town in order to allow the family to stay on the farm.[11]

As life was made easier for the farmwife with the introduction of laborsaving devices, improved technology also altered the way farmers farmed. Two studies conducted in the 1970s in the Palouse, a rich dryland wheat-farming region in western Idaho and eastern Washington, note that accepted roles for men and women have not changed, but the content of their roles has. As Corlann Bush found in "'The Barn Is His, the House Is Mine': Agricultural Technology and Sex Roles," the value or importance of men's work was enhanced as they moved from animal-

powered farming to using mechanized equipment, while new household technology eliminated much of women's traditional work that was
formerly crucial to the economic functioning of the family. Hence, as
the husband/farmer moved from using horsepower and hired men to
purchasing expensive combines, threshers, tractors, and other special-
ized equipment, the farm operation became far more complex. At the
same time, the demands on the farmwife's role as one who "helped out"
by working in the fields and cooking for large harvest crews declined.[12]

Sue Armitage, in "Farmwomen and Technological Change in the
Palouse, 1880–1980," demonstrates the connection between increased
technology on the land and technology that transformed the home. She
found that technological change in the form of tractors and then combines occurred in the farmer's sphere first, resulting in more produc-
tivity and income. The most significant technological change to the
domestic sphere came in the form of electricity, and in the Palouse
region this came later than the technology that transformed farming.
Farm men and women both welcomed changes that made their workday lives easier—he on the tractor and she in a kitchen surrounded by
laborsaving devices. The irony lay in the fact that her increased pro-
ductivity was not in demand, since his technological improvements had
eliminated the basis for her efforts. She no longer was required to feed
farmworkers, since machinery had taken the place of manpower. Hence,
as Bush noted, the value or importance of her role had been eroded.[13]

Yet, according to prevailing cultural values, women's primary postwar role remained that of homemaker. An editorial in *Wallaces' Farmer*
in March 1953 described the farmwife's situation in this way:

> What does the "little woman" do with her time now that she has a
> cleanfuel stove and cake mixes have come on the market? With
> clothes dryers to save trips to the clothes lines, freezers to bring forth
> frozen pies and casseroles for hurry-up meals, a great many women
> hours are spent each year on tractors. Perhaps more important are
> the hours spent on trips to town for repairs for all the new machin-
> ery. . . . And then somebody—guess who—has to take time to make
> the good rolls, and the angel food cakes and the casserole dishes that
> come out of the freezer on busy days.[14]

Still, many farm women resisted the full-time homemaker status.

They saw themselves in partnership with their husbands and believed
that outside farm work, self-described as "helping out," brought more
status and personal satisfaction, and demonstrated their importance to
the family economy. They continued to run errands, pick up machinery parts, shut off the tank, or chase the hogs when they got out. By
"helping out" in these ways, women were able to deny that they actually performed farm work and could then claim that they were living
up to the postwar domestic ideal. Perhaps that is why they supported
decisions to spend family income on new agricultural equipment before
making repairs on the farm home, although new or improved equipment would lead to greater income.[15]

The patriarchal nature of agriculture assumes the male farmer's
control of the labor of women and children. To many farm women, the
phrase, "He's the boss" is of secondary importance to the recognition
that farm women play an important role in farming and in passing that
knowledge on to their children. Farmwife Helen Tiegs of Nampa,
Idaho, would agree, and describes her marriage as a partnership shaped
by distinct gender roles. Her husband works in the field, and she runs
the household, which at one time included six children. Although she
prefers not to get on a tractor—"I have but it's been a disaster!"—and
has never driven the beet truck during harvest, she considers herself
"the hub of the wheel. I kinda keep things going because I'm the one
that chases to town for parts; I really am the 'gofer'. . . . Instead of them
having to leave their jobs, they send me. So I've been the one who has
to run for parts and it gets pretty hot and heavy—they're always breaking chains, they're always breaking something." Tiegs is there to provide the needed labor at a crucial time.[16]

Martha Ascuena of Mountain Home, Idaho, would concur with
Tiegs and, in fact, also referred to herself as a "gofer" as well as a farmer.
Although she did not operate the farm by herself during the years when
her husband also taught school, she helped him irrigate, cut corn, drive
the truck, and work their hundred head of cattle. She views their relationship as balanced, noting that she has supported his decisions regarding farm purchases because "he knows more about those things and
would not buy what we could not afford." Overall, Ascuena praises farm
life and cannot imagine another way of making a living. "I always
thought I would be a farmer's wife. . . . It was all that I knew and I loved
it from the very start."[17]

Few farmwives today are disadvantaged by a lack of utilities (as their mothers and grandmothers were) or by an absence of laborsaving devices such as refrigerators, washing machines and dryers, home freezers, radios, or television sets. They have, like their urban counterparts, become "good consumers." Clearly, consumerism appears to be part of a larger, more complex issue—one that is related to issues of power, to gender roles, and, at a deeper level, to a strongly held belief in agriculture as a way of life. Whether the farmer orders another tractor at the expense of remodeling the farm kitchen is perhaps less important than how both farm people view their roles on the land and their ability to stay on the farm in the face of continuing change.

Lila Hill and her husband, Earl, know firsthand how change can alter gender roles. Hill and her husband live on a 147-acre farm in Meridian, Idaho, west of Boise. Together they operate a dairy farm caring for about a hundred head of cattle. When they married in 1968, they were clear on the division of labor on the farm. Earl was the farmer and worked outside, Lila the farmwife who worked inside with the exception of the garden and yard. For more than fifteen years, Lila gave music lessons to augment the family income, carrying as many as fifty students a week at one time. By the early 1980s, Lila and Earl agreed that Lila would take a job off-farm, one that would produce greater income in a time of rising farm costs and falling dairy prices. To prepare herself for the job market, Lila took a computer course under the Job Training Partnership Act (JTPA), then took a series of jobs serving as secretary for several area churches, a position she continues to hold today.[18]

Now, in the 1990s, their roles have altered as Earl is "easing into" retirement while Lila continues to work off the farm. She still teaches music to a few students after school, both because music defines part of who she is and for the income the lessons produce. She no longer has time to do yard work, so Earl has taken over that responsibility. The farm, originally homesteaded in 1891 by Angus Hill, will pass to the oldest son, Martin, who currently lives in a home on the property. Lila and Earl have already sold several parcels of land and foresee the distinct possibility that the farm will be sold to developers as urban growth creeps up to their property line, a common situation in metropolitan areas in the West today.[19]

Lila Hill is typical of many farmwives who recognize that their most important contribution to farming may be taking a job in town. Working off the farm to augment the farm income is not a new development but one that has been taking place for several decades as American agriculture has undergone dramatic changes. At the turn of the century, almost half the population lived on farms. This figure dropped to 30 percent in 1920 and has declined to less than 2 percent in the 1990s. At the same time, small family farms have given way to very large farms now recognized as part of the sector known as agribusiness. In 1935, there were 6.8 million farms averaging 155 acres. In 1960, there were just under 4 million, and, by 1982 the figure had dropped to 2.4 million farms averaging 433 acres. According to government definitions, however, there is great variation in the type of farms. The current definition, first used for the 1974 census, is any place from which $1,000 or more of agricultural products were produced and sold or normally would have been sold during the census year. On these terms, farms range from the very large ($500,000 or more annual gross farm income) to large, medium, and small family farms (annual gross farm sales ranging from $499,000 to $10,000) to what the USDA classifies as a rural residence with less than $10,000 gross income. The trend in the last half century has been an increase in the very large and large family farms, while medium and small family farms and rural residences have declined. The result is that farming has become more productive, concentrated, centralized, and dependent on hired rather than family labor, with corporate farms accounting for increased farm production.[20]

Still there is a great deal of sentiment among Americans for farming as a "way of life." The notion that small to medium-sized farms are indispensable to American democracy is part of the heritage of the Jeffersonian agrarian ideal. Although the number of small, part-time farms has increased, the total number of farms in the United States has been dropping since the 1930s. Since 1950, it has declined by half, from more than 5 million to fewer than 3 million farms. Still, it is not likely that the family farm will disappear from view despite the "farm crisis" that has persisted for much of the twentieth century, accelerating since World War II. Indeed, one farmwife responded to my query about the farm crisis by commenting that being raised on a farm meant "it was always a crisis, all my life."[21]

One important factor that has allowed family farms to stay in business is working off-farm for wages. Men as well as women have taken jobs off-farm in order to be able to stay on the farm. Martha Ascuena's husband, for example, taught school in Mountain Home for many years while continuing to farm. From the beginning of their marriage, Elizabeth Lloyd's husband did part-time and later full-time work while continuing to raise dairy cattle on their farms in both eastern Idaho and eastern Oregon. When a back injury in 1956 prevented him from returning to farm work, Elizabeth went to work full-time for Ore-Ida Foods in 1957 and continued at the potato processing plant until her retirement in 1986. Still, they continued to farm and to care for a family of seven children. Earl worked the evening shift, while Elizabeth worked nights, which allowed her to see the children off to school in the mornings and be there when they returned later in the day. Equally important, Elizabeth was able to maintain the role of mother and wife that was expected of farm women while contributing to the farm income.[22]

Lloyd is one of many women who fit Katherine Jellison's study of midwestern farmwives between 1913 and 1963. Jellison found that women taking jobs off-farm was a new phenomenon in the 1950s that drew mixed responses. Editors at *Wallaces' Farmer* took the position that wage work was acceptable but only as a temporary measure until the young couple could "establish themselves." By the mid-1950s, however, farm women of all ages were increasingly becoming permanent members of the small-town labor force in midwestern communities. In Illinois, 10 percent of that state's farm women were wage earners, most of them working as retail clerks, teachers, or factory workers. Although wages were low, women could still make more money at town jobs than they could by selling dressed chickens, cottage cheese, or eggs—the traditional types of economic activities for farm women. Nor did they expect to quit their town jobs soon, even when a forty-mile round-trip commute was part of the job. According to the *Wallaces' Farmer* editor, "It isn't for a TV set or a home freezer that Harriet Sellers, R.N. and homemaker, is spending her salary. It's for school clothing, groceries, tractor fuel and farm payments. . . . Practically speaking, it seems that mom has come to town so dad and the kids can stay on the farm." Many Idaho farm families fit this midwestern pattern as well.[23]

More recent studies show that a substantial number of farm women continue to hold full- or part-time jobs off the farm, jobs that benefit both farm families and local businesses. A 1976 survey of rural women in the small communities of Wendell and Jerome in south central Idaho

showed that 45 percent from small farms—those with an annual production below $25,000—were employed away from the farm. Women
on larger farms were less likely to have outside employment. The survey
showed that income from the farmwife's off-the-farm job may be necessary for a small farm to remain in operation. At the same time, such
employment strengthens the bonds between farm and non-farm sectors
of the economy.[24]

Not only is off-farm work important to keep a small farm going; it
can be crucial to establishing a family farm given the high costs of getting into business as a farmer. Linda and Gary Murgoitio of Meridian,
Idaho, struggled and scrimped for nearly fifteen years to build a financial base that would enable them to invest in land and farm equipment.
During this period, when they worked on Gary's parents' farm, Linda
worked off-farm first at a bank, then at a trucking company, and later
at an insurance company, usually for low wages. They delayed starting
a family, again because all their energy and assets were directed toward
building up capital to purchase their own farm. Once their two children
were born, Linda quit work in town to care for them, as well as to help
Gary with farm work, a working relationship she values highly. When
asked if she would work off-farm again, perhaps when the children were
grown, she was hesitant to commit to the possibility, preferring to maintain the warm partnership they have created. She went on to say, "When
I was working outside the home I think my relationship with Gary suffered. Gary and I are terribly close now and I don't want to jeopardize
[that by] going back [to work]. . . . I really like hanging out with him
and doing whatever he's doing. . . . We seem to be pretty close."[25]

Like many others, Linda questions how small farmers today can
amass the capital needed to enter agriculture under present conditions.
Several of the older farm women interviewed for this study spoke of
younger women who work off-farm as a matter of fact rather than necessity. Helen Tiegs described her daughter-in-law, who works for an
insurance company, as "a good farm wife. She knows how to irrigate,
how to do siphon tubes and everything" and is a "very good business
gal" in addition to keeping the books for a local farm organization. In
Martha Ascuena's view, "three-quarters of the girls are [working off-
farm] because the farm just isn't enough to pay expenses. . . . I'm sure
that income is taking care of the house expenses or even the groceries.
It's certainly a different way of life." Elizabeth Lloyd was even more

direct, saying, "The farm was just a place to live really because even people today that have small farms—a lot of their living they get from outside work."[26]

Rosalie Romero of Chacon, New Mexico, was eighteen when she first went to work off-farm at the local hospital in nearby Las Vegas in the early 1950s. There she worked for fifty cents an hour but remembered that "we did a lot with it." Her mother-in-law kept her children while her husband worked his father's land. Gradually Rosalie and Alfonso took over the eight-hundred-acre farm, mostly sheep, and both continued to seek out wage labor to meet their modest expenses. When Alfonso went to work for the Forest Service, the extra income helped buy "coffee, sugar, the basics." Rosalie held a variety of jobs over her lifetime as a maid, a waitress, a nutrition aid to the agricultural extension agent, in the Senior Citizen Center in Mora, and until her retirement in May 1995, as a school bus driver.[27]

The Romeros did not, and still do not, have mechanical equipment, just horses and wagons. When their children were small, Rosalie would take them with her on horseback to deliver lunches to the sheepherders in the mountains. Like most farmwives, she tended to a large garden and canned, although she no longer cans as much as she used to. The family did not install running water in their home until 1982 but carried water from a nearby river and used outdoor plumbing. She recalled washing diapers outside in tubs and cooking over a wood-burning stove. The stove is still present in her kitchen, right next to a modern electric stove. Rosalie is cheerfully optimistic when asked about the character of their lives. She has had a hard life, but it has brought satisfaction as well. The presence of a large extended family nearby has been important to her as a source of support. As her husband did, their children— four sons and one daughter—will take over the farm at their parents' deaths, perpetuating this family farm for yet another generation.[28]

Taking over the family farm is not as clear for many families, given the increasing costs associated with farming. Irene Getz of Elgin, Illinois, married a sheep and cattle rancher in 1930 and came west, to Monte Vista, Colorado, to begin a new life. Initially, her husband, Floyd, worked for his father for cash wages, fifty dollars a month, until they were able to acquire land of their own. At one time, the family farm consisted of two operations of five thousand acres where they raised approximately 500 head of cattle and 1,200 sheep. After Floyd's death in 1975, their four sons continued to run the two operations. Later they sold one ranch. In the 1980s, one son left ranching and moved into town, where he became a businessman and local politician. Although her husband arranged for all five children to inherit the land, Irene is not sure how long the Getz ranch will remain in the family. Her daughter, Marilyn, has two sons, one of whom may go into the family agricultural enterprise; he is currently finishing a college degree. At present, the grandsons represent the only hope that this family farm will continue in its present form.[29]

In cash-poor Mora County in northeastern New Mexico, small family farms dot the high-mountain countryside. Mora, thirty miles north of Las Vegas, is the largest town in the valley at eight hundred people. In 1970, nearly 60 percent of the residents lived in what the federal government officially defined as poverty; nationally less than 11 percent of the population fit that category. Over homemade tortillas, red chile, and *posole*, Alice and Frank Trambley relate some of their forty-two years together. Alice grew up on her family's farm eight miles south of Mora. She met Frank while baling hay (with horses), married him at age twenty-two, and settled into farm life. After three of their six children were born, the family moved into "town," where they have resided since, although they continue to make daily trips to the farm. They raise cattle and hay on about six hundred acres. Half the land is under irrigation; cattle graze the other half.[30]

Like many of the other families in heavily Hispanic Mora Valley, this family has always had income from off-farm work. In the 1960s, they opened a slaughterhouse in Mora, drawing on family labor. All the children went to work when they were small; the sons learned to cut meat at age fourteen. Alice divided her time between raising the children and working at the business. There were long days, especially in the fall, when eighty head of cattle a week were slaughtered. For twenty-five years, she helped with the slaughter on Mondays and wrapped meat on Thursdays. Today she is free of this task, since one of the sons took over full management of the business in 1992. Her "free" labor, unaccounted for in census terms, helped this farm family to survive. The work of family members reduced labor costs, and thus "The slaughterhouse gave them a cushion."[31]

Twenty years ago, the family invested in another income-generating business, a small mobile home park adjacent to their home in Mora.

Today they have space for thirty-three units; they own fifteen units and rent out the remaining spaces. Alice and Frank agreed early on in their marriage that she would do the "inside" work; it is Alice's task to clean the rental units when tenants move out. Despite the discomfort of sometimes noisy, rowdy renters, the extra income has been important. Along with the slaughterhouse business, off-farm work has allowed this family to maintain their agricultural roots through difficult periods and in a challenging environment. Alice made it clear that "we can't make it without these sources of income." As a result, their children will inherit a working family farm, one that has been maintained by outside income. Two of the sons live nearby and are actively involved in the daily management of the cattle and hay operation. Yet they, too, live and work off-farm.

Of the Trambleys' eight grandchildren, will any of them be willing to return to the Mora Valley and commit to the demanding tasks of maintaining the family farm? Frank and Alice are unsure. Reflecting on the reality of farming in the late twentieth century, they suggest that "maybe the grandchildren will be smarter and will sell out." They note the large number of young people who leave the valley because of a lack of jobs: "Even the ones that finish high school and college have to go out and look for jobs." Farm expenses are simply too great. In this valley, as in other agricultural areas, local families sell out to newcomers, people who have retired from jobs elsewhere, saved their money, and can afford to buy up large parcels.[32]

Alice Trambley's willingness to serve as a cheap source of labor is key to the survival of small farm families. Cornelia Butler Flora and Jan L. Flora, in their 1988 study of agriculture and women's culture in the Great Plains, suggest three factors that allow the family farm to survive in a society dominated by capitalist relations of production: provision of a flexible labor force; absorption of risk; and heavy capital investment relative to the profit generated. Women play key roles in each situation. Since agricultural production differs from industrial production as regards a flexible labor force, the family is the ideal basic production unit. As part of a flexible labor force, shaped by the cyclic nature of farming and dictates of weather, women and often children are "available" to "help out" at harvest or calving time, or to serve as the ones to go for parts or supplies. Once the peak season has ebbed, women can then assume the role of "dependent" during the rest of the agricultural cycle, as Alice and her children did after the fall slaughter.[33]

Farm women take pride in "helping out" in this manner and have created a variety of cultural structures around the role of farmwife. Basic to agrarian ideology is the notion that "the family working in harmony as a production unit is the best possible way of life even though that unit may be defined by the male in the household." Unlike in industry, management, labor, and capital are bound up in the agricultural enterprise—the family—so all in the family are expected to contribute to the whole to make it work. Alice Trambley, as well as her children, have been integral to this system, helping to mobilize needed labor at peak periods in the production cycle. At the same time, the demand for labor in "her sphere" continued—cooking, cleaning, child care, laundry, and numerous other tasks associated with being a farmwife. While cultural norms allow women to do men's work, men perform women's tasks less often.[34]

Along with their role as part of a flexible labor force, women play a key role in the absorption of risk through diversification in production. Examples of this diversification include the production and sale of butter, cream, eggs, poultry, and vegetables. Historically, women have been actively involved in some aspect of agricultural production. Dairying, poultry raising, and truck farming were often an integral part of all farm families' work up through the 1950s and 1960s. Women participated in the marketplace and received monetary compensation. Irene Getz was typical: she raised turkeys and sold cream and butter in town to cover household expenses. When insects attacked the crops or drought occurred, profits from selling chickens, eggs, or butter contributed to the family economic base. These diversified enterprises also allowed women to control one portion of family income while reducing risk for the farm operation as a whole.[35]

Another form of diversification is in the off-farm jobs women take to supplement agricultural income. Wage labor has often meant the difference between staying in agriculture and losing the family farm. Lila Hill went to work in town when her family's dairy operation was threatened in the 1980s. She also contributed to diversification by giving piano lessons for many years. Rosalie Chacon's wage labor has been key to her family's stability throughout their lifetime.

Finally, according to the Floras, women's patterns of consumption affect the welfare of the agricultural enterprise. Because the nature of farming is land-extensive, it requires a relatively large investment to reach the volume of production necessary to support a family. Women's willingness to support investment in land and machinery before household improvement is an integral part of their commitment to agriculture. Sometimes that acceptance comes at the expense of their own sacrifice. The house will have to wait, as the Nebraska farm mother and daughter quoted earlier experienced. For Sylvia Ortega of Guadalupita, New Mexico, supporting her husband's decision to buy land rather than install running water in their farm home paid off in time. As she describes it now, "We were buying land and I still didn't have running water. He'd buy more land and I'd complain and get mad, then I'd give in. Which I'm glad I did because otherwise we wouldn't have the land we have. . . . We did get the water eventually." Clearly, her husband prevailed in the larger decision of land purchase. Ultimately, they installed indoor plumbing. Although Sylvia was initially resistant, she eventually acquiesced to the larger use of land as capital for investment.[36]

The lives of the women in this study mirror some of the findings of Rachel Ann Rosenfield's 1980 national study of farm women, published in 1985 in *Farm Women: Work, Farm, and Family in the United States*. This study, carried out through telephone interviews with 2,509 women and 569 men, has provided researchers with material that the federal census did not cover. In general, census data have centered on farms rather than farm families. The Bureau of Census did not ask the sex of the farm operator until 1978. In that year, 128,170 women listed themselves as farmers and farm managers, or 5.2 percent of all American farmers. In the West, 17,037, or 5.9 percent, of the area's farm operators were female. As part of the nationwide trend toward smaller farms, women tend to run even smaller farms than their male counterparts. They also earn less, are older, and are more likely to be full owners of the land they farm. While the majority of women farmers are in the South, western farm women have the largest average-size farm, perhaps due to the large number of commercial farms in the West.[37]

Rosenfeld's work also draws on statistics compiled by Judith Z. Kalbacher. Both studies show the number of women farmers and ranchers increasing between 1950 and 1980, from 3 percent of total operators to almost 10 percent. The largest increase occurred between 1970 and 1980 when the numbers nearly doubled, from 71,000 to over 137,000 female farmers and farm managers. Although not yet completely documented, it is possible that this period of high land prices, easier access to credit, and greater availability of federal programs encouraged women as well as men to expand their agricultural holdings.[38]

Gretchen Sammis exemplifies the modern woman farmer/rancher in the West. She is sole heir to the historic Chase Ranch near Cimarron in northeastern New Mexico. Her great-grandfather, Manley M. Chase, came to New Mexico in 1866. He built a notable reputation as a rancher, businessman, and local politician, while the Chase family women created orchards and poultry flocks. Manley's wife, Theresa, planted fruit trees that developed into one of the finest orchards in the Southwest. Daughter-in-law Nettie Chase built up a prosperous poultry business, while the cattle and sheep enterprise continued to thrive. In the next generation, Zeta Chase, Gretchen's grandmother, ran a dairy. Gretchen, born in 1925, was active in ranching activities at an early age and developed a close working relationship with her grandfather, Stanley Chase. When he died in 1964, she took over management of the family Hereford cattle ranch.[39]

At that time, Gretchen was teaching high school in nearby Cimarron, working on the ranch before and after school. Although her grandfather had relied on animal power, she quickly turned to mechanized equipment as a more efficient and timely way to carry out ranch work. In 1965, she took on a partner, Ruby Gobble, who shares the work and satisfaction of running the Chase Ranch. According to Gretchen, "We do it all. Right now, the ranch is a little over 11,000 acres and we still run straight Hereford cattle. We also farm a little bit, irrigate a little bit, raise alfalfa, oats for the cattle and raise oats for the turkeys—we have lots of wild turkeys. . . . I used to do all of the irrigating and most of the farming and Ruby is really good with heavy equipment . . . we still do all our own cattle work." Gretchen continued to teach and ranch until 1972, when she gave up teaching to give full attention to the ranch, but she "still misses the kids."[40]

Gretchen Sammis fits Kalbacher's profile, which shows that women who farm or ranch are older than their male counterparts. They also inherit a significantly greater proportion of their land than do men. Sammis's situation is unique in that she was much younger than the average heir at time of inheritance. Many women inherit their farm operations after a husband's death, and they usually are older than fifty-five; Gretchen was just thirty-nine when her grandfather died. In 1978, only 5.2 percent of farm operators nationally were female, with a median age of fifty-nine; the median age for men in this category was almost fifty. (Gretchen was then fifty-three.) In 1992, the average age of female operators dropped to 57.6. So, unlike most (older) women farmers or ranchers, Gretchen has been the operator, with Ruby's help, for more than thirty years.[41]

The Chase Ranch, like many other western outfits, has become more than a working ranch. Gretchen has allowed hunting on the ranch since the early 1970s. Deer and elk hunting "pays a lot of the bills. The way cattle prices are right now, we'd be in bad shape if it wasn't for hunting." For the Sammis operation, "It's a secondary income as far as this ranch is concerned, not primary yet but it's pretty close to being as good." Talli Manning of Big Piney, Wyoming, is equally supportive of this form of diversification because "with ranching, there's not a guaranteed income. You have to keep a good nest egg or you could end up out of business."[42]

Obtaining an outfitter's license gives the landowner the right to charge money to take people fishing, on pack trips, or hunting. Gretchen is enthusiastic about combining hunting and cattle ranching, finding them compatible activities. "We lease it to an outfitter and he worries about everything. If we wanted to worry about everything ourselves, we'd make more money but it wouldn't be worth the hassle." In Sammis's view, hunting benefits both humans and animals because "anything that grows has to be harvested. I don't care if it's animals or grass or people or anything. If it grows, it has to be harvested or it falls apart."[43]

Seventy miles south of Cimarron, in the small Mora County village of Rociada, lies the four-thousand-acre Gascon Ranch now owned and managed by Editha Bartley and her son John and his wife, Tamara. The Gascon Ranch is also a diversified operation that includes a sawmill; from the early 1940s until 1989, it also included a guest ranch. Editha's husband, Jim, built the sawmill in 1984; since his father's death in 1993, John has managed the sawmill and the cattle ranch. Adjacent to the Santa Fe National Forest, the ranch has served as a gateway into the wilderness for visitors for five decades. Originally owned by the Gascon family, it has served as a summer respite for midwestern and eastern doctors who came to New Mexico to visit patients they had referred to nearby Valmora Sanitarium early in the twentieth century. Dr. William T. Brown, Editha's grandfather, himself a tuberculosis patient, founded the sanitarium, twenty-five miles from Las Vegas, in 1904; it stayed in family hands until the Bartleys sold it in 1991. The Gascon Ranch, just over the ridge from Valmora, continues to be a working cattle ranch.[44]

Editha Bartley dreamed of becoming a veterinarian; her father, Carl H. Gallenthien, wanted her to become a physician like himself. Instead, Editha met and married Jim Bartley, an electrician, and moved to Las Vegas, New Mexico, although they spent the summer months at Gascon Ranch. After the birth of their three children in the 1950s, they bought the Gascon property and continued to run it as a guest ranch. New to this type of ranch management, they drew on the experiences of other westerners in the same business and quickly developed a loyal clientele, including groups of children who "needed to be in the wilderness for a while." All the Bartley children helped with the enterprise, and Editha "practiced a lot of medicine without a license, especially on animals." Inexperienced in the kitchen when first married, she soon learned to cook for large groups of twenty or more guests and developed into a gourmet cook.

For over twenty-five years, the guest ranch provided the family with extra income and at the same time allowed them to remain on the ranch. In Editha's words, "We make it with moonlighting, with the guest ranch and the sawmill." Although she had to close the facility in 1989 because of her father's illness, she hopes to reopen it as a bed-and-breakfast in the near future, continuing the pattern of diversification that has marked many western operations in the twentieth century.[45]

Clearly, life on a family farm in the 1990s is a challenge. It is apparent from the foregoing accounts that farm women do not make the choice to work off-farm in order to provide the family with luxury items. Instead, farmwives, and some husbands, work at wage labor to increase farm income because the costs associated with farming are so high. Post–World War II accounts demonstrate that farmwives in the 1950s were working to pay bills, clothe their children, buy farm supplies, and generally support their families in ways similar to farmwives four decades later. These farmwives take pride in and find satisfaction with wage work, which in turn brings them a measure of power within the patriarchal structure of agriculture. Similarly, those women who describe their farm work as "helping out" in times of need have made a commitment to agriculture as a way of life. They place great value on this lifestyle despite the hardships. Seventy-four-year-old Elizabeth Lloyd, now living with a daughter, made it clear: "Right now I'd rather be on the farm; that's all I knew." When asked if she had missed anything by living in a rural area, Martha Ascuena responded, "I don't think a thing, no, I think that my life has been just about as complete as anyone's could be." Editha Bartley put it this way: "Those of us that have that feel[ing], I don't think it will ever change. . . . I love being in the country. I love people and working with people, but I love the quiet and isolation. I love this kind of country." Although it may appear that the demise of family farms is at hand, farm and ranch women in New Mexico and Idaho reaffirm a commitment to a way of life that has long shaped our perception of the United States as an agrarian nation.[46]

Sandra Schackel is a professor in the Department of History at Boise State University. She is the author of *Social Housekeepers: Women Shaping Public Policy in New Mexico, 1920–1940* (1992).

NOTES

1. Joan Jensen, *With These Hands: Women Working on the Land* (Old Westbury, N.Y.: Feminist Press, 1981), xxiii.
2. Katherine Jellison, *Entitled to Power: Farm Women and Technology, 1913–1963* (Chapel Hill: University of North Carolina Press, 1993), xx.
3. Ibid., 151–52.
4. Elaine Tyler May, *Homeward Bound: American Families in the Cold War Era* (New York: Basic Books 1988), 165; Susan M. Hartmann, *The Home Front and Beyond: American Women in the 1940s* (Boston: Twayne, 1982), 8.
5. U.S. Bureau of the Census, *Statistical Abstract of the United States: 1957* (Washington, D.C.: Government Printing Office, 1957), 641.
6. Jellison, *Entitled to Power*, 150.
7. Interview with Martha Ascuena, Mountain Home, Idaho, 26 June 1995.
8. Cynthia Sturgis, "'How're You Gonna Keep 'Em Down on the Farm?': Rural Women and the Urban Model in Utah," *Agricultural History* 60 (spring 1986): 182–99.
9. Katherine Jellison, "Women and Technology on the Great Plains, 1910–1940," *Great Plains Quarterly* 8 (summer 1988): 145–57.
10. Mary Logan Rothschild and Pamela Claire Hronek, *Doing What the Day Brought:*

An Oral History of Arizona Women (Tucson: University of Arizona Press, 1992), 85–86.

11. Sandra Schackel, *Social Housekeepers: Women Shaping Public Policy in New Mexico, 1920–1940* (Albuquerque: University of New Mexico Press, 1992), 115; Jellison, *Entitled to Power,* 184.

12. Corlann G. Bush, "'The Barn Is His, the House Is Mine': Agricultural Technology and Sex Roles," in *Energy and Transport: Historical Perspectives on Policy Issues,* ed. George H. Daniels and Mark H. Rose (Beverly Hills, Calif.: Sage, 1982), 235–59.

13. Sue Armitage, "Farm Women and Technological Change in the Palouse, 1880–1980" (paper presented at the Fifth Berkshire Conference on the History of Women, Vassar College, Poughkeepsie, New York, 16–17 June 1981); Bush, "'The Barn Is His, the House Is Mine'," 235–59.

14. Quoted in Jellison, *Entitled to Power,* 164.

15. Ibid.

16. Sarah Elbert, "Women and Farming: Changing Structures, Changing Roles," in *Women and Farming: Changing Roles, Changing Structures,* ed. Wava G. Haney and Jane B. Knowles (Boulder, Colo.: Westview Press, 1988), 245–64; interview with Helen Tiegs, Nampa, Idaho, 29 June 1995.

17. Ascuena interview.

18. Interview with Lila Hill, Meridian, Idaho, 13 September 1995.

19. Ibid.

20. Rachel Ann Rosenfeld, *Farm Women: Work, Farm, and Family in the United States* (Chapel Hill: University of North Carolina Press, 1985), 12; U.S. Department of Commerce, *Census of Agriculture, 1987,* vol. 1, Geographic Area Series, part 51, United States Summary and State Data (Washington, D.C.: U.S. Department of Commerce, Bureau of the Census, 1989); Harold D. Guither and Harold G. Halcrow, eds., *The American Farm Crisis: An Annotated Bibliography with Analytical Introductions* (Ann Arbor, Mich.: Pierian Press, 1988), 2; Rosenfeld, *Farm Women,* 12–13.

21. *Lewiston Tribune,* 7 September 1981, 2B; interview with Elizabeth Lloyd, Ontario, Oregon, at the home of her daughter, Jeanette Moore, in Boise, Idaho, 18 September 1995.

22. Ascuena interview; Lloyd interview.

23. Jellison, *Entitled to Power,* 165–67.

24. *Idahonian,* 21 October 1976.

25. Interview with Linda Murgoitio, Meridian, Idaho, 20 September 1995.

26. Tiegs interview; Ascuena interview; Lloyd interview.

27. Interview with Rosalie Romero, Chacon, New Mexico, 3 October 1995.

28. Ibid.

29. Interview with Irene Getz, Monte Vista, Colorado, 28 September 1995.

30. William Eno DeBuys, *Enchantment and Exploitation: The Life and Hard Times of a New Mexico Mountain Range* (Albuquerque: University of New Mexico Press, 1985), 211; interview with Alice and Frank Trambley, Mora, New Mexico, 3 October 1995.

31. Trambley interview.

32. Trambley interview; DeBuys, *Enchantment and Exploitation,* 210–11.

33. Cornelia Butler Flora and Jan L. Flora, "Structure of Agriculture and Women's Culture in the Great Plains," *Great Plains Quarterly* 8 (fall 1988): 195–205.

34. Ibid., 197.

35. Madeline Buckendorf, "The Poultry Frontier: Family Farm Roles and Turkey Raising in Southwest Idaho, 1910–1940," *Idaho Yesterdays* 37 (summer 1993): 2–8; Jensen, *With These Hands;* Getz interview.

36. Flora and Flora, "Structure of Agriculture and Women's Culture in the Great Plains," 197–98; interview with Sylvia Ortega, Guadalupita, New Mexico, 4 October 1995.

37. Rosenfeld, *Farm Women*, 36; Judith Z. Kalbacher, "A Profile of Female Farmers in America," Development Division, Economic Research Service, *USDA Rural Development Research Report No. 45* (Washington, D.C.: Government Printing Office, 1985); the average size of a female-operated farm in the West is 701 acres; in the South, 226 acres. The national average for women is 285 acres; for men, 423 acres.

38. Kalbacher, "A Profile of Female Farmers," 2; Rosenfeld, *Farm Women*, 3.

39. Interview with Gretchen Sammis, Cimarron, New Mexico, 5 October 1995.

40. Interview with Gretchen Sammis, Cimarron, New Mexico, 25 October 1995.

41. Kalbacher, "Female Farmers," 7–9.

42. Ronnie Farley, ed., *Cowgirls: Contemporary Portraits of the American West* (New York: Crown, 1995), 26.

43. Sammis interview.

44. Interview with Editha Bartley, Rociada, New Mexico, 5 October 1995. For a fuller discussion of dude ranching in the West, see Robert G. Athearn, *The Mythic West in Twentieth-Century America* (Lawrence: University Press of Kansas, 1986).

45. Bartley interview.

46. Lloyd interview; Ascuena interview; Bartley interview.

FARM WIFE

GOLDIE KELTNER FORD (1890–1962)*

Carol Wolfe Konek

I.

Worry never changed the weather
or stopped the coming of children
and knowing this
never stopped me worrying.

Asa had an easy way with drought
with grasshopper clouds
with dust storms that took
the spring seed and good soil.
He was a man who'd laugh
every time I told him
my suspicion, taking no heed
of the time it took to recover
my strength or wean the baby
or whether the midwife was paid
for last time. "There's a lot of land.
We can always use more hands,"
he'd tease and turn away
reaching for the milk pail.

---

*This chapter was originally published as: Konek, Carol Wolfe. "Farm Wife: Goldie Keltner Ford (1890–1962)." In *Frontiers* 12 (no. 1, 1991): 126–40.

When they came
he took the little one
to the fields so early I came
to fear the neighbor's eyes.
Seeing the little girls
tilling the ground, scattering the seed
wearing sunbonnets and work gloves
trying to hide the secret of the sun
wanting so to be like town girls
I'd feel hope shrinking inside me
like a summer squash on a frozen vine.
I wondered if they were learning
to hate the farm, the land
the way he would bring home
hired hands to feed even when
there were no crops to bring in.
Saturdays when we would go to town
little boys on the seat of the wagon
big girls in back, they snuggled
down into their shame, sad litter
of stray kittens.

II.

Once, while washing the blood
from my hands in the cold well water
at the windmill pump, the chicken dancing
crazily away from its stone-still head
I turned to see Helen watching me
with a look I know only from the eyes
of women, my mama, grandma, my sisters
every one, as they leave one house
for another when the crops fail
when the foreclosure comes
when you know only the place
you leave but not the place you go.
She was closed and silent

as an abandoned house after that.
Wouldn't bow her head or fold her hands
for grace or so much as touch
the golden unhatched eggs I stewed
with dumplings in rich broth.
She started piecing a quilt
from scraps cut from flour sacks
working plain muslin into
intricate patterns with stitches
elegant as cobwebs captured
in sunlight. He scolded her
for the cost of kerosene
when he caught her sewing at night
couldn't grasp the need
for worthless work. He was
nettled by her solemn motion
as she did his extra chores
sending her to the henhouse
mornings before the hens
were even off their nests.

The ways of women angered him.
Sometimes I dreamed I took revenge
by birthing only daughters.

III.

Fern was born for work
for waking with the dawn.
Whether she was sowing wheat
or bailing hay or herding cows
she set her will against the heat
or dark or wind or cold
and did her best to be as
brittle as a man. Still
there were things she never
understood, how the ewe

sometimes abandons her lamb
smelling death in the cord
she chews apart. She brought
such a tiny thing into the house
one bitter morning early in March
its new woolen coat glazed
with sleet. I see her the way
she was with her head bowed
warming it with a worn flannel gown
humming a lullaby under her breath.
We took turns holding its wobbly head
forcing the nipple of the nursing bottle
between jaws stubborn for a mother's touch.
Fuel was scarce on that godforsaken plain
but I sat up with her till her papa
had gone to bed, then built a fire
as though for cooking breakfast
and coaxed her on to bed.
I had scarcely closed my eyes
when her scream split the night.
Her papa was by her side
when I reached the door
to see her crying herself
beyond his anger and my sorrow
for the poor frozen life
gone out with the fire
that died before the first light
as the wind turned to the north.
From that time on, I knew
the way Fern worked had to do
with the other children
with the little ones born
and yet to be born, and with
trouble yet to come. It was
her way of earning them
a mother's comfort and
the warmth of a fire
always gleaming till morning.

IV.

Esther was a timid one
who watched and listened
and took things in. She was
given to following her sisters
down narrow furrows, often
distracted from her task
by the sight of any scampering thing
or sudden treasure. She gathered
weed flowers and found bright stones
where others would have seen only
a fallow field against relentless sun.
She was given to finding secret places
and making ceremonies of the usual.
Neither she nor her sisters
would have had a play-doll
had she not fashioned a family
from corn husks she dried
on the back porch. She made
fancy clothes from scraps
of this and that, painted faces
with magic potions of weed juice
and whispered them full of stories
she gathered listening through walls
when mama and my sisters came
to make ready for birthing or
for grieving. I worried that
she grew wise beyond her years
hanging on our every word
and hearing what was never said.
I never told my girls when I was
that way. I always sent them
to Nellie's or Sylvie's or Pearl's
when I suspected my time was come.
Each time their papa fetched them
home to see what we had found
they dressed themselves in

the worn-out clothes of our surprise
as though to please us playing
a grown-up game of make-believe.
I came to wonder if Esther
was shamed by the way I grew
heavier and slower with
each passing season. I sometimes
saw her eyes tracing the curve
of my apron as though she would
iron it flat. Now she says
she grieves for children she never had.
There is a clothes basket of store-bought toys
for family children in the corner
of her neat and barren room. One toy
is a wind-up lady doll dancing with
a man who whispers in her ear as they
twirl to music only Esther hears.

V.

Asa was a man who'd wait
his time and have his way.
He'd dream next spring's harvest
while harsh torrents beat down
clay-baked fields, washing seed
into tiny rivers bound for
gullies beyond our section fence.
He had that kind of stubborn hope
for sons he needed to work
those homestead fields.
Wesley was his wish come true
so like him, defiant in a contest
of any kind, with a stubborn colt
an ornery boy, or bad weather
and hard times. His papa had him
on a horse before he could walk
smiling and gulping dust

as though he couldn't wait
to be a man. There never was
a colt he couldn't break
a machine he couldn't tame
a girl he couldn't court
with just a smile. He was
blessed with a certain ease
that shone on everyone around.
No one told me, and I didn't
think to ask, about the races
at the county fairgrounds.
Then, Fern was unexpected
in the doorway, looking away
telling in a distant voice
of his racing car sideswiped
shattering the grandstand fence
his smile, splintered
his body, broken like stubble
in a hail-punished field.

His hope seemed to have died
for the longest bitter time.
Then, just when I knew
he would never find what
was still whole in himself
his spirit rose again
into those wise, dark eyes
sudden as the scent of April
on Indian summer air.

VI.

The winter of the blizzard
brought days and days without
a glimmer of sun shining through
snowflake lace curtains swirling
closer and closer to the house

and nights upon nights heaping
blankets of new snow on the deep
down comfort of the yard.
We had long since lost sight
of the barn, the hitching post
the railing of the back porch.
We clung silently to the stove's
sparse heat, listening for the sound
of snow stopping. What we heard
shrill as a coyote's wail
was the fierce rising of the wind
as it drove sleet nails into
the walls of the heaving house.
Asa finally had to say, "I reckon
I'll venture out and chip the ice
in the horse tanks beyond the barn."
Turning his back on our fear
he tied a rope around himself
anchoring one end to the door knob
and set out, vanishing in an instant
into thick doom. Who wants to hear
a woman's waiting talk? I remember
the eyes of the children following me
from cupboard to stove and back again
blinking only with the evening
chiming of the clock. Earl would test
the tension of the rope from time
to time. By and by, his eyes slid
past us to his wool cap on the rack.
"Think I'll just give Papa a hand."
We knew without his saying so
the rope had gone limp, knew
with cold certainty Papa was lost
in the wilderness between the house
and barn. Snow-filled darkness
is not night. It glows so your eyes
make ghosts where they remember shadows.
A waiting house will heave and sigh

against the wind as though giving up
the spirit. Then, there they were
ice statues set aglow by the kitchen lamp
Papa leaning into Earl as though
he were the boy and Earl the man.
After three days and nights we would know
how they chose their own lives
leaving the animals to yield their bones
to the cruel spring thaw.

VII.

The boys dared Joy to climb the windmill
when she was no bigger than a minute.
If I so much as turned my back, they
taunted her to ride the skittish mare.
She went careening through the gate
hanging onto the mane, hair flying
eyes serene on a horizon beyond her years.
No matter what she did, she had no fear
as though born to do what she was doing.
She was born knowing how to stare down trouble.
The boys tell, now that she is grown
how once, playing mumbly-peg, the knife
flew off course, striking her in the leg
how Wesley's hand froze in the air
as he took in the terror of his target
and her steady motion, jerking out
the knife, stopping the blood with a kerchief
taking her turn in the game, winning
hiding the scar, never tattling
knowing the secret law of brothers
without being told. I remember
how she took the change in Papa
when Helen had her terrible trouble.
We kept Helen home, hiding our disgrace
hoping for the redemption of a wedding.

Asa decided then and there to tame Joy
to teach her caution. He was after her
whatever she did, to be ladylike
not to go tagging after her brothers
wherever they went, to come in from
the fields before sundown, to walk
and not to ride to school. One thing
after another. She never let on
she noticed any change in him.
He never got a rise from her
no matter what he said or did.
Later, he came to fear her like a wildfire
saying the awfulest things about her
carrying on with the hotel man, divorced
too old for her. Repeating what the townfolks said
as though she were no longer one of our own.

All the time she knew she would
break away in her own good time
setting her own terms for the life
she meant to live. There is no
changing a person who knows better
than anyone who she plans to be.

VIII.

Ray was the orneriest one. He was
a coltish kind of boy with a ready smile
and an urge to tease big sisters
chickens in the yard, plow horse
he wanted to do rodeo tricks. I recall
him leading the others through a maze
he stamped down in a field of near-ripe wheat
making a harmless game. They didn't
ruin more than half a bushel, but
Papa carried on as though Ray
were himself a hailstorm taking

a season's crop. I have to say
no matter what he did to gain
displeasure, he'd work himself even
if given half a chance. He had
the longest arms, could reach
across three hired hands and two brothers
for a plate of hot biscuits. How he loved
gravy and fired pork chops for breakfast.
He'd leave the table already hungry
for noon, forgetting to back out
the door, extra chops sticking
from his hip pocket, innocence
written all over his face. More than once
I found wildflowers inside the churn
or an orphan rabbit in my sewing basket
but he never owned his part in a prank
or gift. When Earl was stricken
he hid it from us as long as he could
the hair covering his pillow
every morning as he woke
slick skin patches on his head
growing while he slept. Poor boy.
Every hair on his body gone and him
a mere sixteen. He was crippled
with shyness after that, but never free
of his talking, teasing brother
so hungry for life, or of Joy
who'd look him in the eye and flirt
telling him she had no beau and
he must take her to the prom to
save her from being a wallflower.

IX.

Mama said till the day she died
it was the evil eye happened to Elvis
poor little strange one that

you didn't know what was wrong
and there was no one to tell you
and never knowing who or how to ask
if it was your fault for
something you'd done or
hadn't done. Asa would look
into his slanted eyes, then
look away, thinking, I thought
how it would be if he were
the runt of a litter.
He was the only one
I bought a toy at the
Elsie Chapel Christmas
Bazaar. I told Elvis
the other children might laugh
at his raggedy clown wearing
its gingham patchwork suit.
And they did, but still
he had the belonging of
riding to the one-room school
in the circle of Joy's arms
with the other boys walking
along beside the old plow horse
with its tiny load. The teacher
was a mere youngster herself
teaching all the grades.
I've no doubt her hands were full
what with some of the rowdy boys.
She called him special
the day she came to say
Elvis couldn't learn and
was turned out of school.
After that, he followed me
from room to room in the house
and from chore to chore in the yard.
He was with me always, so
there was nowhere to take
what I held inside. Now

I know there are others
as though he belongs
to a huge family 'way
beyond the county, and that
I should have told the others
how it was with him. But
this is now, and that was then.
In those days, to speak of such
a burden would have been to complain
of the rain, bringing a never-ending
drought upon the land. I kept
my silence.

X.

Glen was born with questions flowing
in his veins. It was his nature to wonder
what if . . . Asa was determined row crops
would grow in the sand hills south
of the wheat sections. No matter
how often his brothers Harry and Fred
said those hills would never yield
Asa would take the children there
come planting time and try against
all natural odds to bring one crop
and then another to harvest. He would
put a child on a plow horse, warning
him never to stay on a skittish horse
but, then, a boy like Glen couldn't know
the meaning of a runaway horse any more
than he could know the nature of wind.
I can see him in my mind's eye
suffering the monotony of slow circles
the hot sun shining down on his back
making him itch for excitement.
Although he wouldn't mean to tease
the horse, he might have been

distracted by a devil's tail
his discontent the prod.
Fern said the horse and plow and all
went careening crazy through the field
leaving a dust storm in their wake.
His yell, as he somersaulted through
the air, silenced as he landed in a heap.
The girls cried him back to life.
When he came to, he felt himself
between him and sudden death.
I never found the words to tell the girls
I'd come to live with them, leaving Elvis
home to tend the farm with his Papa
or dressing him up and bringing him along.
I worried I might not seem proper
since my ways were so much the ways
farm women have, now the girls
all lived their well-to-do lives
in the same house in different towns.
I knew myself to be heavy and plain
and slow with words, and never
even having a proper dress to wear
to their fancy church weddings.
I knew the startled looking away
of their town children on seeing
the sunken place in my cotton dress
my work-rough hands, my country shoes.
It was as though I never chose to stay
with Asa, but just that no day seemed
long enough to bring the words for going.
The sun came up and went down.
The ground froze and thawed.
Before you knew it, planting time
gave way to harvest, and there were
hands to feed, and hens to set
and eggs to gather, and baking
and mending to be done, and Elvis
and Asa in from the field hungry

for warm bread and smooth churned butter.
Maybe life is no more than a string of days
and maybe one shouldn't complain
living to see most of your children live
and more crops yield than die. At night
I sit on the porch alone and feel the stars
move down to make a canopy over me
and know I am giving myself over
to a certain kind of comfort.
This is the time and place
I can rest a bit.

Carol Wolfe Konek is an assistant professor of women's studies at Witchita State University in Kansas. She is the author of *Daddyboy: A Memoir* (1991) and the co-editor with Dorothy Walters of *I Hear My Sisters Saying: Poems by Twentieth-Century Women* (1976).

Part 4: Uncovering Women's Voices

INTRODUCTION

Uncovering Women's Voices

Since the 1970s, using oral histories to write women's history has become a standard methodology. A not uncontroversial method, the turn toward writing history "plumbed from memory," has, nevertheless, become an important tool in uncovering the voices of women, and other groups, previously silenced or ignored.[1] Based on the premise that people at the low end of the social and economic scale rarely leave records of their own stories, historians have come to value the use of oral testimony to write "grassroots history" or "history from the bottom up." Thus, the popularity today of books with "memory" in their titles. As Devra Weber has noted, however, memories can be problematic. "They can be inaccurate, contradictory, altered with the passage of time and the effects of alienation . . ." for "[m]emory is a fragile construct." The reliability of memory work then requires the researcher/writer to critically examine the value and use of oral history as a guide to the historical past.[2]

Using oral histories, moreover, requires more of the interviewer than asking questions and listening to the answers; it also requires the interviewer to listen for meaning rather than just facts, and to interpret and contextualize the many meanings that are present in tone of voice and gestures. Nor does the work end with the interview but subsequently must be read through the filter of memory and the mediation of the interviewer. Despite the cautionary reminders, those who work in the field maintain that oral narratives are one of the most valuable sources in the historian's quest "to tell what actually happened."[3]

The use of interviews has become so essential to the process of writing women's history that some scholars have labeled it a "particularly feminist methodology," says Emily Honig, author of the first piece in this section.[4] Citing Susan Geiger, "What's So Feminist about Doing Women's Oral History?" Honig agrees that the use of oral interviews itself is not sufficient to label the method feminist. Oral history only becomes a method when it is put to use, that is, when it goes beyond the pleasure of hearing and learning the history being told. And it only becomes "a feminist methodology if its use is systematized in particular feminist ways and if the objectives for collecting the oral data are feminist."[5] Further, oral history should not be considered a narrative truth but one of many possible versions of an individual's past that, in turn, requires explanation.

In 1972, garment workers at the Farah Manufacturing Company in El Paso, Texas, went on strike demanding union representation. In 1977 and again in 1978, Emily Honig and two colleagues interviewed the mostly Chicana workers who struck Farah for two years then published their results in "Women at Farah: An Unfinished Story" in 1979.[6] More recently, Honig reexamined the narratives and discovered, in addition to the story of the strike, the various ways in which the women viewed and gave voice to their personal pasts. Hence, the reminder that oral history "is less about history and experience than about their retelling."[7]

For racial ethnic people whose voices are rarely heard in historical contexts, oral sources are a necessity as, for example, in studying working-class women of color. When Delores Delgado Bernal examined the 1968 East Los Angeles Blowouts through the prism of gender, she discovered that the voices of the young Chicanas involved provided an alternative history of the event. Her interviews with eight grassroots activists rebuke the popular stereotypes of Mexican women as docile, passive, and apathetic. Instead, the oral histories revealed female leadership roles that had gone unrecognized and unappreciated.

In what might be one of the most challenging topics in writing women's history, Debra A. Castillo, María Gudelia Rangel Gómez, and Bonnie Delgado initiated a study of prostitution in Tijuana, Mexico, in 1988. Through interviews with 184 sex workers, and later through in-depth interviews of thirty prostitutes in their workplaces, the sociologists explored "the cultural construction of gender and sexuality—both its dominant stereotypes and its unruly margins . . .."[8] Complicated by the duality of two sets of dominant cultural stereotypes that share underlying assumptions about sex workers, the study shows the many ambiguous and unambiguous ways in which the women tell their stories. The authors cite the advice of Wendy Chapkis in *Live Sex Acts* to listen for meaning rather than just 'fact,' to consider how the speaker shapes the tale, how the audience hears it, and to consider what is at stake politically, personally, and strategically.[9] All three of these essays remind us of other ways to tell women's stories, to move beyond the celebrations of women's lives to a more nuanced understanding of the complexities of women's lives that feminist oral history methodology can provide.

NOTES

1. See the introduction to Sherna Berger Gluck and Daphne Patai, eds., *Women's Words: The Feminist Practice of Oral History* (London: Routledge, 1991).
2. See Brewster L. Chamberlin, *A Review Essay*, "Doing Memory: Remembrance Reified and Other Shoah Business," in *The Public Historian* 23 (summer 2001): 73–82; and Devra Weber, "Raiz Fuerte: Oral History and Mexican Farmworkers," *Oral History Review* 17 (fall 1989): 61.
3. Vicki L. Ruiz and Ellen Carol DuBois, eds., *Unequal Sisters: A Multicultural Reader in U.S. Women's History* 2d. ed. (New York: Routledge, 1994), xv–xvi; and Chamberlin, "Doing Memory," 77.
4. See Susan Geiger, "What's So Feminist About Doing Women's Oral History?" in *Expanding the Boundaries of Women's History*, eds. Cheryl Johnson-Odim and Margaret Strobel (Bloomington: Indiana University Press, 1992), 305–18; and Sherna Gluck, "What's So Special About Women? Women's Oral History," *Frontiers* 2, no. 2 (1979): 3–11.
5. Geiger, "What's So Feminist About Doing Women's Oral History?" 306.
6. Emily Honig, "Women at Farah: An Unfinished Story," *Aztlán* (summer 1979).
7. Emily Honig, "Striking Lives: Oral History and the Politics of Memory," *Journal of Women's History* 9 (spring 1997): 139–57.
8. Debra A. Castillo, María Gudelia Rangel Gómez, and Bonnie Delgado, "Border Lives: Prostitute Women in Tijuana," *Signs: Journal of Women in Culture and Society* 24 (winter 1999): 387–422.
9. Wendy Chapkis, *Live Sex Acts: Women Performing Erotic Labor* (New York: Routledge, 1997), 212.

STRIKING LIVES

ORAL HISTORY AND THE POLITICS OF MEMORY*

Emily Honig

As some of the only means of retrieving the historical experience of non-elite people whose lives are not recorded in historical documents, oral history has played a crucial role in the writing of women's history. Beginning in the early 1970s, the well-known oral historians Sherna Gluck and Daphne Patai observe, the desire to recover a previously ignored women's history "generated an enormous volume of women's oral history, making available in accessible forms the words of women who had previously been silenced or ignored."[1] Oral history, as two other practitioners note, offered a means of retrieving women's voices, allowing "women to speak for themselves, to describe their situation, define their identity, and interpret the meaning of their own lives."[2] Books composed of edited, but uninterpreted, texts of women's oral histories began to appear, the mere recovery and presentation of women's stories considered an essential ingredient of the "new women's history."[3]

Subsequent scholars began to integrate oral history interviews with other historical documents to construct social histories, such as those of cotton mill workers in the U.S. South, Chicana workers in the 1930s, Japanese-American women during World War II, women factory workers in early twentieth-century China, and prostitutes in Kenya during

---

*This chapter was originally published as: Honig, Emily. "Striking Lives: Oral History and the Politics of Memory." In *Journal of Women's History* 9 (spring 1997): 140–57.

World War II.[4] Such histories are inconceivable (or certainly would not boast such rich detail, nuance, and complexity) without the possibility of recording these women's life histories. So integral was oral history to the writing of women's history that some scholars labeled it a particularly feminist methodology.[5]

As oral history has become increasingly central to the writing of women's history, it has also attracted more critical scrutiny. "When examined through the lens of the expanding feminist scholarship of later years," Gluck and Patai acknowledge, "Women's oral history revealed itself to be more problematic than we had imagined."[6] Instead of treating a recorded life history as a straightforward representation of experience, feminist scholars began to problematize power relationships between the historian and interviewee, to see the narration of life history as performance, and to recognize the importance of speech patterns.[7] The role of memory has also come into question. "Oral narratives reflect peoples' memory of the past," Devra Weber points out in her study of Mexicana farmworkers involved in a 1933 cotton strike in California's San Joaquin Valley. "They can be inaccurate, contradictory, altered with the passage of time and the effects of alienation." They may therefore be more indicative of women's consciousness than actual experience, Weber suggests.[8] An even more critical reading of memory in oral history is presented in Luisa Passerini's study of workers in early twentieth-century Italy. In *Fascism in Popular Memory*, she argues for treating oral history interviews not necessarily as reflections of an individual's personal experience, but rather as records of a cultural form, reflections of collective memory and storytelling.[9]

One aspect of oral history has been overlooked in these critical scrutinies, and that concerns the way in which any particular rendition of a life history is a product of the personal present.[10] It is well-recognized that chronicles of the past are invariably a product of the present, so that different "presents" inspire different versions of the past.[11] Just as all historical accounts—the very questions posed or the interpretive framework imposed—are informed by the historian's present, so, too, is a life history structured by both the interviewer's and the narrator's present. As Erik Erikson, reflecting on his effort to write Gandhi's biography, observed, "At best, memories connect meaningfully what happened once and what is happening now."[12] This means that oral history cannot be treated as a source of some narrative truth, but rather as one of many possible versions of an individual's past. It also means that the stories told in an oral history are not simply the source of explanation, but rather *require* explanation.[13]

This essay explores how the narrator's present informs the telling of a life history by focusing on a series of oral histories that two colleagues and I gathered from Chicana garment workers who from 1972 to 1974 were involved in a strike at the Farah Manufacturing Company in El Paso, Texas.[14] The strike involved some four thousand workers, the overwhelming majority of whom were Chicana women. When they walked out on strike, demanding to be represented by the Amalgamated Clothing Workers' Union, they were confronting the city's largest industrial employer and pitting themselves against El Paso's famously anti-union local patriarch. (Willie Farah's family had been operating pants-manufacturing plants in El Paso since 1920.) The two-year strike divided the city politically, destroyed longstanding friendships, and created near-warfare in many households. A union-organized boycott of Farah pants transformed the strike from a local dispute to a national campaign that was critical to the workers' eventual success in winning union recognition.

Concerned that women's experience of this strike was absent from almost all journalistic accounts, we went to El Paso in 1977 to conduct oral histories of some of the strikers. Our initial intent was to record and document women's strike experience, to find out how it had affected their relationships with family and community, and to explore its impact on their political consciousness. We returned in 1978 to focus more extensively on their family histories and their own experiences growing up along the U.S.-Mexico border. The oral histories, we presumed at the time, recorded women's actual memories, experiences, and beliefs.

Yet a critical reading of those narratives reveals the ways in which they are the product of a particular historical moment. In 1977 and 1978, when we conducted the interviews, the aftermath of the strike and the union cause was at the center of women's lives. The two years on strike had jolted their daily routines, social relationships, and self-perceptions. The initial decision to strike had involved taking a public stand in opposition to the factory management, immediate supervisors, as well as friends, relatives, and co-workers who sympathized with the company. Days spent walking picket lines, in front of the factories that produced and the stores that sold Farah pants, exposed women to both community hostility and sympathy. Many went door-to-door, trying to win neighborhood support. Others visited local grocery stores, hoping to collect food donations for striking workers.

For many women the strike provided a unique sense of community, one that transcended the kinds of informal networks that had always existed at work. They often gathered at each others' homes to prepare picket signs; some spent time in the local jail together (having been arrested for "illegal picketing"); many met at the union office to help sort clothes and food that had been donated to the strikers. As Sabina H. put it,

> When we were on strike we learned to make friends, to sit together; we started to talk about our problems: "Ay, my husband here"; "Let's look at my son. . . ." We began to share our problems, our experiences. We started to treat each other like human beings. During the two years that we were on strike it was pure talking, to communicate with each other, to chat with each other about what was happening to one another. We were more animated, like brothers and sisters, like human beings, like children of God.

For some, the sense of community extended beyond Farah strikers to workers throughout El Paso. Many became interested in other strikes taking place in the city, and some went to help out on picket lines at striking plants such as the ASARCO steel mill. For a few women the strike provided an occasion to travel beyond El Paso, to speak at rallies of workers in places ranging from nearby Albuquerque to faraway Chicago and New York.

Finally, for a number of women the strike provided opportunities to study that were not ordinarily available: some attended union-sponsored classes on labor history and union benefits; others became involved in study groups sponsored by the rank-and-file group *Unidad Para Siempre* or by political organizations such as the Revolutionary Communist Party. Many learned about, and some became involved in, organizations such as the Texas Farmworkers' Union and *Chicanos Unidos*.

The successful end of the strike in 1974, for many women, marked the beginning of even more intense involvement in the union cause.

Most of the women we interviewed became shop stewards and spent many of their after-work hours making house calls to solicit workers' grievances, filing those grievances at the union office, attending union meetings, and battling to make the union officials more responsive to workers' needs. Some became even more involved in the rank-and-file group. Their lives, at the time we conducted the oral histories in 1977 and 1978, were devoted to and consumed by the union movement.

Most of the women unequivocally believed that the strike and union experience had transformed their lives, as well it had. But what I want to explore in this essay is a far less visible effect of the strike, which is how it may have affected the ways in which they conceptualized their personal pasts. ("May have," because there are not previous personal accounts with which to compare those they related immediately after the strike.) The point is not to argue that women's personal histories should be treated with suspicion, but rather to stress the ways in which any oral history must be read with an eye to how the personal and historical moment in which it is told invariably shapes its content.

Strike-Speak

There are several obvious ways in which the relationship between the narrative present and chronicled past is evident in the oral histories of Farah strikers. It is hardly surprising, for example, that women who became union activists proudly recounted instances of working-class heroism in their families' pasts. Lilian S., for example, described her stepfather's experience as a union member and striker in the mines of northern Mexico. "He was one of the fighters over there in the mines," she recalled.[15] Juana T., too, clearly saw a direct connection between her father's politics and her union activism. Born in Guanajuato in the late 1880s, he went to work in the mines of New Mexico as a young adult. She was not certain he had ever been involved in labor organizing, "but knowing him, he probably was," she declared. "He was the kind of man that was always speaking for himself and defending himself. He always knew what was going on and what everybody should get." Finally, Sabina H. proudly recounted her father's battles against injustice. As a union leader at the mines where he worked in northern Mexico, he demanded that the company provide, among other things, a school for workers' children. "I heard my father talk about this a lot," Sabina recalled. "'We are making the company rich, so it's only fair that they give us a portion of their wealth for our children!'" She also honored his efforts on behalf of the Indians who lived in the mountains: sympathetic to their poverty, he initially taught them to read and write. Later, when sawmills began logging pine trees on Indian lands, Sabina's father organized them to go to Mexico City and protest.

These stories of union activist fathers could be cited to make a variety of points. One could use them, for example, to argue that some history of labor activism can be identified in most women's families (even if Farah represented the first time that women family members were the ones striking), or that a memory of their father's union struggles provided them a historical context for their own battle. The fact that their "heroes" were all men/fathers might be scrutinized as well. One could also focus on the language of social justice invoked to frame their fathers' experiences as antecedents of their own. Most significant here, though, is the connection between the historical moment when women related their oral histories and the family anecdotes they chose to include. These stories may have seemed particularly salient precisely because the women themselves were passionately engaged in a struggle to build a union. The strike, in other words, may have provided an opportunity for women to celebrate parts of their past that had previously seemed insignificant. In some cases, it may even have provided an occasion for women to learn about parts of their family history that had been previously invisible.

A second obvious way in which women's union activist present may have affected their narration of the past concerns their accounts of work life at Farah before the strike. These accounts are very much shaped by the union's analysis of exploitative conditions that required worker organizing to demand union representation. Women's stories both declared and documented an experience of oppression. "What I do remember [from before the strike]," Lilian S. offered, "is that I didn't like the injustice that was going there." She, along with other women, complained about the relentless pressure to meet high production quotas, the lack of breaks (even to go to the bathroom), the preferential treatment granted workers who were pretty and willing to date supervisors, the belittling requirement of a doctor's note for any work days missed for sickness, the incompetence of the nurses at the factory clinic, and the required savings plan that benefited the company more than the workers. Most women deplored the lack of maternity leave, sick leave, seniority, and a pension plan. "When I was pregnant with my youngest," a typical account of pre-strike work life begins,

> I was working there and my husband was also working there. But what he was making wasn't enough. I worked up to the eighth month. And let me tell you, it was pretty bad because they take no consideration; even if you're pregnant you still have to do the same thing, the same quota. They don't even take you down [from the machine] to rest your legs. If you're standing up you have to stand all day. Then after the baby is born you just take a month off, and that's it. You have to go back to work. If you didn't go back to work exactly a month after, you would just lose your whole seniority. That was another reason we decided we needed a union and we should organize.

The point here is not to deny the veracity of these accounts, for they undoubtedly describe actual conditions at Farah. And a historian certainly could draw on them to document the work experience of Chicanas in the Southwest. But it is important to contextualize these accounts, to recognize them as part of a union discourse about Farah. This discourse was particularly ingrained in women who not only participated in the strike but who then became shop stewards devoted to enjoining their co-workers to become union members. Their accounts of pre-strike work life at Farah, then, must be understood as a product of the immediate post-strike years, with the recognition that somewhat different aspects of pre-strike work life might be recalled or emphasized at other moments.

For some women, there is one final connection between the narrative present and chronicled past, and that concerns their accounts of growing up in the barrios of El Paso. The oldest and best-known barrio, El Segundo (also called "the south side," "the Second Ward," or simply "the barrio"), was the shared childhood home of a large number of women. Crowded between the banks of the Rio Grande and El Paso's encroaching downtown, it had long been the community where people who have just crossed the river find residence. Many of the strikers' parents settled there when they first entered the United States from Mexico. By the time they married, though, most of the strikers had moved to the sprawling neighborhoods of one-story houses on El Paso's east side.

When, in the oral histories, women recalled their experiences growing up in El Segundo, they described the impoverished physical circumstances of daily life: the extremely crowded tenement buildings as well as the lack of indoor bathrooms, hot water, washing machines, telephones, and televisions. Neighborhood gangs posed a constant threat to their physical safety. Some women, such as Juana T., recounted an almost desperate yearning to move away from El Segundo. "We were always talking about getting away from there," she recalled, "because we wanted to better ourselves."

Yet what stands out in a number of women's accounts of El Segundo is the emphasis on the feeling of community that bonded barrio residents. "You would live there for years and years and it would become like one big family," Lina L. explained.

> Everyone would help each other. It was a lot of fun, too, because like for Christmas or New Year's Eve, they would all get together, pitch in, and buy beer. They'd make cakes and *bunuelos*, tamales, and get big tubs of peanuts. The whole block would celebrate. It was real nice. Some of the people say that maybe at that time we didn't live as comfortably as we do now. But they still miss a lot of things from those days. Up to now they say, "There's nothing like the Second Ward."

"It was a lot of fun!" another striker, Lucy C., exclaimed when asked about her memories of El Segundo. "We were all Mexicans. We would go to La Frontera, the swimming pool, and we would play on the streets. It was real nice." She empathized with barrio residents who, in the mid-1970s, mobilized to save their neighborhood from urban renewal and staged repeated protests against the bulldozing of barrio buildings. "They don't want to move," she explained, recalling her own sadness when her family moved from El Segundo. "You live real comfortably there. You get along with everybody."

On the one hand, these stories of El Segundo could be drawn on to illustrate the dual nature of barrio life—the impoverished physical environment and the concomitant sense of community shared by its residents. On the other hand, however, the emphasis on—if not nostalgia for—the barrio community might also be understood as a product of the post-strike "narrative moment." A sense of community or extended family, as noted above, was one of the most profound aspects of women's experience with the strike and union-building years. In this context, it is not surprising that memories of El Segundo would be formulated around a story of community. This is not to deny or diminish the family-like atmosphere of the barrio, but rather to highlight the ways in which sentiments powerfully felt by women at the time the oral histories were conducted may be grafted onto those histories.

One other factor may have affected women's stories of El Segundo: At the time the oral histories were conducted in 1977–78, a campaign was being waged to save El Segundo from developers who saw the barrio as the most likely location for a modern commercial district between Juarez and El Paso. An organization, *La Campaña por el Preservacion del Barrio*, was formed to oppose developers; at one point, when developers actually began razing barrio tenements, residents quickly erected tent cities on the lots where their houses had been destroyed, declaring the integrity of the barrio community and demanding preservation. Meanwhile, walls of remaining tenements were plastered with petitions, announcements of meetings, and slogans such as *"El Segundo Barrio No Morirá"* ("the Second Ward will not die!"). Many of the Farah strikers paid close attention to this struggle, perceiving it as a continuation of the broader battle for social justice in which they, as strikers and union-activists, were engaged. This, too, may have affected the way they framed their memories of El Segundo as they joined barrio activists and adopted their language in emphasizing the value of the El Segundo community.

The stories of El Segundo, recollections of pre-strike work life at Farah, as well as the incidents of working-class heroism in women's family histories illustrate some of the obvious and direct ways in which the substance of the Farah strikers' oral histories is shaped by the moment those histories were recorded. This relationship between the narrative present and chronicled past, however, is not always so linear or predictable, but instead is often replete with contradictions and complexities. Some of these more complicated relationships are evident in women's accounts of their personal experiences as children and young adults. These accounts, punctuated with stories of nonconformity, independence, and rebellion, may in some ways seem as directly and obviously connected to women's union activist narrative present as the stories cited above. The less linear connections, as will be discussed below, become apparent when one recognizes that they are narrated in a context of declaring profound personal changes caused by the strike.

"This Is How Far I've Come"

If there is a commonality to the oral histories of Farah strikers, it is a description of the strike as *the* pivotal event of their lives, one that radically altered their personal identities and relationships as well as their social and political worlds. The act of walking out itself marked this transformation for some. Virgie Delgado, for instance, recalls literally shaking with fear as she contemplated leaving the Farah plant, and then, once she began walking toward the exit, gaining so much courage that she instructed a supervisor to "get out of the way." "Then we saw all the other people outside," she explained, "and we were really happy. We started hugging each other and singing even though we didn't know each other. It was really something."[16]

The transformation from shy, fearful worker to bold, courageous striker was magnified by the two years on strike. Most of the women saw the strike as transforming them from being quiet to outspoken, passive to assertive, dependent to independent. "When we went out on strike we started to be independent, knowing what we wanted for ourselves," Lillian S. explained. "I believe the strike changed me," Chayo P. concurred, emphasizing the ways in which the strike made her more outspoken, outgoing, and involved in community affairs.

> I didn't used to speak up for what I believed. I wouldn't have talked to you if I hadn't changed. I used to be the type that would rather be on the side and not be hurt. The strike changed me completely. I started volunteering for this and for that. . . . Before I wasn't the outgoing type. I would come from work, stay at home, and that's it. I wouldn't bother to associate with other people.

Other strikers, too, highlighted the ways in which the strike made them more aware of and outspoken about their rights, stressing that they "never used to talk to people about their beliefs," or to "fight for what is ours." For some, this translated into political conversion, as suggested by a woman who attributed to the strike her becoming "a revolutionary for *la causa.*"

A number of women experienced the strike as integrating political and personal change. Isela A., for instance, describes how the strike increased her sense of authority vis-à-vis both supervisors at work and her husband at home. "I was a very insecure person, way back then," she explained.

> I felt that I was inferior to my supervisors, who were at the time only Anglo. None of this affects me any more. I have learned that I am an equal and have all the rights they have. [The strike's] changed a lot for me. It made me into a better person. . . . I can stand up and speak if I have to speak. If I have something to say I'm going to say it. This is how far I've come from way back then.

The strike not only changed her attitude toward supervisors at work, but toward her husband as well. Before the strike, she observed, she did nothing without her husband's permission.

> I've been married nineteen years, and I was always, "Hey, can I, or should I. . . ." I see myself now and I think, "Good grief, having to ask to buy a pair of underwear." Of course, I don't do this anymore. The strike is when it started changing—all of it. I was able to begin to stand up for myself.

Women who described themselves as once shy, demure, or subordinate to husbands at home or supervisors at work became, through the strike, assertive about their desires and outspoken about their rights. All of these accounts insist on the formulation of diametrically opposite pre- and post-strike selves. In a sense, the declaration of post-strike independence and political certainty requires a belief in pre-strike dependence and timidity. In order to dramatize this dichotomy, one might expect women to have narrated specific childhood stories of submission to convention and authority. And yet, in spite of their own emphasis on the transformation from quiet submission to outspoken assertiveness, few of these women were ever so entirely timid and passive as their interviews imply. In fact, their childhood narratives are punctuated by stories of nonconformity, assertions of independence, and acts of rebellion.

The quest to identify or emphasize continuities between women's experiences growing up and their behavior during the strike (even if an emphasis on those experiences defies women's own generalizations about their pre-strike "selves") is not an uncommon feminist move. In fact, it has become fashionable among feminist historians to look for instances of rebellion and independence through women's lives, rather than settling for a simpler story of passive victims who almost magically became activist heroines. Likewise, recent studies in women's labor history have highlighted the ways in which women's work culture and family networks have shaped their militant participation in strikes.[17] As Ava Baron puts it, in her excellent review of the historiographical literature, "Feminist scholars showed how women, oppressed or not, used their networks and their culture to control their own lives and to shape the development of their societies."[18]

The following accounts of childhood experiences of Farah strikers could be read as a similar attempt to chronicle histories of independence and rebellion that well precede an explosive moment of militant collective action. But where it departs from that project is in its insistence on a critical analysis of those childhood tales. The content of women's stories, as well as sometimes the language used to relate them, must be seen as products of the moment they were told—in this case, a moment of fierce pride in their battle against political injustice and social conventions.

Perhaps the most vivid example of this is the childhood story told by Sabina H., a story dominated by stubborn determination to defy conventional expectations of women and pursue an education. Sabina was born in a small town located about three hours from Chihuahua in northern Mexico. There, her father worked in the silver mine; her mother managed the house. Most people in the town, including her parents, believed that girls did not need any schooling beyond learning how to read and write. "Then they would raise children," she complained, "wait on the husband, make food so that he could go to work, and have his clothing ready. . . . But I didn't like it at all. I couldn't do that. I don't know why. Maybe the stork made a mistake and dropped me off in the wrong place."

Not willing to stay home once she completed third grade, Sabina began accompanying her father to the mines every day, not to work, but just to listen to the seemingly worldly affairs discussed by the men. She also used the opportunity to lobby her father to let her return to school. Unable to persuade him of the merits of schooling for girls, she subjected him to constant moping until he finally gave in and let her finish primary school (although he refused to let her younger sisters go).

No matter how unusual it may have been for a girl in her town to graduate from primary school, Sabina was not satisfied. She immediately began a campaign for further schooling, which would require leaving the small town in which they lived and defying her father's vision that she remain, marry, and have children. She recounts the ways she schemed to secure the address of her godfather who lived in the city of Chihuahua, and then, behind her father's back, wrote him a letter asking to spend some time living with his family.

Her godfather welcomed the prospect of Sabina's company, as his wife was expecting a child and he imagined Sabina could help with household chores. Sabina did not worry that his agenda differed from hers; her main objective at the time was to get to the city where more schooling was possible. When she arrived at his house in Chihuahua, Sabina revealed her true intentions, specifying her hope to attend a school that trained teachers. Her godfather was taken aback, among other reasons because he had no idea how such schooling could be arranged. Having already anticipated this problem, however, Sabina inquired whether he had any relatives who were teachers, and then suggested that they go meet with the school inspector, who was distantly related. "He was the man who organized all the schools, and I said to him, 'I would like to study but my father won't let me. If you could talk to him, maybe he would let me.'" When he hesitated, Sabina pressed, "Make the effort! If you don't try you won't get anything!"

It is useful to pause here to look more closely at the language Sabina invokes to relate this story. The admonishments to her godfather to "make the effort" seem to foreshadow the exact phrases she would decades later use to persuade co-workers at Farah to join the strike. Yet it is equally possible that this is an instance when she is imposing "strike-speak" onto this story, creating through the narration a childhood version of the adult union activist.

Whatever language Sabina used at the time persuaded the school inspector to obtain her father's permission, although he threatened that if she failed a single course she would have to quit. Having passed all her courses, she graduated in 1951, at the age of twenty, and obtained a job working as a teacher at the same school.

For reasons that are not entirely clear, she married two years later, although her uncle encouraged her to remain single and pursue her education. "This boy's not good enough to be a *compañero* of yours," her uncle advised. "He's from a lower class. . . . Someday you're going to see yourself old, fat, and ugly, with a house full of kids and working in a factory." "Ay," Sabina chuckled, "who would have known that would be the truth!"

Her family moved to El Paso because her husband's job working for the Mexican Telephone Company required him to set up phone poles and wires on the U.S. side of the border. Some years later, in the mid-1960s, Sabina resigned herself to a job at Farah, having been unable to continue her career as a school teacher in the United States. It was only after the Farah strike, when she became a shop steward for the union, that she felt she was continuing the project of educating people that she had previously undertaken in the context of school.

Although the pursuit of an education was the context in which Sabina most persistently expressed defiance and determination, it was not the only one. Sabina displayed a similarly independent and rebellious streak in relationship to the church as well. Although she appreciated and respected her father's "struggles for justice" (he was active, as noted above, in the miners' union, and also worked to improve the plight of indigenous peoples), she found herself much more powerfully attracted to the spiritual offerings of the church. Like her scheme to go to school, she carefully strategized ways to attend church more frequently than her family was prone to do, as well as ways to remain in the church far longer than the mass. "I *always* did what I liked," she later boasted about her successful attempts to stay at church.

These anecdotes illustrate some of the ways in which Sabina, in spite of her post-strike formulation of a submissive past, in fact focused much of her childhood story on incidents of determination. Like Sabina's, Lina L.'s childhood narrative also describes an independent, if not a rebellious and defiant, spirit. She was so determined to quit school at age fifteen that she was undeterred by threats of being sent to a detention home; she left home for several days to protest her parents' restrictions on dating; she defied friends and neighbors who frowned on her having an Anglo boyfriend. Finally, when as a young adult she resolved to learn bullfighting, she did not let any obstacles stand in her way. Her godfather, himself a bullfighter who had trained several prominent women fighters, initially refused to teach Lina. "Would you rather that I go to someone else, or would you rather that you be the one?" she then demanded. "Because I've made up my mind. I want to fight bulls." When he agreed on the condition that she secure her father's permission, she repeated the same tactic. "Would you rather it be him or someone else?" she asked her father. "Well, if you put it that way . . ." he reluctantly conceded. "I was already nineteen," she added, "so I could decide for myself, right?"

His concession was not the end of her assertions. After several years of training, her godfather still had not let her participate in an actual fight, and she began to argue with him. Then, behind his back, she signed a contract with someone else to fight small bulls. "I didn't even think twice about it or what my godfather might say. . . . I'd been waiting for a long time and now I had this opportunity. I was going to take it." Her godfather, enraged, refused to show up for her first public fight. "So, I was on my own," she declared, admitting as well that she had been quite frightened during the fight because she had been thrown to the ground. The bull "hit me with the side of his horn," she recalled.

> I fell on the ground and the cape fell on top of me. And the bull of course went for the cape. And I was under the cape. The only thing I could think of doing was fighting him from the ground. So I grabbed the cape and just as if I was standing up, I threw the cape to my side and he went for the cape. I never knew if he stepped on me; all I knew was that he went over me. Someone came and grabbed me. In less than a second I was standing on my feet. They brought me the cape and I was ready to fight again. I said, "I'm gonna do it!" And the fear was gone. Once I saw I could do it, it felt like an accomplishment. When the *corrida* was over a lot of fans came to congratulate me. They said, "Keep going. . . . You've got what it takes!"

During her brief career as a public bullfighter Lina adopted the name "Rosa," hoping to prevent relatives from knowing of her unauthorized ventures. "I said that if I ever made it I'd use my real name," she explained. "But if I didn't, everybody would forget Rosa and I'd forget Rosa too. And that's what happened. But it was something very uncommon that I did, and it's a satisfaction to know that I did it. I've always like to explore, and that was a great adventure."

Lina's short-lived career as a bullfighter illustrates her fierce determination to pursue her own goals, unconventional as they may have been. It also highlights her willingness to defy authority, in this case, the authority of her godfather/teacher. In subsequent years, she continued to refuse to be intimidated by authority figures, as illustrated by her attitude toward the social worker whom she and her husband had gone to see to cope with his heroin addiction. In spite of the woman's credentials, Lina remained unimpressed.

> She started asking me questions like, "Do you think you're ugly?"
> "Do you think you're pretty? I know that maybe you think you're
> ugly, but get it into your head that you're pretty nice." And I said,
> "Golly, no counselor is going to ever help me like this!"

Lina speculated that the counselor perhaps thought she suffered from an inferiority complex, or had been too affected by her husband's addiction. Her most generous assessment was that the counselor was trying to build Lina's confidence so that she would be better able to cope with her husband's problems. The result was that her husband, equally confused by the counselor's questions, went back to drugs. "I decided if anybody knows my problem it's me," Lina concluded. "I'm not going to a counselor who doesn't know peanuts about this!"

Although few other women told stories of determination and defiance as detailed as Lina's or Sabina's, almost all related some incident that defied their own assertions that only *after* the strike did they become independent and outspoken. Isela A., for example, describes herself as having been an excessively obedient young girl, yet her life history includes many acts of defiance and independence. Protesting her grandmother's strict rein on the household (her parents had both died when she was very young), she ran away from home to live with her older sister in California. Then, when her sister left her husband, Isela (then fifteen years old) unilaterally decided to move back to El Paso rather than stay in California with her brother-in-law and take care of his children. For some time while in high school, she and her brother lived in their family's old house by themselves. Unbeknownst to anyone else, they wrote absence notes for each other, signed each other's report cards, and bought all their own groceries. (And unbeknownst to Isela, her brother was stealing clothes for her—never for himself—from Newberry's department store where he worked part-time.)

As a young married woman, she vehemently objected to her brother's attempts to dictate her behavior, such as when he once scolded her for drinking a beer (although her argument to him was that now her husband, not her brother, was the "boss"). Nevertheless, she was not always subservient to her husband. On another occasion she evoked her brother's wrath by ordering her husband to take her to the laundromat rather than going out with him. "I hate women that tell their husbands what to do!" her brother sniped. In spite of her insistence that only after the strike did she become independent in her marriage, she acknowledges that "I'm kind of independent. There were many times that I was very stubborn. When I wanted to do something, as long as I wasn't doing anything wrong, I used to just do it. And he used to get very angry at me."

Isela's initial decision to get a job working at Farah was one such instance. Home with two young children, she became a self-described nervous wreck. Her doctor diagnosed the problem as being "too young to be shut up in the house with two little kids," and suggested that the best way "to be able to control my nerves would be to get away from the house and from my kids." In spite of her husband's protests, she arranged to take her kids to nursery school and get a job herself.

Chayo P. may not have grown up with a rebellious streak, but she was hardly passive or submissive. Even as a young girl she was indignant at women's subordination in the household. "I used to study my mother," she recalled.

> She was sitting at the table, eating her warm meal, and then here comes my brother, "I want to eat!" She would leave her plate and serve him. I'd say, "Shit, that's not for me! Why don't you get up and serve yourself?"

As a young woman, too, she did not hesitate to assert her own views, well before the strike. During the early years of her marriage, for instance, when she and her husband lived with his parents, her mother-in-law insisted that Chayo, along with the rest of the family, attend church. "I'm not the type that gets up at six o'clock in the morning on Sundays, but there she'd come and knock, 'Time to go to church!'" Chayo refused to go, arguing that her parents had never forced her to attend church. "And you know," Chayo recalled, "everybody stopped going after that, even my brothers-in-law and husband. . . . My habits got to him!"

One could continue to list rebellious moments in women's childhood narratives: a woman who insisted on watching football with her brothers instead of doing the household chores assigned her and who subsequently defied her parents to become the singer for a rock-and-roll band organized by some "guys from high school." Another resisted her father's strict prohibition on dating by sneaking out of the house and making sure she returned before he did. Another, sent to live in a convent when her father died, ran away when the nuns tried to cut her hair. Still another woman recalled her insistence on playing with boys even though she was punished and told to stick with other girls.

All these stories of childhood rebellion, nonconformity, and assertiveness can be interpreted in several ways. First, they might be cited to challenge popular images of Chicanas as passive victims of gender and racial discrimination, who startle their employers and the public by sudden displays of militancy, such as the Farah strike. They might also challenge popular beliefs—ones expressed by many of the Farah strikers themselves—that the strike transformed quiet, submissive women into outspoken labor heroines. Although the strike became emblematic of women's political awareness and self-confidence, not all post-strike acts of assertiveness, independence, and insistence upon one's rights can be mechanistically attributed to the strike experience. They must instead be understood in the context of longer life histories, as all these stories so poignantly illustrate.

In this essay I am trying to suggest a slightly different interpretation of these stories, one that emphasizes their relationship to the narrative present. Although women structured their narratives around a passive and timid pre-strike past versus an activist and self-confident post-strike present, they perhaps unconsciously crafted a story of childhood that explained, or at least contained elements of consistency with, their present. The strike may well have enabled women to acknowledge, emphasize, or even celebrate aspects of their personal histories that they had previously ignored or kept hidden. For example, as Lina relates the story of her pre-Farah bullfighting career, one cannot help but wonder whether it was only during her years as a union activist that "Rosa" the bullfighter was excavated as a memorable story. That she made no reference to bullfighting during the first two times we interviewed her suggests that it was not a part of her personal past about which she was unambivalent. It was only some years later, when she bought a house of her own, that she displayed a large black-and-white photograph of "Rosa, the bullfighter" alongside banners from the Farah strike as exhibits of the two most memorable events of her life. It would be presumptuous to over-read her initial omission and subsequent telling of the story, but it possibly suggests that she saw a connection between Rosa and the political activist she became through the strike.

If the strike allowed a celebration of some childhood experiences, it may have provoked an embellishment of others, a retelling or reformulation of them to fit women's current values. For instance, when Chayo P. describes the rage she felt, as a child, at her mother's subservient role, it is not obvious whether that rage was fully developed before the strike or whether it emerged as her values changed and her self-confidence in herself as a woman developed during the strike. The point, then, is not that these women *have* histories of rebellion or feminist insight, but rather that they have experiences they can draw on to formulate such histories. Women are not *inventing* nonexistent past experiences, but they are retelling them with the language, perceptions, and mandates of their present.

Women's post-strike present may have mandated, or at least provided an occasion to honor, childhood stories of rebellion and determination. It is not surprising that a post-strike oral history would call attention to or try to formulate a childhood version of the adult self. What is curious, then, is that women emphasized a life story of transformation from pre-strike timidity and subordination to post-strike courage and assertiveness. It may be, as noted above, that the declaration of post-strike independence and political certainty mandated a belief in pre-strike dependence, shyness, and passivity. The belief in the strike as a transformative event, in other words, required the framework of dichotomous pre- and post-strike selves. The imposition of this dramatic framework on their childhood stories may also be related to the oral histories themselves, particularly to the women's perception of what we, interviewers there to hear about the "strike experience," wanted to hear. In this sense, the dramatization may represent the kind of interview "performance" that anthropologist Patricia Zavella describes in her study of Chicana cannery workers in California.[19]

That one can simultaneously embrace multiple, and even contradictory, versions of a life history dramatizes the point of this essay, and that concerns how we interpret oral histories. Feminist historians, myself included, have struggled to collect oral histories of non-elite women whose lives might remain otherwise undocumented. This endeavor has often presumed the recovery of women's "true" voice, and scholars, again myself included, have often drawn on oral history as a source of women's actual experience. This has been crucial to the project of recovering women's history as well as challenging histories based on men's experience and perspective.

By focusing on the relationship between the narrative present and personal past, this analysis of the oral histories of Farah strikers is trying to caution against an overly literal reading of oral histories. The point is not to deny that some of the women involved in the Farah strike had fathers who were union activists, that they experienced pre-strike work life at Farah as oppressive, that the sense of community among barrio residents stood out in their memories of the neighborhood where they grew up; nor is it to deny that they were, as children and young adults, very determined, independent, self-confident, and sometimes rebellious. Instead, it is important to recognize that women's narration of those stories is partly a product of their union-activist present—a present that may reveal previously forgotten memories, prompt a celebration of experiences that once seemed insignificant, or compel an embellishment or reformulation of old childhood tales. This does not mean that oral history should be devalued or rejected. Rather, it should be problematized as one of many possible tellings of a woman's life story and not the source of her single, "true" experience. In this context, one of the most important and least recognized legacies of the Farah strike and union struggle is its provision of an occasion for women to remake their personal histories. Ultimately, oral history, like autobiography, is less about history and experience than about their retelling.

Emily Honig is a professor of women's studies and history at the University of California, Santa Cruz. She is the author of *Creating Chinese Ethnicity: Subei People in Shanghai, 1850–1980* (1992) and *Sisters and Strangers: Women in the Shanghai Cotton Mills, 1919–1949* (1986).

NOTES

1. Sherna Gluck and Daphne Patai, "Introduction," in *Women's Words: The Feminist Practice of Oral History*, ed. Sherna Gluck and Daphne Patai (New York: Routledge, 1991), 2.
2. Nancy Grey Osterud and Lu Ann Jones, "'If I must say so myself': Oral Histories of Rural Women," *Oral History Review* 17, no. 2 (fall 1989): 1–2.
3. See, for example, Nancy Seifer, *Nobody Speaks for Me: Self-Portraits of American Working-Class Women* (New York: Simon and Schuster, 1976); Sherna Gluck, *From Parlor to Prison: Five American Suffragists Talk about Their Lives* (New York: Vintage, 1976); Patricia Preciado Martin, *Songs My Mother Sang to Me: An Oral History of Mexican-American Women* (Tucson and London: The University of Arizona Press, 1992); Patricia Romero, ed., *Life Histories of African Women* (London: The Ashfield Press, 1988).
4. See, for example, Jacquelyn Dowd Hall, James Leloudis, Robert Korstad, Mary Murphy, Lu Ann Jones, and Christopher Daly, *Like a Family: The Making of a Southern Cotton Mill World* (Chapel Hill: The University of North Carolina Press, 1987); Vicki Ruiz, *Cannery Women, Cannery Lives: Mexican Women, Unionization, and the California Food Processing Industry, 1930–1950* (Albuquerque: University of New Mexico Press, 1987); Emily Honig, *Sisters and Strangers: Women Cotton Mill Workers in Shanghai, 1919–1949* (Stanford: Stanford University Press, 1986); Luise White, "Prostitution, Identity and Class Consciousness in Nairobi during World War II," *Signs* 11, no. 2 (winter 1986): 255–73.
5. See Susan Geiger, "What's So Feminist About Doing Women's Oral History?" in *Expanding the Boundaries of Women's History: Essays on Women in the Third World*, ed. Cheryl Johnson-Odim and Margaret Strobel (Bloomington: Indiana University Press, 1992), 305–18. Also see Sherna Gluck, "What's So Special About Women? Women's Oral History," *Frontiers* 2, no. 2 (1979):3–11.
6. Gluck and Patai, "Introduction," 2.
7. Ibid., 3. For a discussion of interviews as performance, see Patricia Zavella, *Women's Work and Chicano Families: Cannery Workers of the Santa Clara Valley* (Ithaca and London: Cornell University Press, 1987), 25–26.
8. Devra Weber, "*Raiz Fuerte:* Oral History and Mexicana Farmworkers," *Oral History Review* 17, no. 2 (fall 1989): 61.
9. Luisa Passerini, *Fascism in Popular Memory: The Cultural Experience of the Turin Working Class* (Cambridge: Cambridge University Press, 1987).
10. Discussion of this issue is absent not only from feminist discussion of oral history, but of women's personal narratives more generally. See, for example, Bella Brodzki and Celeste Schenck, *Life/Lines: Theorizing Women's Autobiography* (Ithaca: Cornell University Press, 1988); and The Personal Narratives Group, *Interpreting Women's*

   Lives: Feminist Theory and Personal Narratives (Bloomington: Indiana University Press, 1989).
11. One of the early formulations of this view, was by E. H. Carr, *What is History?* (New York: Vintage, 1961).
12. Erik H. Erikson, *Life History and the Historical Moment* (New York: W. W. Norton and Co., Inc., 1975), 124.
13. This problematizing of oral history accounts is not dissimilar to the critical scrutiny of the invocation of "experience" by historians that Joan Scott discusses in her essay "Experience," in *Feminists Theorize the Political*, ed. Judith Butler and Joan Scott (New York: Routledge, 1992), 22–40.
14. For a detailed account of the strike, see Laurie Coyle, Gail Hershatter, and Emily Honig, "Women at Farah: An Unfinished Story," *Aztlán* (summer 1979).
15. Unless otherwise cited, all quotations are from the interviews conducted by Laurie Coyle, Gail Hershatter, and myself in El Paso in 1977 and 1978.
16. This quote is from an interview with Virgie Delgado published in *Union Drive in the Southwest: Chicanos Strike at Farah*, by The San Francisco Bay Area Farah Strike Support Committee (San Francisco: United Front Press, 1974), 6.
17. Patricia A. Cooper, *Once a Cigar Maker: Men, Women, and Work Culture in American Cigar Factories, 1900–1919* (Urbana: University of Illinois Press, 1987), and Dorothy Sue Cobble, *Dishing It Out: Waitresses and Their Unions in the Twentieth Century* (Urbana: University of Illinois Press, 1991) provide particularly detailed analyses of connections between women's work culture, daily acts of resistance, and more formal labor protest.
18. For an excellent historiographical review of the literature on women's labor history, see Ava Baron, "Gender and Labor History: Learning from the Past, Looking to the Future," in *Work Engendered: Toward a New History of American Labor*, ed. Ava Baron (Ithaca: Cornell University Press, 1991), 1–46.
19. Zavella, *Women's Work and Chicano Families*, 25–26.

GRASSROOTS LEADERSHIP RECONCEPTUALIZED

CHICANA ORAL HISTORIES AND THE 1968 EAST LOS ANGELES SCHOOL BLOWOUTS*

Dolores Delgado Bernal

The 1960s was an era of social unrest in American history. Student movements that helped shape larger struggles for social and political equality emerged from street politics and mass protests. A myriad of literature discusses the social and political forces of the 1960s, particularly the liberal and radical student movements. Yet, as Carlos Muñoz, Jr., argues, there is a paucity of material on 1960s nonwhite student radicalism and protest.[1] He outlines various explanations that have been provided by white scholars for their failure to incorporate nonwhite student radicalism into their work: that the black student movement was not radical enough and that Mexican students were simply not involved in the struggles of the sixties. However, though Muñoz points to the omission of working-class people of color in the literature on 1960s student movements, he neglects to include a serious analysis of gender in his own examination of the Chicano Movement and the politics of identity.

In 1968 people witnessed student demonstrations in countries such as France, Italy, Mexico, and the United States. In March of that year well over ten thousand students walked out of the mostly Chicano schools in East Los Angeles to protest the inferior quality of their

*This chapter was originally published as: Bernal, Dolores Delgado. "Grassroots Leadership Reconceptualized: Chicana Oral Histories and the 1968 East Los Angeles School Blowouts." In *Frontiers* 19, no. 2 (1998): 113–42.

education. This event, which came to be known as the East Los Angeles School Blowouts, has been viewed through a variety of analytical historical perspectives including those of protest politics, internal colonialism, spontaneous mass demonstrations, the Chicano student movement, and as a political and social development of the wider Chicano Movement. None of these historical accounts, however, include a gender analysis.[2] Indeed, even contemporary depictions, such as the important documentary series *Chicano: A History of the Mexican American Civil Rights Movement*, continue to marginalize women's activism; part three of the series, "Taking Back the Schools," fails to tell the stories of young Chicanas and the roles they filled in the East Los Angeles Blowouts.[3]

As an educational researcher and a Chicana, I am interested in the women's voices that have been omitted from the diverse historical accounts of the Blowouts—particularly those women who were key participants.[4] The Blowouts provide an opportunity to rediscover a history that has been unrecognized and unappreciated. In addition, a historical analysis that focuses on the Blowout participation of women allows us to explore how women offered leadership and how that leadership, while different in form and substance from traditional interpretations, was indeed meaningful and essential.[5]

Hence, my purpose is twofold. Through the oral history data of eight women, I provide an alternative perspective to the historical narratives of the 1968 Blowouts that have thus far only been told by males with a focus on males. At the same time, I will use the oral history data to examine the concept of leadership in community activism. I propose that a paradigmatic shift in the way we view grassroots leadership not only provides an alternative history to the Blowouts, but it also acknowledges Chicanas as important leaders in past and present grassroots movements.

Methodology

The relationship between a researcher's methodology and his or her theoretical and epistemological orientation is not always explicit, but these elements are inevitably closely connected. To reclaim a history of Chicana activism and leadership, I utilize a theoretical and epistemological perspective grounded in critical feminisms that are strongly influenced by women of color. Critical feminist theories challenge the dominant notion of knowledge and provide legitimacy as well as a logical rationale for the study of working-class women of color. Chandra Talpade Mohanty points to the importance of traditionally excluded groups, such as Chicanas, breaking through dominant ways of thinking and reclaiming history. She discusses the development of alternative histories:

> This issue of subjectivity represents a realization of the fact that who we are, how we act, what we think, and what stories we tell become more intelligible within an epistemological framework that begins by recognizing existing hegemonic histories.... [Thus,] uncovering and reclaiming of subjugated knowledges is one way to clay claim to alternative histories.[6]

The struggle to reclaim history is a contention over power, meaning, and knowledge. Critical feminisms provide a space within the academy for historically silenced peoples to identify unequal power relations and to take the first steps in constructing alternative histories. In short, my epistemological orientation, which is grounded in critical feminisms, allows for the identification of unequal power relations, the development of alternative histories, and the validation of a methodology based on the lived experiences of Chicanas.

Kenneth Kann writes that there are three types of history: "the kind you live, the kind you hear about, and the kind you read about."[7] The second, when documented as oral history, transforms the first into the third: Lived history becomes written history. In my own attempt to transform lived experiences into written history, my primary method of data collection is the oral history interviews of eight women who as high school or college students participated in the 1968 Blowouts. Oral histories provide a special opportunity to learn the unique perceptions and interpretations of individuals, particularly those from groups whose history has been traditionally excluded or distorted. Oral sources are thus a necessity when studying working-class women of color, though they may be less important when studying topics involving white men of the dominant class who have typically had control over written history and collective memory.[8] Oral histories, grounded in critical feminisms, provide a means of breaking through dominant ways of knowing and reclaiming an alternative history of grassroots activism in the 1968 Blowouts.

The interviews I conducted took place between June 1995 and January 1996 in a place that was most convenient for each woman, usually in her home. Following a network sampling procedure, I interviewed eight women who were identified by other female participants or resource individuals as key participants or leaders in the Blowouts.[9] I followed an interview protocol with open-ended questions in order to elicit multiple levels of data. Though the interview protocol was used as a guide, I realized that as the women spoke of very personal experiences, a less structured approach allowed their voices and ways of knowing to come forth. Although I took interview notes, each interview was also recorded and transcribed, and the full transcription of each interview tape has helped me create a more complete database.

In addition to conducting an oral history interview with each participant, I also conducted a focus group interview that included seven of the eight women together for one interview. The videotaped interview took place at Self-Help Graphics, a community art gallery and studio in East Los Angeles, during February 1996. Focus group interviews incorporate the explicit use of group interaction to produce data and insights that would be less accessible without the interaction.[10] Therefore, my interest in conducting a focus group interview was less on reconstructing the "Truth" of what happened than it was on recording the new information, differing viewpoints, and recurring issues that the group communication generated.

To work within critical feminist scholarship, I provided each woman with a transcription of her individual interview so that she had a chance to reflect and comment on her responses to questions. The women were given these transcriptions prior to the focus group interview, allowing them the opportunity to reflect and bring up concerns at the group interview. During the group interview, I also shared my preliminary analysis with the women and asked for their reaction and input to four themes I had identified from their oral history interviews. Their comments have helped me to better understand the roles they played in the Blowouts and the ways in which we might look at grassroots leadership differently.

Table 1: Family and Personal History

Name	Two-Parent Home	Strong Catholic Family	Family History of Community or Labor Involvement	Named Mother as Influential	Others Named Influential besides Parent
Celeste Baca			X	X	X
Vickie Castro	X	X	X	X	
Paula Crisostomo	X		X	X	X
Mita Cuaron	X		X	X*	
Tanya Luna Mount	X		X	X*	
Rosalinda M. González	X	X		X	X
Rachael Ochoa Cervera	X	X			X
Cassandra Zacarías				X	X

*Indicates that a focus was placed on both her mother and father.

The Women

All eight of the women are similar insofar as they are second- or third-generation Chicanas, first-generation college students, and grew up in working-class neighborhoods on the eastside of Los Angeles. However, these women are not a homogeneous group, nor does their composite lend itself to a "typical Chicana" leader or activist. Two of the women grew up in single-parent households with only two children, while the other six come from two-parent families with four or more children. Four of the women come from families that had been involved in union organizing or leftist political movements since the 1940s. Three women state that they come from strong Catholic families, while three other women state they were raised in families in which their parent(s) had abandoned the Catholic Church. Though six of the eight women are bilingual in Spanish and English today, only one of the women grew up in a predominantly Spanish-speaking home. Three of the women come from mixed marriages and are half white, Jewish, or Filipina. Finally, during high school, six of the women maintained an exceptional academic and extracurricular record as college-tracked students.

Despite the similarities, the notable differences in the women's family and personal histories reflect the complexity and diversity of Chicanas' experiences in 1968 and today (see table 1). Indeed, there are also similarities and differences in the type of participation and leadership each women contributed to the East L.A. Blowouts. While this article is an interpretation based on the personal perceptions and experiences of these women, knowing the historical circumstances of the time provides a clearer picture of the 1968 East L.A. School Blowouts.

The 1968 East Los Angeles School Blowouts

Chicanos' struggle for quality education and the right to include their culture, history, and language in the curriculum is not a phenomenon of the 1960s but instead predates the 1968 Blowouts by a number of decades. In fact, many of the concerns and issues that were voiced by participants and supporters of the 1968 Blowouts—implementation of bilingual and bicultural training for teachers, elimination of tracking based on standardized tests, improvement and replacement of inferior school facilities, removal of racist teachers and administrators, and inclusion of Mexican history and culture into the curriculum—were very similar to those voiced in Mexican communities in the United States since before the turn of the century.[11]

For years, East Los Angeles community members made unsuccessful attempts to create change and improve the education system through the "proper" channels. In the 1950s the Education Committee of the Council of Mexican-American Affairs, comprised of educated Mexican professionals, addressed the failure of schools to educate Mexican students through mainstream channels. They met with legislators, school officials, and community members and attended hearings, press conferences, and symposia to no avail.[12] In June 1967 Irene Tovar, Commissioner of Compensatory Education for the Los Angeles district, explained to the U.S. Commission on Civil Rights that a long list of recommendations to improve the inferior schooling conditions was presented to the Los Angeles Board of Education in 1963 but that "few of those recommendations were accepted and even fewer reached the community."[13] In the years immediately preceding the Blowouts, students and parents participating in one East L.A. high school's PTA specifically addressed the poor quality of education and requested reforms similar to those demanded by the Blowouts two years later.[14] Nonetheless, formal requests through official channels were unanswered.

In 1963, the Los Angeles County Commission on Human Relations began sponsoring an annual Mexican-American Youth Leadership Conference at Camp Hess Kramer for high school students. These conferences were important to the development of the 1968 Blowouts because a number of students who participated in the conference later became organizers in the Blowouts as well as in other progressive movements. Given these outcomes, it is ironic that the camp held an assimilationist perspective, stating that the official goal of the camp was to improve self-image and intergroup relations so that Mexican American students "may be free to develop themselves into the mainstream of Anglo-American life."[15] Students were encouraged to be traditional school leaders, run for school offices, and go on to college. The student participants were selected by either a school, a community person, or an organization based on their ability to contribute to the group as well as on their ability to return and create progress in their own communities.

The weekend camps were held at Camp Hess Kramer in Malibu, California. The student participants were assigned to cabins, and college students served as camp counselors and workshop leaders. Four of the women in my study participated in at least one of the leadership conferences prior to their involvement in the 1968 Blowouts. They remember the camp as a beautiful place where they were given a better framework to understand inequities and where they developed a sense of community and family responsibility. As one woman put it, "These youth conferences were the first time that we began to develop a consciousness." Rachael Ochoa Cervera discusses her memories of the camp:

> First of all, it was a nice experience because you'd get away for a whole weekend and the environment, the atmosphere was quite beautiful, very aesthetic. Being by the ocean, yet you felt you were in the mountains. . . . It was very affirmative. That's where you began to have an identity. You weren't with your schoolmates, you could be more open. You could say what you wanted to.[16]

While the camp fostered civic responsibility and school leadership, many students left motivated to organize around more radical and progressive issues. Rosalinda Méndez González describes how the conferences motivated students to organize:

> Well, when we started going to these youth conferences, there were older Mexican Americans. Now we were high school kids, so older was probably twenties and early thirties. They would talk to us, and explain a lot of things about what was happening, and I remember they were opening up our eyes. After those youth conferences, then we went back and started organizing to raise support for the farmworkers, and things like that.[17]

As a direct result of youth participating at Camp Hess Kramer, the Young Citizens for Community Action (YCCA) was formed. The YCCA (which later became Young Chicanos for Community Action and then evolved into the Brown Berets) surveyed high school students' needs, met with education officials to discuss problems, and endorsed potential candidates for the board of education. YCCA members, still following official channels to bring about improved educational conditions, supported and helped elect the first Chicano school board member, Julian Nava.[18]

Also influential in the development of the Blowouts was the fact that by 1967 a relatively larger number of Chicano students began entering college—though still a small representation of the Chicano population. In that year, one of the first Chicano college student organizations in the Los Angeles area, the Mexican American Student Association (MASA), was formed at East Los Angeles Community College.[19] Student organizations rapidly formed throughout college campuses in California, including United Mexican-American Students (UMAS) at the University of California, Los Angeles; California State University, Los Angeles; Occidental College; and Loyola University. The primary issue of these organizations was the lack of Chicano access to quality education.

Historians have also noted the importance of the community activist newspapers *Inside Eastside* and *La Raza* to the rise of the Blowouts.[20] *Inside Eastside* had an emphasis on social, cultural, and political activities relevant to students and for the most part was written and edited by high school students. In fact, two women in this study wrote articles for *Inside Eastside* and *La Raza*. *La Raza*, aimed at the Chicano community as a whole, was concerned with a spectrum of political activities focusing on the schools, police, and electoral politics. The newspapers provided a forum in which students and community members were able to articulate their discontent with the schools, and frequent themes were the poor quality of East Los Angeles schools and the cultural insensitivity of teachers. The newspapers, the increased number of Chicano college students, and events such as the Camp Hess Kramer conferences were all influential in bringing attention to the poor educational conditions of East Los Angeles schools.

During the 1960s, East Los Angeles high schools had an especially deplorable record of educating Chicano students, who had a dropout/ pushout rate of well over 50 percent as well as the lowest reading scores in the district. In contrast, according to a survey undertaken by the Los Angeles City School System, two westside schools, Palisades and Monroe, had dropout rates of 3.1 percent and 2.6 percent respectively in 1965–1966.[21] According to the State Department of Education's racial survey, Mexican American students were also heavily represented in special education classes, including classes for the mentally retarded and the emotionally disturbed.[22] The classrooms were overcrowded, and most teachers lacked sensitivity to or understanding of the Mexican working-class communities in which they taught. Rosalinda Méndez González recalls:

> There were teachers who would say, "You dirty Mexicans, why don't you go back to where you came from?" So there was a lot of racism we encountered in the school. We had severely overcrowded class-rooms. We didn't have sufficient books. We had buildings that were barrack-type buildings that had been built as emergency, temporary buildings during World War II, and this was in the late 1960s, and we were still going to school in those buildings.[23]

As a result of the poor educational conditions and the fact that numerous attempts to voice community concerns and school reforms were ignored, school strikes took place during the first week of March 1968. Though the Blowouts were centered at five predominately Chicano high schools located in the general eastside of Los Angeles, other schools in the district also participated, including Jefferson High School, which was predominately African American.[24]

The school boycott began on different days during the first week of March and lasted a week and a half, with over ten thousand students protesting the inferior quality of their education. Though there had been weeks of discussions and planning, the first impromptu walkout was prompted by the cancellation of the school play *Barefoot in the Park* by the administration at Wilson High School. Paula Crisostomo, a student organizer at Lincoln High School, comments on the atmosphere at her school preceding the walkout.

> I know tension had heightened, activity had heightened districtwide, a lot of schools were talking about it, everyone knew it was going to happen, everyone was waiting for the sign. But I remember the atmosphere was absolutely tense, I mean it was just electric in school. This had been building for so long, and everyone knew it was going to happen and everyone was just waiting and waiting.[25]

Though there was coordination between the schools, the planning and actual implementation of each school walkout took on a distinct character. High school students, college students, Brown Beret members, teachers, and the general community took on different roles and provided different kinds of support.

Vickie Castro, a Roosevelt graduate, was a college student who played a crucial role in organizing and supporting the Blowouts. Vickie recalls that while she was at Roosevelt trying to help organize students, she was recognized by a teacher and escorted to the gate. The teacher told her, "If I see you on campus again, I'll have you arrested." Vickie later used her old Mazda to pull down the chain-link fence that had been locked to prevent high school students from leaving: "I remember having to back my car and put chains on and pull the gates off." In contrast, her key role at Lincoln was to set up a meeting with the principal and detail him while other college students came on campus to encourage high school students to participate in the walkouts. Vickie recalls the strategy she used at Lincoln, pretending to be a job applicant to get an appointment with the principal:

> I remember we had a whole strategy planned for Lincoln, how we were going to do it. And who was going to be in the halls to yell "walkouts" at the various buildings. And my role was to make an appointment with the principal to meet him, to talk to him about either employment or something. I'm in his office and my job is trying to delay him. He kept saying, "I'll be right with you, I'll be right with you." So I was to just keep him distracted a little bit. Then when the walkouts came, of course, he said, "I have to leave." And then somehow, I don't even recall, I got out of the building too.[26]

Just as the planning and actual implementation of each school walkout took on a distinct character, so did the response by each school administration and by the police. While the student walkouts on other campuses could be characterized as ranging from peaceful to controlled with mild incidents of violence, the students on Roosevelt's campus experienced a great deal of police violence. Police, county sheriffs, and riot squads were called. With a number of students and community members injured and arrested, the student protest turned into a near riot situation. Tanya Luna Mount, a student organizer, points out that even though the students were following the legal requirements of a public demonstration, the situation with the police escalated to the point of senseless beatings with school administrators trying to stop the police:

> They [the LAPD] were treating it like we were rioting and tearing everything up, which we weren't. We weren't breaking, destroying anything. Nobody was hanging on school property and tearing it apart. Nothing, nothing like that happened. And we were told to disperse, we had three minutes. Everybody kept yelling that we had a right to be there. . . . All of a sudden they [the riot squad] started coming down this way. They start whacking people. Now they're beating people up, badly, badly beating people up. Now people, administrators are inside yelling, "Stop, my God. What are you doing?" Once you call LAPD, the school no longer has any jurisdiction. They couldn't even open the gate and tell the kids to run inside because the police were telling them, "Remove yourself from the fence and go back, mind your own business." That's when all of a sudden they [the administrators] realized, "My God."[27]

The student strikers, including those at Roosevelt who were subjected to police violence, were not just idly walking out of school. They proposed that their schools be brought up to the same standards as those of other Los Angeles high schools. The students generated a list of grievances and pushed for the board of education to hold a special meeting in which they could present their grievances. The official list of student grievances to be presented to the board of education consisted of thirty-six demands, including smaller class size, bilingual education, more emphasis on Chicano history, and community control of schools.[28] Many of the grievances were education reforms previously proposed by concerned parents, educators, and community members, and all of the demands were supported by the premise that East Los Angeles schools were not properly educating Chicano students.

The Blowouts generated the formation of the Educational Issues Coordinating Committee (EICC) by parents, various community members, high school students, and UMAS members. With pressure from the EICC and the student strikers, the Blowouts also generated at least two special board of education meetings in which students, the

EICC, and supporters were allowed to voice their concerns. By Friday, March 9, the school strikes had not ended, and the board of education scheduled a special meeting to hear the students' proposals. At this meeting it was decided that another meeting would be held at Lincoln High School and that the board would grant amnesty to the thousands of students who had boycotted classes.[29]

Approximately twelve hundred people attended a four-hour board meeting that was held at Lincoln High School, yet the board of education made no commitments. Students walked out of the meeting in response to the board's inaction. The sentiments of the board were captured by an article in the *Los Angeles Times* stating that "school officials deny any prejudice in allocation of building funds and say that they agree with 99% of the students' demands—but that the district does not have the money to finance the kind of massive changes proposed."[30] At this meeting, the board went on record opposing the discipline of students and teachers who had participated in the boycott. Yet in the late evening of June 2, 1968, thirteen individuals involved in the Blowouts were arrested and imprisoned on conspiracy charges. Though female students were involved in organizing the Blowouts, the "L.A. 13" were all men, including Sal Castro, a teacher from Lincoln High School. With a focus on males, especially those who looked the militant type, females avoided arrest. Though the charges were later dropped and found unconstitutional, Sal Castro was suspended from his teaching position at Lincoln High School. For many months students, community, and EICC members rallied in support of the L.A. 13 and then focused organizing efforts on the reinstatement of Sal Castro.

A Reconceptualization of Leadership

In exploring how and when women participated in the Blowouts, it is important to outline a reconceptualization of leadership that places women at the center of analysis and does not separate the task of organizing from leading. The reconceptualization I put forth comes out of a women's studies tradition that in the last twenty years has produced an impressive body of new knowledge and has contributed to the development of new paradigms on leadership. Rather than using traditional paradigms that view leaders as those who occupy a high position in an organization, feminist scholars have developed alternative paradigms that more accurately consider gender in the analysis of leadership.[31]

In the area of science, Thomas Kuhn's influential work *The Structure of Scientific Revolutions* presents a model for a fundamental change in theories and scientific paradigms, arguing that without major paradigm shifts we may never understand certain scientific phenomena. He gives the example of how Joseph Priestley, one of the scientists said to have discovered the gas that was later found to be oxygen, was unable to see what other scientists were able to see as a result of a paradigm revision.[32] Similarly, a paradigm shift in the way that we understand and study leadership allows us to see how women—specifically the women in my study—emerge as leaders. Perhaps there is something faulty in the previous leadership paradigms that have not allowed us to understand and explain the lived experiences of Chicanas.

Karen Brodkin Sacks indicates that the traditional paradigm of leadership implicitly equates public speakers and negotiators with leaders and also identifies organizing and leading as two different tasks.[33] She challenges this notion of leadership by placing working-class women at the center of analysis. Leadership in this perspective is a collective process that includes the mutually important and reinforcing dynamic between both women's and men's roles. Leadership as a process allows us to acknowledge and study a cooperative leadership in "which members of a group are empowered to work together synergistically toward a common goal or vision that will create change, transform institutions, and thus improve the quality of life."[34] This paradigm of cooperative leadership along with the inclusion of women's voices allows an alternative view of the Blowouts and of different dimensions of grassroots leadership to emerge.

Dimensions of Grassroots Leadership

In previous work, I have identified five different types of activities that can be considered dimensions of grassroots leadership in the 1968 Blowouts: networking, organizing, developing consciousness, holding an elected or appointed office, and acting as an official or unofficial spokesperson.[35] The distinction between these activities is not meant

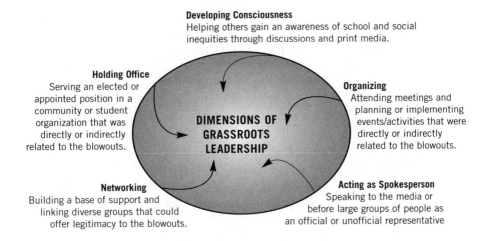

Developing Consciousness
Helping others gain an awareness of school and social inequities through discussions and print media.

Holding Office
Serving an elected or appointed position in a community or student organization that was directly or indirectly related to the blowouts.

DIMENSIONS OF GRASSROOTS LEADERSHIP

Organizing
Attending meetings and planning or implementing events/activities that were directly or indirectly related to the blowouts.

Networking
Building a base of support and linking diverse groups that could offer legitimacy to the blowouts.

Acting as Spokesperson
Speaking to the media or before large groups of people as an official or unofficial representative

Figure 1: Dimensions of Grassroots Leadership

to be a rigid and impermeable one, nor are these activities inclusive of all dimensions of grassroots leadership. Not every leader need participate in every dimension of leadership, and I argue that there is no hierarchical order assigned to the different dimensions. The activities can be viewed as locations on a moving carousel, each location being of equal importance. There are many entry points at which one can get on and off, and once on the carousel one is free to move about in different locations (see figure 1).

Writing about black women involved in the civil rights movement of the same period, Charlotte Bunch points that "while black male leaders were the ones whom the press called on to be the spokesmen, it was often the black women who made things happen, especially in terms of organizing people at the community level."[36] Likewise, when I initially described my research proposal to a male Chicano colleague of the Movement generation, he sincerely encouraged me to pursue the topic, but unassumingly warned that there were no female leaders in the Blowouts and that few women were involved. Perhaps because he views the Blowouts from a traditional leadership paradigm, he overlooked Chicanas as leaders and failed to recognize their important contributions to the Blowouts. Yet in distinct ways and to varying degrees, the women I interviewed participated in these different dimensions of leadership. Their participation was vital to the Blowouts, yet because a traditional leadership paradigm does not acknowledge the importance of those who participate in organizing, developing consciousness, and networking, their leadership remains unrecognized and unappreciated by most historians.

In the following sections, I will discuss each of the five identified, interrelated dimensions of leadership, exploring the ways in which the oral histories of the women in this study further our understanding of the Blowouts and of women's activist leadership.

Participation and Implementation of Meetings, Events, and Activities: Organizing

Organizing includes attending meetings and planning or implementing events and activities that were directly or indirectly related to the Blowouts. There were numerous meetings, events, and activities that took place prior to and after the Blowouts in which students, teachers, parents, and community members raised concerns about the quality of education in the East L.A. high schools. All eight of the women discuss attending and actively participating in PTA meetings, school board meetings, Blowout committee meetings, or community planning meetings that were held in such places as the Cleveland House, the Plaza Community Center, and the home of Tanya Luna Mount's parents.[37]

In an attempt to address and remedy school inequities, activists in these organizations implemented a number of strategies before resorting to a school boycott. For example, Vicki Castro, Paula Crisostomo, and Rachael Ochoa Cervera were intimately involved in YCCA, a community youth group formed by former Camp Hess Kramer participants that took up issues of education. Members of this group met regularly, talked to other youth at government-sponsored Teen Posts, and conducted a needs-assessment survey to find out what was going on in the schools. Vicki discusses her and others' organizing efforts in the years prior to the Blowouts:

> And we even had like a questionnaire that we had made. I wish we had kept all these things. We wanted to compile complaints and I

guess we were trying to develop, even in our simple perspective, like
a needs assessment. We would talk to kids, What do you think about
your school? Do they help you? Do they push you out? Are you going
to college? . . . I know that we compiled quite a bit of complaints and
that's where during the walkouts when you hear about the demands,
a lot of that was based on these complaints. So we had a process in
mind.[38]

After the surveys were returned and tallied up, Vicki, Paula,
Rachael, and other YCCA members decided to actively support and
work on Julian Nava's school board campaign. Paula remembers how
their organizing efforts progressed:

So it was interesting when we got it [the surveys] back and we tallied
it up and again it strengthened our belief of how inadequate we saw
the schools to be. Well, of course, the next question was, "Okay, now
what do we do?" We got involved in a campaign, my first political
campaign that I worked in, for Julian Nava, the first Latino to run
for school board. It was an at-large position before the board was
broken up into districts or regions, and he courted us. We worked
with him, we worked for him, thinking that this was the way, this was
an answer.[39]

When Tanya Luna Mount speaks of her organizing efforts, they
range from the antiwar movement she helped organize at Roosevelt just
prior to the Blowouts to the work she did against police brutality in her
community. In addition, Tanya remembers participating in the planning of what would be presented in discussions with the board of education: "I was on the committee that would decide what would be said
at the board of education meetings. And we'd elect who would do it."
She also speaks of the many Blowout organization meetings that were
held at her home and how "we were open all night . . . [and] people
would come over our house during the walkouts." She remembers that
her home even made the news when George Putnam, a conservative
news commentator, said that there was a house at "126 South Soto
Street in East Los Angeles, in Boyle Heights that is notorious for being
commies, rebel rousers, and anti-government."
    In fact, an important component of organizing the Blowouts was

the active participation in meetings that helped to develop or support the demonstrations. Mita Cuaron remembers actively participating in many community meetings prior to and during the Blowouts in which "we set up a list of demands on various topics and issues that we felt we were being deprived of," and community members decided that these concerns had to be brought before the board of education.[40] Rosalinda Méndez González describes the school board meetings in which she and others protested the suspension of teacher Sal Castro and demanded that the board return him to his teaching position at Lincoln High School. Though the police employed various intimidation techniques, she and others continued to organize and actively participate in these meetings:

> I mean there would be so many hundreds of us that would show up, students, elderly people, some professionals, all kinds of people that would show up to these meetings that we couldn't even fit inside the board room. I mean people were out in the courtyard and they had to have the P.A. system. . . . But I remember also at these meeting all of the intimidation. The police were going around literally, aisle by aisle, snapping, snapping, snapping pictures of everybody who was there. I mean it was pure intimidation. If you're here to testify and you're here to demonstrate, we're going to have you on file.[4]

Without the organizing efforts and persistence of these and other young Chicanas the Blowouts probably would not have taken place, and the attention needed to expose poor educational conditions may not have been garnered. By organizing community people, the women in this study demonstrate the dynamic process and complex set of relationships that comprised the leadership of the 1968 Blowouts. Indeed, this reconceptualization of leadership allows us to consider organizers as leaders in various grassroots movements, including the Chicano Civil Rights Movement.

From Behind the Scenes: Developing Consciousness

A second dimension of leadership is developing consciousness, the process of helping others gain awareness of school and social inequities through discussions or print media. Developing the consciousness of individuals is crucial to generating and maintaining the momentum needed for any social movement. Yet just as organizing is separated from the task of leading, consciousness shaping is often overlooked as part of the dynamic process.

Each of the women I talked with participated in raising consciousness through informal dialogues with her peers, family members, or community members. As young women they challenged others to think about and consider the inequities that they confronted on a daily basis. One woman put it bluntly, "You raised consciousness in any way that you could do it, subtly or outright."[42] Often one of the most difficult and least rewarding tasks of leading, developing consciousness requires one to help others see and understand things like they never have before. Cassandra Zacarías reflects on the difficulty of the task:

> I was talking to students and trying to explain to them, and I remember that was really hard for me because I was a really shy person at the time. I was a real introverted person and this was really difficult to have people actually say, "Oh you're nuts. What the hell is wrong with you?" And I remember feeling sometimes, what have I gotten myself into.[43]

In addition to holding informal discussions about school conditions or social inequities, these women used print media to raise consciousness. Both Tanya Luna Mount and Mita Cuaron's families had mimeograph machines that they used for mass duplication of informational leaflets and flyers that were then distributed throughout the communities and schools. Furthermore, all the women I interviewed were somehow connected to the community activist newspapers *Inside Eastside* and *La Raza*. Celeste Baca worked in the *La Raza* office as a volunteer, Tanya Luna Mount and Paula Crisostomo wrote for and distributed newspapers, and the other women all read and encouraged others to read these newspapers. As high school students, Tanya Luna Mount and Paula Crisostomo contributed to building consciousness by writing articles specifically addressing the poor educational conditions in East Los Angeles schools. Paula recounts her involvement with the community activist newspapers:

I typed and did layouts, and wrote ghost articles about the schools. I would also go to the [Whittier] Boulevard to sell *Chicano Student Movement* or *Inside Eastside*. . . . I would bring a whole stack to school and I would give a few to people, and they would pass them out to their friends. And then the school said we couldn't do it anymore, so I'd get to school early and I'd leave them around the campus. I would go into the bathroom and I would put them in the bathroom, the cafeteria, where I knew kids hung out, and I would tell people where they could find them. People would find them, but I wasn't actually distributing.[44]

Developing consciousness, whether through verbal or written communication, is less public than tasks normally associated with traditional interpretations of leadership. Like organizing and networking, it is work that is done from behind the scenes, often unrecognized and unappreciated. By placing working-class females at the center of analysis, we were able to see this behind-the-scenes work and appreciate its importance in the leadership of the 1968 East L.A. Blowouts.

A Need for a Wide Base of Support: Networking

A third dimension of leadership, networking, refers to activities that link diverse groups in building a base of support. During the time of the Blowouts it was important to have support from community members as well as from those outside of the community who could lend some legitimacy to the students' efforts. Thus, networking involved both transforming community and familial ties into a political force and building a supportive political front by reaching those outside of a comfortable social network. As Brodkin Sacks found in her study of workplace networks at Duke Medical Center, the networks formed during the Blowouts functioned as a sort of "telegraph system, carrying a collective message of protest against unfairness."[45]

Students who were involved in the walkouts were continuously accused of being communist, being organized by outside agitators, or just wanting to skip school. Networking within the community was a way to develop an awareness of the school inequities and develop a political force. Cassandra Zacarías remembers having to defend her own and other students' actions while trying to gain support from teachers, peers, and some family members:

> The issue would come up, well, it's all outside agitators, it's all communists coming in and riling up the little Mexicans and these little teenagers and we'd say, "No it's not. It's within our community." . . . I remember feeling like most of the kids didn't really like us and they'd say, "Oh, you know you guys are communists and you're crazy." . . . I'd tell my family, "No, I'm not a communist," and then start to tell them that there's all these inequities in the system.[46]

Similarly, Vickie Castro, a college student at the time, comments on how important it was that high school students not cause a disturbance or skip school without understanding the issues:

> I remember something that was very important to all of us is that we just didn't want disturbance for disturbance sake. And we were really talking to kids saying, "We want you to know why you're walking out." . . . There was a purpose so that we did meet with groups in the park, in the schools, on the corners and we tried to say, "This is why we're doing this and we need your support."[47]

Cassandra and Vicki's statements exemplify how networking—transforming community ties into a political force—is closely interrelated with raising consciousness—helping others gain awareness of school and social inequities.

During my interview with Sal Castro, he discussed networking strategies that involved the students connecting with individuals outside of the communal or familial social networks. He knew that an endorsement from the church, César Chavez, or politicians would lend legitimacy to the students' cause: "I constantly wanted people of the cloth to support the kids. I was never able to get any support from the Catholic Church. We had to steal a banner of the Our Lady of Guadalupe because we couldn't get any priest."[48] Finally, after a number of phone calls and some pleading, "a major coup" was set in place: Bobby Kennedy agreed to talk to the students and make a statement of support. Kennedy was on his way back to Washington, D.C., from a visit with César Chavez in Delano, California. He had to make a stop at the Los Angeles airport, where he agreed to meet with a group of students that included Paula Crisostomo and Cassandra Zacarías. A picture of Kennedy with the students appeared in local East Los Angeles papers, and Kennedy's endorsement proved to be a helpful networking strategy that increased support for the Blowouts.

During the actual week and a half of the Blowouts, Paula Crisostomo was involved with other students who were building a base of support throughout the city with groups such as the Jewish organization B'nai B'rith and Hamilton High School on the westside. Through speaking engagements, students voiced their concerns and discussed school inequities with others who could offer support and advocate on the students' behalf. Crisostomo recalls:

> We were also doing speaking engagements. I remember we spoke to the B'nai B'rith in West L.A. And we went to Hamilton and they had a rally for us in a park. During that week we were hot items, and a lot of groups were asking us to come and speak, and we were getting more support, so the board had to [listen].[49]

In light of the widespread communist and outside agitator accusations, it was especially crucial to develop a network formation of individuals and organizations who could sanction and endorse the students' actions and demands.

Less Focus on More Visibility: Holding Office

Holding an elected or appointed office is a fourth dimension of leadership. Four of the women I talked with held an elected or appointed office in direct or indirect relationship to the Blowouts. Vickie Castro was the first president of YCCA, the youth organization that focused on education and was a precursor to the Blowouts. Shortly after the school walkouts, Mita Cuaron and Cassandra Zacarías were elected student body officers. Their Freedom Candidate slate was made up of Garfield Blowout Committee members and was based on their ideal of "instituting an educational system in our school which is based on *equality, justice and first-rate education for all*."[50] Months after the Blowouts, Rosalinda Méndez González was one of the youths appointed to the

Mexican American Education Commission, which was originally an advisory board to the school board.

Though these positions probably accorded these women slightly more visibility than other young female participants, the positions seemed to be secondary to their other leadership activities. For the most part, women casually mentioned these positions during their interviews. They spent much more time recalling and talking about the more private tasks that I have included under the dimensions of networking, organizing, and developing consciousness. In other words, they seem to identify their role in the Blowouts more in relation to these dimensions of leadership than in the elected or appointed positions that they held. Yet, though these women gave less focus to the more visible and public roles, documenting this dimension of leadership is important in that it demonstrates that young Chicanas also contributed to the Blowouts (and in other social movements) within the more prevalent notion of leadership that equates elected officers and public speakers with leaders.

A More Public Space: Acting As Spokesperson

The fifth dimension of leadership is acting as an official or unofficial spokesperson. During the Blowouts male participants usually took on this role and were found in front of the camera, quoted in the *Los Angeles Times,* or speaking before crowds. However, there were occasions in which a female student who was active in other dimensions of leadership also took on the role of spokesperson. Rosalinda Méndez González and Paula Crisostomo were both asked to act as official spokespersons by providing testimony about Mexican Americans in education based on their experiences as students. Each of them testified before the United States Commission on Civil Rights at hearings held in Los Angeles. As a recent graduate of Lincoln High School, Rosalinda felt that the school curriculum was primarily responsible for the failure of many Chicano students. The following is an excerpt of Rosalinda's comments before the United States Commission on Civil Rights in June of 1967:

> From the time we first begin attending school, we hear about how great and wonderful our United States is, about our democratic American heritage, but little about our splendid and magnificent

Mexican heritage and culture. What little we do learn about Mexicans is how they mercilessly slaughtered the brave Texans at the Alamo, but we never hear about the child heroes of Mexico who courageously threw themselves from the heights of Chapultepec rather than allow themselves and their flag to be captured by the attacking Americans. . . . We look for others like ourselves in these history books, for something to be proud of for being a Mexican, and all we see in books and magazines, films and T.V. shows are stereotypes of a dark, dirty, smelly man with a tequila bottle in one hand, a dripping taco in the other, a serape wrapped around him, and a big sombrero. But we are not the dirty, stinking wino that the Anglo world would like to point out as a Mexican.[51]

In an effort to return Sal Castro to the classroom, Rosalinda also testified before the Los Angeles School Board, as did Vickie Castro and other young Chicanas.

Though most young women involved in the Blowouts did not fill the role of official spokesperson, several of the women I interviewed described instances in which they spontaneously addressed a group of students or the media in relation to the Blowouts. Mita Cuaron reconstructs a situation in which she was an unofficial spokesperson:

It was just so spontaneous. And I remember picking up an orange cone from the street, and began talking about, we are protesting and this is what's happening. And I don't remember exactly what I said, but I remember physically standing on a car and talking out loud. And for two minutes there was quite a group of students not going back into school and then the police were called and they began to chase us.[52]

Thus, although acting as a spokesperson is a dimension of leadership that was more often filled by males, these examples show that some women did participate in this dimension of leadership while also participating in other dimensions.

The Multidimensional Influence of Gender

How is it that these eight women came to participate in the 1968
Blowouts in the ways that they did? What influenced and shaped their
participation? This study provides evidence suggesting that the dimensions of leadership are not necessarily gender specific, and the same individual may engage in several dimensions.[53] While young women were
more likely to be found participating in the first three dimensions of
leadership—networking, organizing, and developing consciousness—it
is important to look at the factors that shaped their participation rather
than assume that these are gender-specific dimensions of leadership that
are only filled by females. In a study of traditional and nontraditional
patterns of Chicana and Mexicana activism, Margaret Rose concedes
that personalities have shaped female participation in the United Farm
Workers of America (UFW).[54] However, she argues that the pattern of
participation is more greatly influenced by complex factors such as class,
cultural values, social expectations, and the sexual division of labor.
Indeed, the eight women I interviewed discuss similar factors that
appear to have shaped their participation in the school boycotts. In this
final section, I will present the oral history data that speaks to the multidimensional influence of gender.

The influence of gender was perceived in a somewhat nebulous way
by the women in this study. Women made statements ranging from,
"Nobody ever said that you couldn't do this because you were a girl,"
to "I know that the females were not the leaders," and from, "Being a
female was not an issue, it was just a non-issue," to "I'm sure I knew
that there was sexism involved . . . but we probably didn't talk about it."
This diversity of statements, both within interviews and between interviews, leads to a conclusion that these women held no single distinct
and precise viewpoint on the influence of gender. Though the way that
boys and girls were socialized may have reinforced the gender differences in how they exercised leadership in the school Blowouts, the
women's diverse comments reflect the complexity of gender's influence
while also attributing their participation in various leadership roles to
sexism, role-compatibility, choice, and expectations.

The social, cultural, and temporal milieu all contributed to what
was expected of young women in 1968. And though most of these
women ventured from these expectations, they were very aware of

them. For example, one woman stated, "So I think that my home life, in one sense, brought me up very traditional. And I definitely knew what the female role was supposed to be. And that it wasn't college, and it wasn't this and that."[55] Paula Crisostomo also comments on the way that gender expectations, "how it was then," and her personal agency shaped the ways in which she participated in the Blowouts:

> Boys were more outspoken and I think that's just because of, that's how it was then. They were given the interviews more than the girls were. When we would talk about the division of who was going to speak to what group, it was the boys who were chosen and the girls who sort of stayed back. And I think that's just how it was. . . . And I was happy, as I still am today, to be in the background. I'll do what you want me to do, but I'll do it back here. Don't have me stand in front of a mike, or in front of a group of people, I just don't want to do that.[56]

Vickie Castro points out that patriarchy and her own agency were complex forces that interacted to shape her participation. Vickie believes there was a "big gender issue in the family." She grew up in a "traditional" family with a very strong and dominant father who expected her to get married and have children. Her father was an inspiration through his own strength and leadership, yet he often held traditional gender expectations and tried to place limitations on Vicki. On the other hand, her older brothers were always encouraging and supportive, and they urged Vickie to go on to college. Her family's influence gave her the strength to combat the sexism she and other young women found in some of the student organizations:

> Maybe my male friends at the time, in the organization, would try to put me in female roles. Like be the secretary, make the sandwiches, do that. But I think that I had such a strong male influence in my household, you know, four brothers and my father, that among my brothers I was equal. So I always challenged. And when I would see that there were no women involved, boom, I made myself right there.[57]

Rosalinda Méndez González also offers comments that demonstrate how the influence of gender interacted with various structures and social systems to offer a multidimensional influence. First, she acknowledges that few people raised the question or offered a critique of patriarchy in the early part of the Chicano Movement (a point with which most of the women concur), yet Rosalinda experienced sexism in a personal relationship. Second, she points to the fact that it was older males involved in Camp Hess Kramer and other organizations, rather than females, that encouraged her and other young women to become involved in Blowout related activities:

> I think that when we participated in things initially, there wasn't a consciousness of patriarchy. If you were a young man or young woman and you saw injustice, whether in regards to the farmworkers or in regards to our college, you spoke out and got involved. Now in my case, I very early on began to encounter some patriarchal hostilities from my own boyfriend, who very much criticized me for taking an active role and speaking out. But he didn't convince me nor did he succeed in holding me back. I was just very hurt by it, but I didn't accept his arguments or his reason. I encountered it at a very personal level. At the same time there were a lot of men, older men that were encouraging me to speak out and participate.[58]

Rosalinda explains that after the Blowouts, as the Movment began to gain momentum, she encountered increasing evidence of sexism and that women began addressing patriarchy as a system of domination. In fact, she argues that in many cases it was the female students who were at the forefront of the Movement and that male students tried to hold young women back and move into the more visible leadership positions.

Though sexist gender expectations were prevalent within the existing patriarchal relations, Vickie Castro also points to how she and other female and male students were conscious of gender stereotypes and used them to their advantage. They would strategize the roles that students would take based on individual characteristics and resources. For her, that meant different things at different times. At one point it meant using her car and a set of chains to pull open the gates around Roosevelt High School; at other times it meant using her "goody-two-shoes image":

> So we knew that if we needed someone who didn't look threatening, that looked like a nice person, I was to go in. I was the, you know, I'm

a little bit more *güera*. I didn't really dress, I didn't really look *chola*.
If we wanted somebody to be aggressive and very vocal then that was
David's [Sanchez] role. . . . I always had the look to get out of it. I
always looked real straight laced. And I knew that. And I used it. I
never looked the militant type, the *chola* type.[59]

In other words, she did not embody what some school officials
feared most in Mexican American students. As a fair-complexioned
female who dressed "appropriately," she was not threatening to the
white mainstream community nor to the older or more conservative
Mexicans in her own community. Vickie's physical appearance influenced the type of participation and leadership she offered to the
Blowouts, and she used it to gain support for the Blowouts.

Gender interacted with sexism, patriarchal relations, personal
agency, and the family to shape the participation and leadership of
young women in the Blowouts. And while the women in this study
acknowledge the impact gender expectations had on their participation,
they link their participation in the Blowouts to the discrimination and
oppression of the community as a whole rather than to that of women.
One woman stated, "I felt as a whole, in terms of my peers and I, we
were being discriminated against, but, personally, as a woman, I didn't
feel that there was a differentiation."[60] This echoes the findings of Mary
Pardo's study of the Mothers of East L.A. in which she points out that
working-class women activists seldom opt to separate themselves from
men and their families.[61] As the women in my study reflect back, they
too view their participation in the school Blowouts as a struggle for their
community and quality education.

Conclusion

The oral history data I present challenges the historical and ideological
representation of Chicanas by relocating them to a central position in
the historical narrative. Through a cooperative leadership paradigm
that recognizes diverse dimensions of grassroots leadership, we are able
to move beyond the traditional notion of leadership and identify ways
in which women offered leadership to the Blowouts. Though their
stories are often excluded in the writing of history, I confirm that

Chicanas have been intimately involved with and have offered leadership to the ongoing struggle for educational justice. The experiences of Celeste Baca, Vickie Castro, Paula Crisostomo, Mita Cuaron, Tanya Luna Mount, Rosalinda Méndez González, Rachael Ochoa Cervera, and Cassandra Zacarías rebuke the popular stereotypes of Mexican women as docile, passive, and apathetic, and demonstrate that women's leadership in events like the 1968 East Los Angeles School Blowouts has often been unrecognized and unappreciated.

Through the oral history data of these eight women, I illustrate that looking at grassroots leadership within a cooperative leadership paradigm leads us to an alternative history of the 1968 East Los Angeles School Blowouts—a history that makes the invisible visible. This alternative history of women's participation and leadership also pushes us to consider how we can redefine the categories for studying and participating in community activism. By redefining the leadership paradigm, we may be able to break through dominant ways of thinking and doing and reclaim histories that have been silenced in our communities, as well as shape our future histories to be more inclusive of traditionally silenced voices. Indeed, there is something faulty in previous leadership paradigms that have not allowed us to acknowledge Chicanas as leaders in the 1968 Blowouts, the Chicano Movement, and in other grassroots movements. A cooperative leadership paradigm allows us to address the erroneous absence of Chicanas as participants and leaders in history and contemporary life.[62]

Dolores Delgado Bernal is an assistant professor in the Department of Education, Culture, and Society and the Department of Ethnic Studies at the University of Utah. She is the author of numerous articles on Chicana/o education.

NOTES

I would like to thank the many individuals who provided me with supportive criticism during the different stages of analyzing, conceptualizing, and writing. The completion of this article benefited from the feedback and encouragement of Ramona Maile Cutri, Claudia Ramirez Weideman, Anne Powell, Amy Stuart Wells, Freddy Heredia, Mary Pardo, Danny Solorzano, Octavio Villalpando, and the readers at *Frontiers*, including Vicki Ruiz. A special thanks also to Sal Castro. I am especially indebted to the eight women who allowed me to transform their lived history into a written history—*muchisimas gracias.*

1. Carlos Muñoz, Jr., *Youth, Identity, Power: The Chicano Movement* (New York: Verso, 1989).

2. The following scholars have studied the Blowouts from theoretical perspectives: Myron Puckett, "Protest Politics in Education: A Case Study in the Los Angeles Unified School District" (Ph.D. diss., Claremont Graduate School, 1971); Carlos Muñoz, Jr., "The Politics of Chicano Urban Protest: A Model of Political Analysis" (Ph.D. diss., Claremont Graduate School, 1972); Louis R. Negrete, "Culture Clash: The Utility of Mass Protest as a Political Response," *The Journal of Comparative Cultures* 1:1 (1972): 25–36; Juan Gómez-Quiñones, *Mexican Students Por La Raza: The Chicano Student Movement in Southern California, 1967–1977* (Santa Barbara, Calif.: Editorial La Causa, 1978); and Gerald Rosen, "The Development of the Chicano Movement in Los Angeles from 1967–1969," *Aztlán* 4:1 (1973): 155–83.

3. Luis Ruiz (executive producer) and Susan Racho (segment producer), "Taking Back the Schools," part 3 of *Chicano: A History of the Mexican American Civil Rights Movement* (Los Angeles: National Latino Communications Center & Galán Productions, Inc., 1996).

4. In this paper "Chicana" is used when referring to female persons of Mexican origin living in the United States—irrespective of generational or immigration status. "Chicano" is used when referring to both male and female persons; I specifically indicate when the term refers only to males. Terms of identification vary according to context and it should be noted that during the period of interest in this paper, 1968, these terms were especially prominent within the student population as conscious political identifiers. The term Chicano was not prominent prior to the 1960s and is therefore used interchangeably with "Mexican" when referring to pre-1960s history.

5. In the last fifteen to twenty years there has been a relative increase in the works that look specifically at the grassroots leadership, community activism, and historical struggles of Chicanas. The following are but a few examples: Adelaida R. Del Castillo, ed., *Between Borders: Essays on Mexicana/Chicana History* (Encino, Calif.: Floricanto Press, 1990); Rosalinda Méndez González, "Chicanas and Mexican Immigrant Families, 1920–1940," in *Decades of Discontent: The Women's Movement, 1920–1940*, ed. Lois Scharf and Joan M. Jensen (Westport, Conn.: Greenwood Press, 1983), 59–83; Magdalena Mora and Adelaida R. Del Castillo, eds., *Mexican Women in the United States: Struggles Past and Present* (Los Angeles: Chicano Studies Research Center Publications, University of California, 1980); Vicki L. Ruiz, *Cannery Women, Cannery Lives: Mexican Women, Unionization, and the California Food Processing Industry, 1930–1950* (Albuquerque: University of New Mexico Press, 1987); Adaljiza Sosa-Riddell, "Chicanas and El Movimiento," *Aztlán* 5:2 (spring

and fall 1974): 155–65; Adela de la Torre and Beatriz M. Pesquera, eds., *Building With Our Hands: New Directions in Chicana Studies* (Berkeley: University of California Press, 1993); Mary Pardo, "Identity and Resistance: Mexican American Women and Grassroots Activism in Two Los Angeles Communities" (Ph.D. diss., University of California, Los Angeles, 1990); and Patricia Zavella, "Reflections on Diversity Among Chicanas," *Frontiers: A Journal of Women Studies* 12:2 (1991): 73–85.

6.   Chandra Talpade Mohanty, "On Race and Voice: Challenges for Liberal Education in the 1990's," in *Between Borders: Pedagogy and the Politics of Cultural Studies*, ed. Henry A. Giroux and Peter McLaren (New York: Routledge, 1994), 148.

7.   Kenneth Kann, "Reconstructing the History of a Community," *International Journal of Oral History* 2:1 (1981): 4.

8.   Alessandro Portelli, "The Peculiarities of Oral History," *History Workshop Journal* 12 (1981): 96–107.

9.   Patricia Gándara defines a networking sampling procedure, which is sometimes called a "snowball" procedure, as one in which participants identify other potential participants based on an informal social or professional network (*Over the Ivy Walls: The Educational Mobility of Low-Income Chicanos* [Albany: State University of New York Press, 1995]).

10. Richard A. Krueger, *Focus Groups: A Practical Guide for Applied Research* (Thousand Oaks, Calif.: Sage Publications, 1988).

11. For different interpretations of the Blowout demands see Puckett, "Protest Politics in Education"; Rosen, "The Development of the Chicano Movement"; Carlos Muñoz, Jr., "The Politics of Protest and Chicano Liberation: A Case Study of Repression and Cooptation," *Aztlán* 5:1/2 (1974): 119–41; and Jack McCurdy, "Frivolous to Fundamental: Demands Made by East Side High School Students Listed," *Los Angeles Times*, March 17, 1968, 1, 4–5. For an overview of educational concerns and issues of Mexicans during the first half of the century, see Gilbert G. González, *Chicano Education in the Era of Segregation* (Philadelphia: Balch Institute Press, 1990), and "The System of Public Education and Its Function Within the Chicano Communities, 1910–1950" (Ph.D. diss., University of California, Los Angeles, 1974).

12. Kaye Briegel, "Chicano Student Militancy: The Los Angeles High School Strike of 1968," in *An Awakened Minority: The Mexican-Americans*, ed. Manuel P. Servín, 2nd ed. (New York: Macmillan Publishing Co., 1974), 215–25.

13. California State Advisory Committee to the United States Commission on Civil Rights, "Education and the Mexican American Community in Los Angeles County," CR 1.2: Ed 8/3 (April 1968), 16.

14. Rosalinda Méndez González, personal interview, October 8, 1995.

15. "Conference Fact Sheet: Fifth Annual Mexican-American Youth Leadership Conference, 1967."

16. Rachael Ochoa Cervera, personal interview, December 10, 1995.

17. Méndez González, interview.

18. Rosen, "The Development of the Chicano Movement."

19. Gómez-Quiñones, *Mexican Students Por La Raza*.

20. Briegel, "Chicano Student Militancy"; and Rosen, "The Development of the Chicano Movement."

21. California State Advisory Committee, "Education and the Mexican American Community."

22. California State Advisory Committee, "Education and the Mexican American Community."

23. Méndez González, interview.

24. Based on the Los Angeles Unified School District's "Historical Racial Ethnic Data 1966–1979," the percentage of "Hispanic" students in each of the five schools in 1968 was as follows: Garfield, 96 percent; Roosevelt, 83 percent; Lincoln, 89 percent; Wilson, 76 percent, and Belmont, 59 percent.

25. Paula Crisostomo, personal interview, November 16, 1995.

26. Victoria Castro, personal interview, June 8, 1995.

27. Tanya Luna Mount, personal interview, January 31, 1996. For a historical analysis of patterns of police brutality in East Los Angeles, see also Armando Morales, *Ando Sangrando/ I Am Bleeding: A Study of Mexican American Police Conflict* (La Puente, Calif.: Perspectiva Publications, 1972).

28. McCurdy, "Frivolous to Fundamental."

29. Jack McCurdy, "School Board Yields on Some Student Points," *Los Angeles Times*, March 12, 1968, 1, 3.

30. McCurdy, "Frivolous to Fundamental," 1.

31. Karen Brodkin Sacks, *Caring By the Hour: Women, Work, and Organizing at Duke Medical Center* (Urbana: University of Illinois Press, 1988), and "Gender and Grassroots Leadership," in *Women and the Politics of Empowerment*, ed. Ann Bookman and Sandra Morgen (Philadelphia: Temple University Press, 1988), 77–94. These works have greatly influenced my conceptual analysis of grassroots leadership. See also Helen S. Astin and Carole Leland, *Women of Influence, Women of Vision: A Cross-Generational Study of Leaders and Social Change* (San Francisco: Jossey-Bass, 1991).

32. Thomas S. Kuhn, *The Structure of Scientific Revolutions*, 2nd ed. (Chicago: University of Chicago Press, 1970).

33. Brodkin Sacks, *Caring By the Hour*, and "Gender and Grassroots Leadership."

34. Astin and Leland, *Women of Influence, Women of Vision*, 8.

35. Dolores Delgado Bernal, "Chicana School Resistance and Grassroots Leadership: Providing an Alternative History of the 1968 East Los Angeles Blowouts" (Ph.D. diss., University of California, Los Angeles, 1997).

36. Charlotte Bunch, foreword, Astin and Leland, *Women of Influence, Women of Vision*, xiii.

37. Tanya Luna Mount's parents had a long history of labor, civil rights, and peace activism. Her mother, Julia Luna Mount, was actively involved in a labor resistance movement at one of the largest food processing plants in Los Angeles that included a massive walkout and a twenty-four-hour picket line to end deplorable working conditions. See Ruiz, *Cannery Women, Cannery Lives*.

38. Castro, interview.

39. Crisostomo, interview.

40. Mita Cuaron, personal interview, January 23, 1996.

41. Méndez González, interview.

42. Ochoa Cervera, interview.

43. Cassandra Zacarías, personal interview, December 7, 1995.

44. Crisostomo, interview.

45. Brodkin Sacks, "Gender and Grassroots Leadership," 81.

46. Zacarías, interview.

47. Castro, interview.

48. Sal Castro, personal interview, February 6, 1996.

49. Crisostomo, interview.

50. Election campaign materials, Garfield Blowout Committee, 1968.

51. California State Advisory Committee to the United States Commission on Civil Rights.

52. Cuaron, interview.

53. See Brodkin Sacks, "Gender and Grassroots Leadership," who suggests that grassroots leadership roles need not be gender specific.

54. Margaret Rose, "Traditional and Nontraditional Patterns of Female Activism in the United Farm Workers of America, 1962 to 1980," *Frontiers: A Journal of Women Studies* 11:1 (1990): 26–32.

55. V. Castro, interview.

56. Crisostomo, interview.

57. V. Castro, interview.

58. Méndez González, interview.

59. V. Castro, interview.

60. Mita Cuaron, interview conducted by Susan Racho, December 3, 1994.

61. Mary Pardo, "Mexican American Women Grassroots Community Activists: 'Mothers of East Los Angeles,'" *Frontiers: A Journal of Women Studies* 11:1 (1990): 1–7.

62. The following provides the reader with a quick snapshot of where the eight women are today:

Today, **Celeste Baca** lives in Sonoma County, California, with her husband. She holds a Master's in Education from the Claremont Graduate School and a Master's in Computer Technology in Education from California State University, Los Angeles. She has taught elementary school for twenty-four years and currently teaches in a Spanish two-way immersion classroom in Roseland School District. She has been a member of the National Association of Bilingual Education throughout most of her teaching career. In addition, Celeste teaches computer courses as a part-time lecturer in the Mexican American Studies Department at Sonoma State University.

Vickie Castro obtained her bachelor's degree from Cal-State, Los Angeles, her teaching credential from the University of California, Santa Cruz, and a Master's of Science in School Management and Administration from Pepperdine University. She has worked as an employee of the Los Angeles Unified School District for twenty-eight years. Throughout her career, Vickie has been very active in the Association of Mexican American Education (AMAE), serving as the East Los Angeles local chapter president and then the state president in 1981. In 1993, Vickie was elected to the Los Angeles City Board of Education, the second largest school district in the nation. Vickie continues to volunteer as a sponsor or workshop facilitator to various Latino youth leadership conferences in the Los Angeles area. A resident of the Echo Park community, Vickie is mother to an adult daughter and grandmother to a new grandson.

Paula Crisostomo graduated from California State University, Sonoma, with a major in liberal studies. Today she lives with her husband and two teenage children in the Los Angeles area. For a number of years Paula was a fund developer for the National Association for the Advancement of Colored People (NAACP) Legal Defense. For more than five years, she has been working in the field of social marketing—selling public service ideas—and is currently working on public housing and economic development issues for Los Angeles County. Paula contin-ues to participate in various community-based activities and over the years has remained very active in the Mexican American Youth Leadership Conferences at Camp Hess Kramer. As a member of the nonprofit Educational Issues Coordinating Committee and acting director of the conferences, Paula has been involved in fund-raising to maintain the conferences since 1988.

Mita Cuaron's social activism has often been displayed through her work as a nurse and an artist. Beginning in the late 1970s, she was a member of the "Flying Samaritans," a group of medical professionals who made monthly trips to Baja California, Mexico, to administer free medical care. In the early 1980s, she went to Nicaragua to participate in the International World Health Tour. More recently, Mita has also served as a volunteer nurse for the Mexican American Youth Leadership Conferences at Camp Hess Kramer. She has exhibited her artwork at various sites, including Self-Help Graphics, Plaza de La Raza, and University of California, Riverside. She recently donated a piece of art to a silent auction benefiting the Rigoberta Menchu Fund. Today Mita continues to reside in the Los Angeles area with her husband and four-year-old son. She works at White Memorial Hospital in East Los Angeles as a registered nurse specializing in the area of psychiatry.

Throughout college and her career as a professor, **Rosalinda Méndez González** has been active in movements against gender, class, and ethnic/racial oppression. She and another graduate student, Linda Apodaca, created and then cotaught with a third woman the first course in women studies at University of California, Irvine, "The History of Women's Oppression." She has conducted and presented research at various regional and national conferences such as the National Association for Chicana and Chicano Studies and the Latin American Studies Association. She was awarded the Woodrow Wilson Fellowship for Women's Studies for her dissertation research, and in 1980 she was invited to be a delegate to the International Conference on Women in Copenhagen, Denmark. Today Rosalinda is a mother of two adult children and is a college professor at Southwestern College in Chula Vista, California. Most recently, she has been very involved in issues of culture and the empowerment that comes from reclaiming family roots and community history; she is currently working with two other historians on a book on the history of Chicanos in San Diego County.

Over the years **Tanya Luna Mount** has worked and volunteered in various political and social justice movements. In the 1970s, she took undergraduate courses at California State University, Los Angeles, and worked as a teaching assistant in the bilingual/ESL program at a junior high in East L.A. She was active in the anti-Vietnam movement, La Raza Unida, and organizing against police brutality. She worked with the Barrio Defense Committee, which was a support and advocacy organization that brought attention to police brutality in East Los Angeles communities. During the 1980s Tanya remained active in developing a third political party through the Peace and Freedom Party. She also worked at the East Los Angeles Health Task Force, which is a multiservice social agency. Today Tanya has an eighteen-year-old daughter and a twenty-one-year-old son and continues to live in the Los Angeles area. She works at a junior high in East Los Angeles as a cafeteria clerk for the Federal Lunch Program. She actively supports the Los Angeles Catholic Worker Brittania House, which is a progressive Catholic social service organization in East Los Angeles.

After graduating from Cal-State, Los Angeles, **Rachael Ochoa Cervera** attended the Claremont Graduate School to earn her Master's in Education and a Bilingual Specialist Teaching Credential. During her early teaching career she was very involved in the Association of Mexican American Educators (AMAE) and served on its state executive board. Rachael has been teaching elementary school for twenty-four years. She is a bilingual teacher in the Garvey School District and teaches evening adult education classes at the El Monte/Rosemead Adult School. She is active in the California Teachers Association (CTA) and was recently appointed to be a Reading Recovery Specialist and a member of the Mentor-Teacher Selection Committee by her district. She continues to live in the Los Angeles area with her husband and two school-aged children, and over the years she has remained actively involved in Roosevelt High School's Class Reunion Committee.

Cassandra Zacarías attended the Claremont Graduate School while working on her teaching credential. However, after teaching for a short period, she realized teaching was not for her and left the program. She worked for a while outside of the educational field and then returned by attending graduate school and obtaining her Master's in School Counseling and her Pupil Personnel Services Credential from California State University, Los Angeles. Early in her high school counseling career, Cassandra was involved with the Association of Mexican American Educators (AMAE), attending monthly meetings and participating in scholarship fund-raisers for Latino students. Today, Cassandra is a high school counselor in the Whittier Union High School District. She continues to live in the Los Angeles area with her husband, who is an elementary school administrator, and her elementary-school-aged daughter.

BORDER LIVES

PROSTITUTE WOMEN IN TIJUANA*

Debra A. Castillo
María Gudelia Rangel Gómez
Bonnie Delgado

Con el nombre que quieras, tú pagas.
(With whatever name you like, you're paying.)
  —*Mexico City prostitute (Aranda Luna 1990, 101)*

Pues me llamo como me llamo ¿eh? Y soy quien soy,
simplemente.
(I call myself what I am, right? And I am who I am, just that.)

Eso (trabadajora sexual) se escucha muy feo, ¿no? Desde cuando
trabaja Ud. en el ambiente de noche, mejor digo.
(That [sex worker] sounds really ugly, right? Better say: How
long have you been working in this scene at night?)
  —*Tijuana prostitutes to Rangel Gómez*

This article is explicitly concerned with trying to understand the concrete social situation of women working in prostitution in Tijuana,
Mexico. Nothing in this seemingly simple statement is either simple or

---

*This chapter was originally published as: Castillo, Debra A., María Gudelia Rangel
Gómez, and Bonnie Delgado. "Border Lives: Prostitute Women in Tijuana." In *Signs:
The Journal of Women in Culture and Society* 24 (winter 1999): 387–422.

straightforward, however. To talk about the "social" immediately embeds our study in a complex dynamic of competing institutional discourses and practices in which the traditional sociological methodology of participant observation is compromised a priori. To talk about working women opens the topic of work (that of both the researcher and the research subject) as an emancipatory, nonhierarchical, theoretical, activist practice, as vociferously theorized by both Anglo-European and Latin American feminists in various, competing, and often mutually contradictory ways. To talk about women involves a necessary exploration of the cultural construction of gender and sexuality—both its dominant stereotypes and its unruly margins. To talk about prostitution is to evoke what Wendy Chapkis calls a "'magic sign' whose meaning always exceeds its definition" to such an extent that it begins to resemble a degree-zero space of representation, an empty screen onto which people project their desires and anxieties (1997, 211). To talk about Tijuana invokes a complex history in which all of these magic signs, discourses, practices, and struggles are filtered through a particular border site with its own metaphorical overlay of feminization and abjection, its own legal history, its own racially inflected past and present, its own biculturally determined exchanges. And when we as researchers try to understand the concrete situation of real women in that city, we are thrown back on ambiguously framed narratives about their lives that implicitly or explicitly rub up against all these social, theoretical, cultural, historical frames in a sometimes complicitous, often contestatory manner. The interplay between theory and methodology has produced a certain familiar discourse of ethically driven personal engagement, ironically reproduced in its (our) critique; the interplay between interviewer and interviewee opens onto another space of negotiated identities, a counterdiscourse of the sort evoked in the epigraphs to this article by which narratives and selves are continually reinvented in ways neither unmotivated nor naïve. Our aim, finally, is to try to understand the articulations among these competing social and cultural formations, and our tactic is to move back and forth between the staging of methodology and the performance of identity, between the theoretical and the thematic, with the goal of exploring the concomitant complicities and appropriations.

A Problem of Method

In 1993, Lynn Sharon Chancer published an article that asked the reader to imagine a hypothetical sociologist involved in participant observer fieldwork on prostitution in Chicago. The theoretical grounding of Chancer's article rests on the reader's and the author's shared perception of the impossibility of such a project—or at least, the extreme ambivalence of its reception—within U.S. academic settings. The responses to Chancer's scenario led her to conclude that "something about sex work is especially threatening, putting the researcher socially/sociologically at risk above and beyond the dangers attaching to the researched activity itself" (Chancer 1993, 167).[1] This perception of a risk that is both personal (participant observation with sex workers is frequently dangerous because of the social spaces in which these women work) and professional (Chancer's colleagues, when approached about this hypothetical project, all asked her in confidence if she had once been a prostitute) leads to a paradoxical positioning of the researcher that undermines her work on at least two levels. The highly charged social connotations of this kind of study associate the researcher with a stigmatized subject community, to her professional detriment. Of even greater concern is the degree to which the work itself is compromised. More intensely, perhaps, than in other participant observer situations, the academic researcher has an important stake in maintaining a distance between herself and the women she studies, such that "the benefits of participant observation are seldom brought to bear" (Chancer 1993, 153). Maintaining distance is important both for the researcher and for the women themselves, whose difficult lives have taught them to distrust strangers who may want only to use them.[2]

Chancer's observations serve as important cautionary reminders in our study, the result of collaborative work by a public health researcher, a social activist, and a literary critic. Experience in Mexico shows that the first reaction of people working in prostitution when approached by researchers is to ask, "Why are you interested in us?" "Do you have AIDS?" If they are not satisfied with the answers to these questions, they will not participate in the interviews and will influence companions not to participate. Published research in Mexico, as elsewhere, frequently marks the difficulty of securing useful material: commercial sex workers are "reluctant to talk about their trade—especially to outsiders identified with public institutions" (Zalduondo, Hernández Avila, and Uribe Zúñiga 1991, 167), and researchers often have to adjudicate the accuracy of the information gathered; as one article delicately puts it, referring to the veracity of a particular statement, "doubt exists" (Uribe-Salas et al. 1996, 124).[3]

Recent studies such as that by Michael Schwalbe and Douglas Mason-Schrock on "Identity Work as Group Process" further compli-cate this discussion by inquiring into the ways that "identities are cre-ated, used, and changed in interaction" (1996, 114). Schwalbe and Mason-Schrock remind us that interviews and questionnaires tend to assume that people report to researchers on their (singular) identity, when identity work can more accurately be defined as a process, a sit-uationally based performance, and a mechanism for describing a moral position with respect to society. They emphasize "how people adopt and adapt various rhetorical strategies for presenting themselves as they want to be seen in a given situation" (1996, 117). These strategies include defining, coding and policing, and affirming an individual's per-ceived/chosen/imagined identity. Schwalbe and Mason-Schrock con-clude that "any identity can be made into a moral identity" that offers an individual the possibility of creating a personal, symbolic resource base that supports her in the face of a hostile dominant culture (1996, 137). Following on Schwalbe and Mason-Schrock's discussion, then, we could say that the Tijuanan woman working in prostitution defines her-self both in her work and in her home life in ways that allow her to set the limits and boundaries of her variously assumed moral identities. These identities, in the interview context, are put into play situation-ally and performatively in response to her understanding of who she is in a particular moment, her symbolic capital vis-à-vis the interviewer, and her assumptions about the interviewer's stake in the conversation.

This article derives from ongoing, published work, primarily in education and public health policy, with both male and female prosti-tutes and from our own two-phase qualitative project. The first phase involved ethnographic work in 1988, including interviews with 184 women working in prostitution in Tijuana to evaluate their knowledge of HIV/AIDS and to take blood samples to test for seropositivity, as well as visits to different zones of the city to study the social character-istics and dynamics of each of these places. During this process, we (1) made a complete census of all the places where prostitution is practiced in Tijuana, (2) observed the working dynamics in each site, (3) through participant observation, studied the characteristics of women working both in establishments and on the street, and (4) classified the prostitution zones based on their social characteristics and those of the women who work in them. This information has been continually updated by the researchers.

The second phase took place in 1994–95 and consisted of in-depth interviews with thirty Tijuanan prostitutes in their workplaces; these women were chosen to represent the places in which prostitution is practiced and the types of services offered. While a qualitative study of this sort does not lend itself to the kinds of generalizations that can be drawn from data collected using the tools of statistical analysis and larger, quantitatively determined samples, every effort was made to guarantee that we interviewed women of different ages and from different socioeconomic classes within the world of prostitution, from different types of establishments and from the street, who had migrated from different regions of the country, and who had been working in prostitution for periods of time ranging from a few months to many years. Material drawn from these interviews serves as the basis for the discussion that follows, and the findings are consistent with other, related research and with the prostitutes' responses in workshops and meetings organized for and by them in Tijuana both before and after these interviews were recorded.[4]

While we too could say of our focus and data that "doubt exists," we intend this article to supplement Chancer's picture of the ambivalence about serious sociological study of prostitution in the U.S. academy and to contribute to an interdisciplinary conversation about the social construction of prostitution within Tijuana. In the latter respect we also respond to a call by Patricia Uribe, Laura Elena de Caso, and Víctor Aguirre (1996) for further multidisciplinary study of prostitution in Mexico: "There is little published research that can contribute to expanding knowledge about the groups engaged in prostitution; there is also limited work with an interdisciplinary focus which deals with the phenomenon from an epidemiological, biomedical, ethnographic, anthropological, socioeconomic, or cultural perspective" (185). Our purpose in this article is thus twofold: (1) to look at the way that metropolitan methodology and theory intertwine to produce/ invent a discourse on prostitution that spills over into ethical and political concerns in Mexico as well as in the Anglo-European sites of theory production and (2) to analyze interviews with prostitute women in Tijuana to show how their identity narratives complicate typical social science discussions of prostitution and constitute an implicit—if ambiguously sited—counternarrative to them.

Mexican Research on Prostitution

Discussions of prostitution in Mexico range from historical studies, like those of Sergio González Rodríguez (1993) and Xorge del Campo (1974), to published memoirs or *testimonios* of women who have worked in prostitution, such as Eduardo Muñuzuri's *Memorias de la Bandida* (1967) and Antonia Mora's *Del oficio* (1972), to studies of attitudes toward prostitution and the relationship between prostitution and society, such as those by culture critics Carlos Monsiváis (1977, 1980, 1981) and José Joaquín Blanco (1981). In addition to such popular culture materials on prostitution, there is also a body of professional studies on women who work in "el ambiente" in Mexico. Current studies in this field tend to one of four types: historical, sociological, medical, or legal. Uribe, de Caso, and Aguirre find that investigators associated with the field of public health have greater and more reliable access to women working in prostitution in Mexico than do people in other academic specialties, thus ameliorating the kind of distrust between sex workers and academic investigators pointed out by Chancer and Chapkis, among others, as a persistent problem in this kind of research (Chapkis 1991, 1997; Chancer 1993). At the same time, while we support the Mexican researchers' recommendation that research ties with public health and nongovernmental organizations be strengthened (Uribe, de Caso, and Aguirre 1996, 201)—and despite our own commitment to public health issues—we recognize that such a focus often tends to limit research questions too narrowly to reproductive health issues and epidemiological concerns. One currently popular research topic is the relationship between the behavior of the prostitute and the propagation of venereal diseases and, particularly, AIDS. For example, articles by Luis Alfredo Juárez-Figueroa et al. (1993) and Felipe Uribe-Salas et al. (1996) address only one of the issues concerning sex workers in Mexico, basically limiting the objectives of the study to providing epidemiologically oriented information of use to policy makers in public health.

Because of the concern about AIDS, the scientific community has been increasingly interested in the relationship between prostitution and infection, both as a topic of investigation for health authorities and as a response to generalized concern in the society as a whole. However, one of the most important limiting factors of this research is that it does not explicitly analyze the social context of prostitution. A more nuanced study, for example, would address more of the many variables affecting how women enter prostitution—including geographic locations, economic class structures within prostitution, client bases, patterns of migration into and out of prostitution, and intravenous drug use. Current epidemiological studies, unfortunately, tend to flatten out or ignore such crucial differences. While they have provided much valuable information, their focus skews the results by reducing the sex worker to a risk category and imagining her workplaces as a site of infection.

Valerie Sacks's review of Western literature notes that similar studies done in the United States and Europe routinely assume a link between HIV and prostitution, despite consistent evidence that the rate of infection is no higher for sex workers than for nonprostitute women, with the notable exception of women with a history of intravenous drug use (1996, 61). Gail Pheterson, too, complains of this bias, citing one study among many in which "the authors are cognizant of the 'peculiar methodological problems' of research related to prostitution. . . . And yet they do not question whether the status 'prostitute' is indeed the variable under study" (1990, 403). Inevitably, we are led to the conclusion that epidemiological study of AIDS is as much about inherited prejudices as it is about disease transmission. Such work evokes and participates in a long tradition in middle-class culture of associating sex workers with a femme fatale stereotype and stigmatizing female sexuality as contaminated. Leo Bersani points out that such cultural phenomena "'legitimate' a fantasy of female sexuality as intrinsically diseased; and promiscuity in this fantasy, far from merely increasing the risk of infection, is the *sign of infection*" (1998, 211). According to such models of promiscuity as the linguistic/scientific sign of infection (which is implicit in works with the premise that prostitution is a risk category) sexually transmitted diseases such as AIDS are marked as and associated with the female, and with transmission to innocent male victims via her ostensibly unrestrained and unnatural sexual activity.

As Barbara O. de Zalduondo, Mauricio Hernández Avila, and Patricia Uribe Zúñiga point out, an understanding of the social context of paid sex requires the perspectives of clients, pimps, bar and rooming house owners, and police and other authorities (1991, 173). Likewise, a fuller social characterization of the sex worker would include, minimally, the perspective of her family. By focusing on the sex worker as a deviant or marginal member of society, commentators greatly simplify a very complex issue that cuts directly to the heart of how men perceive women and how women perceive themselves in variously adumbrated social and narrative interactions. Even though the sex worker's livelihood "depends on the maintenance of the very ideology which degrades her and makes her into a social outcast" (Davidson 1995, 9), her liminal status in society casts a revealing light on questions of the social construction of gender and on issues of control and consent in human relationships.

Furthermore, like Chancer, we found that neither the historical nor the social and legal studies provided the grounding necessary to answer our fundamental questions about the integration of prostitute women into their communities. Worse, the material is spotty and incomplete, plagued with evidence of researchers' preexisting stereotypes and prostitutes' distrust. Mexican scholars have tended to fill these theoretical and empirical gaps with historical surveys and large chunks of paraphrased material from writers as diverse as Carlos Fuentes, Susan Sontag, and Simone de Beauvoir (see, e.g., Poniatowska 1988; Careaga 1990, 98, 108–11), with only postscripts to indicate their relevance to a Mexican social model. The result is a somewhat vague and unfocused essay style that depends for its effect on dubious analogies, on shock value and self-analysis, and on the empirical evidence of a database constructed from a very few, often ambiguous, questions asked of an inadequate sample of the population. One such essay, admittedly an extreme example, involves a single conversation between journalist Javier Aranda Luna and a Mexico City prostitute in which the journalist has paid for her time (which makes the essay particularly suspect since researchers in Mexico are prohibited by law from offering any monetary compensation to interviewees) (Aranda Luna 1990).

Thus, Mexican investigations into prostitution tend to one of two poles: the narrowly conceived scientific study or the generally oriented discursive essay. In trying to negotiate our way between these equally unsatisfactory solutions, we are brought back again and again to the theoretical, methodological, political, and practical concerns that undergird them and to the voices of the Tijuanan women whose narrative constructions of their own lives and strategies for survival are often at cross-purposes to the researchers' concerns. What is most powerful in these interviews is the glimpse they permit into the lives of these women—as women, not as symbols of evil, metaphors of disease, or displaced representatives of a narrative style. Their stories speak to the pervasive silence about the image of the prostitute in modern Mexico and open up a new space for continued study. In these interviews with Tijuana prostitutes we are confronted continually by the need to understand the dynamics of the interview process itself, which inevitably constructs dialogic and situational narratives about the self, both for the interviewee and for the interviewer.

James Clifford describes the predicament of postcolonial ethnography as an unnerving process of negotiating across resistances while at the same time dealing with the moral tensions, inherent violence, and tactical dissimulations of modern fieldwork. His comments seem apposite to the way we undertake a study of socially marginalized persons in society as well: "Some 'authentic encounter,' in [Clifford] Geertz's phrase, seems a prerequisite for intensive research; but initiatory claims to speak as a knowledgeable insider revealing essential cultural truths are no longer credible. Fieldwork . . . must be seen as a historically contingent, unruly dialogic encounter involving to some degree both conflict and collaboration in the production of texts. Ethnographers seem to be condemned to strive for true encounter while simultaneously recognizing the political, ethical, and personal cross-purposes that undermine any transmission of intercultural knowledge" (1988, 90). Existing scholarship on prostitutes in Mexico does not capture well the complexities of social practices or explore the relationship of these practices to the women's complex sense of personal identity as shifting and reconstructed according to the multiple spaces they inhabit. For example, a 1993 article by Marta Lamas, informed by international feminism and published in her prestigious journal *Debate feminista*, frames a discussion of street prostitution in two areas of Mexico City—Cuauhtémoc and Miguel Hidalgo—through a debate on symbolic violence and stigmatized behaviors. For a number of researchers involved directly in the field, the potential and actual consequences of this study have been particularly unfortunate because of its author's privileged location in Mexican society and government circles and because the journal's international readership guarantees the article a certain influence. In a trenchant critique of Lamas's work, Armando Rosas Solis of the Universidad Autónoma de Baja California writes, "The article has a very unclear structure, since it leaps from a moralistic presentation, without specifying whether it refers to the Mexican or the international context, connecting it immediately to the context of labor and from there to politics, in order to tie in the international prostitutes' movement, concluding with a series of statements which, depending on how they are interpreted, are very risky. . . . The whole of the text depends on quotes to make proposals, and on the analysis of [Lamas's] feelings towards Claudia [a sex worker who assisted in the project] and not about prostitution" (Rosas Solis 1996, 2). Lamas's article, then, purports to offer a new perspective on female prostitution based on the author's experience with government-sponsored research groups and confirmed by her own participant observer status in the prostitutes' community. However, as Rosas Solis comments, her work remains structured by the moral codes it decries, unconsciously speaking to the stereotypes that derive from a particular Mexican upper-middle-class, dominant-culture location.

Most strikingly, in typical middle-class parlance the category of "womanhood" is decoupled from the adjectives "evil" or "decent" to hover unambiguously over only a certain type of female behavior, pushing other female persons into a discursive abyss. Note, for example, the interview of Mexican middle-class women in a book by Roberto Martínez Baños, Patricia Trejo de Zepeda, and Edilberto Soto Angli, in which freedom of sexual expression is immediately translated by the middle-class women interviewed into a de facto definition of prostitution that presupposes the incompatibility of sexual freedom and womanhood. The interviews further describe the essential characteristic of the prostitute not as the exchange of sex for money but as an immoral and degenerate enjoyment of sexual relations

> *Corazón:* Yo conozco a muchas muchachas que salen con uno tres días
> y al cuarto, a la cama. Y esto pienso que es negativo porque esa mujer

ya no es mujer; ya es otra cosa, ya es una mujer que se vende: para mí es una prostitute, es una mujer de la calle.

Patricia: Si por puro placer, sin sentir amor, se acuestan con el primero que se encuentren, pues, realmente sí, son prostitutas.

Corazón: Y está peor, porque ni le pagan. (1973, 91)

(*Corazón:* I know a lot of girls who go out with a guy for three days and on the fourth, to bed. And I think this is negative because that woman is no longer a woman; she becomes something else, she becomes a woman who sells herself: for me she's a prostitute, a streetwalker.

Patricia: If they go to bed with the first guy they meet just for pure pleasure, without love, then, well, yes, they really are prostitutes.

Corazón: And it's worse, because they aren't even getting paid.)

This exchange does not just manifest an internalization of the traditional double standard by which women are divided into two camps, decent and evil; it also shows that those who refuse to fit easily into either category are stripped of womanhood itself. For Patricia and Corazón, "woman" is defined not only in opposition to "man" but also in contradiction to that other-gendered being, the whore. In their conversation, the two women echo novelist Federico Gamboa's famously elliptical description of his prostitute protagonist, Santa, "¡No era mujer, no; era una . . . !" (She was not a woman, no; she was a . . . !) (Gamboa 1903, 15). Curiously, the interviewees find the women they describe most morally reprehensible if they do *not* participate in the single most traditional definition of the prostitute—the exchange of sex for money. Thus, the sexually liberated woman poses a particular threat to society if she has sex only for pleasure; because traditional notions posit decent women as indifferent to sex, the prostitute who accepts money for a service she finds unpleasant fits more readily into the social norm.

Recognizing her own preexisting prejudices, which she claims were dispelled by her work with women in prostitution, Lamas concludes her article with a call for more equitable treatment: "A struggle to establish better social conditions has to include the task of deconstructing this symbolization of prostitutes as evil or sin, so linked to religious thought and so far from libertarian and democratic aspirations" (1993, 132).

Rosas Solis points out that Lamas does not in fact deconstruct the model describing women as either decent or whores but rather reinstates the stereotypes that her rhetoric apparently rejects, in that she asks not for a more nuanced understanding of the multiple roles and spaces of Mexican prostitutes but for a revision of the symbolic structure by which the dominant class appropriates images of them. In other words, the discussion that Lamas promotes retains a single moral horizon and does not recognize alternative structures into which the figure of the prostitute can interpolate herself—or be interpolated—on terms other than evil/not evil. This negative typing of the prostitute suggests to Rosas Solis that Lamas has a theoretical/structural stake in discussing prostitution in terms of marginality and stigma; her perspective, despite her six months of fieldwork on Mexico City streets, remains that of her upper-class background and does not take into account in a more than anecdotal way the perspective of the women who work within the very different class structures of prostitution.

The difference of opinion between Lamas and Rosas Solis has important material effects on how studies of prostitution in the Mexican context are conducted and by whom. In Mexico, where competition for scarce resources is often fierce, and where the different regions of the country vary widely (with respect to economics, culture, and education), current research has tended to be so narrowly focused that the results neither yield generalizations of wider import nor are able to influence public policy at a national level. Furthermore, prostitution has seldom been studied as a social phenomenon in itself at any level, creating a lacuna in knowledge about a population that, with the appearance of AIDS, has come under increased fire. More nuanced studies addressing the concrete social realities of men and women working in prostitution will require shifts of focus and resources. It is not irrelevant in this context that Lamas enjoys an important position in Mexican government and runs an influential, widely circulated journal, while Rosas Solis occupies a less privileged position in Tijuana, expressing his views via personal fax. One of the frustrations of the existing material is that it inevitably returns to the consolidation of stereotypes about the essential nature of women and the social construction of femininity in other similarly politicized contexts. Alternative constructions of femininity—produced by women and men of all class backgrounds and overlapping to varying degrees with dominant culture imaginings of women as middle-class, heterosexual wives and mothers—resolve into mere verbal evocations, at best pointing to ongoing struggles about gender in popular culture. In any case, the social phenomena of prostitution and the lives of the women involved in it are perceived as liminal to the larger social context.

The paucity of serious work on the personal contexts and social constructions of prostitution is particularly ironic in places like Tijuana, where geographic and moral marginality have always been tightly linked. Because of the "Black Legend" of Tijuana's development as an outpost of Mexican culture and a gigantic brothel at the service of the United States, both its population growth and economic development have gone hand in hand with activities that are stigmatized or prohibited in other places, and in Tijuana the tight imbrication of (provincial) identity and (deviant) female sexuality is particularly pronounced. Tijuana's infamous international image as a meat market for the United States—in which U.S. men cross the border to purchase sex from Mexican women, while Mexican men cross the border to sell their labor in U.S. fields—suggests that in both central Mexico and the United States there is a tendency to feminize Tijuana in a particularly marginalizing and stigmatized manner. One result of this process is a generalized conception of the city as, variously, a generous lady who allows a better standard of living for her inhabitants; a frivolous young woman who attracts men only to cause them to lose their souls; and, finally, a decadent and grotesque prostitute who abuses the unfortunate souls who pass through in either direction. Tijuana, in this respect, confirms centrist notions about the provinces as unattractive at best and degraded at worst. Even more curiously, in view of Tijuana's notorious image of undomestic femininity, writers and social scientists have tended, until very recently, to avoid analysis of the actual women who work in the night clubs as waitresses, dancers for pay, strippers, and prostitutes. As Patricia Barrón Salido astutely comments, even in respected studies of marginal figures from Tijuana, "it seems that prostitution remains in the ellipsis" (1995, 9).[5]

Complicating this picture further are the ambivalent attitudes evident in commentaries by women working in prostitution—attitudes determined in part by a woman's background, her geographical location and place in the class hierarchy of sex workers, her relationship to her interlocutors (readers, interviewers, clients) and presumptions about their desires and expectations, the space of utterance (whether interviewed in the work place, in her home, or in a clinic or other third location), and whether her words will be published. For example, Mexico City sex worker Claudia Colimoro, president of an organization called Mujeres por la Salud en Acción contra las Enfermedades de Transmisión Sexual y el SIDA (Women for Health in Action against Sexually Transmitted Diseases and AIDS) (MUSA, formed in 1985), presents an image of sex workers very different from that encoded in popular stereotypes. In contrast to the glamorous and terrible fatal woman image of "la dama del alba" ("the lady of the morning," singer Víctor Manuel's code term for AIDS in a popular song), or the women inappropriately attracted to sexual pleasure, Colimoro points out that 80 percent of Mexican female sex workers are mothers, a reality that "hace que las mujeres tengan que llevar una vida doble para satisfacer las necesidades de sus hijos y ocultar su ocupación y diciendo en su casa que trabajan de meseras o enfermeras" (forces women to live a double life to meet the needs of their children and hide their profession by saying at home that they work as waitresses or nurses) (quoted in Ojeda 1994, 78). Colimoro's observation hints at a tense and often bitter renegotiation of accepted roles within the community, in which the prostitute and the saintly mother occupy the same social space, rendering both home and bar environments more complicated. Yet, even Colimoro's references to a "double life" and "hiding their profession" suggest that women in prostitution uniformly accept the strictures of the dominant culture's moral rhetoric, which condemn them as immoral within the home space while covertly demanding their sexual availability within recognized zones of tolerance.

A somewhat different picture emerges from a large sample study of over 1,600 prostitutes in six cities in 1987–88, in which researchers with la Secretaría de Salud (the Ministry of Health) asked women working in prostitution about their attitudes toward a variety of sexual practices. The women were asked to respond to a number of statements and to discriminate between what they find acceptable for themselves and what for others. Clearly, these women know the codes of dominant cultural moral rhetoric; however, their own sense of appropriate behaviors does not always coincide with those norms. Evidence of this lack of fit appears in the results of the May 1988 interviews with 783 of these women. Their responses evoke a picture of their social context that is not strictly bound by dominant culture's moral strictures but instead looks a good deal more fluid. For instance, a high percentage of the women agree with the statement that faithfulness to one's partner is a positive good both for themselves and for others (80 percent/70 percent; however, about one-third of the women also find nothing particularly reprehensible in extramarital relationships), yet there is almost equally high acceptance of the practice of receiving money in exchange for sexual favors for both themselves and others (82 percent/69 percent). Likewise, a surprising number (42 percent) of the almost 800 women interviewed also evince approval of sexual relations with strangers for society in general (Secretaría de Salud 1989, 4:6–7). Just as one would hesitate to draw conclusions from the Colimoro interview about the degree to which prostitute women share normative middle-class views, so one should reserve judgment about the very different narrative constructed in the Secretaría de Salud surveys. Reading the two side by side demonstrates that the questions undergirding much social/ethnographic/public health research—of good versus bad information, or of presumptions about reaching a single "truth" about the research subject—need to be complicated by a recognition that narratives about the women's lives (both the ones implicitly created in the research paper and the ones provided in interview responses) are constructed in dialogue and situationally.

Another component of the confusion about prostitution's status in Mexico is that, while it is decried as an inescapable social evil and prostitutes are considered both immoral and pathological, the act of selling one's body for money falls into a legislative gray area—not quite illegal, and more or less regulated depending on local politics and statutes.[6] In the section of the Mexican penal code dealing with "los delitos contra la moral pública" (crimes against public morality), the following are identified as criminal acts: "contempt of public morality or good customs, corruption of minors, procuring, inciting crime, and defense of this or another vice" (González de la Vega 1968, 304; Moreno 1968, 239). Thus prostitution is technically legal, while houses of prostitution are outlawed under the prohibition against procuring. Despite these federal regulations, however, some individual states have legalized and regulate houses of prostitution in so-called *zonas de tolerancia* (tolerance zones or red-light districts). As José Salazar González notes, these functioning state laws are in conflict with the federal code and thus seem to be unconstitutional (1986, 99, 122). Likewise, one state authority comments that "even though prostitution is not legally defined as a crime, that does not imply that the subjects who dedicate themselves to its practice can do it without any restrictions" (CONASIDA, 1995b, 22). Because of prostitution's ambiguous legal status, officials' continuing harassment of streetwalkers in most of the country is technically based not on their act of exchanging sex for money but on their personal appearance, for which they can be charged with "un atenado contra las buenas costumbres" (an assault on good customs) and held for thirty-six hours (Lamas 1993, 111). In the eyes of the dominant society, as represented in the national legal code, the prostitute, then, embodies an immoral but legal vice, a crime more against middle-class good taste than against the social order.

Prostitution in Tijuana

Perhaps because Tijuana itself has so often been stigmatized in centrist Mexican rhetoric as a whore of a city and a particularly loathsome blight on the national self-image, it is an apt locus for exploring the assumptions behind social and cultural codes and how these codes affect the form of investigations into prostitution. Whether overtly political, covertly moralistic, self-consciously "p.c.," or detachedly scientific, studies of prostitution tend to frame it as a borderline experience, excluded from centrist concepts of self and nation. Tijuana almost too neatly conflates symbolic geographic and moral exclusions from the healthy body of the state. From both sides of the border, Tijuana represents that tacky and vile and threatening thing that middle-class morality must resist but cannot stop talking about.

This contemporary image is deeply rooted in the city's volatile past. Its growth in the early part of the century had a good deal to do with the prevailing prohibitionist rhetoric in the United States. When Los Angeles prohibited bars and horse racing in 1911, the small Mexican town across the border experienced a sudden influx of bars, liquor stores, and night clubs, and in 1916 the Hippodrome opened its gates, so increasing tourist traffic that by 1920 the United States ordered the border closed between 6:00 P.M. and 8:00 A.M. With the opening of the Agua Caliente Casino in 1928, Tijuana's attractions for tourists increased dramatically. At the same time, the city's prevailing industries contributed to serious social problems on the border, exacerbated by the Great Depression of 1929. Mayo Murieta and Alberto Hernández note that "Hollywood glamour displaced itself to Tijuana. It was the refuge of harassed revolutionaries, of Cristeros pursued by the Law, of farm workers expelled from the United States by the crisis of 1929 and of Mexicans who arrived to populate it, seduced by its growth and distance" (1991).

The "Black Legend" of Tijuana as a giant brothel for U.S. tourists, soldiers based in San Diego, and transient Mexicans on their way to California's prosperous agricultural fields makes the study of prostitution in this city both necessary and exceptionally difficult. An additional complicating factor is the widespread disdain in Mexico's centralized power structure for border issues. For example, Carlos Monsiváis underlines the political, social, and cultural cost of the traditional division between Mexico City and the rest of the country: "A play of opposites was sanctified: civilization and barbarism, capital and provinces, culture and desolation. Since the beginning of the century . . . the idea has propagated that the province is 'unredeemable,' that to stay is to be condemned" (Monsiváis 1992, 197). From Mexico City's point of view, the northern border is imagined as perhaps the most "unredeemable" of all the provincial outposts. It is, from a centrist perspective, the region most affected by the cultural, linguistic, and moral corruption of Mexico's unfortunately proximate and powerful neighbor, the United States.

One of the most ambiguously negotiated social sites from either side of the border is that of female sexuality. In the bars and streets of Tijuana at least two dominant-culture (U.S., Mexican) and two marginalized (underclass) versions of male and female stereotypes meet in the grating of two sets of cultural mores against each other. In this manner, the already problematic category of womanhood becomes even more unstable, and at the same time, the clash of cultural expectations highlights and sharpens our understanding of the limits of research paradigms that prematurely limit the scope of their own analyses. In Tijuana there are an estimated fifteen thousand women working in prostitution on the street (in some sectors) and in 210 night clubs/brothels. The women range in age from their twenties to their fifties, have been involved in prostitution for a period ranging from a few weeks to many years, and work in a variety of establishments, from the least exclusive to the more expensive venues. While family circumstances vary, most indicate that they come from the countryside, often from situations of extreme poverty. Family violence (mothers beaten by fathers, children beaten by parents) is common, and the women frequently seek to escape abusive homes either by forming partnerships with young men at a very early age (often as young as thirteen or fourteen) or by seeking work. They tend to fall into prostitution, which they may or may not drop in and out of over the years, in response to economic necessity propelled by the failure of a relationship or by intolerable working conditions in other jobs. Some of the women are on their own and others have partners; most have children. Some of their children and partners know about their jobs; others do not. Their attitudes toward the sex industry vary widely, but most women indicate that they insist on certain boundaries and specific practices that allow them to establish a comfort zone within their profession. At the same time, they often point to the failure of other women in the same community to do so—which they commonly see as a contributing factor to drug addiction and venereal disease.

A number of the women indicate that their first sexual experience was rape. One describes being kidnapped in a car by a young man she knew only by sight and being so injured by the rape that her attacker took fright and dropped her off at a hospital. Another describes being coerced into having sex when she was thirteen. A third describes an acquaintance rape by her employer:

> Pues como fue tan frío, tan cruel. No me la vas a creer, pero ese señor después de violarme me pagó. Sí, me botó el dinero. Y yo lo necesitaba. Yo estaba estudiando en ese entonces en Hermosillo y trabajando y este señor era el gerente de la empresa, me ofreció raite y de ahí en lugar de ofrecerme un raite, y yo le acepté raite porque estaba lloviendo mucho, entonces, de ahí me llevó a un hotel. Así con todo lujo de violencia y prepotencia me metió a un cuarto a empujones hizo lo que quiso, todavía me amenazó, y pues. Nosotros habíamos sido de una condición no precisamente humilde, sino clase medio pero muy retraídas por mi mamá. Entonces, la educación que nos habían dado, ¿no? No fui capaz de reclamar ni nada de eso, ¿no? Me sentía avergonzada, me sentía humillada, impotente. Y lo tomé con

tranquilidad, no me podia quejar con nadie. Y ya después, pues seguí, seguí más o menos la misma ruta nomás que seguí cobrando.

(How it was so cold, so cruel. You are not going to believe me, but that man after raping me he paid me. Yes, he threw money at me. And I needed it. I was studying in Hermosillo at that time and I was working and that man was the manager of the business. He offered me a ride and then instead of giving me a ride, well, I accepted the ride because it was raining hard, and then he took me to a hotel. There, with a lot of violence and superior strength he forced and shoved me into a room, did what he wanted to do, and even threatened me afterwards and then. . . . We had come from a background that was not precisely poor, more like middle class, but very repressed by my mother. So the education that she had given us, well, I wasn't able to file a complaint about any of this, right? I felt ashamed, I felt humiliated, powerless. And I took it calmly, I couldn't complain to anyone. And afterwards, then I continued, I continued more or less down the same path only now I began charging.

This woman's story of rape by her employer is but a more violent form of the many stories of sexual harassment in the workplace, confirming a widespread machista stereotype that unattached women are fair prey for sexual advances. One of the interviewees says she became a prostitute "porque no tengo estudio y cualquier parte que vaya el caso es lo mismo" (because I don't have any schooling and wherever I go it's the same story). Another woman describes moving from job to job in order to avoid overfamiliarity on the part of male bosses and expresses her frustration when it is assumed that a young widow with a child will be sexually available as one of the normal perks of the boss's job. Eventually, she concludes that there is no way to avoid being forced into sexual relations, so she decides to prostitute herself voluntarily, and for pay: "y resulta que al final de cuenta tienes que hacerlo . . . y ya no tienes hasta donde libertad de hacer" (and it turns out that you have to do it after all . . . and you don't even have the freedom to do it). Over and over again the women describe a societal structure based on male dominance in the workplace and male rights to women who are perceived as stepping out of their traditional roles, whether by remaining unattached to a male protector or by attempting to enter the realm of paid labor. The options—to have sex with male coworkers or to change jobs constantly—are seen as increasingly unviable and unstable.

The women freely admit that prostitution provides a better living than other unskilled labor, since a minimum-wage job does not provide even enough to buy sufficient food to support themselves and their families, much less to pay the rent. Furthermore, in addition to paying the bills, the relatively high wages earned in sex work allow for a measure of discretionary income, and consequently a certain freedom. Thus, while many of the women indicate that circumstances forced them into sex work, the narrowing of employment options paradoxically offers certain advantages to a woman who is able to use the system to her benefit. A sex worker can choose the number of days and hours in a day she works; she can choose the number of clients to meet and select specific ones from among the men soliciting her services; she can save her money and leave prostitution entirely or just drop out for a period of time. Sex work, while tension-wrought and exhausting, allows for this flexibility, and several of the women describe holding other jobs in the informal economy as well as selling sexual favors; they talk about buying and selling items from the other side of the border, working in shops, or selling foodstuffs.

A number of women see in prostitution the opportunity to live an autonomous life, in which they are no longer dependent on an abusive, unreliable, or unfaithful partner. As one woman says, "no me gusta depender de nadie, ni que se posesionen de mi mente, de mi tiempo, de mi persona. No me gusta que me manejen por el hecho de estarme dando un cantidad a la semana o al mes" (I don't like to depend on anyone, nor to have anyone own my mind, my time, my body. I don't like them to control me by the fact of giving me so much per week or per month). Another woman says that she has come to Tijuana from her home in the countryside for a few months only, to earn the money to pay off a debt. Still another came out of retirement to pay for expenses incurred by her previous partner. Others are saving money to establish a small business or to buy a truck. Yet another is working for a time because she wants to be able to give her children the kinds of presents she missed as a child. Several women indicate that they are the sole support of extended families including their own children, their parents, and the families of siblings, and that they may work longer hours or quit working for a time, depending on family necessity. As one woman notes, "no me gustaba al principio pero me hice la idea de que me tenía que gustar porque tenía que atender a mi mamá, a mi hermana y dos niños que tengo" (I didn't like it at first but I told myself that I had to like it because I had to take care of my mother, my sister, and my two children).

This attitude of looking at the positive side of an experience that is otherwise unpleasant is common to all the women interviewed. Importantly, the women, almost invariably, describe themselves and the attitudes they bring to their work as exceptions to the general rule within communities of prostitutes. Women who are egotistical or uncertain of their motives and goals are, according to the women interviewed, the ones most likely to destroy themselves through substance abuse. Women like themselves, however, who are able to step outside their immediate environment and focus on the positive side of their jobs, are the ones who survive, remain healthy, and have the intelligence to use the system against itself. Most important among the positive aspects are the rewards that accrue from seeing the family better itself; many of the women point with pride to how well their children and their nieces and nephews have done, precisely because of the assistance that they have been able to provide: these are children with enough to eat and decent clothes to wear, children who have finished high school, technical school, or even college. In this respect the interview responses are astonishingly consistent with the findings of therapist Clara Coria in her therapeutic practice with middle-class women and suggest the degree to which the Tijuanan prostitutes interviewed narrate themselves according to dominant-culture models of good and bad motherhood, ironically finding support in and complicating a value structure that degrades them. Coria speaks of "prostitution fantasies" in her middle-class clients that manifest themselves as "modesty [*el pudor*] about money. . . . To speak of money immodestly would be like evoking a prohibited sexuality" (1986, 45). To avoid association with this prostitution fantasy, says Coria, "women are capable of postponing or renouncing personal interests so as not to suffer from this stigma" (74). The prostitute women interviewed here also divide money into good money (used for altruistic purposes like supporting family) and bad money (used for self-gratification by women who consequently become prone to other vices such as drugs and alcohol), allowing them to distance themselves from the necessities of their work. However, if we follow Coria's line of reasoning, the Tijuanan prostitutes are finding strength, paradoxically, in an ideological position that explicitly excludes them—an indication of the way that even explicitly marginal identities (or, at least, self-representations in the interview exchanges) are bound up in the value system that dominant culture dictates.

At the same time, these women remind us that their job need not be wholly unpleasant, thus challenging the middle-class prostitution fantasy that associates desire, female sexuality, and money along quite different lines. In the dominant culture fantasy, a prostitute is less morally reprehensible if she suffers endlessly in her work and more degenerate if she enjoys it; the good mother, or good money, could never be linked to transgressive sexuality and even less to the satisfaction of illicit desires. A number of the actual prostitutes, however, comment that they find sexual satisfaction with their clients, particularly with repeat customers or with men who treat them as human beings, with kindness and thoughtfulness. One woman even sees human development prospects within prostitution itself, when it is approached with the right attitude: "Realmente es una escuela . . . si se toma de una manera positiva. . . . A mí me ha servido mucho en que he aprendido a volorar a la gente, a volorarme yo misma, a comprender, a entender, a investigar también" (Really it's a school . . . if taken in a positive way. . . . It's helped me a lot in that I have learned to value people, to value myself, to comprehend, to understand, and to investigate as well).

Yet, if the job has its positive aspects with respect to human development, the rewards nevertheless fall into a familiar realm. Chapkis says it succinctly: "Women are expected to do emotional labor and to do it willingly" (1997, 81). Thus, many of the Tijuanan women prize the caretaking and emotional maintenance work that more commonly characterize long-term relationships outside the commercial exchanges of prostitution. Paradoxically, what oppresses them in one setting alleviates oppression in another and can serve as a survival strategy and a basis for what Schwalbe and Mason-Schrock (1996) see as a socially acceptable moral identity. Complicating this picture, of course, are client expectations. Clients include two large groups: returning Mexican nationals and foreign visitors from the United States and, increasingly, other countries; and internal migrants from other states in Mexico (over 94 percent of migrant workers are men, particularly concentrated in the age group of 25–34). The Mexican underclass client shares a common language and presumably common culture with the prostitute; however, he tends to be a transient customer rather than a repeat client. For clients from the United States who come to Mexico looking for the old-fashioned caretaking absent in their understanding of dominant-culture U.S. women, the prostitutes' emotional labor fulfills stereotypical expectations of another sort. Complicating the picture still further is the implicit contrast of this emotional labor with the stereotypical image of the hardened prostitute who detaches herself from her work. If, as Chapkis notes in her research with prostitutes in Amsterdam, professionalism is favorably associated with an ability to distance oneself from one's work (1997, 78), then the positive valence that our interviewees' narratives give to emotional involvement with clients suggests that some of them wish to align themselves with dominant-culture stereotypes of the good woman as a defense mechanism against the deadening professionalism of the evil whore stereotype.

Of course, the women interviewed do not lose sight of the ugly aspects of their lives, complicating and showing the inevitable cracks and inconsistencies in their self-narratives. They freely recognize the potential for women to lose themselves if they are not strong enough to overcome the ugly and depressing environment. One woman describes how difficult it is to work on a daily basis, "hagas o no hagas el acto sexual" (whether or not you do the sex act). She explains: "Es la tensión, es la desvelada, es el alcohol, es, aunque no fumes, ya estás fumando" (It's the tension, it's the lack of sleep, it's the alcohol, it's, even if you don't smoke, you're smoking anyway). Another adds the stress of pretending to be happy and having to laugh when she least wants to do so. Still another comments on the high degree of alcohol and drug use among the women: "A veces yo comprendo a las muchachas cuando yo las veo que se dan su pase de coca o de cristal y sus acá todos lo que traen. Yo las considero porque yo sé que tienan que aguantar a cualquiera, a cualquiera. Y para aguantar a cualquiera hay que, no hay que andar en sus cinco sentidos. Apenas tomándose unos tragos o la droga para que así pueda uno soportar a cualquier" (Sometimes I understand the girls when I see them and they shoot up their coke or their rock or their whatever it is that they bring. I feel sorry for them because I know that they have to put with everyone, with everyone. And to put up with everyone, you can't go around sober. Only by drinking a few glasses or with drugs can one survive it). In this manner, the women talk indirectly about their own drug or alcohol problems, while directly and specifically describing themselves as exceptions to the general rule of exhaustion, violence, and substance abuse.

Frequently, the women shift from first person to second or third person at crucial points in their narration, thus distancing themselves from disagreeable personal experiences. For example, in the passage that follows, a woman describes her experiences in the bar where she works in the second person, displacing and generalizing her experiences, while her comments on her home life are expressed in the first person:

> Y va de todo, y tanto pues tienes que soportar un viejo borracho que anda hasta las mangas y te diga cosas y tienes que aguantarte porque estás ahí. No vas a darle una cachetada, pues no, ¿cómo te verías? todo el mundo te corre. Te aguantas y te quitas nada más del lugar. . . . Sales ya aquí, piensas, a respirar aire fresco. Es lo que te digo. Yo llego a la casa y quisiera . . . pero como llego tan cansada, tan malhumorada, a veces fastidiada. Duermo, descanso y al día de mi descanso lo primero que hago, me levanto, me doy un regaderazo, y me voy a caminar al parque.

> (All kinds go there, and so many that you have to put up with an old drunk who's falling all over himself and tells you things and you have to put up with it because you're there. You aren't going to slap his face, oh no, how would that look? everyone would throw you out. You put up with it and you just move from that spot. . . . You are getting out of here, you think, to breathe fresh air. That is what I am telling you. I arrive home and I wish . . . but I arrive so tired, in such a bad mood, sometimes disgusted. I sleep, I rest, and on my day off the first thing I do is I get up, I take a shower, and I go for a walk in the park.)

There is a certain poetry to this passage, which falls so neatly into two parts. The second-person narration of the first few sentences evokes a restricted space, where movement is limited, as are options for verbal responses to provocative remarks. In the bar, the woman feels dirtied and yearns for fresh air. The second half of the passage provides the counterpart to the first; here is the cleansing of the body and soul: the shower, the walk in the park, the recuperation of the "I."

This division of the self in language—of the first-person voice shifting to second or third person and back again—duplicates a common division in the essential spaces of the women's lives. Many of them hide their real jobs from their families, saying that they are waitresses, cashiers, assembly plant workers, salespeople or street vendors, or that they clean houses, in some cases using an actual secondary source of income as a disguise for their primary one. Many prostitutes, especially those with children, avoid the topic of their jobs with their families; as one woman says, "yo no les voy a dejar el trauma a mis hijos" (I am not going to leave my children with that trauma). More realistically, perhaps, it is often difficult for their children not to guess what is going on at some point: as one woman says, "Posiblemente cuando era niño pues lo podía engañar. Yo sé que hoy siendo él un adulto no lo voy a poder engañar porque en primer lugar una persona que no tiene un empleo, que es una mujer, que se ve más o menos físicamente y que trae mucho dinero en la bolsa y compra carro y hace esto y hace lo otro, pues es muy díficil de que alguien se la trague" (Maybe when he was a child I could fool him. I know that now that he is an adult I will not be able to fool him because in the first place a person who doesn't have a job, who is a woman, who is more or less good looking, and who carries around a lot of money in her purse and buys a car and does this and that, well, it's difficult for someone to swallow). Similarly, while extended families may receive a distanced and buffered version of the women's employment history, their long-term live-in partners generally know the truth, although considerations of "respect" make that profession an open secret that is not discussed. One woman says specifically, in response to the question "Would you tell your son about your job?": "No, porque yo sé que él lo tiene sobrentendido. Y si él guarda silencio es por respeto. Entonces, si yo hablo, ¿qué caso tiene?" (No, because I know that he implicitly understands. And if he maintains silence, it is out of respect. Thus, if I speak, what purpose would it serve?). Here, the delicate dance of silenced mutual understanding creates a relationship with her child in which each of them respects implicit distances established by love and custom.

In any case, for most of the women the topic of their work is more or less taboo outside their working environment; whether out of shame, concern about showing the children a bad example, or simply a kind of unspoken respect for privacy on their partners' and their children's part, their profession remains unacknowledged: "A veces digo yo, no tiene por qué saber de mi vida cualquier persona. . . . Tengo muchas . . . amistades pero no, muchas no saben ni la mitad de mi vida porque soy muy reservada" (Sometimes I say, not just anyone has the right to know about my life. . . . I have many . . . friends but, no, many don't know even half of my life because I am very reserved). Once again, virtues valued by the dominant society—reserve, respect, caretaking—are reinscribed with a difference in the double life of the prostitute, where what is spoken and what remains unsaid, both at work and in the home, constitute the very warp and woof of her life.

This double-voiced silence around an open secret is not always the rule. One of the women indicates that the relationship she has built with her children has allowed them to go beyond the tacit recognition of her profession, in which the mother's job becomes an unspoken matter of concern. The woman indicates that all her children know exactly what she does for a living and that their support is extremely important to her in maintaining an integrated life. She argues reasonably that since her children know exactly what their mother is doing and why, they will never feel the betrayal or shame that afflict some families whose mothers try to maintain the secret of their real jobs. She also uses her life as an object lesson for her children on the values of education and points proudly to their success in school. Likewise, another woman comments that her children have always known about her profession; however, now that her daughters are reaching the age of having boyfriends they have decided as a family that they do not want the boyfriends to know, for fear that it would lead to misinterpretations that could only be awkward.

While most of the women indicate that they prefer to keep the two halves of their lives completely separate, common themes running through the interviews are the economic necessity of working in prostitution in order to support a family and, in a parallel commentary, the importance of maintaining a focus on the family when working so as to preserve their health and self-respect. Thus, paradoxically, the same forces that propelled them into prostitution are the ones that give them the strength to survive its destructive aspects. Because Tijuana so visibly offers an alternative to prostitution for the unskilled laborer—that is, through work in the *maquiladoras* or assembly plants—these narratives of family necessity are even more forcefully inscribed, as is the women's need to imagine their basic identity as that of the good, self-sacrificing mother. For many of these women, maternity is both a precondition of the work and the single most important factor in defining their sense of self. "Yo me dediqué por entero a mi hijo" (I dedicated myself entirely to my child), says one woman. Another adds, "Sea yo una prostituta, siempre las tuve bien cuidadas" (I may be a prostitute, but my daughters were always well taken care of), implicitly recognizing the dominant-society prejudice that women working in prostitution are irresponsible and evil. Another woman, whose children know that she works in prostitution, uses her own life as an object lesson to motivate them to work hard at their studies. In reproducing one such conversation for the interviewer, she cites what she would tell her child: "Yo no quiero que Ud. sea lo que yo soy. Si Ud. sabe que está mal lo que yo estoy haciendo por esto y esto otro, yo quiero que estudie y que Ud. sea muy diferente a mí" (I don't want you to become what I am. If you know that what I am doing is wrong because of this or that, I want you to study so that you can be different from me). In this instance, the woman marks out for the interviewer a clear distance between who she is (a responsible mother) and what she does (sells her body to pay for her children's education).

The responsible mother is not only valued as an absolute social good; the prostitutes perceive her as a provider and survivor in the otherwise destructive world of the red zone, which always threatens her maternal role. One woman's stance represents that of many:

> Pero he visto muchas mujeres que nada más se prostituyen para drogarse y ni siquiera se dan cuenta de como están sus hijos. Nos les importa su alimentación, ni estudio, ni nada. Nada más ellas se prostituyen para el beneficio de ellas, para satisfacer los deseos que ellas traen. Y eso es lo que a mí en la prostitución no me admira de nada. Simplemente uno se metió a esa clase de vida pues hay que sacarle provecho y cuidarse uno.

> (But I have seen a lot of women who just prostitute themselves for drugs and don't even notice their children. They don't worry about their food, their schools, or anything. They just prostitute themselves

for their own benefit, to satisfy their desires that they carry around. And that is something about prostitution that I don't care for at all. Simply put, if one has gotten into that kind of life, one has to get the best out of it and take care of oneself.)

The pathos evoked in these comments is too strong to be ignored. The speaker eloquently defines the constraining qualities of a prostitute's life; in order to work in the dehumanizing world of the red zone, self-respect and respect for others are the keys to survival. At the same time, to be able to function at all, the women must separate within themselves the roles of mother/caretaker and commercial sex worker. If the separation is too absolute, however, they may fall prey to the dangers of the prostitute's world: the drugs, the egotism.

And yet, of course, the process of interviewing brings together the two parts of the women's lives, and the resulting picture, whether a consequence of the questions asked or not, is strikingly consistent with other understandings of professional women in other, more traditionally accepted venues. Overwhelmingly, stories about professional women—whether Tijuana street prostitutes or prominent lawyers—at some point place emphasis on the woman's concept of herself with respect to her home and her children, a feature generally elided in stories of professional men. Conventional wisdom assumes that a woman's identity is most clearly articulated with respect to her home life, whereas a man's identity is wrapped up in his profession. This story of women's identity allows Tijuana prostitutes distance from their profession, for whatever good they see in it has to do with service to others, and it is only the weak or the unwary who are consumed and hence destroyed by the profession.

It is also important to recall that the work of these women occurs in an ambiguous space, not quite licit, not entirely illegal. Within the red zone certain behaviors are accepted; outside that space both clients and prostitutes enter into other sets of social, familial, and sexual relationships that may or may not reflect very different expectations for gendered behavior. It is, says Angie Hart about a Spanish red zone, precisely the permeability of the boundary between what is allowed and what is prohibited that makes the space of prostitution so titillating for clients: "Many clients . . . describe their presence in the barrio as 'vice.' However, they were able to enjoy this 'vice' in an atmosphere in which this was accepted as a leisure pursuit" (1995, 219). For the men and the women, then, relationships established within the red-light district are ambiguously coded. The men see their behavior as leisure activity, often imagined not as strictly evil but as playing at transgression, practicing a "vice" imagined within ironic quotation marks; for the women it is a temporary and generally unpleasant job. If the clients sometimes express interest in crossing the boundaries between differently coded spaces—wanting home addresses or even begging to marry prostitutes—it is the women themselves who make an effort to retain separation in the two parts of their lives, rejecting overtures, and only infrequently allowing men they have known as clients to become members of their lives outside their work.

Infection-Free Sites

In order to exert some control over their circumstances, the women describe their techniques for creating personal comfort zones in the midst of the tense, uncertain environment. They mark out boundaries within prostitution by using specific practices to create reserved spaces, often spaces on their bodies. For instance, all of the women interviewed insist that they require condom use, and, uniformly, any woman who admits to having a venereal disease at some time in her life insists that it occurred outside of work, with a partner who was not a client and with whom, hence, she was less careful about safe sex practices. One of the women says that her only experience of sexually transmitted disease dates from her youth, before she was a prostitute, when she was infected by a boyfriend and did not even realize why she was sick. Another woman comments that her infection was the result of her desire for a social life outside of work, one involving going out for dinner and to movies and showing affection to a man. However, "los hombres andan sueltos como las mujeres de las maquiladoras" (men run around loose like the women from the assembly plants), which causes all the problems because, unlike responsible sex workers, unprofessional women and men who act promiscuously tend to spread disease. Still another describes her disgust upon finding out that her partner had gonorrhea. She immediately had herself tested for the disease and was able to prove exactly where the guilt lay when her test turned out negative. In response, she not only threw her erstwhile boyfriend out of her life on the spot but even refused to give him a ride home from the clinic in her car: "No, no, no, le dije, no vayas a dejar aquí microbios" (No, no, I told him, you aren't going to leave your microbes in here). These stories are not so much an accurate account of the relative safety from contagion within prostitution as they are modern myths, cautionary tales that reverse the dominant culture's story of prostitution as a site of infection.

In these revisionary stories, unlike the more familiar middle-class tales of the evil women who make men sick by passing on their vile female-associated diseases, it is the hypocritical dominant culture that victimizes women, who must be constantly alert to the persistent dangers of a contaminated space outside formal sex work. Certainly, this image of the knowledgeable professional holds true only for a certain subset of Tijuana prostitutes; it is also true that, whatever fantasies a male client may bring to his encounter with a prostitute, in most cases the woman has far more experience than the man, which partially offsets the power differentials inherent in patriarchal expectations and paid-sex relationships.

In an analogous manner, the boundaries of the specific sexual practices in which the women say they will engage are also indications of physical and mental reserve, or even a kind of patriotic *pudor* (modesty). When the women are asked about sexual practices, the responses are surprisingly uniform: they consistently indicate a preference for "normal" vaginal sex. Some express ignorance about other sexual practices; some say that under special circumstances they will perform oral sex, albeit reluctantly; all vehemently deny that they ever agree to anal sex. When that inquiry is made, one woman says she typically responds, "Soy mujer, no maricón" (I'm a woman, not a fag). Another hints that such unnatural perversions could come only from foreigners or contagion by foreign practices: "Todavía soy muy Mexicana, ¿verdad? Yo sexo anal no lo realizo por ningún concepto" (I am still very Mexican, right? I don't perform anal sex under any circumstances). Another indignantly responds to the inquiry about sexual practices other than vaginal sex with "¡Jamás! Te estoy diciendo que yo soy limpia en todo aspecto sexual. . . . Nunca jamás en la vida permití que me hicieron cochinadas ni que me dijeran que yo tenía que hacerlo" (Never! I am telling you that I am clean in every sexual aspect.

. . . I never ever in my life permitted anyone to do dirty things to me nor to tell me that I had to do it). Still another describes her technique for dealing with insistent clients: she tells them, "Mira, la verdad es que quiero llegar virgen de un lado de mi cuerpo para el día que yo me case" (Look, the truth is that I want to arrive virgin on one side of my body for the day I get married). In these comments too the women are delineating a certain comfortable social space, perhaps real, perhaps constructed in the imaginary exchanges of interview expectations. Clearly, demands for oral and anal sex are extremely common. As one woman interviewed in Mexico City by another researcher notes, "Me imagino que como la novia o su mujer no pueden vienen con una a ver si pega" (I imagine that since the girlfriend or the wife can't, they come to one of us to see if they can talk us into it) (Aranda Luna 1990, 99), and other evidence suggests that in Tijuana, as elsewhere, the most commonly offered service is the half-and-half (oral stimulation followed by vaginal sex), which most efficiently gets a client out of the room in twenty minutes. What the Tijuanan women are signaling in this interview situation is a particular personal reserve, a chastity within prostitution that implicitly functions as a differentiating quality that the women interviewed believe separates them from the mass of other prostitutes, whom they see as perhaps less stable, less moral, more prey to the destructive side of their jobs. Again, what is crucial here is the way these women construct a consistent and moral identity with respect to the interview situation. We are less concerned with whether they actually pronounce the ugly and all-too-prevalent offer of "sucky-fucky" to their clients than with how their sense of self and their fragile boundary maintenance conspire to exhibit a desired identity that intersects with, and occasionally runs at odds to, their professional lives.

On another, discreet level the sex workers are indirectly addressing dominant Mexican culture's concerns about the prostitute as a site of infection, since they know that AIDS is associated with homosexuals and particularly with anal sex. In defining themselves as professional *and* chaste, they implicitly position themselves as outside simplistic dominant-society perceptions, where, in Chapkis's words, "the lack of interest in the 'contamination of prostitutes'—rather than *by* them—exposes the belief that prostitutes (like homosexuals) are always already 'sick'; their eventual literal infection by a sexually transmitted disease does not represent a significant change of status. The message appears to be that for the 'whore' who has abandoned proper womanhood through money-driven promiscuity, . . . disease and death are the natural, the expected, the sanctioned punishment" (1997, 166). In Tijuana, again the nature of border consciousness comes into play; not only are anal intercourse and homosexuality expelled from the repertoire of usual practices, they are rejected as explicitly *foreign* perversions—a clear contestation of dominant culture's expectations and understandings of prostitution as illness. Thus, these women insist that contamination is not localizable on their bodies or in the geographical space of the Zona Norte, nor can it be ascribed to Mexican national identity; it resides outside, across the border, in the other culture against which they must be vigilant. In each case, the delimitation involves a construction of borders against a threat that must be kept out—to protect body, community, nation—as well as an implicit recognition of the counterdiscursive quality of these assertions. Mexican dominant culture serves Tijuanan prostitutes alternately as a model and as a menace, as a myth against which to measure survival strategies and as a harsh reality. At the same time, these shifting values interact with perceptions about the United States so that two sets of dominant-culture stereotypes and two sets of marginalized responses resonate against each other in the tales the women tell. Each culture's discourse also allows for slippage, for the woman who does not protect her boundaries and slips from one narrative construction into another, from myth to myth.

Condom use is one of the most contested problems in establishing the boundaries and ground rules between a woman and her client. While Lamas's study of street prostitution in Mexico City arrives at the conclusion that "no girl would refuse to do it without a condom, since that would mean losing the client" (1993, 123), the Tijuanan women we interviewed are far more united and adamant about condom use, to the degree that they commonly exchange stories on the topic and suggest methods for persuading reluctant clients to comply.[7] As one of the women notes, it is important to have an unbreakable agreement among the women that they will accept only clients with condoms, since, she says, 99 percent of the men try to get out of using them: "Vamos a suponer que yo aceptara irme con un cliente sin condón, al ratito ya le gustó otra y también sin condón. Y es donde va el contagie" (Let's suppose that I agreed to go with a client without a condom, and then after a while he likes another woman and also without a condom. And that is where contagions start). One common argument is that the woman knows she is disease-free because of her regular checkups but that the client can give no such assurances. This argument reinforces the message that the professional woman offers advantages to a man careful of his health and that the red zone is a safer environment for nonmonogamous men than the larger community. The opposite argument is also common: the client may believe he is disease-free, but since he cannot have the same confidence about the prostitute, condom use is in his best interest.

Ninety-five percent of the prostitutes surveyed for the 1989 national *Informe técnico* feel that they should use condoms. Fifty-seven percent actually used condoms in the nine months preceding the study and approximately 15 percent use them at all times (Secretaría de Salud 1989, 4:4, 8, 11). Obviously, the responses of the women interviewed in depth in Tijuana, in their uniform insistence on an unwavering commitment to consistent condom use with their clients, do not accord with the national statistics. Studies by Mauricio Hernández Avila et al. and Uribe-Salas et al. remind us that questions about condom use are particularly loaded ones and that the responses need to be evaluated with respect to behavioral, social, and political contexts (Hernández Avila et al. 1991, 185, 187–88; Uribe-Salas et al. 1996, 124).[8] We do not attempt to resolve the question of whether the women's responses are truthful; more important is that their emphasis on condom use indicates consciousness of safe sex practices and the important ideological representations of themselves as wholesome and intelligent and of the space of prostitution as an infection-free site where safe-sex knowledge is put into practice, in contrast to the practices of the general population.

Conclusions

What then, finally, can we say about the perspective of the prostitute apart from how she frames her life story for consumption by the privileged classes, whether in the form of a *testimonio* or a research interview? Rosas Solis—who draws from personal experience and from professional interviews with hundreds of prostitutes in more than two dozen Mexican cities in seventeen states over a period of thirty years—

suggests that the familiar stereotypes do not always function as expected:

> Symbolizing prostitutes as evil, sin, or social trash is not something directed towards women who hold this job. . . . It is used for women who are not prostitutes and who are interested in sexual pleasure. . . . On the other hand, this symbolism, which so worries social scientists, does not bother the majority of the women who work in prostitution.
>
> The other symbolism . . . of prostitution as a job like any other, is something that most of the time doesn't worry them either.
>
> The problem of prostitution should not be focused from the point of view of male demand. . . . The problem should be addressed from the point of view of education in families and in schools, of the influence of the social setting; these things determine conduct and the stereotypes people follow; from these derive the creation of necessity, and for this reason opens the space for it to become a business.

Rosas Solis points out the curious fact that it is within so-called decent society that women are excoriated for expressing sexual desires. Thus, if a woman comes from a class background and upbringing that would seem to locate her within the category of "decent women," she may be stigmatized with the hurtful epithet of "whore" if her behavior is understood within her social context as overly sensual or sexual. Within the social space of the prostitute's community, however, such an accusation would be irrelevant; it is only in relation to the stigmatized and abjected female other that the insults acquire their force. Likewise, the question of prostitution's relation to other forms of labor—a concept encapsulated in the term "sex worker"—only intermittently inflects these women's understanding of themselves. While they frequently insist that prostitution is "un trabajo como cualquier otro" (a job like any other), and while they underline their professionalism, they also move in and out of prostitution with great fluidity and with little sense of themselves as a potential collective of workers. Strikingly, then, the typical research framings of prostitution as either a social problem or as a labor movement fall drastically short of the women's narrative reality.

Again and again, we are reminded of the situational quality of our own work and its realignment of the fantasies that permeate the social imaginary, in which the prostitute (or one of her metaphors) stands for whatever corrupting, dangerous quality needs to be expelled from society at a given time and for whatever threats of corruption continue to menace society. In this article we have begun the project of interrogating these social forms, looking at the shadows of the narratives behind methodological and theoretical texts and exploring the inventions and reinventions of self and culture that take place in the dialogues between interviewer and interviewee. In the interstices of these half-spoken, half-formulated shadow texts, we glimpse the engagements of and slippages from dominant discourses both Mexican and metropolitan. In this respect, we subscribe to the concern that Chapkis so eloquently voices in *Live Sex Acts:* "We need to develop the capacity to listen to these stories without reducing them to competitors for the status of Truth. We need to listen for meaning rather than just 'fact,' to ask why a story is told in this way, how the location of the speaker shapes the tale, how the position of the audience affects what is heard, and to carefully consider what is at stake politically, personally, and strategically in invoking this particular version at this moment in this context" (1997, 212). Chapkis reminds us that discussions of prostitution—even when they pass for or are disguised in the rhetoric of objective, value-free scientific research—tend toward the dissimulation of highly charged political agendas.

These agendas are not the same in Mexico as in the United States, but the cultures share underlying assumptions about a contained category called "sex worker." However, the narratives of Tijuana prostitutes that we discuss in these pages pose a continuing challenge to theoretical and methodological recuperation. Our task is complicated by the continual reinvention of narratives and selves in ways neither unmotivated nor naïve, but even in our narrative subsumption of these voices, they remain unruly and recalcitrant and resist categorization. One anonymous reviewer of an earlier version of this article commented, for instance, that some of the stories "counter popular stereotypes, some don't." Some of the interviewees reinscribe specific stereotypes (about women, about prostitutes); some live at odds with conventional expectations. Their narratives remain uncontainable, and in this important respect they function most crucially not as indices

to or even recuperations of dominant culture's expelled and contained
Other but as its shadow supplement. It is this complicity that most
threatens standard categories and thus is so often silenced or reduced
to unintelligible cacophony. These Tijuanan prostitutes' border lives,
read in the context of cultural studies practices and social scientific
theory, remind us that appeals to "knowledge" and "understanding"—
the terms we proposed at the outset of our modest study—inevitably
raise the stakes in a complex game of contested meanings. Their
conjunction has forced us to rethink the question of the social; their
presence shadows every theoretical turn. In trying to understand the
articulations among these competing social and cultural formations we
are reminded again of Schwalbe and Mason-Schrock's conclusion that
"any identity can be made into a moral identity" (1996, 137), even if
this morality may not coincide at all points with that of the hostile
dominant culture. If a fuller understanding of these processes still eludes
us, we have at least some hints about where to go to raise the deeper
questions that need to be asked.

Debra A. Castillo is a professor in the Latin American Studies Program at
Cornell University. Her previous books include *Easy Women: Sex and Gender
in Modern Mexican Fiction* (1998), *Talking Back: Toward a Latin American
Feminist Literary Criticism* (1992), and *The Translated World: A Postmodern
Tour of Libraries in Literature* (1984). María Gudelia Rangel Gómez is a
professor in the Departamento de Estudios en Salud Pública at Colegio de
la Frontera Norte. Bonnie Delgado is a professor at Escuela de Idiomas,
Universidad Autónoma de Baja California.

NOTES

The authors gratefully acknowledge the following sources of support for this project: internal grants from the Latin American Studies Program and the Society for the Humanities at Cornell University and from the Colegio de la Frontera Norte in Tijuana, as well as a Presidential Faculty Fellowship Award (National Science Foundation grant DEB 925370) to Carlos Castillo-Chavez. All translations from Spanish in this text are our own.

1. One of the symptoms of the disquiet provoked by studies of prostitution is the plethora of terms surrounding it, each with particular connotations and ideological baggage. Wendy Chapkis's introductory chapter to *Live Sex Acts*, "The Meaning of Sex," offers a lucid analysis of how specific terms such as *prostitute, whore,* and *sex worker* play themselves out relative to the position of the researcher. The Tijuanan women interviewed for this study also differ with respect to the terms they prefer to describe themselves and their work; some say "call me what I am," while most prefer less explicit references to "el ambiente" (loosely equivalent to "the scene"). There is a general (but not universal) dislike among them for the term "trabajadora sexual" (sex worker), which they see as an academic affectation. Because it is not the purpose of this article to engage these debates, we merely try to remain consistent with these shifting perspectives in our choice of vocabulary used to paraphrase the interviewees' comments.

2. This issue is also addressed by Chapkis 1995, which responds to the same theoretical/methodological problem posed by Chancer 1993 with respect to participant observation research in California and Amsterdam. Chapkis's work has been further developed in her 1997 book, *Live Sex Acts*. We thank an anonymous reviewer at *Signs* for bringing this important work to our attention.

3. The issue of doubt has always been present in cultural studies, though its implications are seldom explored. Davidson and Layder's book on methodology in the social sciences comments that "while all manner of methodologists have a lot to say about how best to get people to give truthful, or full and sincere replies, less is said about how a researcher can tell whether an interviewee *is* telling the truth," allowing such questions to fall back onto an assertion about good rapport as a foundation for the interview process (1994, 116, 122). Chancer, Zalduondo et al., and Uribe-Salas et al. put pressure on methodological concerns at precisely this level; in studies of prostitution, where both the rapport and the responses are always in doubt, the data must be evaluated very carefully indeed. Furthermore, we must take seriously the concerns of feminist writers (Chapkis and Davidson are excellent examples in the Anglo-European scene, as is Lamas in Mexico) about the masculinist bias in social research and the way that "the orthodox methodologist's emphasis on control, hierarchy and the impersonal nature of scientific research reflects a masculine view of the world and of human relationships more generally" (Davidson and Layder 1994, 125). Even here, however, doubt persists and cannot be alleviated by our assurances of a good interview rapport or by a nonhierarchical format for interviews of women by women since, inevitably, class and the educational differentials between interviewer and interviewee reinstate a hierarchical relationship.

4. In addition to these studies, and informing the general content of our work, we would like to recognize Patricia Barrón Salido's fieldwork (in 1995–96) on an

organized group of Tijuanan street prostitutes, the "María Magdalenas," and her recently completed master's thesis on the social reproduction of the families of prostitute women. Barrón's particular interest is on the double stigmatization they experience. Both of these projects were completed under the direction of María Rangel Gómez.

5. Barrón Salido is referring to a specific report on the situation in Tijuana. She quotes Martín de las Rosa's (1985) extensive list of marginal persons: "Vamos a ocuparnos en este apartado de los peones, los albañiles, meseros, lavacoches, periodiqueros, las 'marías,' los que 'ya volvieron del otro lado' (metedólares), los que 'quieren ir al otro lado,' las empleadas domésticas, las 'que lavan ajeno,' los yonkeros, los 'cholos,' los barrenderos, los artesanos, los vendedores ambulantes, . . . los desocupados" (We are going to concern ourselves in this report with the peons, the construction workers, the waiters, the car washers, the newspaper sellers, the indigenous women workers, those who came back from the other side [bringing dollars], those who want to go to the other side, the servants, the washerwomen, the junkies, the gang members, the street sweepers, the handicraft makers, the street vendors, the unemployed) (quoted in Barrón Salido 1995).

6. Debates in the federal congress in January 1997 about regulating prostitution within Mexico City have heightened national awareness of the contradictions and inconsistencies in federal and local codes. These ambiguous legal codes importantly affect the circumstances under which studies of prostitution are carried out in Mexico; most notably, unlike in the United States, the prostitution researchers are not dealing with a legally criminalized population.

7. Lamas's conclusion is also consistent with other local studies, although not with the statements made by the women we interviewed in depth for the Tijuana study. For example, the CONASIDA report on sex workers in the area of Tuxtla Gutiérrez in the south of Mexico indicates that women in that area "do not include negotiations about condom use as part of their daily practice, and their experience is slight. They reiterate a rejection of condom use in almost all types of clients, except 'rich boys'" (CONASIDA 1995b, 13). Similarly, clients interviewed in Ciudad Hidalgo, also in the south of Mexico, tell interviewers that sex workers there report inflated rates of condom use. The prostitutes themselves know that they ought to use condoms but, when pressed, cannot explain exactly *why* they should (CONASIDA 1995a, 19). Women in Jalisco complain that while they are aware of the health risks, they are unable to use condoms because their clients refuse (Rivera, Vicente-Raldo, and Lucero 1992, 77). The information from southern border cities is especially interesting, as the majority of prostitutes in Ciudad Hidalgo, e.g., are Central American women who immigrate illegally to Mexico and use that city as a jumping-off point to earn enough money to move to Mexico's northern border.

8. It is important to remember that rates of HIV infection differ significantly in the major Mexican cities, although there is no consistent correlation between the rate of condom use and the risk of infection. One explanation for the relatively high reported condom use rate in Tijuana would be the effectiveness of education and prevent programs, particularly among the client base in southern California cities. Anecdotal evidence from Internet newsgroups suggests that U.S. clients of Tijuanan prostitutes are aware of, and support, the women's universal requirement of condom use at all times.

REFERENCES

Aranda Luna, Javier. 1990. "Una también es gente." In *El nuevo arte de amar: Usos y cos-tumbres sexuales en México*, ed. Hermann Bellinghausen, 99–106. Mexico: Cal y Arena.
Barrón Salido, Patricia. 1995. *Las "María Magdalena": El oficio de la prostitución y su estrategía colectiva de vida*. Bachelor's thesis, Colegio de la Frontera Norte, Tijuana.
Bersani, Leo, 1988. "Is the Rectum a Grave?" In *AIDS: Cultural Analysis, Cultural Activism*, ed. Douglas Crimp. Cambridge, Mass.: MIT Press.
Blanco, José Joaquín. 1981. *Función de medianoche: Ensayos de literatura cotidiana*. Mexico: Ediciones Era.
Careaga, Gabriel. 1990. *Mitos y fantasías de las clase media en México*. Mexico: Cal y Arena.
Chancer, Lynn Sharon. 1993. "Prostitution, Feminist Theory, and Ambivalence: Notes from the Sociological Underground." *Social Text* 37 (winter): 143–71.
Chapkis, Wendy. 1991. "Suggestive Language: On Sex Workers and (Other) Feminists." *Sub/versions* (winter): 1–6 (Working paper series, University of California, Santa Cruz).
———. 1995. "Too Close for Comfort: Prostitution, Participant Observation, and Sexual Stigma." Society for the Study of Social Problems. April 3.
———. 1997. *Live Sex Acts: Women Performing Erotic Labor*. New York: Routledge.
Clifford, James. 1988. *The Predicament of Culture: Twentieth-Century Ethnography, Literature, and Art*. Cambridge, Mass.: Harvard University Press.
CONASIDA (Consejo Nacional para la Prevención y Control del SIDA). 1995a. "Análisis de la situación de Ciudad Hidalgo, Chiapas." Internal technical report.
———. 1995b. "Resultados del análisis de la situación y propuesta para desarrollar una intervención para aumentar la seguridad del sexo comercial, en Chiapas, area de Tuxtla Gutiérrez." Internal technical report.
Coria, Clara. 1986. *El sexo oculto del dinero: Formas de la dependencia feminina*. Buenos Aires: Grupo Editor Latinoamericano.
Davidson, Julia O'Connell. 1995. "The Anatomy of 'Free Choice' Prostitution." *Gender, Work and Organization* 2(1):1–10.
Davidson, Julia O'Connell, and Derek Layder. 1994. *Methods, Sex and Madness*. New York: Routledge.
de la Rosa, Martín. 1985. *Marginalidad en Tijuana*. Tijuana: Cuadernos CEF-NOMEX.
del Campo, Xorge. 1974. *La prostitución en México*. Mexico: Editores Asociados.
Gamboa, Federico. 1903. *Santa*. Mexico: Fontamara.
González de la Vega, Francisco. 1968. *Derecho penal en México: Los delitos*. Mexico: Porrua.
González Rodríguez, Sergio, ed. 1993. *Los amorosos: Relatos eróticos mexicanos*. Mexico: Cal y Arena.
Hart, Angie. 1995. "(Re)constructing a Spanish Red-Light District: Prostitution, Space, and Power." In *Mapping Desire: Geographies of Sexualities*, ed. David Bell and Gill Valentine, 214–28. New York: Routledge.
Hernández Avila, Mauricio, Patricia Uribe Zúñiga, and Barbara O. de Zalduondo. 1991. "Diversity in Commercial Sex Work Systems: Preliminary Findings from Mexico City and Their Implications for AIDS Interventions." In *AIDS and Women's Reproductive Health*, ed. L. C. Chen, 179–94. New York: Plenum.
Juárez-Figueroa, Luis Alfredo, Mauricio Hernández Avila, Patricia Uribe Zúñiga, George Smulian. 1993. "Prevalencia de anticuerpos contra *Pneumocystis carinii*

en sujetos con prácticas de alto riesgo de SIDA." *Revista de Investigaciones Clinicas.* 45:229–31.

Lamas, Marta. 1993. "El fulgor de noche: Algunos aspectos de la prostitución callejera en la ciudad de México." *Debate feminista* 8:103–33.

Martínez Baños, Roberto, Patricia Trejo de Zepeda, and Edilberto Soto Angli. 1973. *Virginidad y machismo en México.* Mexico: Era.

Monsiváis, Carlos. 1977. *Amor perdido.* Mexico: Era.

———. 1980. "La mujer en la cultura mexicana." In *Mujer y sociedad en América latina,* ed. Lucía Guerra-Cunningham, 101–17. Irvine, Calif.: Editorial del Pacífico.

———. 1981. *Escenas de pudor y liviandad.* Mexico: Grijalbo.

———1992. "De la cultura mexicana en vísperas del TLC." In *La educación y la cultura ante el Tratado de Libre Comercio,* ed. Julio López et al., 189–209. Mexico: Nueva Imagen.

Mora, Antonia. 1972. *Del oficio.* Mexico: Editorial Samo.

Moreno, Antonio de P. 1968. *Curso de derecho penal mexicano.* Mexico: Porrua.

Muñuzuri, Eduardo. 1967. *Memorias de "La Bandida."* Mexico: Costa-Amic.

Murrieta, Mayo, and Alberto Hernández. 1991. "Puente México: La vecindad de Tijuana con California." Working paper, Colegio de la Frontera Norte, Tijuana.

Ojeda, Néstor L. 1994. "Prostitución en los noventa." *Nexos* 17(203):76–80.

Pheterson, Gail. 1990. "The Category 'Prostitute' in Scientific Inquiry." *Journal of Sex Research* 27(3):397–407.

Poniatowska, Elena. 1988. "Xaviera Hollander o las glorias de las prostitución." In *Fem: Diez años de periodismo feminista,* 74–78. Mexico: Planeta.

Rivera, George, Jr., Hugo Vicente-Ralde, and Aileen F. Lucero. 1992. "Knowledge about AIDS among Mexican Prostitutes." *Sociology and Social Research* 76(2):74–80.

Rosas Solis, Armando. 1996. "Comentarios." Unpublished manuscript.

Sacks, Valeria. 1996. "Women and AIDS: An Analysis of Media Misrepresentation." *Social Science and Medicine* 42(1):59–73.

Salazar González, José Guadalupe. 1986. *Reglamentación del trabajo de las mujeres en los centros nocturnos.* Law thesis, Universidad Autónoma de Baja California, Tijuana.

Schwalbe, Michael L., and Douglas Mason-Schrock. 1996. "Identity Work as Group Process." *Advances in Group Processes* 13:113–47.

Secretaría de Salud. 1989. *Informe técnico. Evaluación del impacto de la estrategía educativa para la prevención del SIDA en México 1987–1988.* 5 vols.: *Mujeres dedicadas a la prostitución, Hombres homo-bisexuales, Estudiantes universitarios, Personal de salud,* and *Público general.* Mexico: Secretaría de Salud.

Uribe, Patricia, Laura Elena de Caso, and Víctor Aguirre. 1996. "Prostitución en México." In *Mujer: Sexualidad y salud reproductiva en México,* ed. Ana Langer and Kathryn Tolbert, 179–206. New York: World Health Organization, the Population Council, and EDAMEX.

Uribe-Salas, Felipe, Carlos de Río Chiriboga, Carlos J. Conde Glez, Luis Juárez Figueroa, Patricia Uribe Zúñiga, Ernesto Calderón James, and Mauricio Hernández Avila. 1996. "Prevalence, Incidence, and Determinants of Syphilis in Female Commercial Sex Workers in Mexico City." *Sexually-Transmitted Diseases* 23(2):120–26.

Zalduondo, Barbara O. de, Mauricio Hernández Avila, and Patricia Uribe Zúñiga. 1991. "Intervention Research Needs for AIDS Prevention among Commercial Sex Workers and Their Clients." In *AIDS and Women's Reproductive Health,* ed. Lincoln C. Chen, Jaime Sepúlveda Amor, and Sheldon J. Segal, 165–77. New York: Plenum.

INTRODUCTION

Reshaping Cultural Images and Ideas

By the end of the twentieth century, American popular culture, a powerful medium of persuasion, had become a worldwide mass commodity. There are probably few places left on the planet unaware of the power of capitalist consumer culture represented by such American iconic images (and icons) as Coca Cola, Nike, Madonna, Elvis, or McDonald's hamburgers. Popular culture allows us to imagine our possibilities for identity through film, television, advertising, music, books, magazines, and other forms of popular media materials. Unfortunately, the same sources also create stereotypes that limit and define women and men in unfair and misleading ways. One has only to think of the Marlboro Man/rugged cowboy and the half-naked Plains Indian on horseback racing across the prairie to recognize the power of stereotyping. The pioneer woman, the "China doll," the "whore with a heart of gold," the Indian princess and her sister, the squaw, evoke instant images of a wild and colorful American West. In the twentieth-century West, popular culture has introduced us to the rodeo queen, the "surfer girl," and the "valley girl," images that are equally limiting and misleading. The West, perhaps due to the rich diversity here, serves as a site of experimentation where women and men negotiate their identities amid cultural constraints and changing systems.

Our ideas of who we are are formed at a deeper cultural level, however, and are shaped by the ways in which we understand and internalize cultural symbols and practices. Often these practices include disapproval, discrimination, and rejection. Members of the dominant Euro-American culture, for example, may feel quite comfortable "in their skins" in situations where racial ethnic people may not. Early in the twentieth century, African Americans knew which water fountains to use, where to sit in movie theaters (the balcony), and which hospitals would accept them for care. In pre–World War II Seattle, Japanese-Americans knew landowners in certain "white" neighborhoods would not rent to "Japs."[1] Our notions of who we are and how we are expected to act are deeply embedded in this larger cultural matrix. When forces outside this sphere exert pressure, such as increasing rates of immigration at the turn of the century and again in the 1980s, cultural change results, either through choice or coercion. Sometimes, conflict results over issues of dress, food, religion, intermarriage, or names, ways in which newcomers attempt to "fit in" with the larger culture. The tensions produced when ethnic racial peoples meet and mix reflect the larger, underlying cultural issue, that of unequal power relationships among them.[2]

This fifth and last section examines how identities and cultures are created, a complex and multilayered process. Historically, women's identities were constructed or prescripted for them, i.e., "the Republican Mother," the Victorian woman, the "working girl."[3] Early in the twentieth century, however, women began to move toward a process of self-identification, discarding or disregarding images and roles previously expected of them. More recently, the construction of identity has become a dialogue in which cultural identities converge around body issues and behaviors.[4] Mexicanas/Chicanas, for example, may choose to practice birth control even if such usage is disapproved by the Catholic Church. Teenage girls confront (and often confound) their elders when they bare their bellies and pierce various body parts. Clothing, cosmetics, and behavior as markers of identity allow women to push the boundaries of "acceptable" appearance and "appropriate" behavior.[5] The last four articles in this collection address the construction of identity in several forms.

In the first article, Mary Murphy reveals the social changes and opportunities that Prohibition created for women in "wide open" Butte, Montana. In an ironic twist, Murphy discovered that the behavior that women had long campaigned against, the abuse of alcohol, had, with the passage of the Eighteenth Amendment, created new social spaces (literally, saloons and bars) that some women readily occupied, both in their own consumption patterns and for economic opportunities. In the second article, building on an exchange between President Theodore Roosevelt and Navajo weaver Elle of Ganado in Albuquerque in 1903, Laura Jane Moore reveals the role Indian art played in the national market economy. To do so, Moore moves Elle, not the President, to the center of her story. In doing so, Moore demonstrates the significant roles Elle and other Native American artists played in integrating their art into the larger commercial and cultural context of the times. In the third essay, Valerie Matsumoto chronicles the uncertainty and confusion of young, second-generation Japanese Americans (Nisei) as they tried to find their identity in American culture without losing their connection to their parents' (Issei) world. The study of ethnic experiences such as this can illuminate the way in which real and imagined identities are reflected within shifting cultural contexts. Finally, Judy Tzu-Chun Wu looks at the phenomenon of the Miss Chinatown U.S.A. Beauty Pageant in San Francisco in the 1950s through the controversies of the Civil Rights Movement and up to the present. Tzu-Chun Wu found that the pageant serves multiple purposes, which include enlightening the public about Chinese American culture, attracting tourists and, hence, business for Chinatown merchants, and providing "insights into Chinese American efforts to construct both gender and ethnic identity during the post-World-War II era." She notes, as well, how idealized versions of womanhood reflect broader concerns about power and culture, issues that permeate this section overall.

NOTES

1. See Monica Sone's discussion of this form of discrimination in her book, *Nisei Daughter* (Seattle: University of Washington Press, 1979).
2. I have drawn some of the ideas in this paragraph from the authors' insightful introductory remarks to part six, "Culture and Identities" in *Writing the Range: Race, Class, and Culture in the Women's West*, eds. Elizabeth Jameson and Susan Armitage (Norman: University of Oklahoma Press, 1997), 457–60.
3. The classic work based in Euro-American prescriptive literature is Barbara Welter, "The Cult of True Womanhood: 1820–1860," *American Quarterly* 18 (summer 1966): 151–74.

4. See chapter 3, "The Flapper and the Chaperone," in Vicki L. Ruiz, *From Out of the Shadows: Mexican Women in Twentieth-Century America* (New York: Oxford University Press, 1998). Also see her article, "'Star Struck': Acculturation, Adolescence, and Mexican American Women, 1920–1950," in *Small Worlds: Children & Adolescents in America, 1850–1950*, eds. Elliot West and Paula Petrik (Lawrence: University Press of Kansas, 1992), 61–80.

5. Joan Jacobs Brumberg, *The Body Project: An Intimate History of American Girls* (New York: Vintage Books, 1997). For an understanding of the power of cultural ideas, consult Rose Weitz, ed., *The Politics of Women's Bodies: Sexuality, Appearance, and Behavior* (New York: Oxford University Press, 1998). Also informative around the issue of cosmetics and gender is Kathy Peiss, "Making Faces: The Cosmetics Industry and the Cultural Construction of Gender, 1890–1930," in *Unequal Sisters: A Multicultural Reader in U.S. Women's History* 2d. ed., eds. Vicki L. Ruiz and Ellen Carol DuBois (New York: Routledge, 1994), 372–94.

BOOTLEGGING MOTHERS AND DRINKING DAUGHTERS

GENDER AND PROHIBITION IN BUTTE, MONTANA*

Mary Murphy

Late one evening in 1922, as Federal Prohibition Officer Ben Holter drove along Nettie Street in Butte, Montana, his car broke down. He asked to use a phone at a nearby house, but his attention quickly shifted from the stranded car to "demon rum." The woman who answered his knock, Mrs. Maud Vogen, aroused Holter's suspicions when she denied having a phone, although one sat in plain view. Holter returned a short time later with two other police officers, and his hunch paid off—they found Mrs. Vogen and another woman tending a twenty-gallon still and a quantity of whiskey and mash. A few days after Vogen's arrest, police apprehended her husband Andrew, who was living at another address, on the assumption that he had been in charge of the bootleg operation. Subsequent investigation, however, revealed that Maud and Andrew Vogen had not been living together as husband and wife for some time. Maud Vogen was "in sole charge" of the still, and the woman with her at the time of her arrest was her mother.[1]

In the 1920s, Butte women made, sold, and drank liquor in unprecedented fashion. Decades later, a Butte woman recalled the many evenings she donned her flapper finery and headed to the dance halls where she and her friends shimmied to jazz tunes and slipped outside

---

*This chapter was originally published as: Murphy, Mary. "Bootlegging Mothers and Drinking Daughters: Gender and Prohibition in Butte, Montana." In *American Quarterly* 46 (June 1994): 174–94.

to share a pint of moonshine. In 1929, a Butte judge, Dan Shea, proposed a city ordinance calling for police matrons in all the city's dance
halls; his action was prompted by the number of women carrying
whiskey flasks into the popular nightspots.[2]

Until the advent of Prohibition, drinking in Butte was governed
by clearly defined and understood social rules. Saloons were male preserves and reflected the ethnic and occupational strata of the community. Any woman who drank in a saloon was assumed to be a prostitute
at worst, "loose" at best. When reputable women drank, they did so at
home. Prohibition rattled these traditional patterns. It curbed some
drinking, but, more significantly, it changed the drinking habits of
youth and women. Blatant flouting of the law during Prohibition created new social spaces for drinking, and women began stepping up to
the bar along with men, albeit in speakeasies and nightclubs rather than
in the old corner saloons. Prohibition accelerated the advent of heterosocial night life as new watering holes welcomed young couples and
groups of women, as well as men.

Prohibition also allowed ethnic groups and women to capitalize on
the underground economy by launching new businesses in the
manufacturing and sale of liquor. Women cooked liquor on the kitchen
stove to supplement the family income. Husbands and wives running
"blind pigs," "moonshine joints," and "home speaks" competed with
saloons hastily converted into soft drink parlors. A few women operated bustling roadhouses. In the 1920s, judges and juries, whose previous
contact with female criminals had been almost exclusively with
prostitutes, were confounded by grey-haired mothers appearing in their
courts on bootlegging charges. In all aspects of the liquor business,
women moved into spaces that had once been reserved exclusively for
men. Prohibition allowed women to rewrite the script of acceptable
public behavior and to transform one arena of commercial leisure
bounded by rigid gender roles.[3]

Drinking in the late nineteenth and early twentieth centuries was
one of the most gender-segregated activities in the United States. No
one denied that women drank. Some researchers estimated that women
comprised between one-tenth and one-third of the problem drinkers
during this period. However, with the rise of the saloon, men had begun
drinking in public, commercial arenas, while women were relegated to
drinking at home. Changes in industrial capitalism doomed "kitchen

grog shops," traditionally operated by women. Increases in working-class income and free time, coupled with a search for relief from the monotony of more-regimented work, led to the growth of public saloons for male workers. Women, meanwhile, stayed at home, losing both the income from their small businesses and the companionship of husbands and male neighbors.[4]

Recent studies exploring the "cheap amusements" of young working-class women have uncovered evidence of some public drinking in the early twentieth century. But these youthful pleasure seekers were not drinking in traditional corner saloons. They strutted into new institutions such as dance halls, beer gardens, amusement parks, and cabarets. Significantly, these entertainments were phenomena of very large cities, cities that had jobs that attracted girls from surrounding farms and small towns. These urban migrants lived in furnished-room districts on their own. Or, if they lived at home, they sought their pleasures in places that were perhaps a trolley ride away from their own neighborhoods and the judgmental gazes of parents and neighbors. Most of America, however, was not like Chicago or New York. In small and middling cities there were fewer of the new commercial amusements and few places women could go where someone would not know them or their families. Quite simply, most women lacked the anonymity that emboldened their urban sisters. Changes in traditional gender roles thus took place more slowly in the hinterlands. Not until Prohibition altered the institutional basis of nightlife and public drinking were women able to expand the boundaries of recreational behavior and still retain respectability. Even in Butte, Montana, the "wide open town" of the northern Rockies, change awaited Prohibition. In order to understand the magnitude of that change, it is necessary to understand just what a "man's town" Butte was.[5]

Butte, Montana bore three monikers in the early twentieth century. To capitalists, it was "the richest hill on earth," a treasure trove of copper ore, control of which made the Anaconda Copper Mining Company one of the most powerful corporations in the country. Workers knew it as "the Gibraltar of Unionism," where nearly every working person from theater usher to hoist engineer belonged to a labor union. And everyone recognized it as a "wide open town," meaning that a man could buy a drink, place a bet, or visit a prostitute at any hour of the day or night without worrying about being arrested. On the eve of

World War I, Butte, Montana—seat of Silver Bow County—was the largest metropolis between Spokane and Minneapolis-St. Paul: a hardrock mining city, home to nearly 95,000 residents, the majority of them men. In 1910, the population was 57-percent male; in 1920, it was still 54-percent male. Butte was rollicking, gritty, and famous for its nightlife, which was by no means confined to the hours of darkness. The city's main crossroads at Park and Main streets anchored a commercial district bustling with department stores, groceries, hotels, banks, cafes, saloons, poolrooms, and gambling halls. The red-light district, where prostitutes charged a dollar for a bottle of beer and a dollar for a trick, was just two blocks south. Everyone from newly arrived Finnish muckers living in boarding houses on the East Side to Irish-American girls housekeeping for West Side families came through uptown Butte and witnessed its pleasures and vices. The majority of the population probably never approved of prostitution, and many had reservations about gambling. Drinking, however, was such an accepted habit that it took a national movement to present any challenge to its dominion.[6]

In November 1916, Montanans voted on statewide prohibition. The measure passed with a comfortable margin of 58 percent of the vote, only three urban counties dissenting: Deer Lodge, the site of the smelter city Anaconda; Lewis and Clark, home of Helena, the state capital; and Silver Bow. In fact, Silver Bow County neatly reversed the statewide referendum with 58 percent of its voters opposing the measure, registering the largest vote against prohibition in the state. The real strength of the Prohibition movement rested in the rural counties, several of which passed the referendum by 60 to 70 percent. Silver Bow County's vote against prohibition was hardly surprising. Butte was the largest city in the state; drinking was an integral part of its male-dominated, urban culture. At the time of the referendum, Silver Bow County had three breweries and 250 saloons.[7]

Saloons were endemic to the urban culture of the nineteenth century as centers of male conviviality; on the mining frontier, they were multifunctional institutions. Often the first nonresidential buildings constructed, saloons predated fraternal lodge halls, hotels, churches, schools, and city halls. Men used them as banks, employment agencies, and post offices. As urban institutions developed, most saloons shed their many skins and returned to their original form as places where men drank, talked, and argued. However, in newly minted western cities, saloons were more likely to accommodate billiards, gambling, and prostitution than were more strictly regulated eastern taverns. In poor and immigrant neighborhoods, saloons often continued to hold workers' savings in their safes, to distribute foreign-language newspapers, and to let people from the neighborhood use their toilets. One saloon in Butte—known as a hobo retreat—served only beer and whiskey, always had a pot of stew on the stove, was festooned with clothes drying after a wash in back-room tubs, and served at night as a flophouse.[8]

Despite their many community functions, western saloons were first and foremost places for men to drink and socialize. A cross-cultural study of North American and Argentine frontier saloons refers to both as "theaters of excessive machismo." On their stages, men played out ritualized roles of masculine culture: camaraderie and conflict, communality and competition. The denouement was often violence. Strong cultural links between manliness and drinking existed in both societies, as evinced in nineteenth-century Idaho, where a man was scarcely able to do business if he was "a lemonade son of a bitch."[9]

Taking a drink was also a public proclamation of a boy's entry to manhood. In his autobiographical novel *Singermann*, set in early twentieth-century Butte, Myron Brinig charted young Michael Singermann's journey to adulthood. On the day he first donned long pants at age thirteen, he marched into the corner saloon, went straight up to the bar, and ordered a beer. Chastened because the bartender refused to serve him, he was about to retreat in humiliation when a man at the bar bought him a schooner. As Michael took his first sip, "The beer ran down his throat, into his stomach, down his thighs and seemed to love the feel of his long pants. Beer was good now that he was drinking it in his long pants. It was a man's drink, filling a man with a golden glow, lighting little torches all over his body until he was aflame for life." Drinking became Michael's rite of passage, and he soon adopted his companion's stance: "with one foot on the brass rail, his left elbow propped on the bar, his right hand holding the schooner of beer."[10]

Although the law forbade the presence of minors in saloons, parents often sent their children to the bar with a pail, smeared inside with lard to keep down the foam, to be filled with beer and brought home. Pat O'Leary stopped at the back door of Stripey's saloon every night, handed over his money, and got a bucket of beer for his father and a Hershey bar for himself. Newsboys and messengers, hoping to earn a few cents running errands, plied their trade in saloons. Frank Carden remembered accompanying his father on rounds of Saturday chores and persuading him to take him to the Atlantic Bar for a liverwurst sandwich, a glass of milk, and a chance to watch the goings on. These childhood forays contributed to young boys' socialization into the masculine club of the saloon. Mike McNelis realized early on that the measure of man, at least by a saloon's standards, had more to do with size than age. A boy was old enough to drink "if you were tall enough to put the money up on the bar."[11]

In Butte, the masculine nature of the saloon grew not only from a long tradition of American drinking habits and the frontier experience but also from patterns brought over from Europe—especially from Ireland, the country that provided the single largest group of immigrants to Butte. Historians and other investigators have observed that Irishmen traditionally used drinking as a safety valve for sexual tensions, the depressions of poverty, the frustrations of parental authority, and their hatred of the English. As long as he did not threaten his family's income, a hard-drinking man was admired by his peers or treated with maternal affection as "the poor boy." In the local tavern or *shebeen*, a man's status was secure, unchallenged by his father, unthreatened by women. Both married and single men belonged to a "bachelor group," who spent their evenings in the *shebeen*; this demonstrated that sexual divisions were far more significant than those between old and young or married and single. One historian has observed that when the Irish-American Catholic Church attacked whiskey and took up the temperance cause, it pulled "the keystone from the arch which was traditional male culture."[12]

Naturally the Irish were not the only ethnic group with established drinking patterns transplanted to Butte. Far fewer Italians were saloonkeepers, but the community was well known for its homemade wines and grappa, a potent brandy. Slavs, Germans, Finns, Greeks, English, and French all kept and patronized saloons. Unlike Irish women, who did not socialize in Irish *shebeens* or American saloons, Slavic women occasionally patronized ethnic saloons in America, which resembled the eastern European inns that had doubled as shops and served both sexes. Accustomed to light wines and liquors, and having taken to beer "like ducks to water," many Slavic immigrants, especially industrial workers, drank daily.[13]

While Old World customs influenced New World drinking, living and working conditions in Butte also drove men to saloons. Myron Brinig captured the feelings that many miners probably shared when he described the appeal of the saloon: "when you dig for copper all day in the moist drifts underground, and you come up, and there is no sunlight, no waves beating against a rocky shore, why, a saloon, is a heaven then." When miners finished work and headed home, they frequently traded one unpleasant environment for another. Miners' families created cozy homes where they could, but the lack of sanitation in the densely packed neighborhoods was a serious problem. Throughout the early 1910s, the county and city health departments reported filthy alleys full of refuse and rotting food, unkempt animals, and privies dangerously close to houses. Garbage, standing water, and dead animals had grown to such a heap in one vacant East Side lot that nearby residents kept their windows closed to minimize the stench. The majority of miners returned not to family homes but to cabins where they "batched" with a few other men, to furnished rooms in the upper stories of commercial buildings, or to boarding houses. Men who worked all day in the dark underground were reluctant to retire to small, inhospitable sleeping rooms. In fact, a County Board of Health study demonstrated that the physical environment of some working-class saloons was far healthier than that of the men's boarding houses. It was not surprising that men sought the warmth, lights, and company of saloons, cigar stores, or fraternal lodges in uptown Butte.[14]

East Park Street was "a beehive" of working-class social life. Miners shopped for boots and overalls in Jewish dry-goods stores, ate at Greek restaurants, and drank in Irish saloons. Butte's drinking establishments ran the gamut from "saw-dust joints" to places such as the Atlantic, which had a bar a block long and fifteen bartenders working each shift. Saloons were working-class institutions, but, within their ranks, hierarchies and divisions based on ethnicity, occupation, and income prevailed. Electrical workers congregated at the Park Saloon; smeltermen favored the Atlantic. Pedestrians passing Tickell and Spargo's on West Broadway delighted in the harmonizing of Cornish and Welsh singers. The *Anaconda Standard*, reviewing Butte's saloon business on the eve of Prohibition, revealed its prejudice when it compared uptown, established saloons where "the talk is never loud and where order always maintains itself" to the rougher places owned by "Finlanders and other foreigners" on the East Side who served poor liquor and scarcely noticed fights. Journalist Byron E. Cooney, in a homage to Butte saloons, observed, "everyone who drank at all had their own pet saloon. Personally I felt very much at home in all of them."[15]

On the other end of the scale from even the plushest working man's saloon was Butte's Silver Bow Club, organized by copper magnate William A. Clark and several colleagues in 1882 and incorporated in 1891. In 1905, the club bought a lot adjacent to the courthouse, hired Montana's most prominent architects, and built a four-story edifice replete with massive fireplaces, murals of English country life, copper and leaded glass chandeliers, and a bar decorated with stained-glass panels of lush grapes and sinuous vines.[16]

The Silver Bow Club admitted women for special events, and they no doubt sampled its wine cellar, but, for the most part, public drinking remained a male privilege until Prohibition. Even in freewheeling Butte, as Aili Goldberg declared, "you just didn't see a woman in a saloon." Alma and Lillie Muentzer were born above their father's brewery and saloon. Alma recalled that the Butte Brewery and Saloon had "a little room in case the ladies wanted anything . . . [but] it was never used much because women at that time didn't go to bars." Lillie remembered that the California Bar featured "booths for ladies," but she also noted, "you weren't a lady if you went in." Throughout the West, the only women to frequent saloons openly were prostitutes. As custom became entrenched, any woman who entered a saloon was assumed to be of dubious character. Men in Denver capitalized on the universality of that assumption to taunt female reformers. When members of the Woman's Christian Temperance Union (WCTU) tried to enter saloons to record the condition of drinkers, they were met by guards who shouted "Whore!"[17]

In 1907, Montana institutionalized the taboo against women drinking in saloons. That year, the Republican-dominated state assembly enacted a program of progressive legislation designed to protect the physical and moral health of Montanans. Abolishing the "wineroom evil" targeted prostitution and garnered nearly unanimous legislative support. Winerooms—the partitioned areas in which some saloon owners permitted women to drink—were considered incubators of prostitution. The new law banned women from saloons and compelled saloon owners to dismantle any accommodations designed to provide space for female drinkers. Proprietors were instructed to remove signs that advertised a ladies' entrance or a private entrance and to demolish winerooms, private apartments, or screened areas. Butte complied with the state legislature and passed a complementary city ordinance the same year.[18]

Nevertheless, while the law barred women from saloons, it was not designed to stop them from purchasing alcohol. Women who never drank in saloons commonly bought liquor there. Catherine Hoy recalled neighborhood women in Dublin Gulch going themselves or sending their children to the back doors of saloons for their buckets of beer. Many Slavic women, who apparently preferred wine, would also have a little glass at home. Women's drinking habits, barely recorded by historians, were widely recognized by contemporaries. Indeed, during the campaign for prohibition in Montana, at least one dry advocate chastised "mothers in Butte who won't vote for prohibition because you want to have beer on your own tables in your own homes." Until the reconstruction of social drinking during Prohibition, reputable women, with few exceptions, continued to drink at home while men drank in public.[19]

Factions for and against prohibition in Montana paralleled divisions in other states. The dry forces were led by the WCTU and the Anti-Saloon League. Enrollment in Montana's WCTU, founded in 1883, peaked during the prohibition campaign of 1916. Nevertheless, the WCTU's stalwart campaigners waged a losing battle. On their program in 1920 was the question, "Does Prohibition Prohibit in Butte?" Reluctantly, they had to answer "no." By 1923, 156 of the 250 saloons that had operated in Butte in 1916 and 1917 were in the same locations, under the same proprietorships, thinly disguised as soft drink parlors. The city directory advertised another 44 new soft drink parlors, and it is impossible to estimate the number of clandestine speakeasies. Frank Carden observed that "the saloons all stayed open and dispensed 'bootleg' whiskey, homemade wine and homemade beer, brandy, gin. . . . If they were raided by Federal officers they would just pause long enough to get in another stock of liquor and start over again." As federal judge George M. Bourquin proclaimed, "shabby, dingy holes in the wall, labeled 'soft drink parlors' do not fool anybody, least of all the court," especially when they were in the same location as former saloons. Clearly such parlors neither operated for the sale of ice cream and pop nor catered to women and children. Nevertheless, community-side acceptance of illegal activity was a major factor encouraging women to get into the liquor business.[20]

To be sure, during the first few years of Prohibition, Montana authorities made some attempt to enforce the law. Statements from county attorneys across the state showed varying rates of success in prosecuting violators. In Butte, however, cooperation between the local authorities and state and federal officers was notoriously lacking. Affidavits by state enforcement agents attested to the fact that the Cyrus Noble saloon was run by a former police chief and patronized by uniform and plainclothes detectives. During a two-year period from November 1920 to November 1922, Silver Bow County's attorney won convictions in 59 percent of his liquor cases. But, during that time, only 105 cases were prosecuted—compared to 271 in Cascade County, site of Great Falls, and 168 in Lewis and Clark County, both with smaller populations. Despite almost daily newspaper accounts of confiscation of stills and illegal liquor, law enforcement officials were not collecting sufficient evidence to convict. Even when they did, Butte juries remained unsympathetic to the law. In 1928, Judge Bourquin replaced a jury that had been hearing prohibition cases and admonished the twelve new men to bring in verdicts in accordance with the evidence: "I don't want men sitting in the jury box who have no regard for their oaths. We have had two such juries and I don't want anymore if we can escape it."[21]

By 1926, a majority of Montanans agreed with Helen Raymond, who thought "it was a shame they ever had [prohibition] because I think it broke down a morale of the people. . . . Cause once you think you can break a law, you're in worse shape than if you'd never done it." Montanans judged the noble experiment a failure, and that year voters repealed their state prohibition law with 53 percent of the vote. (Silver Bow County tallied 73 percent in favor of repeal.) Federal agents became entirely responsible for enforcement, and their efforts at times seemed farcical. In 1928, the newspaper reported a "dry sleuth" who had adopted a disguise to entrap young Butte fraternity men from the School of Mines. Bartenders noted that raids often followed the appearance of a hatless young man "flaunting white flannel trousers and black coat or corduroy pants and skin-tight sweater [with] hair . . . greased back from forehead and smile of sophistication . . . spread on his face." The alleged agent would gain the confidence of Butte youths "whose entry to the drink parlors is never questioned," buy them drinks and leave. Shortly afterward, a raid commenced.[22]

Prohibition did not appear to change the habits and economy of uptown drinking. And, contrary to its intent, it created economic opportunities for people who had never been involved in the liquor business. At one end of the bootlegging chain were children who collected empty bottles outside dance halls and sold them back to moonshiners or who discovered bootleggers' stores and pilfered a few bottles of liquor to sell on their own. Italians, who had traditionally made wine for their own families, expanded production for commerce. The commission houses ordered freight-car loads of grapes—the largest anyone remembered was thirty-four cars—and had them brought directly to a siding near the Italian suburb of Meaderville. Italians who lived in Brown's Gulch, northwest of the city, also made wine and grappa. Dorothy Martin, who taught school in the Gulch, recalled that a sudden cloudburst would sometimes flood a bootlegger's cache and barrels of wine and grappa would come rolling down by the schoolhouse.[23]

It may well have been profits from bootlegging that led to the creation of a zone of restaurant-nightclubs in Meaderville in the late 1920s and early 1930s. These nightclubs bore little relation to pre-Prohibition saloons, and it was within their walls that a new heterosocial nightlife emerged. The first clubs opened during the last years of Prohibition, and, by the time liquor again became legal, they were Butte institutions. The Rocky Mountain Café, Aro, Golden Fan, Copper Club, and Pera Café, among others, attracted all classes of men and women for drinking, dancing, gambling, and one- or two-dollar multicourse dinners. As in New York City's cabarets, the design of Butte clubs gave women social and physical protection. They offered privacy and distance not provided in open barrooms, where there were few tables or chairs and where patrons freely mingled and jostled one another. In the Rocky Mountain Café, for example, booths lined the walls around a central dance floor and the gambling operation was in a back room. Many people patronized the clubs exclusively as restaurants and did not sample their other attractions. But Meaderville's nightclubs also created an atmosphere in which women felt comfortable drinking and gambling, if they so chose. As one customer observed, "Meaderville's night clubs lack the vigor, the hairy chests and the call of the wild that you'll find in the city. Women may gamble side by side with their men and loll at the bars with them." Unlike saloons, where women were welcome only at the back door, nightclubs encouraged women's attendance and trade.[24]

While the Meaderville clubs provided a spectrum of entertainment, more common throughout the city were "home speaks," which marked a return of kitchen grog shops run by women or families. Mike Erick and his wife, for instance, owned a small dance hall and soft drink parlor that catered to fellow Slavic immigrants. Mr. and Mrs. Charles Martin, African Americans, ran a home speak on New Street. Pat O'Hara sold beer and moonshine in his cabin and denied that it was a dance hall, although he did admit that his customers sometimes danced to the music of a phonograph.[25]

Bootlegging, in fact, provided a new vehicle for women, especially widows and wives, to supplement their incomes. Slavic women began making wine and selling it to boarders with their dinners. Many working-class women in Dublin Gulch, on the East Side, and in gulches outside the city had their own stills or cared for family stills while their husbands were at work. One of the most elaborate outfits confiscated, a three-hundred-gallon-capacity still, was operated by eighty-year-old Mrs. Lavinia Gilman. The court gave Mrs. Kate Farlan, "a gray-haired mother" convicted of manufacturing liquor in her home, a suspended sentence on condition she obey the law for one year. Shortly after sentencing, agents found another still in her house. Mrs. Michael Murray, who had two children and claimed she could not work outside the home, confessed to being the "cook" in an operation in which her husband and a friend marketed her liquor. Widow Nora Gallagher told police she set up a still on her kitchen stove in order to outfit her five children for Easter. Police arrested women selling liquor and beer in grocery stores and boarding houses and others attempting to destroy incriminating evidence by dumping liquor and mash into cellars.[26]

Home bootlegging was, for the most part, a working-class practice, but at least a few middle-class women set up their own stills, presumably more for the thrill than from any economic need. Arriving home one day to find a peculiar odor in the house, Dr. Carl Horst traced it to the basement where he discovered his wife had assembled a still.

He demolished it over her protests but allowed her to keep one gallon for her ladies club. The public did not expect the middle class to manufacture their own liquor. When police found a still "within a stone's throw of the class halls of the School of Mines and surrounded by residences of men of high standing in the community," it was "an astounding revelation."[27]

The independence of female bootleggers also challenged male notions of women's place. While police and judges had long experience with prostitutes and women drunkards, bootlegging women were beyond their ken. When police arrested Susie Gallagher Kerr along with two men, Kerr admitted that the seized still was her operation, but the police preferred to believe that the men were in charge. The judge who tried eighty-year-old Lavinia Gilman felt her son was the "real culprit" and hoped that he would come forward to save his mother. The younger Gilman apparently did not share the court's chivalrous attitude and never appeared. Judge Bourquin, a staunch upholder of the law, did not like to commit women to jail, but, in the case of twice-caught Kate Farlan, he felt compelled to carry out the court's order and reluctantly locked her up for six months.[28]

Many writers in the 1920s and early 1930s commented on the appearance of women in speakeasies; most portrayed their actions as silly or comic. But caricatures of well-to-do young flappers or matrons, with their high heels hooked over the brass rail of a smoky speakeasy, trivialized an important and, certainly for some, disturbing change in women's behavior and values. Butte author Reuben Maury, writing in *Scribner's Magazine* in 1926, captured the anxiety of a mining-city mother, whose daughter seemed to care more for "comfort and an automobile and an able bootlegger" than for the prospect of marriage and children. Mothers feared that their daughters were eschewing domesticity for frivolity.[29]

Men shared an uneasy feeling that more was at stake than a woman having a drink. Indeed, male writers' caustic remarks about ladies lunching in speakeasies were a defensive response to women's invasion of traditional male territory. As one scholar of drinking habits noted, men defined the use and abuse of alcohol as a male privilege, a symbol of power and prestige. What bothered men was not that women drank but that they drank in public commercial institutions. It was not only the anti-saloon thrust of the Prohibition movement but also the heterosociability of new watering holes that seemed to spell doom for that long-cherished male bastion, the saloon.[30]

Women who made whiskey and those who patronized speakeasies were breaking both custom and the law. Their actions were deliberate and self-conscious. For working-class women, bootlegging was a logical extension of the many kinds of home work they had traditionally undertaken to supplement family income; admittedly, it carried some risks but presumably offered greater rewards. For unmarried women—both working- and middle-class—drinking and visiting speakeasies were open acts of rebellion, since "nice girls" did not do such things.

The speakeasy culture that gave more freedom to young women also became associated with other symbols of independence not necessarily connected to drinking, such as cigarette-smoking and bobbed hair. These gestures in some ways became rites of passage for young women in the 1920s. Peer pressure, as well as the lure of the forbidden, was clearly at work. Alma Muentzer Hileman recalled that none of her girlfriends drank until Prohibition, "then everybody ha[d] to taste and see what it [was]. . . . That's the first that any of us ever knew what a highball and all that stuff was. And we were born in a brewery."[31]

Many daughters deliberately violated long-held conventions defining respectability and tested the strength of familial bonds. Both Helen Harrington and Dorothy Martin spent a considerable amount of time preparing their parents for the day they came home with bobbed hair. Dorothy's father had initially dissuaded her from having her hair cut when he told her that only prostitutes wore bobbed hair. She persisted, but it was only after her mother saw that nearly all Dorothy's friends were having their hair cut that she succeeded in getting a bob. For several weeks as she came home from work each day, Helen Harrington told her mother that she was going to get her hair bobbed. Her sister remembered the day she finally did: Helen came home and said, "'Ma, I got my hair bobbed,' and Ma never looked at her. Finally after a while, she peeked over her 15-cent-store glasses and all she said was, 'I guess you'll be going to the roadhouses next.'"[32]

Josephine Weiss Casey did go to the roadhouses. Wearing her "pretty dress," she and her boyfriend and two or three other couples would drive over from Anaconda to eat, drink, and dance in the Meaderville clubs. For a dollar, they could get a chicken dinner and two highballs; the third was, by custom, on the house. Other nights after a movie they would go to a speakeasy that served "the best gin fizzes in the world." It was not just the quality of the liquor but the fact that they were "swanky drinks," served in "tall nice glasses," in a place that was "packed, packed and not all [with] kids like us" that made the evening so tantalizing.[33]

For young women, the speakeasies often seemed mysterious and thrilling. Dorothy Martin recalled that going to the clubs "was probably the most daring and frightening thing that I did." She remembered climbing down a ladder to get in one place. "You couldn't see through the smoke because everybody smoked. And I thought, 'Oh, boy, what a wonderful place for tragedy.'" But Dorothy didn't like liquor and she ended up dumping her drinks in the spittoon when no one was looking. Clearly, it was not alcohol but adventure that drew her and perhaps many of her peers to the "downright honest-to-God bootleg joints."[34]

The Meaderville nightclubs eventually posed a challenge to women's traditional forms of leisure. In the late 1930s, the Daughters of Norway engaged in a considerable discussion over the relative merits of having their annual picnic or going to a Meaderville café for a ravioli dinner. Ravioli triumphed over tradition, and the women had such a good time that they made it an annual event. Club minutes record their pleasure. "We all had a glorious evening, an evening that will live in our memory for a long, long time; after a hi-ball or two, Mrs. Sontum got hot clear down to her feet, & [if] that wasn't enough, she also emptied their slot machines." In an addendum to the minutes, the secretary noted, "It was moved and seconded that we should take the dollar Mrs. Larsen & Mrs. Langstadt gave us to treat ourselfs [sic] to some wine, which we did."[35]

Prohibition's new speakeasies, nightclubs, and roadhouses catered to couples and sanctioned and encouraged drinking for women. Young women who ventured into these new institutions knew they were crossing a divide between an old set of assumptions about behavior and morality and a new code they were creating. Some faced the divide with a bittersweet knowledge of the price of innovation. As Dorothy Martin recalled, when she finally got her hair cut, "I kind of cried myself when I looked at me with my short hair. But, it was done." The actions of Dorothy Martin, a schoolteacher, Helen Harrington, a shop clerk, and hundreds of other young women forced changes in the public perception of female drinking. Female patrons of speakeasies were neither "loose women" nor "floozies." They were "good" women and they compelled people to acknowledge that they could retain their respectability while taking a drink in public.[36]

There is great irony in Prohibition. The law had, in effect, created a vacuum of rules, and women exploited the opportunity to slip into niches in the economy of liquor production, distribution, and consumption. Women had been in the vanguard of the Prohibition movement, a movement designed to restrict male behavior by abolishing the vice-ridden retreat of the saloon and curbing male drinking. Yet, a decade after legislative success, some of the very same women led the campaign for repeal of the Eighteenth Amendment, having concluded that some kind of regulated liquor trade was preferable to moral anarchy. Much to their dismay, during Prohibition, drinking had become an equal-opportunity vice. True, many saloons closed their doors forever and the consumption of alcohol did decrease. But, during Prohibition, men and women reconstructed social drinking habits, and the greatest change was women's newfound penchant to belly up to the bar. Unforeseen by proponents and opponents, Prohibition effectively created new social spaces in speakeasies and nightclubs; this allowed a redefinition of sex roles in one of the most gender-segregated arenas of leisure—getting together for a drink. Behavior followed structural change. Public drinking was not on the list of rights demanded by twentieth-century feminists. Indeed, the seemingly frivolous activities of young women in the 1920s dismayed feminists who saw them diverting energy from politics. Nevertheless, the reorganization of drinking did increase women's autonomy. Whether they spent an evening drinking and dancing with their boyfriends, husbands, or members of their ladies club, doors that had been closed to them now opened in welcome. Prohibition provided women with new economic opportunities, greater choices of public leisure, and a chance to broaden the definition of reputable female behavior.[37]

Mary Murphy is an associate professor of history at Montana State University. She is the author of *Mining Cultures: Men, Women, and Leisure in Butte, 1914–41* (1997).

NOTES

My thanks to David Emmons, Jacquelyn Dowd Hall, Dale Martin, Laurie Mercier, Susan Rhoades Neel, and Anastatia Sims for their generous and incisive reading of this essay. Special thanks to Alice Finnegan for sharing her Anaconda interviews and to Joyce Justice for assistance with the District Court records.

1. *United States v. Maud Vogen*, Judgment Roll 928, U.S. District Court, Montana, 11 Nov. 1922. U.S. District Court, Montana, District of Montana Criminal Register and Dockets. Record Group 21, National Archives, Pacific Northwest Region, Seattle, Wash. Between 1920 and 1934, 134 Butte women were prosecuted in the District Court for violations of the Volstead Act.
2. Anonymous letter to John Hughes, Butte-Silver Bow Archivist, 27 Sept. 1982; *Montana Standard*, 11 Apr. 1929, 1.
3. On changing gender roles in the 1920s, see Loren Baritz, "The Culture of the Twenties," in *The Development of an American Culture*, ed. Stanley Coben and Lorman Ratner (New York: St. Martin's Press, 1983); Gerald E. Critoph, "The Flapper and Her Critics," in *"Remember the Ladies": New Perspectives on Women in American History*, ed. Carol V. R. George (Syracuse, N.Y.: Syracuse University Press, 1975); Peter G. Filene, *Him/Her/Self: Sex Roles in Modern America* (Baltimore: Johns Hopkins University Press, 1986); Estelle B. Freedman, "The New Woman: Changing Views of Women in the 1920s," *Journal of American History* 61 (Sept. 1974): 372–93; Ruth Freeman and Patricia Klaus, "Blessed or Not? The New Spinster in England and the United States in the Late Nineteenth and Early Twentieth Centuries," *Journal of Family History* 9 (winter 1984): 394–414; John D. Hewitt, "Patterns of Female Criminality in Middletown: 1900 to 1920," *Indiana Social Studies Quarterly* 38 (autumn 1986): 49–59; J. Stanley Lemons, *The Woman Citizen; Social Feminism in the 1920s* (Urbana: University of Illinois Press, 1973); James R. McGovern, "The American Woman's Pre–World War I Freedom in Manners and Morals," *Journal of American History* 55 (Sept. 1968): 315–33; Carroll Smith-Rosenberg, "The New Woman as Androgyne: Social Disorder and Gender Crisis, 1870–1936," in *Disorderly Conduct: Visions of Gender in Victorian America* (New York: A. A. Knopf, 1985); June Sochen, *The New Woman: Feminism in Greenwich Village, 1910–1920* (New York: Quadrangle Books, 1972); and Kenneth A. Yellis, "Prosperity's Child: Some Thoughts on the Flapper," *American Quarterly* 21 (spring 1969): 49–64.
4. Mark Edward Lender and James Kirby Martin, *Drinking in America: A History* (New York: Free Press, 1982), 117; Albert J. Kennedy, "The Saloon in Retrospect and Prospect," *Survey Graphic* 22 (Apr. 1933): 206. Thomas Brennan discusses the growth in the diversity of public drinking places in *Public Drinking and Popular Culture in Eighteenth-Century Paris* (Princeton: Princeton University Press, 1988), 14–19. Perry R. Duis discusses gender-segregated drinking along public-private lines in *The Saloon: Public Drinking in Chicago and Boston, 1880–1920* (Urbana: University of Illinois Press, 1983), 105–7. Roy Rosenzweig describes the demise of kitchen grog shops in *Eight Hours for What We Will: Workers and Leisure in an Industrial City, 1870–1920* (New York: Cambridge University Press, 1983), 41–49, 63.
5. For working-women's commercial amusements and the changing gender use of public spaces, see Kathy Peiss, *Cheap Amusements. Working Women and Leisure in*

Turn of the Century New York (Philadelphia: Temple University Press, 1986); Joanne
J. Meyerowitz, *Women Adrift: Independent Wage Earners in Chicago, 1880–1930*
(Chicago: University of Chicago Press, 1988); and Elizabeth Ewen, *Immigrant
Women in the Land of Dollars: Life and Culture on the Lower East Side, 1890–1925*
(New York: Monthly Review Press, 1985); Christine Stansell, *City of Women: Sex
and Class in New York, 1789–1860* (Urbana: University of Illinois Press, 1986); and
Michael Schudson, "Women, Cigarettes and Advertising in the 1920s: A Study in
the Sociology of Consumption," in *Mass Media Between the Wars: Perceptions of
Cultural Tension, 1918–1941*, ed. Catherine L. Covert and John D. Stevens
(Syracuse, N.Y.: Syracuse University Press, 1984), 71–83.

Peiss specifically notes the absence of reputable women from saloons, 20–28.
On this topic, see also Madelon Powers, "Decay from Within: The Inevitable
Doom of the American Saloon," in *Drinking: Behavior and Belief in Modern History*,
ed. Susanna Barrows and Robin Room (Berkeley: University of California Press,
1991), 115; Hutchins Hapgood, "McSorley's Saloon," *Harper's Weekly* 58 (25 Oct.
1913): 15; Royal L. Melendy, "The Saloon in Chicago—I," *American Journal of
Sociology* 6 (Nov. 1900): 300; and Travis Hoke, "Corner Saloon," *American Mercury*
22 (Mar. 1931): 313–15.

Lewis A. Erenberg in *Steppin' Out: New York Nightlife and the Transformation of
American Culture, 1890–1930* (Chicago: University of Chicago Press, 1984) discusses the rise of New York cabarets at the turn of the century as a place where
reputable, well-to-do women could drink in public. Cabarets were not, of course,
common outside the largest of American cities.

6. In 1900, the sex ratio between men and women was 147.7 to 100; in 1910, it was
132.4 to 100; and, in 1920, it was 119.6 to 100. Bureau of the Census, *Thirteenth
Census of the United States* (Washington, D.C.: Government Printing Office, 1910),
2:1147; Bureau of the Census, *Abstract of the Fourteenth Census of the United States*
(Washington, D.C.: Government Printing Office, 1920), 131.

For general works on Butte, see Ray Calkins, comp., *Looking Back from the Hill:
Recollections of Butte People* (Butte, Mont., 1982); Jerry W. Calvert, *The Gibraltar:
Socialism and Labor in Butte, Montana, 1895–1920* (Helena: Montana Historical
Society Press, 1988); David M. Emmons, *The Butte Irish: Class and Ethnicity in an
American Mining Town, 1875–1925* (Urbana: University of Illinois Press, 1989);
Michael P. Malone, *The Battle for Butte: Mining and Politics on the Northern Frontier,
1864–1906* (Seattle: University of Washington Press, 1981); Writers' Program,
Work Projects Administration (WPA), *Copper Camp: Stories of the World's Greatest
Mining Town, Butte, Montana* (New York: Hastings House, 1943). On the red-light
district, see Mary Murphy, "Women on the Line: Prostitution in Butte, Montana,
1878–1917" (M.A. thesis, University of North Carolina, Chapel Hill, 1983).

7. Louis J. Bahin, "The Campaign for Prohibition in Montana: Agrarian Radicalism
and Liquor Reform, 1883–1926" (M.A. thesis: University of Montana, 1984),
94–96; *Butte City Directory*, 1916.

8. On the multifunctional nature of western saloons, see Edison K. Putnam, "The
Prohibition Movement in Idaho, 1863–1934" (Ph.D. diss., University of Idaho,
1979), 54, 403; Elliott West, *The Saloon on the Rocky Mountain Mining Frontier*
(Lincoln: University of Nebraska Press, 1979), 131–32; Thomas J. Noel, *The City
and the Saloon: Denver, 1858–1916* (Lincoln: University of Nebraska Press, 1982),
13, 65; David Brundage, "The Producing Classes and the Saloon: Denver in the
1880s," *Labor History* 26 (winter 1985): 30–32; Ann Burk, "The Mining Camp

Saloon as a Social Center," *Red River Valley Historical Review* 2 (fall 1972): 385; Jon M. Kingsdale, "The 'Poor Man's Club': Social Functions of the Urban Working-Class Saloon," in *The American Man*, ed. Joseph H. Pleck and Elizabeth H. Pleck (Englewood Cliffs, N.J.: Prentice-Hall, 1980), 265, 267; and WPA, *Copper Camp*, 83.

9. Richard W. Slatta, "Comparative Frontier Social Life: Western Saloons and Argentine Pulperias," *Great Plains Quarterly* 7 (summer 1987): 158–59; West, *Saloon*, 19–21; and Putnam, "Prohibition Movement," 10.

10. Myron Brinig, *Singermann* (New York: Farrar & Rinehart, 1929), 292–93.

11. On children in saloons, see Noel, *City and Saloon*, 89; Robert Alston Stevenson, "Saloons," *Scribner's Magazine* 29 (May 1901): 571, 577; and "The Experience and Observation of a New York Saloon-Keeper," *McClure's Magazine* 32 (Jan. 1909): 311. Pat O'Leary, interview by Ray Calkins, 22 July 1980, transcript, 17–18, Butte-Silver Bow Public Archives (hereafter cited as BSBA); Frank Carden, "A Walk from 228 S. Gaylord Street to Park and Main Streets and Beyond in Butte, Montana in the 1920's and 1930's," typescript, ca. 1987, 6–7, BSBA; Mick McNelis, interview by Alice Finnegan, 18 Oct. 1985, transcript, 8.

12. On Irish culture and drinking, see Robert F. Bales, "Attitudes toward Drinking in the Irish Culture" in *Society, Culture, and Drinking Patterns*, ed. David J. Pittman and Charles R. Snyder (New York: J. Wiley, 1962), 157–87; James R. Barrett, "Why Paddy Drank: The Social Importance of Whiskey in Pre-Famine Ireland," *Journal of Popular Culture* 11 (summer 1977): 155/17–166/28; and Dennis Clark, *The Irish Relations: Trials of an Immigrant Tradition* (East Brunswick, N.J., 1982), chap. 4. Richard Stivers discusses Irish bachelor culture in *A Hair of the Dog: Irish Drinking and American Stereotype* (University Park: Pennsylvania State University Press, 1976), 76–97. Colleen McDannell, "'True Men as We Need Them': Catholicism and the Irish-American Male," *American Studies* 27 (fall 1986): 24.

13. On Slavic drinking habits, see Emily Greene Balch, *Our Slavic Fellow Citizens* (New York: Charities Publication Committee, 1910), 95, 365–69; quotation is on 365. On Slavic drinking habits in Montana, see Anna Zellick, "Fire in the Hole: Slovenians, Croatians, and Coal Mining on the Musselshell," *Montana Magazine of Western History* 40 (spring 1990): 24–26.

14. Myron Brinig, *Wide Open Town* (New York: Farrar & Rinehart, Inc., 1931), 15–16. Silver Bow County Board of Health, "Report on Sanitary Conditions in the Mines and Community, Silver Bow County, December, 1908–April, 1912," typescript, Montana Historical Society Archives, Helena, Mont. (hereafter cited as MHSA); Silver Bow County Board of Health, "Report Showing Results of Inspection of Dwellings, Hotels, Rooming Houses, and Boarding Houses and Their Surroundings," typescript, 1912, MHSA; *Annual Reports of the City Officers, City of Butte for the Fiscal years Ending April 30, 1908–09* (n.p., n.d.), 175–76; *Annual Reports of the City Officers, City of Butte for the Fiscal Years Ending April 30, 1910–11* (Butte, Mont., n.d.), 163; and *Annual Reports of the City Officers of the City of Butte, Montana, Fiscal Year Ending April 30, 1912* (Butte, Mont., n.d.), 80; Emmons, *Butte Irish*, 152. For a comparable situation regarding boarding house life and patronage of saloons, see Rosenzweig, *Eight Hours*, 56.

15. Brinig, *Singermann*, 34; Joe H. Duffy, *Butte Was Like That* (Butte, Mont., 1941), 41, 47; WPA, *Copper Camp*, 74; George Butler, "Impressions of a Hobo," *Pacific Review* 11 (Sept. 1921): 205; *Montana Standard*, 25 Oct. 1959, 9B; *Anaconda Standard*, 14 Jan. 1917, pt. 2, p. 1; and Byron E. Cooney, "The Saloons of Yester-Year," *Montana American*, 18 July 1919, 64.

Several Butte saloons are described in *North American Industrial Review, Montana* (Butte, Mont.: n.d.), 16, 24, 25 40, 78; and Bill Burke depicted the flavor of Butte saloons in 106 verses in "The Saloons of Old Time Butte," *Rhymes of the Mines* (Vancouver, Wash.: 1964), 65–75.

16. Jon Hopwood, "History of the Silver Bow Club," 1980, Montana State University Libraries, Special Collections.

17. Aili Goldberg, interview by Mary Murphy, 29 Feb. 1980, transcript, 18, BSBA; Alma E. Hileman, interview by Ray Calkins, 27 June 1980, transcript, 7, BSBA; and Noel, *City and Saloon,* 112.

18. *Laws, Resolutions and Memorials of the State of Montana Passed at the Tenth Regular Session of the Legislative Assembly* (Helena, Mont., 1907), 434–37; William E. Carroll, comp. *The Revised Ordinances of the City of Butte, 1914* (Butte, Mont.: McKee Ptg. Co., 1914), 463–64. Richard B. Roeder discusses the Progressives' thinking in "Montana in the Early Years of the Progressive Period" (Ph.D. diss., University of Pennsylvania, 1971), 202–5. Other cities and states passed or attempted to pass similar laws: see Edison K. Putnam, "Travail at the Turn of the Century: Efforts at Liquor Control in Idaho," *Idaho Yesterdays* 33 (spring 1989): 15–16; Duis, *Saloon,* 254.

In at least two cases, Butte tried to enforce the law. In 1912, the city revoked the liquor license of the Canteen saloon for violating the city ordinance and, in 1917, sheriffs arrested the owners of a roadhouse for permitting females to frequent the establishment. "Petition of Centennial Brewing Company, Revocation of Liquor license at 27 1/2 West Granite St.," 17 Jan. 1912, City Council Petitions, BSBA; and *Butte Miner,* 6 Apr. 1917, 7.

19. Catherine Hoy, interview by Ray Calkins and Caroline Smithson, 11 May 1979, transcript, 10–11, BSBA; Ann Pentilla, interview by Ray Calkins and Caroline Smithson, 27 Apr. 1979, transcript, 53, BSBA; and *Butte Miner,* 10 Apr. 1916, 6.

20. Mary Long Alderson, *Thirty-Four Years in the Montana Woman's Christian Temperance Union, 1896–1930* (Helena, Mont., 1932), 14. Bahin discusses the role of the ASL in *Butte Daily Bulletin,* 10 Jan. 1920, 4; *Butte City Directory,* 1916, 1917, 1923; Carden, "A Walk," 9; *Butte Miner,* 3 May 1923, 6.

For works on Prohibition in western states, see *Official Records of the National Commission on Law Observance and Enforcement, Enforcement of the Prohibition Laws,* vol. 4, *Prohibition Surveys of the States,* 71st Cong., 3d sess., S. Doc. 307 (Washington, D.C.: Government Printing Office, 1931). Studies of prohibition enforcement were conducted in several northern Rockies states, including Colorado, Wyoming, and Idaho. Unfortunately, no study was conducted in Montana; however, reports of these states provide valuable insights into the problems of enforcement in the West. Also see Jody Bailey and Robert S. McPherson, "'Practically Free from the Taint of the Bootlegger': A Closer Look at Prohibition in Southeastern Utah," *Utah Historical Quarterly* 57 (spring 1989): 150–64; Helen Z. Papanikolas, "Bootlegging in Zion: Making and Selling the 'Good Stuff,'" *Utah Historical Quarterly* 53 (summer 1985): 268–91; Norman Clark, *The Dry Years: Prohibition and Social Change in Washington,* 2d ed. (Seattle: University of Washington Press, 1988); Edmund Fahey, *Rum Road to Spokane: A Story of Prohibition* (Missoula: University of Montana, 1972); David J. McCullough, "Bone Dry?: Prohibition New Mexico Style, 1918–1933," *New Mexico Historical Review* 63 (Jan. 1988): 25–42; Walter R. Jones, "Casper's Prohibition Years," *Annals of Wyoming* 48 (fall 1976): 264–73; Gary A. Wilson, *Honky-Tonk Town: Havre's*

Bootlegging Days (Helena, Mont.: Montana Magazine, 1985); Patrick G. O'Brien, "Prohibition and the Kansas Progressive Example," *Great Plains Quarterly* 7 (fall 1987): 219–31; Gilman M. Ostrander, *The Prohibition Movement in California, 1848–1933* (Berkeley: University of California Press, 1957); and four studies by Kenneth D. Rose, "Booze and News in 1924: Prohibition in Seattle," *Portage* 5 (winter 1984): 16–22; "The Labbe Affair and Prohibition Enforcement in Portland," *Pacific Northwest Quarterly* 77 (Apr. 1986): 42–51; "'Dry' Los Angeles and Its Liquor Problems in 1924," *Southern California Quarterly* 69 (spring 1987): 51–74; and "Wettest in the West: San Francisco and Prohibition in 1924," *California History* 65 (Dec. 1986): 284–95, 314–15.

21. "Report of County Attorneys for 2 years from November 30, 1920 to November 30, 1922 on liquor cases," Box 15, Folder 16; Agents' reports, Box 7, Folder 11, Montana Attorney General Records, 1893–1969, MHSA; and *Montana Standard*, 20 Dec. 1928, 18.

22. Helen Shute Raymond, interview by Laurie Mercier, Butte, 9 Oct. 1981, MHSA; Bahin, "Campaign for Prohibition," 133; and *Montana Standard*, 12 Sept. 1928, 1.

23. Calkins, *Looking Back*, 15–17; James Blakely, interview by Ray Calkins, 15 Nov. 1979, transcript, 4, BSBA; Camille Maffei, interview by Russ Magnaghi, 4 May 1983, MHSA; *Montana Standard*, 4 Nov. 1962, 1B; and Dorothy A. Martin, interview by Mary Murphy, 23 May 1988, transcript, 29–30, MHSA.

24. Teddy Traparish scrapbook, Teddy Traparish Papers, BSBA; *Montana Standard*, 4 Nov. 1962, n.p.; Calkins, *Looking Back*, 71. Quotation is from Walter Davenport, "The Richest Hill on Earth," *Collier's* 6 Feb. 1937, 53.

On the rise of restaurant-nightclubs after the repeal of Prohibition, see Lewis A. Erenberg, "From New York to Middletown: Repeal and the Legitimization of Nightlife in the Great Depression," *American Quarterly* 38 (winter 1986): 761–78. On economic gains made by Italians during Prohibition, see Gary Ross Mormino, *Immigrants on the Hill: Italian-Americans in St. Louis, 1882–1982* (Urbana: University of Illinois Press, 1986), chap. 5. On business aspects of bootlegging, see Mark H. Haller, "Philadelphia Bootlegging and The Report of the Special August Grand Jury," *Pennsylvania Magazine of History and Biography* 109 (Apr. 1985): 215–33.

25. *Butte Miner*, 31 July 1922, 1; *Butte Miner*, 27 Aug. 1922, 6; and *Montana Free Press*, 21 Jan. 1929, 13. John Chapman Hilder notes "home speaks" as a phenomenon of the West in "New York Speakeasy, A Study of a Social Institution," *Harper's Monthly Magazine* 164 (Apr. 1932): 591.

26. Pentilla interview, 54; *Butte Miner*, 23 Nov. 1924, 6; *Montana Standard*, 28 Dec. 1928, 1; *Butte Daily Post*, 14 Mar. 1921, 1; *Anaconda Standard*, 26 Mar. 1921, 5; *Montana Standard*, 23 Dec. 1928, 19; *Butte Miner*, 4 Dec. 1920, 3; 5 Sept. 1928, 5.

John Kobler, in *Ardent Spirits: The Rise and Fall of Prohibition* (New York: Putnam, 1973), 252, relates the concern of a priest in Pennsylvania who attributed women's unfaithfulness and penchant to run off with star boarders to tending home stills.

27. Betty Horst, unrecorded interview by Mary Murphy, 23 May 1988; and *Butte Miner*, 3 July 1924, 5.

28. *Butte Daily Post*, 9 Apr. 1927, 11; *Butte Miner*, 23 Nov. 1924, 6; and *Montana Standard*, 28 Dec. 1928, 1. Bourquin usually placed female first offenders who pleaded guilty on probation. *Montana Standard*, 18 May 1929, 1.

29. Reuben Maury, "Home," *Scribner's Magazine* 79 (June 1926): 640. According to the New York City Investigating Committee of Fourteen, in 1925 the number of

women seen in places illegally selling liquor was "astounding." Cited in George
E. Mowry and Blaine A. Brownell, *The Urban Nation, 1920–1980*, rev. ed. (New
York: Hill and Wang, 1981), 25. On women in speakeasies, see Frederick Lewis
Allen, *Only Yesterday: An Informal History of the 1920s* (New York, 1931), 211;
Hilder, "New York Speakeasy," 591–601; Margaret Culkin Banning, "On the
Wagon," *Harper's Monthly Magazine* 163 (June 1931): 11–21; and Ida M. Tarbell,
"Ladies at the Bar," *Liberty* (26 July 1930): 6–10.
30. Joseph R. Gusfield, "Status Conflicts and the Changing Ideologies of the American
Temperance Movement" in *Society, Culture and Drinking Patterns*, ed. David. J.
Pittman and Charles R. Snyder (New York: J. Wiley, 1962), 102.
31. Hileman interview, 32.
32. Martin interview, 8–9; Julia McHugh, "The Gulch and I," typescript, ca. 1986,
20–21, BSBA. The press contributed to the notion that the fashions of the 1920s
were linked to prostitution. For example, a prostitute, who charged her husband
with assault after he broke her jaw for not earning enough money on the street,
was described as "a pretty girl with bobbed hair and dressed in the style of a flapper." *Butte Miner,* 29 Aug. 1922, 6.
33. Josephine Weiss Casey, interview by Alice Finnegan, 18 May 1989, transcript, 17.
34. Martin interview, 30–31; Casey interview, 17.
35. Minutes, 3 January 1939, Daughters of Norway, Solheim Lodge No. 20 Records,
BSBA.
36. Martin interview, 9.
37. Women's attempts to repeal the Eighteenth Amendment were coordinated by the
Women's Organization for National Prohibition Repeal (WONPR). On the
WONPR, see David E. Kyvig, *Repealing National Prohibition* (Chicago: University
of Chicago Press, 1979); Kyvig, "Women Against Prohibition," *American Quarterly*
28 (fall 1976): 564–82; Grace C. Root, *Women and Repeal: The Story of the Women's
Organization for National Prohibition Reform* (New York: Harper & Brothers, 1934);
and the Papers of the Association Against the Prohibition Amendment and the
Women's Organization for National Prohibition Reform in the Eleutherian Mills
Historical Library, Wilmington, Delaware.

ELLE MEETS THE PRESIDENT

WEAVING NAVAJO CULTURE AND COMMERCE IN THE SOUTHWESTERN TOURIST INDUSTRY*

Laura Jane Moore

During the spring of 1903, President Theodore Roosevelt included a two-hour stop in Albuquerque while on a speaking tour through the western territories. The Commercial Club of Albuquerque chose a Navajo woman, called Elle of Ganado, to weave a gift for the president—a textile rendition of his honorary Commercial Club membership card. Club members provided the design, which Elle wove quickly in hand-spun red, white, and blue yarn. During his tour of Albuquerque, Roosevelt visited the Commercial Club, where he received Elle's blanket, and he stopped by the Alvarado Hotel's Indian Building, where he met the weaver herself. An Albuquerque newspaper reported that upon meeting the weaver, the "president gave her a hearty shake and told her how much he appreciated her work. The little speech was interpreted and pleased the Indian woman beyond expression"[1]

Although her own thoughts were apparently "beyond expression," Elle's image spoke volumes to turn-of-the-century Americans, showing New Mexico was not only conquered but commercialized, safe for investment and safe for statehood. Indeed, Commercial Club members orchestrated this performance as part of a statehood campaign, a drive

---

*This chapter was previously published as: Moore, Laura Jane. "Elle Meets the President: Weaving Navajo Culture and Commerce in the Southwestern Tourist Industry." In *Frontiers* 22, no. 1 (2001): 21–43.

for integration into the social, economic, and political life of the United States, an effort that would not pay off for nearly ten more years. Elle and the president's meeting suggests ways in which race and gender, regional and national politics, culture and commerce interacted and were inextricably linked as the twentieth century began. The pivotal role that Elle played in Roosevelt's visit reveals that while we tend to think of women like Elle as marginalized historical figures, they were far from peripheral to the unfolding of twentieth-century American history. Not only can we better understand such women by placing them within the larger economic, cultural, and political context of their times, but we can better understand that context by putting a woman like Elle at its center.

Elle of Ganado, also called Asdzaa Lichii' (Red Woman) in Navajo, was born to the Black Sheep Clan and lived in the southern part of the Navajo Reservation near the Hubbell Trading Post in Ganado, Arizona. She might have been about fifty years old at the time she met Roosevelt, and she lived until 1924. At the suggestion of trader John Lorenzo Hubbell, she and her husband Tom began spending substantial periods of time in Albuquerque beginning in 1903 after the Fred Harvey Company opened its Indian Building as part of the Alvarado Hotel complex at the Santa Fe Railroad depot. Together with other Navajo and Pueblo families, they worked as arts and crafts demonstrators within the burgeoning southwestern tourist industry.[2]

Most scholarly literature on southwestern tourism examines the ironies and complexities of images of Indians portrayed as purely nonindustrial producers of "traditional" handcrafts, "outside history, outside industrial capitalism" that had begun to emerge at the turn of the century.[3] Elle's Commercial Club blanket, however, unabashedly declared the link between Indian art and turn-of-the-century capitalism. It is a reminder that those who worked as demonstrators were, like all Americans at the time, entering new kinds of economic relationships that would affect their work and their communities in profound ways. Beyond their ideological implications, then, these tourists sites were workplaces to which a number of Native Americans agreed to travel for extended periods of time. The sites were also cultural crossroads at which negotiations took place between employers and employees, between young corporate and rural America, between white men and Indian families, between metropolitan and peripheral economies. This essay explores the contours of these crossroads, the compromises demanded and the benefits promised various participants.[4]

The Fred Harvey Company, it has been said, "invented" the Southwest as "America's Orient." Fred Harvey was an English immigrant who opened his first restaurant along the Santa Fe Railroad line in 1876 in Topeka, Kansas. From there the company grew into the first chain of restaurants and of railroad hotels. Harvey built his company's reputation on the notion of civilizing rail travel to the West by selling good food served by respectable young, white, single women called "Harvey girls." Combining hot meals, Harvey girls, and Indian images in their advertising, the company presented the West as an exotic but accessible tourist paradise. By the time of Harvey's death in 1901, his empire consisted of twenty-six restaurants, sixteen hotels, and twenty dining cars.[5]

The Harvey Company went into the Indian art business at the instigation of Harvey's daughter, Minnie Harvey Huckel, an avid Indian art collector. In 1902 she suggested that a display of Indian art be included in Albuquerque's new Harvey hotel, the Alvarado. Her husband, J. F. Huckel, a New Yorker who had been in the publishing business and was now a Fred Harvey vice president, began to commute from Harvey headquarters in Kansas City to Albuquerque, where he created the Fred Harvey Indian Department. The Huckels' collaboration with Harvey employee Herman Schweizer ensured the success of this venture. Schweizer, a German immigrant, had found his way to the Southwest in the 1880s, had jobbed silver and turquoise to Navajo silversmiths, and while working at the Harvey restaurant in Coolidge, New Mexico, had begun buying and selling Navajo arts and crafts—a successful sideline that caught Minnie Huckel's attention. Schweizer spent the rest of his life managing the Fred Harvey Indian Department. He had an eye and a taste for the Indian art business and soon built the Harvey Indian collection into a premiere showcase. This success was further facilitated by the architect Mary Colter who helped to design the Indian Building at the Alvarado and subsequently went to work full time for the company. Colter was an important force in developing a regional architectural style inspired by local, native design—spaces for the "staged authenticity" that became fundamental to southwestern tourism, and spaces designed for commercial transactions that also offered a seemingly behind-the-scenes view of Indian homelife.[6]

The development of southwestern tourism thus depended on diverse players who illustrate the various and complex forces at work at the turn of the century: Minnie Huckel, a wealthy woman and art patron; Mary Colter, a professional woman finding a career in the Southwest; J. F. Huckel, an elite eastern businessman; Herman Schweizer, a young, ambitious, Jewish immigrant; and a number of Native American artists, including Elle, worked together to invent the modern Southwest and to find a place for themselves within it. Each brought her or his own goals, background, and economic and cultural logic to their meeting. They did not always act out of positions of equality, but each were crucial players in the story. Most analyses of the Harvey Company and southwestern tourism in general tell the story from the Anglo participants' point of view, even when critiquing their use of Indians and Indian imagery. Although the individual, private thoughts and reactions of Indian workers such as Elle may never be known, careful reading of sources left mostly by those Anglo participants can help us examine their roles and experiences within the larger context of turn-of-the-century Navajo and American history.

Much recent scholarship has explored the elevation of Indian imagery in this period, even as Native Americans remained culturally, politically, and economically marginalized. Indian artisans were central figures in the invention of the Southwest. Traveling in the comfort of a berth on the Santa Fe railroad, white Americans could see exotic pockets of the nation where the industrialization, urbanization, and bureaucratization of the era had not yet, it seemed, taken hold. Yet in this period, as industrial capitalism spread and the Southwest was incorporated into the nation and the national market economy, it became, as Leah Dilworth explains, "increasingly clear that the development of the American West would depend on the metropolis for capital and cheap immigrant labor." Ironically, she continues, "The spectacle of Indian artisanal labor resurrected an ideology that declared precisely the opposite: that the rural artisan and the farmer were the backbone of the nation's economy."[7] The presence of hardworking, artistic Indians provided tourists with a heavily mediated—indeed artificially constructed—arena in which to feel they had safely encountered the real West through a glimpse of Indian homelife. Barbara Babcock, Marta Weigle, and others have shown that the prominent place of female Indian artisans and their children in locales like the Fred Harvey Indian Building was crucial to the domestication of the image of the "wild" West. They called such sites "ethnic sets for exotic performances" or "human showcases" where "the companies staged authenticity by controlling the architectural setting, 'live' demonstrations and other expressive performances, museum and sales displays, publications, and virtually all associated exegesis."[8]

Tourists viewed Indians purportedly practicing their naturally artistic, premodern everyday lives, but the artists, too, were travelers who had moved from their rural homes to these tourist spaces in order to incorporate income from such work into their families' economic strategies. The idealized domestic tableaux offered at the Harvey House obscured a gender organization and economic system that differed markedly from that of Euro-Americans. It also ignored the cultural meanings that the Diné, or Navajos, themselves found in their textiles. Weaving was, and is, a highly respected activity that reflects and reinforces Navajo women's economic, cultural, and social centrality.[9] Navajo textiles had long been both market objects and unique cultural expressions embodying *hozho*, the central Navajo philosophical concept that connotes harmony, balance, goodness, and beauty. Weaving also reflects the power of thought and the combination of autonomy and cooperation that is so important to the Diné. Husbands build looms for their wives, and weavers sometimes work side by side at the same loom. At the same time, the design of a rug, as one weaver explains, "just has to be you," and, to quote Mary Lee Begay, "takes a lot of hard thinking."[10] Weavers do not generally sketch out designs but rather conceive and then hold them in their minds as they work. A leading scholar of contemporary Navajo textiles, Ann Lane Hedlund, explains that weaving "represents a proper way to make a living or, putting it more exactly, to live"; weavers practice their art while "caring for their families, homes, and herds . . . and remembering the sacred stories, prayers, and songs that 'go with weaving.'"[11]

Those "families, homes, and herds" are organized around the principle of motherhood, a term that refers not just to biological mothers, but to the women of one's clan, the family's sheep herd, and the family's land. The Diné are matrilineal, tracing descent from the female side of the family, and matrilocal, with daughters living with their husbands and children near their mother. The primary familial bond is between a mother and child (not between a husband and wife); Navajos belong or are "born to" their mother's clan; and other clan members are their closest relatives. Individual women, men, and children own livestock and other property but share the care of herds and fields. Women generally control range land, and land use is typically inherited from mothers. Weaving, too, has always been dominated by women (though men can, and some do, weave), and weaving knowledge passes from generation to generation through kinship bonds.[12]

At the turn of the twentieth century, livestock products were the primary source of subsistence and of income, supplemented by farming and by trading other items, most importantly textiles, at the local trading post. Living in an often harsh and unpredictable environment, the Diné pooled resources along kinship lines. Economic specialization was not practical, but varied economic strategies and adaptability to changing environmental and historical forces were. Even while becoming more dependent on the national market economy, the Diné did not abandon their diversified subsistence economy or reciprocal economic expectations revolving around matrilineal kinship ties.[13]

Long before trading posts or Harvey houses, weaving had been one of the many activities through which women contributed to the household economy. Between the seventeenth and nineteenth centuries, the Diné had increasingly oriented their economy and culture around sheep herds while developing much of what is now considered traditional Navajo culture. Navajo women used their sheep's wool to weave blankets and clothing for family use and for inter- and intratribal trade. By the early nineteenth century, Navajo blankets were prized within a wide regional market for their quality—so tightly woven they were waterproof—and their beauty.[14]

In 1865 U.S. troops that had wrested control of the region from Mexico two decades earlier implemented a scorched-earth policy, massacring herds and burning crops, in order to impoverish and defeat the Diné. Elle probably joined the approximately eight thousand Navajos who were moved to a tiny reservation near Fort Sumner in southeastern New Mexico called Bosque Redondo, or *Hweeldi* in Navajo. There they faced disease, death, and emotional and economic turmoil. Even though they were short on wool and given manufactured blankets and clothing, Navajo women nevertheless "set up looms and created blankets of strength and beauty."[15]

To the army officers at Bosque Redondo, Navajo women's

commitment to their looms appeared not as evidence of resilience but proof of conquest. Long accustomed to the association of femininity, domesticity, and textile production, Anglo observers thought weaving augured well for Navajos' ability to adopt "civilized" gender roles. When American officials offered Navajos Anglo-style looms and spinning wheels, however, the Navajo women refused to use them or to work with the white women hired to instruct them, insisting on continuing with "their old plan of spinning and making blankets."[16] Weavers readily adopted some newly available materials, including commercial dyes and yarns, but insisted on controlling the means of production. Nor did they adopt Euro-American gender roles, but continued to ground their social organization and identity in matrilineal kinship relations. Despite cultural misreadings of the Navajo, weaving became a critical point of contact, valued by both groups but for different reasons.

After four years, American officials decided that relocating the Diné to Bosque Redondo had been a costly mistake, making a once self-sufficient tribe an unnecessary economic burden on the federal government. In 1868, eager to return home, a group of Navajo headmen signed a treaty establishing a reservation carved out of their traditional homeland. As soon as they returned, they set about resurrecting a pastoral economy using sheep and goats provided by the federal Office of Indian Affairs and taking advantage of a national boom in the wool market. White traders appeared in Navajo country to broker the sale of wool from Navajo herds to eastern markets. Trading posts sprouted along the new railroad lines and deeper within Navajo country. The Diné traded wool, sheep, textiles, and other products for flour, coffee, sugar, and other items they could not produce at home. Traders thus helped introduce the national market economy to the Diné while becoming cultural brokers as well. During the 1890s drought and a severe national depression lowered wool prices and ended the Diné's economic recovery, but they continued to center their lives around their sheep herds, grafting elements of the national market economy onto their subsistence economy.[17]

Weavers left traces of these historical changes and continuities in their textiles. They adopted designs from manufactured Pendleton blankets from Oregon that they bought at trading posts, experimented with serrate style designs inspired by Hispanic weaving, and increasingly used commercial yarns and dyes. The Indian Office provided finely spun yarn manufactured in Germantown, Pennsylvania, that allowed weavers to develop ever more intricate and complex designs. Some weavers began to include figurative elements such as trains in their textiles in a new "pictorial" style. When wool prices dropped in the 1890s, women apparently turned increasingly to weaving as a way to increase the value of their wool. New designs reflected changing concerns of the weavers and the changing market. Traders encouraged weaving styles they thought would sell well and regional styles named after neighboring posts emerged. For the most part, Navajos stopped weaving clothing and instead created what would come to be called rugs, meant not to be worn, but to be souvenirs of the West. Military personnel were among the first Anglo collectors, followed by growing numbers of explorers, scientists, government personnel, and finally tourists arriving with the new railroads.[18]

Railroads altered the economic, cultural, and social contours of the region. By the turn of the century, Santa Fe dominated Albuquerque's economy and had practically built a whole new town around its depot. Railroads also shifted the region's perspective from a local economy oriented along the north-south axis facing Mexico to an east-west trajectory incorporated into the U.S. national economy. One of the byproducts of this process was the introduction of wage work and migrant labor to Native American communities. Many Navajo and other Indian men added income from railroad work to the contributions they made to their household economy. Meanwhile, as the Navajo economy became increasingly incorporated into the modern industrial economy of the United States, the inter- and intratribal blanket trade evaporated as southwestern Indians adopted white-style clothing and factory-made blankets. Navajo weavers adopted their art to a new and changing market that, though it did not generally pay producers well, yet could be crucial to the household economy. Navajo textiles had become a key commodity in southwestern economic development and were central to the income of traders and the growing tourist economy.[19] One of the most famous and successful trading posts, for example, was John Lorenzo Hubbell's in Ganado, Arizona, in the southern part of Navajo country near the New Mexico border. The Hubbell family eventually opened several other posts and became the main suppliers for the Harvey Company. They also became

employment brokers, recruiting Navajos and Hopis, including Elle and
Tom of Ganado, who were willing to work at Harvey houses as arts and
crafts demonstrators.[20] Within the growing trading post economy,
Navajo weavers found new and different customers, and they experimented with new materials and designs while maintaining traditional
production techniques and continuing to create uniquely Navajo
textiles.

While the railroad introduced industrial capitalism to the rural
Southwest, it also introduced the Southwest, or a particular image of
the Southwest, to the world. Ironically, while some Indian men learned
to participate in industrial wage work, the Santa Fe's tourist business
perfected the image of Indians as naturally artistic preindustrial crafts-
people. Upon disembarking at Albuquerque, train travelers passed
through the Harvey Indian Building on the way to the Alvarado lobby.
The first thing they saw were weavers, potters, silversmiths, and basket
makers, and Fred Harvey sales increased appreciably as a result of this
encounter.

The Indian workers' primary job was to be on display for the
tourists. In making arrangements for the demonstrators, Harvey Indian
Department manager Herman Schweizer explained to the trader John
Lorenzo Hubbell that "the principal thing [is] for them to be at work
when trains are in. They should be working from 7:30 A.M. to noon.
They can work as much or as little as they want to in the afternoon but
must come back after supper for about one hour for evening trains." In
exchange the Harvey Company provided room and board and on at
least one occasion Schweizer promised "double of what they are getting for their stuff on the reservation." This was a good enough deal,
apparently, to entice a number of artists and their families away from
their homes, farms, sheep, corn, and kin for two or three months at a
time, long enough for good weavers to complete a large weaving project "if they bring blankets already started."[21]

Schweizer and Huckel always preferred a mix of women, men, and
children to provide scenes of domestic, familial, artistic comradery. The
ideal Navajo couple would include a weaver and a silversmith. Navajo
women would weave, care for the children, cook, and perform janitorial
duties, though accomplishing the latter out of the view of tourists.[22]
Navajo silver work was still a somewhat new craft, and silversmiths were
harder to find than weavers. Back in Navajo country, economic

specialization in weaving or silversmithing would be unusual. Instead arts and crafts work was integrated into diversified economic strategies. Even the Harvey men did not rely on their demonstrators for quality silver work. More important to them was to have a man who knew enough to act like a silversmith while being "a good man," that is, reliable, honest, and hardworking. His tasks would include cleaning and upkeep on the buildings and usually translating.[23]

Many Indian artists worked at some point for the Fred Harvey Company. The San Ildefonso Pueblo potter Maria Martinez and her husband Julian worked as Harvey demonstrators early in their careers, before developing the black pottery style that brought so much fame. The Hopi-Tewa potter Nampeyo also worked for the Harvey Company on a few occasions, demonstrating her Sikyatki revival style. Nampeyo had already begun to make a name for herself, which the Harvey Company cashed in on when they hired her.[24] Elle, in contrast, was not well known until her work for the Harvey Company made her one of the only other Indian artists with name recognition in the early twentieth century. Elle's willingness to stay away from home for long periods of time and to be photographed over and over again made her one of the Harvey Company's favorite employees.[25] She and her husband were local celebrities in Albuquerque, their activities documented regularly in the town's newspapers. They met and were photographed with numerous national celebrities, too, from the Chicago Cubs to "America's sweetheart," Mary Pickford. Encouraged by their success in Albuquerque, the Harvey Company began employing demonstrators for other sites as well. Elle and other artists traveled around the country representing the company at expositions in San Francisco, Chicago, and elsewhere. They also worked in other Harvey houses, most notably at the Grand Canyon, where living exhibits of Indian "homelife" were built into the tourist spaces.[26]

Architect Mary Colter based the architecture of the Grand Canyon's Hopi House on that at Oraibi, one of the oldest inhabited villages in the United States. Hopi demonstrators lived upstairs, Navajos camped nearby, and downstairs salesrooms also invoked Indian "homelife." By emphasizing art, and deemphasizing other economic activities carried out in actual Hopi villages, the Hopi House helped to define Native American culture narrowly by its marketable, artistic products. While Harvey publications extolled the Hopi House as a "reproduction of the homes of this tribe as they are found on their reservation," it was not a reproduction but an interpretation of Indian life in which certain characteristics stood in for Indian culture. The inaccuracy of this "staged authenticity" is highlighted by the number of Navajos who enacted their artistic domestic life at the *Hopi* House, where Navajo weaving and silver were especially important commodities.[27]

Authenticity was itself constructed, and it changed over time. At the Grand Canyon, Huckel insisted that Navajo women "have and *use* some of their homemade pots to cook." At the same time, Schweizer and Huckel solicited Hubbell's help in securing an "old Navaho forge . . . . perhaps a piece of steel rail or whatever there may be that is homemade" for silversmiths working at the Hopi House.[28] Authenticity, then, did not require the complete rejection of technology or industrialization; Navajo silver work, in fact, was not a traditional craft and relied on modern technology, in this case steel. What seemed to be most important in indicating authenticity was the word "homemade," which suggested self-sufficiency: that a Navajo man could build a forge out of a piece of steel rail; that a Navajo woman could feed her family out of homemade pots; that for these Indians art and labor were integrated into everyday life. Such items as Navajo pottery might merely serve as decoration in modern white American homes in which the art of self-sufficiency had been lost, but for Indians they must still be *used*. Harvey images of Indian artisans played off concerns emerging from the arts and crafts movement about the alienation of art from labor in the modern industrial world, the growing dichotomy between the traditional and the modern, and a nostalgia for a mythological past.[29] Still, the art itself did not (yet) have to be so pure: "Modern" designs were especially popular, and weavers could use manufactured yarns and dyes as long as they wove them by hand.

As for the Diné, their identity was less tenuously tied to material objects such as stoves or pots than was the Anglo definition of an "authentic" Indian. On one occasion Tom and Elle asked a Harvey manager to provide buckskin and other materials so that Tom could make moccasins for Elle.[30] This story suggests an impressive level of self-sufficiency that might reinforce Anglo understandings of Indian authenticity: Even if they did not hunt the buck and cure the hide them-selves, they also did not buy the manufactured product. But the cost of a pair of shoes may have been less of an issue for the couple than a deeper cultural undercurrent. As a Navajo woman interviewed in the 1990s explained, moccasins "were first worn by the holy people and reflect our culture and our identity as Diné. . . . It is by a Navajo's moccasins the Holy People recognize that a person is a Diné and who that person is." Indeed, establishing this identity may have been especially important to demonstrators like Elle who had journeyed so far from home. Moreover, the construction of the moccasins is critical because the sole "represents mother earth" and the top, which is "dyed red to represent the rainbow . . . is father sky." The sinew that ties together the sole and the top represents lightning and thus the "union of mother earth and father sky [which] brings forth all life." As when a Navajo weaves, the process of making moccasins expresses hozho, harmony between nature and the supernatural, and the power of thought: "We think about how we are going to make the moccasins, we plan out how best to make the moccasins, we use our thinking and planning put into action when we make the moccasins, and when we are done we have moccasins to protect our feet and give us comfort."[31] In other words, the material, the color, and the process of constructing the moccasins would have been more important to Elle and Tom than that the finished product was "homemade."

Diné identity depended on relationships to land, kin, and livestock, relationships that income from weaving could help maintain. In contrast to Elle and Tom, most weavers were unwilling to stay away from home for long periods of time. For that reason, most of the rugs sold in Harvey houses were woven not by demonstrators, who could not in any case have produced the necessary volume, but by women back in Navajo country who combined weaving with their other daily activities. Often these weavers bought packaged dyes at their trading post. Sometimes they spun and carded wool from their own sheep, but often they received wool from a trader as an advance on their rug, or perhaps they paid another woman to process wool for them. Weaving was thus part of both a local and national economy, combining traditional means of production with materials and marketing strategies made available by industrial capitalism.

Presenting "authentic," "traditional," "ancient" Indian culture to the tourist market was crucial to the economic development of the Southwest, yet in both practical and ideological ways it could clash with official federal Indian policy. In day-to-day business practice, for example, the Harvey people took Navajo polygamy—the bane of Christian missionaries—in stride. In fact, polygamy might have made Harvey managers' job easier by providing more adults, especially weavers, per family to take care of various chores. Similarly, the disjuncture between educating Indian children in the Protestant, individualistic, capitalist work ethic that lay at the heart of assimilationist policy ran counter to Huckel and Schweizer's desire for demonstrators to being along their children who were "one of the chief attractions to the traveling public."[32] The Harvey men had to obtain Indian agents' permission for the children to accompany their families. The agents were employees of the federal Indian Office whose policy was to wean Indian children *away* from traditional culture, the very culture that was being preserved, commodified, and marketed at the Grand Canyon.

Meanwhile, Harvey managers also found some elements of traditional culture trying, and they worried frequently about "spoiled" Indians having a bad influence on other demonstrators.[33] While Indians were asked to demonstrate the appearance of self-sufficiency, attitudes of independence could get them sent home. Demonstrators were to be viewed by, but not interact with, tourists, except within prescribed limits. Most importantly, the Harvey employers wanted demonstrators to act as passive producers rather than active participants in the Indian art market. As anthropologist John Hudson explained to his wife Grace Hudson about the Pomo demonstrators he helped the Harvey Company hire, what "the Harvey's [*sic*] want is the attraction to visitors and monopoly of all work done."[34]

Demonstrators who tried to take business into their own hands, as did a silversmith called Taos, threatened this monopoly. "He is making silver for other Indians and they are selling it," Huckel complained to Hubbell. "He is going over town and selling it and also selling it to our guests on the quiet. Taos has been spoiled by his experience at St. Louis" during the world's fair and, though a "silversmith is quite an attraction," he was becoming uncontrollable. In the end, they sent him home with his wife even before she had completed the blanket she was weaving, which they bought for $20.00. Taos received $31.00, although he asked for $36.50. Harvey manager Snively refused him the additional $5.50 "as I thought he was trying to skin me." He also refused "to pay him $12.50 for putting Pins in 50 buttons for Hat Pins which was about two days' work" but "compromised with him at 12 1/2 cents each."[35]

The dispute with Taos was not the only time that these tourist spaces, primarily dedicated to the commodification of women's work, became arenas for conflicts among men. Shortly before sending Taos home, another Navajo called Long Man, who in Schweizer's opinion had not been working out well anyway was "getting troublesome and stubborn. . . . He is pretty much of a mischief maker."[36] "I've had a lot of trouble with the Indians lately in little petty ways," Schweizer wrote Hubbell late in May of 1905 from the Grand Canyon. "The Longman sort of queered the whole bunch, he seems to be a sort of evil spirit reads the stars and all that sort of thing."[37]

This last complaint indicates that although demonstrators willingly traveled into these white tourist sites, they maintained ways of looking at the world that did not always mesh well with their employers' assumption about market forces and employee responsibilities. Elle and Tom may have been the Harvey Company's favorite employees, but they were not particularly acculturated. Although willing to stay for several months each year, they would go home for reasons that mystified the Harvey people, for example, when Schweizer wrote Hubbell that, "Elle has rheumatism and Tom says Long mans saw the sign and she'd die if she didn't get medicine."[38] In this case, Tom, Long Man, and Elle did not mean western medicine to be found in pills or at hospitals, but the Navajo medicine around which their religious beliefs were organized. Indeed, because the Navajo worldview centers on maintaining well-being through hozho, cultures could clash most irrevocably around the issue of health.

At Harvey houses different worldviews grounded in different economic and gender systems collided. Within this context, it should come as no surprise that even a woman's body could become the site of conflict, as happened to one of the favorite demonstrator families headed by Maria Antonio and Miguelito during the summer of 1905. In May the family began planning to return to the reservation in anticipation of another of Miguelito's wives, Agippa, giving birth. Huckel and Schweizer were not happy with their decision to leave. In a letter to Hubbell, Huckel wrote: "It seems to me he would be much better off if he stays where he is. He is earning a pretty fair salary," and the family was "doing well." Their young daughter, Tonsi-pah, also a weaver, had been ill, but was "quite recovered. Of course, if he is set on going home,

I presume it is not advisable for us to object or persuade him not to."[39] The timing was not good for the Harvey Company, as other demonstrators were also "restless," "lonesome," and "homesick," and Elle and Tom were also away.[40] During June, Schweizer and Huckel, with Hubbell's help, tried to make arrangements for replacements while waiting eagerly for Elle and Tom's return.[41]

Then in mid-June Agippa gave birth, probably prematurely. The Harvey people called in a Dr. Pearce who had attended demonstrators before with success. This time he predicted that the baby would not live a month. Huckel told Hubbell, "Agippa was not very ill in Dr. Pearce's opinion, but he would be obliged to attend to her and take her to the hospital."[42] Later Huckel explained, "We have had so much hospital and other work connected with Migelito's family that I think he believes thoroughly in the 'white man's' doctor."[43] They did not anticipate any problems. Still, Huckel suggested that the family return to the reservation once Agippa was well enough: "I feel if this baby should die at Albuquerque or Agippa should get very ill there the Indians might think it was on account of their living there." He apparently had some understanding of Navajos' need to avoid places associated with death and realized that a death at a Harvey House could be disastrous for the demonstrator program. But Agippa never recovered sufficiently to return home, and as she got sicker, the limits of this family's acceptance of white ways were severely tested. Schweizer informed Hubbell, "Migelito took his wife out of the hospital and he has her down by the river in a grove of cottonwoods where he built a temporary shelter for her and says he is going to cure her."[44]

Though angry at Miguelito and reprimanded by his boss, Schweizer apparently did not know how to stop this retreat to traditional medicine. In fact, the Harvey men knew that Miguelito was a singer, that is, a Navajo doctor and religious leader. Just the previous fall he had performed a healing ceremony for Tom when doctors at Albuquerque's St. Joseph's Hospital failed to cure his pneumonia. On that occasion Miguelito and Tom's traditional ways brought Fred Harvey good publicity as the Albuquerque paper followed Tom's progress.[45] Born during the Navajos' confinement at Bosque Redondo in the 1860s, Miguelito must have been about forty in 1905.[46] During the 1930s, he and his family would act as important informants for the anthropological work then undertaken with increasing frequency in

Navajo country. In her classic studies from that period, anthropologist Gladys Reichard would celebrate Miguelito's knowledge of Navajo religion and Maria Antonio's knowledge of weaving.[47] In the summer of 1905, Miguelito knew what he was doing in that cottonwood grove on the banks of the Rio Grande, although a full-scale sing back home surrounded by a crowd of relatives and friends would surely have been more effective.

When Agippa died, Schweizer, furious, wrote Hubbell, "You can tell Miguelito when he returns that there is no one to blame for her dying but himself." Schweizer insisted that the doctors had told them that she "was bound to die unless she was operated on *immediately*." In fact, Schweizer finally got her to the hospital, but "It was too late. . . . Dr. Pearce told me that there was no excuse whatever for her dying." He insisted that from then on, they would have a stricter policy in which demonstrators "will have to take [their] physician[']s orders or go back to the reservation on the first train."[48]

Miguelito, Maria Antonio, and Tonsi-pah hurried home after Agippa's death, "too nervous" even "to finish their blankets."[49] But they soon returned. As demonstrators, they moved between their rural homes and Harvey houses and occasionally on longer trips to expositions, integrating demonstration work into their diversified economy. Their movement provides yet another example of the back and forth between "farm and factory" that marked the daily lives of so many Americans in the early twentieth century. But Harvey houses were unusual factories. Rather than wholesale celebrations of technological progress, they were meant to be oases from the modern world. More than mere workplaces, they presumed to display the artistic homelife of what the Harvey Company termed "America's First Families." But for the Indian demonstrators, home was not the Hopi House.[50]

Because the Harvey Company's business *was* tourism, the demonstrator program was, in a sense, far more important to them than to their Native American employees. Schweizer liked "to see my factory in full blast," but he constantly struggled to keep enough demonstrators on hand: "Everybody going to the Hopi House is asking where the Hopi Indians are," he moaned to Hubbell on one occasion, ignoring the fact that many of his favorite Hopi House demonstrators were Navajo. With Miguelito's family gone after Agippa's death, only Tom and Elle remained at the Grand Canyon, making "the Indian proposition . . .

really a farce." He pleaded with Hubbell to persuade Miguelito to return or to make some other, really "any arrangement," just, "get some Indians to the Canyon at once."[51]

"It was up to the family when they wanted to quit and go home," remembered one woman who as a child had accompanied her mother to Albuquerque for two months.[52]

And so they did, for dramatic reasons such as Agippa's death or in response to more quotidian or seasonal necessities plant their corn, check in with family and friends, attend ceremonies, take care of business, because they just wanted to, or, in the case of one man called the "Old Silversmith," because "people are bothering too much trying to take his picture."[53] Demonstrator work provided some welcome income as well as travel and adventure. It may even have appealed to a few demonstrators as a way to practice and preserve traditional crafts. Most demonstrators, however, were likely less concerned with facilitating cross-cultural exchange than in the satisfaction of earning decent money for work that was of both economic and cultural value to them and their communities. For some, such as Agippa, this decision could lead to tragedy. For others, such as Elle, it may also have entailed sacrifice that was deemed worthwhile. In any case, in the early twentieth century such craftwork was integrated into Navajos' diversified subsistence economy even when practiced in the "staged authenticity" of Albuquerque's Indian Building or the Grand Canyon's Hopi House.

While the Diné brought economic assumptions based on that diversified subsistence economy and reciprocal economic obligations to Harvey houses, their employers maintained faith in market forces and economic specialization. Part of the justification for the marketing of tradition was, according to the Harvey people, that it would benefit all concerned: "The railroad company is very much interested in the success of this project," Huckel wrote Hubbell, "and the tourists are as much so, and I think it will help eventually the . . . Indians by creating a market for their goods."[54]

Through their art, it seemed, Indians could be incorporated into the national market economy and could find a future in modern America, as long as there was a market for their goods. "Staged authenticity" thus suggested an alternative to assimilation: Indian cultures had unique contributions to make, and perhaps they were worth preserving, at least in part. It also served to define Indians as "naturally artistic," a positive but ultimately constraining view.

The conquest of Indian America included not only military force and boarding schools but also the ideological reduction of native cultures to their marketable artistic products—an example, perhaps, of what Barbara A. Babcock calls "modern power," replacing "violence and force with the 'gentler' constraint of uninterrupted visibility, 'the gaze.'"[55] A woman like Elle would not languish in prison like Geronimo, but she was captured many times—on film.

Yet while in the tourist literature Indians were presented as silent, "beyond expression," a woman like Elle was hardly mute, even if she did not speak English. Remembered decades later as "the boss of the weaving outfit in Albuquerque"[56] she, like her husband Tom and Miguelito and Maria Antonio, found a role in the modern world and a way to support herself by embodying the traditional Indian artisan yearned for by modern Americans. She took on that employment and even met the president without abandoning her ties to her rural home, her kin, her language, her Navajo name, or her religion. In his speech in Albuquerque the day they met, Roosevelt praised those with "adventurous temper and . . . iron resolution . . . who first tempted the shaggy wilderness and turned it into habitations for man." His meeting with Elle is a reminder that the West had been inhabited by "man"—men and women—long before the Anglo conquest, and that diverse groups would continue struggling to make a home there in the twentieth century, a task that might take an even stronger resolution and more adventurous spirit than those manly pioneers Roosevelt had in mind.[57] Historically and historiographically, we have tended to examine more closely the perspective that Roosevelt brought to his meeting with Elle, but just because we do not know what Asdzaa Lichii' said about this encounter does not mean that she said nothing. Despite the lack of written sources from her perspective, we can shift our frame of reference to make the central actor in the story the weaver instead of the president. In doing so, we can deepen our understanding of the ways in which diverse Americans entered the twentieth century and forged our common history.

Much rural women's history has analyzed how women adapted products of domestic labor to the early twentieth century's expanding national industrial economy. The Navajo rug trade fits neatly into this larger historiographical context, but it is worth remembering that

Navajo textiles had always been commodities as well as cultural expressions. As Navajo weavers became symbols of the modern Southwest,
Navajo women who wove found new markets for the craft. Such mar-
ketplaces were sites of compromise and confusion, exploitation and
resistance. But, as Diné, weavers continued to expect both financial
remuneration and cultural respect for their work. One professional
weaver, following in Elle's footsteps, explained in 1986: "Your mind and
prayers are connected" to weaving; a rug "just has to be you. . . . I want
the Navajo weaver to get lots of money for their weaving. I go several
places to teach that." Weaving remains a good way to help face difficult
economic circumstances, despite the low return per hour of labor.
Younger women, she predicted, will continue to take up weaving
because if "there are no jobs for them . . . they think about weaving."
Echoing the words of many Navajo weavers over the centuries, she
explained, "I raised my children" with weaving, and "with my weaving
I get what I want."[58]

Laura Jane Moore received a Ph.D in U.S. History in 1999 from the University
of North Carolina at Chapel Hill. This chapter is drawn from research she did
for her dissertation, "The Navajo Rug Trade: Gender, Art, Work, and Modernity
in the American Southwest, 1870s–1930s."

NOTES

I first told the story of Elle meeting the president at the Fifth Annual Conference on
Rural and Farm Women in Historical Perspective held in 1995 in Chevy Chase,
Maryland. I would like to thank Lu Ann Jones and Anne Effland for making my partic-
ipation there possible. Since then the paper has been through many permutations. My
thanks go to Jacquelyn Hall, Nancy Hewitt, John Kasson, Marla Miller, and Molly
Rozum for their help on the dissertation chapter from which this article is drawn.
Participants in the Duke-UNC Feminist History Group and Nancy Shoemaker, as panel
commentator, at the 1999 Western History Association meeting provided useful suggestions and lively discussions of earlier versions. Finally, I am grateful to Kathleen
Howard, Joan Jensen, Marla Miller, Kathleen Tabaha, and an anonymous outside reader
for their thoughtful comments on drafts of the present article and to John Moore and
Roberto Mosheim for crucial aid in its completion.

    1. Kathleen L. Howard, "Weaving a Legend: Elle of Ganado Promotes the Indian
Southwest," *New Mexico Historical Review* 74:2 (1999): 130–31; *McKinley County*

(Gallup) *Republican*, April 30, 1903; and *Albuquerque Journal-Democrat*, May 6, 1903, 5.

2. For what little biographical information is available on Elle of Ganado see Howard, "Weaving a Legend," 127–53.

3. Barbara A. Babcock, "A New Mexican Rebecca: Imaging Pueblo Women," *Journal of the Southwest* 32:4 (1990): 404. A large literature is available on southwestern tourism and on its relationship to the Indian art market. See, for example, Barbara A. Babcock, ed., "Inventing the Southwest," special issue, *Journal of the Southwest* 32:4 (1990); J. J. Brody, "The Creative Consumer: Survival, Revival, and Invention in Southwest Indian Arts," in *Ethnic and Tourist Arts: Cultural Expressions From the Fourth World*, ed. Nelson H. H. Graburn (Berkeley: University of California Press, 1976), 70–84; Kathleen L. Howard and Diana F. Pardue, *Inventing the Southwest: The Fred Harvey Company and Native American Art* (Flagstaff, Ariz.: Northland Publishing, The Heard Museum, 1996); Louise Lamphere, ed., "Women, Anthropology, Tourism, and the Southwest," special section, *Frontiers: A Journal of Women Studies* 12:3 (1992): 5–12; Molly H. Mullin, "Consuming the American Southwest: Culture, Art, and Difference" (Ph.D. diss., Duke University, 1993); Scott Norris, ed., *Discovered Country: Tourism and Survival in the American West* (Albuquerque, N.Mex.: Stone Ladder Press, 1983); Sylvia Rodriguez, "Art, Tourism, and Race Relations in Taos: Toward a Sociology of the Art Colony," *Journal of Anthropological Research* 45:1 (1989): 77–100; Edwin L. Wade, "The Ethnic Art Market in the American Southwest, 1880–1980," in *Objects and Others: Essays on Museums and Material Culture*, ed. George W. Stocking, Jr. (Madison: University of Wisconsin Press, 1985), 167–91; and Marta Weigle and Barbara A. Babcock, eds., *The Great Southwest of the Fred Harvey Company and the Santa Fe Railway* (Phoenix: The Heard Museum, 1996).

4. Scholars have usually viewed the impact of the tourist industry, and the larger market economy of which it was part, on Native American artists and their communities as highly detrimental. See, for example, Edwin L. Wade, "Straddling the Cultural Fence: The Conflict for Ethnic Artists Within Pueblo Societies," in *The Arts of the North American Indian: Native Traditions in Evolution*, ed. Edwin L. Wade (New York: Hudson Hills Press, 1986), 243–54; Tessie Naranjo, "Cultural Changes: The Effect of Foreign Systems at Santa Clara Pueblo," in Weigle and Babcock, *The Great Southwest*, 187–96; and Kathy M'Closkey, "Marketing Multiple Myths: The Hidden History of Navajo Weaving," *Journal of the Southwest* 36:3 (1994): 185–220. Such analyses parallel and sometimes intersect with scholarship on rural women that views Native Americans as losing out as they adopt items of domestic production to an expanding national market economy, and with analyses in Native American women's history that argue that the European and Euro-American economic system disrupted indigenous gender roles to the detriment of women. For an article that combines these themes, see Terry R. Reynolds, "Women, Pottery, and Economics at Acoma Pueblo," in *New Mexico Women: Intercultural Perspectives*, ed. Joan M. Jensen and Darlis A. Miller (Albuquerque: University of New Mexico Press, 1986). In other words, the market economy has long been a villain in Native American studies. Recently, however, historians of Native American women have noted the depth and resilience of cultural systems, evidenced in particular by the fundamental maintenance of gender roles, even as Native Americans adapted to significant historical and material pressures. Other Native American historians have also examined the variety of Native responses to

changing economic circumstances and the ways in which Indians brought their own economic rationales to interactions with Euro-Americans, adapting and adopting aspects of a complex, historically constructed market economy. For an example, see Theda Perdue, *Cherokee Women: Gender and Cultural Change, 1700–1835* (Lincoln: University of Nebraska Press, 1998); and Arthur J. Ray, *Indians in the Fur Trade: Their Role as Trappers, Hunters, and Middlemen in the Lands Southwest of Hudson Bay, 1660–1870* (Toronto: University of Toronto Press, 1974).

5. About the Fred Harvey Company I rely particularly on two publications generated by the Heard Museum's recent exhibit on the company: Howard and Pardue, *Inventing the Southwest;* and Weigle and Babcock, eds., *The Great Southwest.* On orientalist southwestern discourse, see Weigle and Babcock, *The Great Southwest,* 6–7. On the Fred Harvey Company and the Santa Fe Railroad, see also Keith L. Bryant, *History of the Atchison, Topeka, and Santa Fe Railway* (New York: Macmillan Publishing Company, 1974); T. C. McLuhan, *Dream Tracks: The Railroad and the American Indian, 1890–1930* (New York: Harry N. Abrams, 1985); and Lesley Polling-Kempes, *The Harvey Girls: Women Who Opened the West* (New York: Paragon House, 1989).

6. Howard and Pardue, *Inventing the Southwest,* 9–15, 103. See also Kathleen L. Howard, "'A Most Remarkable Success': Herman Schweizer and the Fred Harvey Indian Department," in Weigle and Babcock, *The Great Southwest,* 87–101; Matilda McQuaid with Karen Bartlett, "Building an Image of the Southwest: Mary Colter, Fred Harvey Company Architect," in Weigle and Babcock, *The Great Southwest,* 24–35; Virginia L. Grattan, *Mary Colter: Builder Upon the Red Earth* (Flagstaff, Ariz.: Northland Press, 1980); and Marta Weigle, "Exposition and Mediation: Mary Colter, Erna Fergusson, and the Santa Fe/Harvey Popularization of the Native Southwest, 1902–1940," *Frontiers: A Journal of Women Studies* 23:3 (1992): 117–50. On using the concepts of "staged authenticity" and "backstage" views of Indian life in analyzing Mary Colter's architecture, concepts drawn from Erving Goffman's and Dean MacCannell's work, see Weigle, "Exposition and Mediation," 120–30.

7. Leah Dilworth, *Imagining Indians in the Southwest: Persistent Visions of a Primitive Past* (Washington, D.C.: Smithsonian Institution Press, 1996), 147–48, 151.

8. Weigle and Babcock, *The Great Southwest,* 12.

9. Ruth Roessel, "Navajo Arts and Crafts," in *Handbook of North American Indians,* vol. 10, *Southwest* (Washington, D.C.: Smithsonian Institution Press, 1983), 595.

10. Interview no. 27, Hubbell Trading Post National Historic Site Oral History Collection (hereafter HTPOHC), Ganado, Arizona; and Ann Lane Hedlund, *Reflections of the Weaver's World: The Gloria F. Ross Collection of Contemporary Navajo Weaving* (Denver, Colo.: Denver Art Museum, 1992), 30. When the interviews were conducted for HTPOHC in the late 1960s and early 1970s, consent forms were not obtained for the interviews to be used in subsequent research. Kathleen Tabaha, the assistant curator at the Hubbell Trading Post National Historic Site, is in the process of contacting interviewees' family members in order to obtain such permission. In the meantime, she has asked that I not use interviewees' names.

11. Ann Lane Hedlund, "'More of a Survival Than an Art': Comparing Late Nineteenth- and Late Twentieth-Century Lifeways and Weaving," in *Woven By the Grandmothers: Nineteenth-Century Textiles from the National Museum of the American Indian,* ed. Eulalie H. Bonar (Washington, D.C.: Smithsonian Institution Press, 1996), 47–48. A voluminous literature is available on Navajo weaving. In addition to those works cited above, I am relying particularly on Ellen F. Elsas and Ann Lane Hedlund, *"Well May They Be Made": Navajo Textiles from the Coleman Cooper*

Collection of the Birmingham Museum of Art (Birmingham, Ala.: Birmingham Museum of Art, 1987); Ann Lane Hedlund, *Beyond the Loom: Keys to Understanding Early Southwestern Weaving* (Boulder, Colo.: Johnson Books, 1990); Ann Lane Hedlund, "Contemporary Navajo Weaving: An Ethnography of a Native Craft," (Ph.D. diss., University of Colorado at Boulder, 1983); Kate Peck Kent, *Navajo Weaving: Three Centuries of Change* (Santa Fe: School of American Research Press, 1985); Marian E. Rodee, *One Hundred Years of Navajo Rugs* (Albuquerque: University of New Mexico Press, 1995); Joe Ben Wheat, "Documentary Basis for Material Changes and Design Styles in Navajo Blanket Weaving," in *Proceedings of the Irene Emery Roundtable on Museum Textiles* (Washington, D.C.: The Textile Museum, 1976); Joe Ben Wheat, *The Gift of Spiderwoman: Southwestern Textiles, the Navajo Tradition* (Philadelphia: University Museum, University of Pennsylvania, 1984); and Roseann W. Willink and Paul G. Zolbrod, *Weaving a World: Textiles and the Navajo Way of Seeing* (Santa Fe: University of New Mexico Press, 1996).

12. Gary Witherspoon, "Navajo Social Organization," in *Handbook of North American Indians*, vol. 10, *Southwest*, 525–26; and Elsas and Hedlund, *"Well May They Be Made,"* 29–30.

13. Garrick Bailey and Roberta Glenn Bailey, in *A History of the Navajos: The Reservation Years* (Santa Fe, N.M.: School of American Research Press, 1986), argue that even in the twentieth century, as "Navajos diversified into commercial stock raising and wage labor" they did not totally commercialize their herds but "successfully maintained high subsistence value while raising the market value of their livestock. . . . In large part rug weaving enabled them to achieve this balance" because it "gave a dimension to their herding economy that Anglo-American and Spanish-American ranchers lacked" (179–80). David Aberle contends in "Navajo Exogamic Rules and Preferred Marriages" (in *The Versatility of Kinship: Essays Presented to Harry W. Basehart*, ed. Linda S. Cordell and Stephen Beckerman [New York: Academic Press, 1980]) that "traditional kinship organization is maintained because of, rather than despite, changes in the Navajo economy—that traditional kinship organization, oriented to the multiple, fluctuating resources of the traditional economy, preserves the same orientation now that the Navajos are marginal participants in the larger United States economy. Relying on multiple, fluctuating resources, which include flocks, farms, crafts, wage work, and welfare, most families have no single source of livelihood sufficient in quantity or reliability to induce them to give up the others. . . . By and large, the nuclear family provides insufficient labor power for all these activities" (123–24). On the maintenance of matrifocal kinship institutions in the midst of a dramatically changing political economy, see also Klara B. Kelley, "Navajo Political Economy before Fort Sumner," in Cordell and Beckerman, *The Versatility of Kinship*, 315, 317–18, 329. On change and persistence of Navajo women's roles and status, see Laila Shukry Hamamsy, "The Role of Women in a Changing Navaho Society," *American Anthropologist* 59:1 (1957): 101–11; Mary Shepardson, "The Status of Navajo Women"; and Christine Conte, "Ladies, Livestock, Land, and Lucre: Women's Networks and Social Status on the Western Navajo Reservation," *American Indian Quarterly* 6:1/2 (1982): 105–24; and Louise Lamphere, "Historical and Regional Variability in Navajo Women's Roles," *Journal of Anthropological Research* 45:4 (1989): 431–56.

14. Richard I. Ford, "Inter-Indian Exchange in the Southwest," in *Handbook of North American Indians*, vol. 10, *Southwest*, 721.

15. Hedlund, "'More of a Survival Than an Art,'" 54.

16. Bailey and Bailey, *A History of the Navajos*, 51.

17. Ibid., chapter 2. On the Navajo economy and trade networks, see also Klara Bonseck Kelley, "Commercial Networks on the Navajo-Hopi-Zuni Region," (Ph.D. diss., The University of New Mexico, 1977).

18. Bailey and Bailey, *A History of the Navajos*, 59–60; Kent, *Navajo Weaving*, 17–18, 83, 85–86; and Dilys Winegard, ed., *A Burst of Brilliance: Germantown, Pennsylvania and Navajo Weaving* (Philadelphia: University of Pennsylvania Press, 1994). A large and growing literature is available on trading posts in Navajo country. The story of traders and Navajo weavers has often been told as change directed by traders with weavers passively accepting white men's suggestions. Recent scholarship has emphasized weavers' agency and analyzes trading posts as complex sites of transculturation. Three classics are Frank McNitt, *The Indian Traders* (1962, reprint, Norman: University of Oklahoma Press, 1989); William Adams, *Shonto: A Study of the Role of the Trader in a Modern Navaho Community* (Washington, D.C.: Smithsonian Institution, Bureau of American Ethnology, Bulletin 188, 1963); and Willow Roberts, *Stokes Carson: Twentieth-Century Trading on the Navajo Reservation* (Albuquerque: University of New Mexico Press, 1987). Recent studies include Martha Blue, *Indian Trader: The Life and Times of J. C. Hubbell* (Walnut, Calif.: Kiva Publishing, Inc., 2000); Laura Graves, *Thomas Varker Keam, Indian Trader* (Norman: University of Oklahoma Press, 1998); Laura Ruth Marcus, "Moving Towards Nizaad: Exploring the Dynamics of Navajo-Anglo Interaction Through Trading and Art" (Ph.D. diss., Indiana University, 1998); Nancy Peake, "Trading Post Tales: Biography of an Indian Trader on the Navajo Reservation, 1930–1980" (Ph.D. diss., University of New Mexico, 1992); and Teresa Jo Wilkins, "Producing Culture Across the Colonial Divide: Navajo Reservation Trading Posts and Weaving" (Ph.D. diss., University of Colorado at Boulder, 1999). A good recent description of the trading post economy is in Robert "Skip" Volk, "'Red Sales in the Sunset': The Rise and Fall of White Trader Dominance in the United States' Navajo Reservation and South Africa's Transkei," *American Indian Culture and Research Journal* 24:1 (2000): 69–97.

19. Marc Simmons, *Albuquerque: A Narrative History* (Albuquerque: University of New Mexico Press, 1982), 234, 275–77, 329; Bradford Luckingham, *The Urban Southwest: A Profile History of Albuquerque, El Paso, Phoenix, and Tucson* (El Paso, Tex.: Western Press, 1982), 19, 35–36; and Bailey and Bailey, *A History of the Navajos*, 156, 157–58. On ways in which Navajos combined wage work with a kin-based household economy that often conflicted with their employer's expectations, see Colleen O'Neill, "Navajo Workers and White Man's Ways: Negotiating the World of Wage Labor, 1930–1970" (Ph.D. diss., Graduate School-New Brunswick, Rutgers, The State University of New Jersey, 1997); and Colleen O'Neill, "The 'Making' of the Navajo Worker: Navajo Households, the Bureau of Indian Affairs, and Off-Reservation Wage Work, 1948–1960," *New Mexico Historical Review* 74:4 (1999): 375–405.

20. The Hubbell Trading Post in Ganado is still in operation today, owned by the National Park Service as a National Historic Site. Weavers still visit the trading post's rug room to bargain with the trader in Navajo, while others demonstrate their art for tourists in the visitor's center. These weavers carry on in Elle's tradition, but much has also changed, and tourists are instructed not to photograph demonstrators without their permission.

21. Herman Schweizer to John Lorenzo Hubbell, March 13, 1903, April 29, 1903, and March 6, 1903, Fred Harvey File (hereafter FHF), Incoming Correspondence, box

36, Harvey Trading Post Collection (hereafter HTPC), Special Collections, University of Arizona.

22. Juana Sangre of Isleta Pueblo, interviewed in 1994, remembered constantly cleaning the pots and the floors between trains. She said, "And when they tell us a train is about to be here we used to quit so they wouldn't find us [cleaning]" (quoted in Howard and Pardue, *Inventing the Southwest*, 24).

23. See, for example, Huckel to Hubbell, June 9, June 26, July 1, and July 20, 1905, FHF, HTPC. Unlike weaving, silver work continued to be an important trade item among the Diné. The heavy silver jewelry that Navajos used was inappropriate for the tourist market, so the Harvey Company encouraged some silversmiths to develop a lighter, cheaper style that they could sell in their stores. See John Adair, *The Navajo and Pueblo Silversmiths* (Norman: University of Oklahoma Press, 1944).

24. Howard and Pardue, *Inventing the Southwest*, 74, 76, 105–10.

25. Elle and Tom had no children together, which might have lessened their responsibilities back home. Still, they often brought some of Tom's grandchildren with them to Albuquerque, and Elle was frequently photographed surrounded by children. She was an ideal demonstrator because she could afford to stay away from home while still providing a matronly image (Howard, "Weaving a Legend," 132, 128).

26. Howard and Pardue, *Inventing the Southwest*, 64, 66, 68.

27. *The Great Southwest Along the Santa Fe* (Kansas City, Mo.: Fred Harvey, 1914), n.p., quoted in Marta Weigle with Kathleen L. Howard, "'To Experience the Real Grand Canyon': Santa Fe/Harvey Panopticism, 1901–1935," in Weigle and Babcock, *The Great Southwest*, 21.

28. Huckel to Hubbell, March 4, 1905; and Schweizer to Hubbell, November 17, 1904, FHF, HTPC.

29. I am touching here only lightly on the relationship between "antimodernism," the arts and crafts movement, and Indian art, a relationship that I discuss in more depth in "The Navajo Rug Trade: Gender, Art, Work, and Modernity in the American Southwest, 1870s–1930s" (Ph.D. diss., University of North Carolina at Chapel Hill, 1999). Besides those already cited, related works include T. J. Jackson Lears, *No Place of Grace: Antimodernism and the Transformation of American Culture, 1880–1920* (New York: Pantheon Books, 1981); Eileen Boris, *Art and Labor: Ruskin, Morris, and the Craftsman Ideal in America* (Philadelphia: Temple University Press, 1986); J. J. Brody, *Indian Painters and White Patrons* (Albuquerque: University of New Mexico Press, 1971); W. Jackson Rushing, *Native American Art and the New York Avant-Garde: A History of Cultural Primitivism* (Austin: University of Texas Press, 1995); Wendy Kaplan, ed., *"Art That is Life:" The Arts and Crafts Movement in America, 1875–1920* (Boston: Little, Brown and Company for Museum of Fine Arts, 1987); Miles Orvell, *The Real Thing: Imitation and Authenticity in American Culture, 1880–1940* (Chapel Hill: The University of North Carolina Press, 1989); Melanie Herzog, "Aesthetics and Meanings: The Arts and Crafts Movement and the Revival of American Indian Basketry," in *The Substance of Style: Perspectives on the American Arts and Crafts Movement*, ed. Bert Denker (Winterthur, Del.: Henry Francis du Pont Winterthur Museum; Hanover: University Press of New England, 1996), 69–92; Margaret D. Jacobs, "Shaping a New Way: White Women and the Movement to Promote Pueblo Indian Arts and Crafts, 1900–1935," *Journal of the Southwest* 40:2 (1998): 187–216; Molly H. Mullin, "The Patronage of Difference: Making Indian Art 'Art, Not Ethnology,'" *Cultural Anthropology* 7:4 (1992):

395–426; and Teresa J. Wilkins, "The Creation of a Usable Past," in *Diné Baa Hané Bi Naaltsoos: Collected Papers from the Seventh through Tenth Navajo Studies Conferences*, ed. June-el Piper (Window Rock, Ariz.: Navajo Nation Historic Preservation Office for the Navajo Studies Conference, 1999), 203–10.

30. Sweizer per Snively to Hubbell, July 9, 1903, FHF, HTPC.

31. Interview no. 20: 567 098, in Michael Joseph Francisconi, *Kinship, Capitalism, Change: The Informal Economy of the Navajo, 1868–1995* (New York: Garland Publishing, 1998), Appendix A, 220.

32. Huckel to Hubbell, October 4, 1905, FHF, HTPC.

33. See, for example, Huckel to Hubbell, April 26, 1905, and April 21, 1905, FHF, HTPC.

34. Letter from John Hudson to Grace Hudson, February 6, 1903, quoted in Howard and Pardue, *Inventing the Southwest*, 59.

35. Huckel to Hubbell, April 21 and 26, 1905; and J. Snively to Hubbell, May 6, 1905, FHF, HTPC.

36. Schweizer to Hubbell, April 29, 1905, FHF, HTPC.

37. Schweizer to Hubbell, May 31, 1905, FHF, HTPC.

38. Schweizer to Hubbell, April 6, 1905, FHF, HTPC.

39. Huckel to Hubbell, June 9, 1905, FHF, HTPC.

40. Huckel to Hubbell, June 26, 1905, and May 31, 1905, FHF, HTPC.

41. They got to the Canyon on June 25.

42. Huckel to Hubbell, July 1, 1905, FHF, HTPC.

43. Huckel to Hubbell, July 20, 1905, FHF, HTPC.

44. Schweizer to Hubbell, July 19, 1905, FHF, HTPC.

45. *Albuquerque Morning Journal*, October 3 and October 21, 1904, cited in Howard and Pardue, *Inventing the Southwest*, 61.

46. Interview with Marie Curley, Doris Duke Number 678, the American Indian History Project, Western History Center, University of Utah, September 10, 1970, copy in the HTPOHC, Ganado. Curley says that her father, Miguelito, was four, and her mother, Maria Antonio, was two, when they left Fort Sumner.

47. Gladys Reichard, *Navajo Shepherd and Weaver* (1936; reprint, Enumclaw, Wash.: MacRae Publications, 1977), *Spider Woman: A Story of Navajo Weavers and Chanters* (1934; reprint, Glorieta, N.Mex.: Rio Grande Press, 1968), and *Navajo Medicine Man: Sandpaintings and Legends of Miguelito* (New York: J. J. Augustin, 1939).

48. Schweizer to Hubbell, July 24, 1905, FHF, HTPC.

49. Schweizer to Hubbell, July 27, 1905, FHF, HTPC.

50. In the 1920s the Fred Harvey Company issued a series of lavishly illustrated publications edited by J. Huckel titled "American Indians: First Families of the Southwest."

51. Schweizer to Hubbell, March 15, 1903; Huckel to Hubbell, May 23, 1905; and Schweizer to Hubbell, September 13, 1905, FHF, HTPC.

52. Interview no. 40, n.d., HTPOHC.

53. Schweizer to Hubbell, May 31, 1905, FHF, HTPC.

54. Huckel to Hubbell, March 23, 1905, FHF, HTPC.

55. Babcock, "A New Mexican Rebecca," 429. Babcock is paraphrasing Michel Foucault's discussion of "the gaze" in *Discipline and Punish: The Birth of the Prison* (New York: Pantheon Books, 1977).

56. Interview no. 7, November 15, 1971, HTPOHC.

57. *Albuquerque Journal-Democrat*, May 6, 1903.

58. Interview no. 1, January 20, 1986, Ganado oral history rug study interviews, HTPC.

REDEFINING EXPECTATIONS

NISEI WOMEN IN THE 1930S*

Valerie Matsumoto

In 1934, a nineteen-year-old Japanese American woman stirred read-ers of the San Francisco *Hokubei Asahi* newspaper with seven essays regarding women's roles in family and society. "Japanese Nisei girls," she announced, "have very little freedom in self-expression. They are bound in skirts and girdled to convention. . . . The social convention has chloroformed them. They are dead to worldly freedom and accom-plishments."[1] "Mary M. N.," as the young writer prudently styled her-self, further railed against the inequities between men and women, and specifically at the male ego:

> To a woman's eyes, he [man] is nothing but a hot-dog rolled in mus-tard, though he may imagine himself to be a lion—a stuffed lion at the most. . . . If a woman actually told a man or boy what he really is, this world would be unsafe for the wiser sex.[2]

Mary urged Japanese American women to "be strong and be a fighter. . . . Our civilization does not call for women to stick forever to sewing and washing. Our life must not be spent in dingy kitchens. . . . the world is too large a place for womankind to squander their lives in foolishness and trifles. . . . Be a woman of the world!"[3]

---

*This chapter was previously published as: Matsumoto, Valerie. "Redefining Expectations: Nisei Women in the 1930s." In *California History* 73 (spring 1994): 44–53.

Mary M. N.'s essays provoked a flurry of response from other second-generation Japanese Americans. Her ideas on gender roles, interracial marriage, and the pursuit of individual fulfillment catalyzed the transformation of a general "letters to the editor" column into the newspaper's popular advice column, which was presided over by another Nisei woman. From 1935 to 1940, Mary Oyama Mittwer—writing under the pseudonym "Deirdre"—provided a sympathetic ear for personal problems, dispensed etiquette tips, and pondered the place of the Nisei (second-generation Japanese Americans) in U.S. society.[4]

Advice columns such as Deirdre's and juvenile pen-pal correspondence clubs—both geared largely toward female readers—provide a valuable window into the concerns and roles of second-generation Japanese American women in the pre–World War II community. Few such personal records have survived the turmoil of the wartime uprooting of the Japanese Americans. These columns serve as a useful gauge indicating the influence of both the ethnic community and the dominant European American society on the position of Nisei women. They also reveal the ways in which second-generation women tried to mediate conflict between American mainstream expectations and the wishes of their immigrant parents.

Only a handful of works by writers such as Monica Sone, Evelyn Nakano Glenn, Jeanne Wakatsuki Houston, and Yoshiko Uchida shed light on what it meant to be a Nisei woman coming of age on the brink of war. For the most part, scholars have focused on Japanese American history during World War II. Certainly the concentration camp experience played a crucial part in altering women's roles and family life, but to what extent had these changes already begun? The prewar newspapers provide evidence that gender role and cultural shifts were already in progress, changes that would accelerate in the pressure-cooker environment of camp life. Japanese American newspaper columns reveal the interplay of ethnic and mainstream cultures, as well as the dreams and realities of young Nisei women, through the decade of the 1930s. The lively Nisei discussion of these topics, particularly the development of an ethnic peer network and issues associated with heterosexual love and marriage, demonstrates second-generation women's efforts to integrate the different social worlds that shaped their perceptions and choices and underscores as well the significance of peer affirmation.

The Japanese-language press served as an important information source and unifying agent for the immigrant enclaves in the U.S. West, enabling the Issei (first generation) to keep abreast of community, national, and international events. In northern California, several newspapers vied for community support, including the *Hokubei Asahi* and the *Shin Sekai*. By the 1930s, both newspapers started English-language sections for the benefit of the growing second generation, most of whom did not read Japanese. These English-language sections initially gave limited coverage to sports news and church events. By 1935, when the two papers merged to form the *New World-Sun*, the English-language sections had expanded to include youth-oriented pen-pal clubs, advice columns, reader-submitted poetry and fiction, recipes, fashion news, and comic strips. By the eve of World II, their offerings included more extensive reporting of Japanese American political concerns and close coverage of U.S.-Japan relations. Reader submissions revealed the popularity of the newspapers among both urban and rural Nisei throughout the West and beyond.

Japanese immigration to the United States had begun in the late nineteenth century with the arrival of male laborers. The "Gentlemen's Agreement" of 1908 restricted the entry of additional male Japanese workers but permitted the immigration of the families of Japanese already living in the United States. The majority of Japanese immigrant women entered the country between 1908 and 1924. The Immigration Act of 1924, however, ended the influx of Japanese men and women altogether. Many of the Issei immigrants settled in the U.S. West, working on railroads, in lumber mills, and in agriculture. Those in urban areas developed small businesses that primarily catered to the ethnic community.

The young 1930s readers of the *New World-Sun*—the children of the Issei—were in age and training representative of their Japanese American peers. The majority of the Nisei were born between 1910 and 1940. Both sons and daughters, particularly those living on farms, played an important role in the family economy from an early age. Country Nisei hoed weeds, irrigated fields, drove tractors, and tended their younger siblings. In addition to fieldwork, girls were expected to fulfill domestic duties. Their urban counterparts helped in their families' small businesses, which provided goods and services to the ethnic community.

The values of Meiji Japan and the American Protestant ethic meshed in the upbringing of the Nisei. Although rural families were more apt to maintain traditional Japanese practices, all Nisei shared common training and ideals. Their Issei parents stressed the importance of education, industriousness, and respect for authority and reminded them of their role as representatives of their family and community. In addition, the Issei sought to instill in their children a strong sense of Japanese values such as *oyakoko* (filial piety) and *on* (obligation).

The Nisei grew up synthesizing both American mainstream culture and the Japanese customs of their parents. Most of the second generation spoke Japanese with their parents and English with their siblings and friends. When the regular school day ended, their parents sent them to *nihongakko* (Japanese school) to learn Japanese language and ethics. Whether Buddhist or Christian, they celebrated a round of Japanese and American holidays, including New Year's Day, Thanksgiving, and Christmas. Nisei girls learned knitting and crocheting as well as *odori*, or traditional Japanese dance. Like their non-Japanese American peers, they followed the adventures of their favorite comic-strip heroes and collected photographs of screen idols such as Deanna Durbin and Clark Gable.

The young women who wrote to Deirdre and solicited pen-pals through the newspaper's "Rendezvous Club" feature were teenagers or in their early twenties by the eve of World War II. Most were single but likely to marry within a few years.[5] Some, like Monica Sone, author of *Nisei Daughter*, dreamed of going to college or business school, and a small minority did so. As they considered their futures, they turned to their peers for empathy and encouragement.

The Nisei were a highly organized group within the ethnic enclave. During the war years, they relied on strong support networks of friends and kin in seeking work and reestablishing families dislocated by wartime internment. Examination of Nisei pen-pal clubs facilitated by the *New World-Sun* in the 1930s affords the opportunity to trace one facet of the development of these peer networks even before the war. These clubs gave Nisei in isolated areas a sense of community and a preliminary bridge between urban and rural experiences, fostering new peer bonds.

The Rendezvous Club, nicknamed the "Rendie" by members, was the longest-running column in the English-language section of the *New World-Sun*. It first appeared in the *Shin Sekai* in 1933 and persisted until the advent of war closed the press. A sense of extended family relationship was fostered by the structure of the pen-pal club, which was supervised by a series of fictive "unkles" and "aunts" like Unkle Oski, Unkle Jimmy, Aunt Tsugi, and Aunt Susan. These supportive adult characters, themselves Nisei, were only a few years older than their enthusiastic "nieces" and "nefs." In the column, the "unkles" and "aunts" wrote travel sketches, exchanged breezy banter with their readers, and introduced new members. In the first several years, the majority of responses to the Rendezvous Club came from girls like Sara Imura, who wrote to the newspaper from Crichton, Alabama, that "I have chosen the name DEW DROP INN because I want all of you to drop in with letters. . . . I am fourteen and will be a junior next year, but have never seen or heard from any Japanese of my age except [a] few of my relatives."[6]

Club participation allowed the Nisei a secure channel in which to experiment with self-definition and identity, since they could choose the information they would present about themselves and invent pseudonyms. Indicative of their engagement with popular youth culture, in the first years, the "Rendites" used pen names such as "Dixie," "Lollypop," "Raggedy Ann," "Rebecca of Cupertino Farm," and "Ratspudding the Vampire." They described to their newfound "cousins," "aunts," and "uncles" their experiences of ice-skating in Utah, cutting spuds in Idaho, and attending girls' finishing schools in Japan. The sense of belonging to a family network was furthered by the circulation of a photograph album in which new members could see their "cousins" and add their own pictures.

As the Nisei matured, the Rendezvous Club began to serve an additional social purpose in facilitating the meeting of young women and men. More flirtatious pseudonyms appeared, such as "Glamour Puss," "Handsome Romeo," "Lonesome Cavalier," and "Hot Time Susie." By 1938, however, pen names began to fall into disuse as the older Nisei sent in their real names and provided more detailed descriptions of their physique and character. It is not certain how much socializing the

Rendie initiated, but its undiminished popularity up to the outbreak of World War II and the announcement in 1938 of the wedding of two readers testify to its importance in providing an ethnic social and romantic outlet for the second generation.

If the "Rendezvous Club" provided an ethnic social network for the second generation, the newspaper's "I'm Telling You, Deirdre" column constituted a forum for inquiries and advice about how Nisei readers might maintain harmonious interaction both with their Japanese elders and persons of the dominant society. For the Nisei, who were sometimes uncertain as to the etiquette that was expected of them by their parents and non-Japanese American contemporaries, Deirdre provided kindly optimism and clues to proper behavior. Her column also offered discussion of the Nisei's most intimate and thorny concerns. When Deirdre took charge of the "I'm Telling You" column, she promised to address the social problems facing the second generation and stated that she would be "happy to answer any question put her concerning family affairs, love and other sex problems, social etiquette and other personal questions."[7] Those who wrote in could rely upon the secrecy of their pseudonyms and on the empathy of their peers. Here Deirdre displayed her skill not only as an arbiter but as a confidante.

The "I'm Telling You" column is a particularly rich source for exploring the lives of prewar Nisei women. As evidenced by letters and postcards sent from all areas of California, Colorado, Idaho, Illinois, Michigan, Nevada, Oregon, Texas, and Washington, D.C., Deirdre reached a wide readership. Women comprised the majority of writers to the column until 1937, when Deirdre reported that the letters she received were now equally divided between men and women. Cities, small towns, and rural districts were all equally represented in her incoming mail. Some of the issues of concern to Deirdre's readers were "boy and girl relations," the "Nisei problem," intergenerational conflict, careers, marriage, and etiquette.

The two kinds of social etiquette information Deirdre dispensed constituted a link for the Nisei between the carefully regulated world of their parents and the sometimes bewildering customs of their non-Japanese American peers. The Nisei strove to adapt to the ways of the larger society, but for many of them it was unfamiliar terrain, and the prospect of committing social errors was mortifying. Through her advice column, Deirdre tried to demystify the social conventions of the middle-class European American world for the urban and rural Nisei. For example, she advised young men about what would be considered proper gifts they might give women friends and warned them, "Never walk down the street with one girl on each arm—like a gigolo."[8] She also cautioned the Nisei that excessive gum-chewing was unattractive.

Attempting to smooth relations between two generations, Deirdre also advised the Nisei regarding Issei expectations of correct behavior. For instance, she devoted one column to the mechanics of a proper bow. "There is nothing more graceful, charming and poiseful to look at than a well-executed bow," she assured her readers. She instructed gentlemen to bow from the waist "rather than bobbing the head from the neck like a chicken."[9] Women, on the other hand, should bow from the hips, slowly and deliberately, sliding the hands down from thighs to kneecaps, holding the position for three seconds. She advocated practice in front of a mirror to perfect the technique.

Often, Deirdre's advice reflected the mixed social environment in which her Nisei readers moved. In an essay devoted to the importance of "small courtesies," Deirdre's list of appropriate behaviors included not sprawling on the couch, going to the door to call for a girlfriend rather than honking the auto-horn, and saying *"Gomen kudasai"* when entering someone's home. Upon leaving, the thoughtful Nisei should say to the host or hostess, "I've had a pleasant time, goodbye," or *"O-jama itashi mashita."*[10] This Nisei "Miss Manners" was well aware of the varied social demands confronting her readers.

Although Deirdre addressed a variety of general issues that were not gender specific, the bulk of her writing was aimed at female readers. She admonished young women to avoid "little white lies" and false sophistication, and advised that men preferred "good sports" to "davenport sirens" or "reclining Cleopatras." Deirdre's advice to Nisei women was mixed, perhaps reflective of the ambivalent position of middle-class European American women in the larger society during the interwar doldrums of feminism. On the one hand, she extolled the importance of finding one's lifework; on the other, she bluntly asserted that "brainy women are not as accepted as brainy men" and must therefore conceal their intelligence. Deirdre's advice-giving was complicated, moreover, by the fact that she was directing it to ethnic minority women in a racially discriminatory society that imposed limitations on their opportunities and aspirations.

The subject of marriage and marriage practices, which reveals the juncture of Japanese traditions and U.S. socioeconomic conditions in the lives of Nisei women, was a recurring topic for Deirdre and her readers. In one column, Deirdre proclaimed that modern sophisticates were daring to break away from superstitious custom and "doing away with rings and titles." Indeed, the economic hardships of the depression years necessitated for many couples a shift away from showy weddings to civil ceremonies.[11] However, the issue of planning a simple wedding was sometimes complicated for the Nisei by the desire of their parents for an elaborate traditional Japanese celebration. "If a bowl of sake and hilarity is what they wish," one sympathetic Nisei asked, "need we deny them?"[12] At stake was not merely an issue of monetary expense, real as that was, but, on another level, a question that pitted Japanese community tradition against American individualism.

The concerns of feminism and conservative economics merged in the matter of engagement and wedding rings. Deirdre informed her readers that, like the flashy wedding, "rings are also being dispensed with as being too much like a 'yoke of bondage,' 'a badge of slavery,' an unnecessary added expense."[13] Deirdre added, thirty years in advance of the women's liberation movement, "The inescapable 'Mrs.' would be dropped for a term as neutral as 'Mr.' if it could be done—but as yet no good substitute title has been found. Usually the young matron is introduced as 'Katherine Allen' rather than the uninteresting 'Mrs. Allen.'"[14]

Marriage in general was a complex issue for the Nisei women. The majority, like their non-Japanese American sisters, expected a future revolving around marriage and family.[15] This expectation was complicated by Issei parents' preference for arranged matches such as their own. Many of the older Nisei who married before World War II had arranged marriages. To their younger siblings, however, such unions represented the antithesis of the companionate marriage extolled by their peers and the popular media. The tensions surrounding this issue were increased in the mid-1930s by the dearth of career opportunities for racial ethnic women and growing racial hostility that Nisei faced outside the Japantowns and Little Tokyos.

Like their mothers, Nisei women anticipated a future of marriage and domesticity. Many would have agreed with "Voice of the Rockies," a reader who wrote to Deirdre in 1937, that "after all is said and done, no career in the world offers ANY woman the satisfaction of the job of motherhood, really and truly well-done. . . . No matter what we may do in life, until we've married, borne children, we are immature in many ways."[16] For a Japanese American woman, adult status derived in large part from her role as wife and mother.

At least a few of the second-generation women, however, took up their pens in favor of career dreams. "Modern Miss" wrote to the newspaper in defense of Nisei "bachelorettes": "All women are NOT necessarily 'born for marriage.' Most women, yes, I grant; but NOT all women. . . ." "There are women who are married to their much beloved work," she continued, "and women who prefer their independence to the drudgery of domesticity. If they prefer to be single, why try to force them into an unwilling marriage merely because of public opinion?"[17] She contrasted mainstream and Japanese American society with regard to the status of single women:

> In the sensible American society of today there is no stigma attached to the unmarried woman. In conservative Japanese society and in our backward Nisei society, there seems to be a sort of 'unwritten question mark' hovering over the unmarried misses' heads like a sort of invisible halo.[18]

"Modern Miss" argued that all bachelorettes were not "dying to get married," but rather cherished their work and independence, and did not plan to marry until they found the "RIGHT man."[19]

The Nisei women's goal of personally locating the "right man" and their romantic expectations of courtship and marriage differentiated them from their mothers and indicated the influence of popular American culture on their attitudes. Historians Mary Ryan and Elaine Tyler May have noted that by the 1920s, American women were turning from the nineteenth-century ideals of purity and sacrifice to those of individuality and independence. In addition, the new woman had higher expectations of her relations with men.[20] The Japanese American women's letters of the 1930s reflect these changes as well. Many of the younger Nisei would agree with "Voice of the Rockies," who said of marriage, "Without love, it's an altogether different story. I, myself, cannot tolerate alliances for 'convenience' only. Without love, marriage is only a sham."[21] In her response to the writer, Deirdre expressed whole-hearted agreement, and reiterated her view that "a lot of busy-bodies and well-meaning Isseis are needlessly worrying about the so-called 'old maid problem.' They are so anxious to get everyone married off before they are twenty that they do not stop to think that not all girls are alike and that different girls mature at different ages."[22] While not downplaying the importance of marriage, Deirdre reflected the Nisei concern with individuality and personal choice.

The Nisei women's image of the "right man" also reflected generational change and the importance of choice. In the early twentieth century, a Japanese immigrant woman was thankful if her husband worked steadily and did not drink or gamble; her daughters looked for additional qualities for which an Issei woman could only hope.[23] "Miss Perplexed" told Deirdre's readers that among her criteria for a partner were personality, intelligence, manners, neat appearance, ambition, superior education, and consideration of women.[24] Certainly the focus on charm and physical attractiveness in the later Rendie columns also indicates changing female expectations.

As the proportion of male readers of "I'm Telling You, Deirdre" increased, the advice columnist could address similar issues, but from the Nisei men's perspective. What did Japanese American men expect in the women they married? One "Nisei Youth" sent Deirdre a description of the "ideal Nisei girl." "A person of my type," he explained,

> likes a girl who is natural, smart, . . . talented or accomplished, . . . fairly sophisticated. . . . She must know how to meet the problems of the world and of life, and with common sense she can face any situation. . . . Young in heart—pleasing and charming as a child, old in wisdom—[with] the understanding of a mature woman. . . . [25]

At the end of this litany, he prompted rhetorically, "Do I ask too much?" and then proclaimed that his girlfriend was just such a paragon. This "Nisei Youth" may have reflected an urban ideal rather than a rural one; still, his "wish list" of female attributes reveals that American mainstream thinking also influenced the men of the second generation. Clearly Nisei women and men had growing expectations of intimacy and emotional satisfaction in marriage. For marital models, they looked less and less to their parents and increasingly drew on the values of American popular culture.

Sociologist Evelyn Nakano Glenn has noted the critical role played by the middle Nisei cohort—those born between 1911 and 1919—in the transition from arranged marriage to "love" marriage, or *jiyu kekkon* (free marriage).[26] Many Nisei, in accordance with their parents' desires, had arranged marriages in the prewar period. However, newspaper articles and letters to Deirdre reflect increasing Nisei resistance to this custom.

The conflict between obedience to parental wishes and personal inclinations rendered the issue of arranged marriage particularly difficult for the Nisei. Deirdre's advice in this arena reflects the numerous considerations to be weighed, and also evidences the extent to which the ideal of companionate marriage had taken root among the Nisei by the mid-1930s. A young woman who entered an arranged marriage because of a sense of family obligation wrote that "This was absolutely not of my doings! I was forced to it. That's why I was always feeling low lately. You understand, don't you? To have to marry a man I've never known in my whole life, and not in love!"[27]

The man this writer *did* profess to care for submitted the letter to Deirdre with a plea for words of encouragement. Deirdre's response, which presented a forum for her views of both arranged and romantic marriages, was positive but not completely sympathetic to the writer. Her advice revealed the degree to which the American mainstream belief in free will had taken hold. The unhappy newlywed, who signed herself "Girl Friend," was first reminded by Deirdre of the eugenic advantages of arranged matches. "You are not just getting anybody," Deirdre said, "that is, if the third parties have seen to it to carefully investigate his family and circumstances. If the *baishakunin* [go-betweens] are good friends of yours, they would at least try to pick out a fairly decent person for you." It is questionable how much comfort "Girl Friend" derived from the columnist's assurance that "unless a man is an inveterate drinker, or of a violent temper, or one of perverse habits, the ordinary man cannot be such an ogre of a creature."[28]

Deirdre then proceeded to question whether "Girl Friend" had been truly coerced into marriage. "Were you 'forced' under pressure of disgrace, threat of bodily harm or torture, or being disowned from your family, or something equally dire?" she asked. Deirdre admitted that parental pressure constituted a powerful force, but insisted that "there must have been some way out of it IF you really wanted to get out."[29] The advice columnist's final words, however, were antithetical to the values the Issei sought to instill in their daughters—and very much the message of mainstream America:

> If you want a thing badly enough, you must be willing to sacrifice anything to attain it. You must be willing to lose your own family even, to face the so-called "disgrace," to endure poverty—hunger—starvation for your "love." If you are unwilling to go through these things . . . then we are afraid that you will have to forego love and marriage with the person of your choice.[30]

While it is not possible to determine how many Nisei women were willing to make such a stand in the prewar years, Deirdre's advice and the sentiments of her readers make clear the growing strength of the dominant society's ideals of heterosexual love and individual choice among the Nisei.

In the realms of love and marriage, Japanese American women confronted the tensions between the Japanese ways of their parents and the values of American mainstream culture. They faced pressure from within and outside the Japanese American community to maintain an ethnic identity and cultural support networks, as well as to prove themselves American citizens. Both the ethnic community and the dominant society influenced women's roles and expectations. Nisei women, like their Issei mothers, anticipated a future of marriage and family; however, like their contemporaries, they also expected to choose their own marital partners, and many prepared for wage-earning jobs outside their family economy.

As reflected by the response of the Nisei readers of the *Hokubei Asahi*, women's growing independence and the debate over female roles drew criticism as well as spirited advocacy. Mary M. N., the young writer whose essays sparked debate in 1934, may have been less representative of her generation than an "Older Mary" who wrote to express her disapproval of what she viewed as the younger Nisei's selfish individualism. "We want," she said, "society with a code that can make people keep a moderate norm."[31] It was with envy, however, that she also stated, "You have dashed the cobwebs from the many sleepy eyes that flounder in these communities. . . . You can only be explained in your own words that you are a high school girl with a streak of 'red flare.' God, how I wish I were like you!"[32]

The issues that had fueled Mary M. N.'s incendiary essays in 1934 echoed in the articles and advice column of the *Shin Sekai*, the *Hokubei Asahi*, and the *New World-Sun* throughout the rest of the 1930s. Prewar newspapers reflect the complexity of the Nisei's cultural integration, particularly with regard to gender roles. The prewar emergence of advice columns evidenced the adoption of a popular mainstream format, as did the more eerie appearance of fashion sections in the wartime internment camp newspapers. Advice columns and correspondence clubs also served to extend ethnic ties, providing a way for isolated rural Nisei youth to make friendly and romantic contact with their peers. These columns, geared to both men and women in the 1930s and primarily toward a female audience during World War II, serve as a gauge of the influence and meaning of mainstream trends and ideals for second-generation women. They make clear the importance of ethnic bonds, as well as the extent to which, by the 1940s, Nisei women's notions of love and marriage separated them from the expectations of their mothers.

Valerie Matsumoto is an associate professor of history at UCLA, where she teaches and researches Asian American history and U.S. women's history. She is the author of *Farming the Home Place: A Japanese American Community in California, 1919–1982* (1993).

NOTES

1. *Hokubei Asahi*, October 15, 1934. I thank Noriko Sawada Bridges, Peggy Pascoe, Vicki Ruiz, and Stan Yogi for their insightful assistance in the preparation of this article.
2. Ibid., October 14, 1934.
3. Ibid., October 15, 1934.
4. For more information about Mary Oyama Mittwer, see my article "Desperately

Seeking 'Deirdre': Gender Roles, Multicultural Relations, and Nisei Women Writers of the 1930s," *Frontiers: A Journal of Women Studies* 12 (1991): 19–32.

5. Evelyn Nakano Glenn, *Issei, Nisei, War Bride: Three Generations of Japanese American Women in Domestic Service* (Philadelphia: Temple University Press, 1986), 58.

6. *Hokubei Asahi*, June 15, 1934.

7. Ibid., January 5, 1935.

8. Ibid., January 7, 1935.

9. Ibid., May 28, 1935.

10. Ibid., January 6, 1935.

11. Ibid., March 28, 1935.

12. *New World-Sun*, March 23, 1937.

13. *Hokubei Asahi*, March 28, 1935.

14. Ibid.

15. Glenn, *Issei, Nisei, War Bride*, 58 and 221.

16. *New World-Sun*, February 10, 1937.

17. Ibid., September 12, 1936.

18. Ibid., September 15, 1936.

19. Ibid.

20. Mary Ryan, *Womanhood in America: From Colonial Times to the Present*, 3rd ed. (New York: Franklin Watts, 1983), 251.

21. *New World-Sun*, February 10, 1937.

22. Glenn, *Issei, Nisei, War Bride*, 214. Both the Japanese American community and the dominant society assumed that the Japanese American woman's "Mr. Right" would be another Nisei. Interracial marriages were illegal in California until 1948. For information on this anti-miscegenation law, see Megumi Dick Osumi, "Asians and California's Anti-Miscegenation Laws," in *Asian and Pacific American Experiences: Women's Perspectives*, ed. Nobuya Tsuchida (Minneapolis: Asian/Pacific American Learning Resource Center and General College, University of Minnesota, 1982), 1–37.

24. *New World-Sun*, October 10, 1935.

25. Ibid., September 30, 1936.

26. Glenn, *Issei, Nisei, War Bride*, 55 and 217. As Glenn points out, arranged marriages were the norm in rural areas until World War II; many urban Nisei also had arranged marriages, although the ideal of romantic love had become popular among them by the mid-1930s.

27. *New World-Sun*, March 14, 1937.

28. Ibid., March 18, 1937.

29. Ibid., March 19, 1937.

30. Ibid., March 20, 1937.

31. *Hokubei Asahi*, October 24, 1934.

32. Ibid., October 20, 1934.

"LOVELIEST DAUGHTER OF OUR ANCIENT CATHAY!"

REPRESENTATIONS OF ETHNIC AND GENDER IDENTITY IN THE MISS CHINATOWN U.S.A. BEAUTY PAGEANT*

Judy Tzu-Chun Wu

In February 1958, seventeen young women came from throughout the country to compete in the first Miss Chinatown U.S.A. Beauty Pageant. Sponsored by the San Francisco Chinese Chamber of Commerce (CCC) as part of the Chinese New Year celebration, the competition sought to find "the most beautiful Chinese girl with the right proportion of beauty, personality and talent." The organizers promised that "honor, fame and awards . . . is [sic] ahead for her majesty in this, the most Cinderella-like moment of her young life." June Gong, a twenty-one-year-old senior majoring in Home Economics at the University of New Hampshire, captured the title of the first Miss Chinatown U.S.A. Although she expressed surprise at winning, Gong had a history of competing successfully in beauty contests. She had won the titles of freshman queen and football queen at college. In 1957, she placed second in the Miss New Hampshire beauty pageant, a preliminary for the Miss America competition. She also won the 1957 Miss New York Chinatown title, which provided her with the opportunity to compete in the national pageant. Years later, she explained that the Miss

*This chapter was previously published as: Tzu-Chun Wu, Judy. "'Loveliest Daughter of our Ancient Cathay!': Representations of Ethnic and Gender Identity in the Miss Chinatown U.S.A. Beauty Pageant." In *Journal of Social History* 31 (fall 1997): 5–31.

Chinatown U.S.A. pageant was not "a beauty contest"; it was "more like a matter of ethnic representation." Having grown up in Miami, Florida, with only a few Chinese families, Gong's participation in the San Francisco event provided her with the opportunity to come into contact with the largest community of Chinese people outside of China and to learn about her ancestral culture.[1]

The popularity of the first Miss Chinatown U.S.A. beauty pageant made the event one of the highlights of the Chinese New Year celebration, which it continues to be today. Without it, one organizer explained, there would be no focus to the celebration: no pageant, no coronation ball, no Miss Chinatown float for the annual parade, and no fashion show. These Chinese New Year events draw hundreds of thousands of tourists into San Francisco's Chinatown, serving the dual purposes of educating the public about Chinese American culture and attracting business for Chinatown merchants.

The Miss Chinatown U.S.A. Beauty Pageant has served as a beauty competition, a promotional event to attract tourism, and a means for exploring and celebrating ethnic identity. Because of its multiple purposes, an analysis of the pageant provides insights into Chinese American efforts to construct both gender and ethnic identity during the post–World War II era. In defining the ideal woman to represent Chinatown, pageant organizers responded to developing cultural, economic, and political tensions within the Chinese American community and the broader American society. In turn, these efforts to represent Chinese American womanhood generated a variety of responses, which reflected community conflicts surrounding not only gender roles and ethnic identity but also class divisions and international politics.[2]

Using pageant publications, oral histories, and Bay Area and Chinese American community newspapers, this paper analyzes the Miss Chinatown U.S.A. beauty pageant from its origins and popularization in the late 1950s and the 1960s, through the growing controversy that surrounded it in the late 1960s and 1970s. During the height of the cold war and the era of racial integration, pageant supporters successfully balanced tensions within the Chinese American community and with the broader society by depicting their ethnic identity as a non-threatening blend of Eastern Confucian and modern Western cultures. However, with the rise of social movements during the late 1960s and 1970s, this conception of ethnic identity came under attack for presenting an outdated and exotic image of Chinese Americans in general and women in particular. Critics argued that Miss Chinatown did not represent the "real" Chinatown women who tended to be working class or the revolutionary Asian women in the third world. Pageant supporters responded by emphasizing the importance of beautiful and articulate Chinese American women as role models for promoting respect for the community.[3]

Ethnic beauty pageants, a subject rarely explored by scholars, provide an opportunity to examine how idealized versions of womanhood reflect broader concerns about power and culture. In a recently published collection of essays devoted to the study of beauty pageants, *Beauty Queens on the Global Stage*, the editors, Colleen Ballerino Cohen, Richard Wilk, and Beverly Stoeltje, argue that pageants:

> showcase values, concepts, and behavior that exist at the center of a group's sense of itself and exhibit values of morality, gender, and place. . . . The beauty contest stage is where these identities and cultures can be—and frequently are—made public and visible.

In studying the formation and evolution of a community ceremony, I had the opportunity to not only examine how the pageant publicly and visibly reflects the community's identity and culture, but also how the event shaped and developed community values. In other words, the history of the pageant and the community dialogue that the event generated provide insight into evolving conflicts concerning ethnic and gender identity as well as class divisions and international politics.[4]

Furthermore, the study of the Miss Chinatown U.S.A. beauty pageant suggests the need to reevaluate dichotomous models of gender and ethnic systems. Beauty pageants do not simply victimize women through male domination; both women and men supported, as well as criticized, the pageant. Similarly, the cultural content of the pageant cannot be evaluated in terms of ethnic assimilation versus retention. Rather, both pageant supporters and critics defined ethnic identity by synthesizing elements of both Chinese and American traditions. While contending groups questioned their opponents' cultural authenticity and commitment to women's advancement, their conflicts often arose because they advocated different strategies to advance similar goals of gender and racial equality.

A Melting Pot of the East and the West

From the very beginning of the pageant, organizers had an ideal image of Miss Chinatown contestants as the perfect blend of Chinese and American cultures. Businessman and community leader H. K. Wong, who is credited with coming up with the idea of the pageant, explained that contenders for the crown must have the "looks that made China's beauties so fascinating" as well as the language skills to answer "key questions" in their own native dialect during the quiz portion of the competition. In addition to these Chinese attributes, contestants had to display modern American qualities. They needed "adequate education, training and the versatility to meet the challenge of the modern world." The Cheongsam (long gown) dresses that contestants wore symbolized this theme of "East-meets-West." First introduced by Manchu women of the Qing Dynasty, the Cheongsam, "the figure-delineating sheath dress with high-necked collar and slit skirt," became "the national costume of Chinese women." For the purposes of the pageant, modern dressmakers modified the design of the Cheongsam to emphasize the cleavage area, creating "the 'poured-in' look so highly desired." Furthermore, the slit up the side of the dress was increased "to endow the basically simple Cheong-sam with a touch of intrigue . . . [,] a tantalizing suggestion about the beauty of its wearer." This conception of Chinese American identity as a blend of East and West allowed pageant supporters to negotiate cultural, economic, and political tensions within the Chinese American community and with the broader community during the late 1950s and 1960s.[5]

Organizers argued that the beauty pageant demonstrated both the assimilation of the Chinese American community and their need to preserve Chinese culture. CCC leaders explained that they wanted to organize "something western" to attract the interest of the American-born generations as they became more assimilated. After nearly a century of racial exclusion and segregation, Chinese Americans became increasingly integrated into American society during the post–World War II era. Because of the alliance between China and the U.S. during the war, Chinese Americans for the first time gained the right to become naturalized citizens. With changes in segregationist residential restrictions after the War, middle-class Chinese Americans began moving out of Chinatown. They also gained access to white-collar jobs as occupational racial barriers decreased. These opportunities encouraged college-educated Chinese American women to join the labor force. The pageant provided a means for Chinese Americans to demonstrate their assimilation by inviting young, educated women to participate in an event that was becoming popular in American society during the post-War era, the beauty pageant.[6]

At the same time, the pageant also sought to preserve Chinese culture among those who were merging into the mainstream. For contestants like June Gong, San Francisco Chinatown represented their first contact with a large population of Chinese Americans. She exclaimed upon her arrival in San Francisco, "I had never seen so many Chinese people." Her unfamiliarity with Chinese culture made the event exciting and educational. She recalled that "it was even fun discovering Chinese food." Other contestants expressed similar sentiments about the pageant. One contestant from Glendale, Arizona explained that she came to San Francisco to catch "her first glimpse of Chinese life." She told a reporter, "When you're born and raised in Glendale, China doesn't mean too much to you. . . . To me, San Francisco's Chinatown is China."[7]

In addition to promoting awareness of Chinese culture among contestants, organizers pointed out that the beauty pageant fostered a more cohesive sense of identity among Chinese Americans across generations and throughout the country. Because the pageant successfully attracted young Chinese American women and encouraged their interest in Chinese culture, the event helped bring together generations that might have been separated by cultural differences. One organizer explained that H. K. Wong thought of the pageant as "a joyful event to get the families and the parents involved in the New Year show." In addition, the pageant fostered cooperation among Chinese Americans nationwide. In order to attract contestants from diverse geographical regions, pageant organizers sought the assistance of Chinese Chambers of Commerce, merchant organizations, and families' associations in other cities. Some areas that already had community beauty pageants began sending their representatives to San Francisco. Others initiated contests in order to participate in the Miss Chinatown U.S.A. beauty pageant. The solidification of these networks helped foster a sense of a national Chinese American identity.[8]

The pageant and the New Year festival not only promoted an

awareness of ethnic identity among Chinese Americans, but the events also educated the general public about the value of Chinese culture. As the embodiment of the positive aspects of ethnic identity, Miss Chinatown U.S.A. held symbolic importance in promoting greater acceptance of Chinese Americans. Historically, the white community viewed Chinatown as a disease-ridden society populated by unattached men. The stereotypes of Chinese American women as exotic slave girls or sequestered women with bound feet symbolized the moral corruption of the community. The pageant offered an alternative view of Chinese American women, which in turn emphasized the progress of the community. First, the pageant demonstrated the demographic changes of the community from a "bachelor society" to a "family society." By presenting beautiful, charming, and intelligent Chinese American women, the competition also paid tribute to the families of these contestants, as implied by the lyric from the official pageant song, "loveliest daughter of our Ancient Cathay." Second, the pageant also demonstrated the modernization of Chinese American gender roles. One pageant booklet charted the advances of women "from dim memories of wee bound-feet to present day stiletto heels." In this statement, the accessory of high heels is supposed to symbolize the advancement and independence of Chinese American women. While bound feet suggests the enforced debilitation of women by outdated cultural practices, the ability to wear high heels suggests women's economic power to purchase modern commodities. Chinese American women, like their American counterparts, were becoming part of a commercialized world.[9]

These images of Chinese American women and the conception of ethnic identity as a blend of the East and the West not only served to educate the broader American public but also helped draw tourists to Chinatown. While the pageant was usually attended by Chinese Americans, the proceeds from the event helped fund the annual New Year Parade, which attracted hundreds of thousands of non-Chinese people. In addition, pageant contestants served as models for advertisements for the festival, and their presence at various New Year events helped attract tourists, who shopped in Chinatown stores and ate in Chinese restaurants.

The developing commercial viability of Chinatown coincided with broader social interest in Asian culture following World War II. The military presence in the Pacific theater during the war and the political, commercial, and military interest in Asian countries during the cold war led to increased contact between Western and Asian peoples. American popular culture reflected this fascination with the "Orient," which also included "Orientals" in the U.S.; San Francisco officials and business leaders actively supported the Chinese New Year festival and the Miss Chinatown U.S.A. Beauty Pageant for commercial purposes. As early as 1957, political and civic leaders expressed interest in promoting the festival as a distinctively San Franciscan cultural event that would draw tourists into the city. They wanted a festival "to rival Mardi Gras." The presence of ethnic beauty queens constituted an important component of the plan to encourage tourism. One non-Chinese festival organizer envisioned that "we'll have floats from Siam, Japan and Korea and we'll have pretty Chinese girls from all over the world . . . [and] I really think we will have an attraction to equal the Mardi Gras in five years."[10]

The joint interests of the CCC and city officials in promoting the commercial benefits of Chinatown fostered tensions as well as cooperation. Ironically, while Chinatown organizers sought to promote the compatibility of East and West through their events, white organizers cautioned Chinese Americans against over-assimilation. In a speech to the Chinese Historical Society of America, journalist Donald Canter, who regularly covered the Chinese New Year festival and Miss Chinatown U.S.A. beauty pageant, explained that the annual parade had become so Americanized that, "I wasn't quite sure whether I was viewing the Rose Parade in Pasadena or a New Year's parade of the largest Chinatown outside the Orient." To promote more tourism for the community, he encouraged organizers to highlight Chinese cultural practices. Instead of having the Miss Chinatown queen and princesses ride in floats for the parade, he suggested the "possibility of having the Queen, and possibly her court, carried in sedan chairs with the carriers performing their chore in relays." He argued that this practice would be "much more Chinese" and would appeal:

> much more to the imagination of the hundreds of thousands viewing this annual spectacle. . . . Wouldn't they write their folks and friends across the country about that eerie spectacle of a Chinese Queen and Chinese princesses being carried in Chinese sedan chairs?

... And consequently, with a proper Chinese sense for reality, would-n't [that] lure more tourists and their dollars into San Francisco and Chinatown?

To attract white tourists interested in seeing the "bizarre," Canter encouraged CCC leaders to emphasize an "Orientalist" image of Chinatown by creating cultural practices that were not relevant to Chinese Americans.[11]

CCC leaders did not entirely disagree with this approach of portraying Chinatown as something "exotic" and "foreign" in order to maintain its commercial viability. Pageant publications regularly invited tourists to visit San Francisco Chinatown because of its resemblance to "the Orient." The souvenir booklet explained that "if you have not been to the Orient, your trip to Chinatown will be as if you were visiting Formosa or Hong Kong." At the same time that pageant organizers promoted a positive conception of Chinese American identity to encourage self-pride and cultural awareness, they also consciously promoted an exotic image to fulfill the expectations of white tourists.[12]

The CCC efforts to balance their agenda of ethnic representation and commercial viability were further complicated by the international political context of the cold war, which ignited immense hostility toward Communist China. The *San Francisco Chronicle* regularly placed its coverage of the New Year events next to articles on the People's Republic of China (PRC). To distance themselves from the negative images of "Red China," pageant and festival organizers emphasized a non-aggressive conception of Chinese culture. One CCC publication explained that the Chinese:

> seldom express their passion, particularly in public. This, combined with the Confucian doctrine of the dignity of man, makes them a calm and pacific race. Fatalism plays an important role in the Chinese mind. Generally they are quite content with their station in life. For this reason, the western sense of the word "revolution" has no appeal to the Chinese mind.

This portrayal of Chinese American identity as orderly and content with the existing order also encompassed cold war conceptions of gender identity. Pageant founder H. K. Wong explained that the pageant represented a quest by "Chinatown Elders . . . for [a] Queen with Ancient Virtues of Chinese Womanhood." He defined the ideal Chinese woman as obeying the patriarchal figures of the Chinese family. She must respect "first your father, then your brother, then your husband." This emphasis on female submissiveness was part of a more general portrayal of Chinese people as culturally passive. Both conceptions of ethnic and gender identity were consciously promoted to counter the notion that all Chinese were potentially red subversives. Furthermore, pageant supporters also implied that their version of Chinese culture was more authentic than the changes taking place in the PRC, because they traced their cultural origins to "Confucian" doctrines.[13]

CCC organizers simultaneously claimed Chinese cultural authenticity and emphasized their loyalty to America. They argued that the ability to celebrate their culture in the U.S. demonstrated the superiority of American society. According to James H. Loo, president of the CCC in 1962,

> In the turmoil of the world situation, we citizens of Chinese ancestry want to take this opportunity to demonstrate to the peoples of the world, particularly those who are living behind the iron and bamboo curtains, how American democracy really works. . . . We, like many Europeans, who came to settle in this free land, are also proud of our ancient culture and endeavor to retain the best of our heritage. The New Year celebration exemplifies the expression of such a love of freedom and liberty.

The close affiliation of the Taiwanese government (ROC) with the pageant and the festival reinforced CCC antagonism toward communism. Members of the ROC Consulate participated regularly in the festival and the pageant. Officials were presented as dignitaries during the beauty pageant and the New Year parade. The wife of the consul also served several times as a judge for the Miss Chinatown U.S.A. contest. Chow Shu-Kai, ROC Ambassador to the U.S., explained that his country supported the pageant and the festival as a reminder to "our compatriots on the mainland of China, who do not have the means to celebrate nor the freedom to commemorate occasions significant and meaningful according to the traditions of the old country." The ambassador as well as CCC officials emphasized the freedom of Chinese Americans to celebrate their culture and the authenticity of their version of Chinese culture compared to communist China.[14]

To support their argument that the beauty pageant represented an expression of authentic Chinese culture, organizers pointed to a Chinese tradition of appreciating female beauty. Although the more conservative Chinese philosophers emphasized female modesty and advocated the seclusion of women to the inner quarters of the home, poets, playwrights, as well as folk storytellers celebrated the beauty of famous women. H. K. Wong drew on these literary traditions to describe the standard of beauty used to select Miss Chinatown. He suggested that

> the elusive memory of ancient China's greatest beauties might lurk in the judges' minds as they ponder their decision. Their thoughts might linger on the centuries-old Chinese concept of beauty such as melon-seed face, new moon eyebrows, phoenix eyes, peachlike cheek, shapely nose, cherry lips, medium height, willowy figure, radiant smile and jet black hair.

Interestingly, the modern beauty pageant did resemble certain Chinese cultural practices. During the Northern Sung, Ming, and Qing dynasties, the imperial court instituted a female draft to select palace maids, consorts, and wives. Choices were based on both the girl's personal appearance and on her family status. Pageant organizers used these Chinese traditions of appreciating feminine beauty to justify the Miss Chinatown U.S.A. competition as an expression of Chinese, as well as American, culture.[15]

The conception of ethnic and gender identity promoted by the Miss Chinatown U.S.A. and Chinese New Year Festival during the 1950s and 1960s emphasized the blend of the exotic, passive Confucian East and the modern, democratic West. This interpretation of Chinese American culture allowed pageant supporters to negotiate tensions within the community and with the broader society during the post–World War II era. Reacting to the integrationist impulse among Chinese Americans, Chinatown organizers used an "American" event to attract the interest of the younger generation and to encourage the maintenance of Chinese culture. The pageant's emphasis on modern Chinese American women also served to educate the broader public about the "progress" of the community, even as the exotic foreignness of the events attracted tourists for Chinatown. The community's ability to celebrate their ancestral culture demonstrated the freedom that existed within democratic societies, while the pageant's emphasis as a non-revolutionary, Confucian notion of Chinese culture allowed Chinese Americans to claim cultural authenticity while also distancing themselves from the negative images of Communist Chinese.

The formulation of gender and ethnic identity presented by the Miss Chinatown beauty pageant suggests the vulnerability of the Chinese American community during the 1950s. While the aftermath of World War II brought increased economic and social opportunities, Chinese Americans also sensed the possibilities of community dispersion and political persecution. In this context, the pageant represented a means to promote a sense of community among Chinese Americans and between Chinese Americans and the broader American population.

The ability of the Miss Chinatown U.S.A. beauty pageant to reconcile tensions within the Chinese American community and with the broader society helped the event achieve widespread popularity. Throughout the 1960s, spectators annually filled the Masonic Auditorium, which seated over three thousand. One organizer for the New Year parade recalled that the pageant was the premier event for Chinatown, attracting the "who's who" of the community. Because of the popularity of the pageant, people often complained of the difficulties of obtaining tickets for the event. Those who could not get tickets either watched the pageant as it was televised to another auditorium or else listened to the program on radio. By the 1960s, then, the pageant had become a recognized tradition in the community.[16]

"China Dolls" and "Iron Girls": Contending Images of Chinese American Women

During the late 1960s and 1970s, a generation of Chinese Americans who became involved with grassroots social movements increasingly criticized the popular Miss Chinatown U.S.A. beauty pageant. Influenced by the civil rights, Black liberation, anti-war, and women's movements, college-educated and community youth began organizing to address social problems within Chinatown. While some advocated social reform, others questioned the fundamental assumptions of American capitalism and sought inspiration from third-world and socialist movements. Their criticisms of the Miss Chinatown U.S.A. beauty pageant and the Chinese New Year Festival demonstrated their attempts to redefine the ethnic and gender identities of Chinese Americans.

The rise in political consciousness among a young generation of Chinese Americans coincided with changing demographic trends in the Chinatown community. In 1965, the U.S. Congress abolished discriminatory national-origins quotas, allowing immigrants from Asian countries to come to the U.S. in the same proportions as Europeans. The new Chinese immigrants followed preexisting demographic patterns. Educated professionals and technicians settled in areas outside of Chinatown, while unskilled workers and those with limited English facility became part of the older community. The heavy influx of working-class immigrants into San Francisco's Chinatown, estimated at "two to four thousand new residents" annually, both revitalized the community and exacerbated its social problems. With this rise in population, Chinatown's poverty level increased, its housing conditions deteriorated, and health and social services became inadequate. Both parents in Chinese immigrant families were likely to work long hours in service and light manufacturing jobs for low wages. Immigrant women also worked a "second shift, which included taking care of children and doing housework. Because of the crowded conditions in Chinatown and the poor quality of housing available, immigrant families were likely to live in small tenement rooms with inadequate plumbing facilities, no central heating, communal kitchens and bathrooms. These poor and overcrowded living conditions increased the health risks among community residents.[17]

Like other ghetto communities, however, Chinatown lacked the resources to respond to the needs of its residents. Government programs like the San Francisco Equal Employment Opportunity Commission were reluctant to allocate funds to assist immigrants or to address systemic problems within the community. Chinese Americans also lacked the political clout to combat the widespread belief that Asian Americans constituted model minorities who could succeed solely through hard work and perseverance.

In reaction to the ghettoization of Chinatown, young activists advocated new solutions to address these problems. They sought to educate themselves and the broader public about the needs of the community, and they demanded the reallocation of government and community resources for social services. During the 1960s and 1970s, liberal and radical activists formed agencies to serve the economic, educational, cultural, and social concerns of Chinatown residents. They also initiated grassroots campaigns to mobilize Chinese Americans to demand better living and working conditions. As part of their broader agenda to fundamentally change the existing social structure, they began criticizing the popular Miss Chinatown U.S.A. beauty pageant. The new generation of activists questioned the role of tourism in the community, the images of Chinese American women promoted by the pageant, and the appropriateness of Confucian values and the ROC in representing Chinese culture. For them, Miss Chinatown represented a symbol of a commercialized, anti-revolutionary, middle-class Chinese American identity, exactly what reformers, radicals, and feminists sought to change in the community.

During the 1960s and 1970s, critics of the pageant and New Year festival increasingly questioned the use of community resources to promote tourism and the educational benefits provided by tourism. *East West*, a liberal Chinese American newspaper, noted that Chinese New Year

> is the time when people near and far come to visit the Chinatown. . . .
> But would the visitors be able to see the real Chinatown? Would they
> have a chance to meet our residents? Would they begin to understand
> our many community problems? At the moment, what we are show-
> ing the visitors are the rides in the carnival, beauty contestants, an
> occasional cherry bomb, and busy restaurants where service could best
> be described as chaotic.

Because of the enormous crowds that the Chinese New Year attracted, keeping peace and order proved difficult. While the city's fire chief annually threatened to ban firecrackers to lessen chances of injury and fire, the police chief increased security during Chinese New Year to prevent fights and public disturbances. In 1969, a full-fledged riot broke out, resulting in thirty-five arrests and eighty-nine injuries. An observer's account suggests that Chinese New Year did not necessarily inspire greater appreciation of Chinese culture. George Chu, who described himself as "a square middle-class Chinese," explained that Chinese New Year was a particularly volatile time in the community. Because of racial tensions, fights between Chinese and whites had the potential to escalate. These tensions were exacerbated by the behavior of white tourists, who indiscriminately threw firecrackers without watching for people around them. Others strolled through the community, "tearing posters and paper lanterns from the booths for souvenirs, [acting] as if Chinatown was theirs for the picking." Police security for the festival did not help the situation since officers tended to ignore these incidents: When they did intervene, they tended to assume the Chinese were at fault. Even Chinatown residents who volunteered to help patrol the streets were warned that "when the cops come, stay out of it; they can't tell the Chinese apart." Some Chinese Americans, angry about the racist treatment by the police and the disrespect of tourists, criticized the CCC for promoting the festival.[18]

The tensions between business leaders and activists came into focus when the Holiday Inn decided to build a hotel to provide luxury accommodations for tourists in Chinatown. As part of the hotel's promotional campaign, they sponsored a contestant, Celeste Wong (alias), for the Miss Chinatown U.S.A. beauty pageant. As a publicity stunt for the gala grand opening of the Holiday Inn, Wong jumped out of a giant fortune cookie. Across the street, members of the Red Guard Party, a radical organization of Chinatown youth, and other Asian Americans staged a rally protesting the "invasion of Chinatown's territory" by the Holiday Inn. Citing the crowded conditions of San Francisco's Chinatown, protesters asked "how many of our people have had to move out of their shops and homes to make way for the growing financial district?" Questioning the displacement of Chinatown people for commercial enterprises like the Holiday Inn, the protesters demanded "low cost housing for our people!" During the New Year Parade, some protesters went so far as to throw eggs at Celeste Wong for representing the Holiday Inn. In the end, she had to be removed from the float because of public hostility. Activists criticized the Miss Chinatown U.S.A. beauty pageant for helping to promote a false commercial image of Chinatown in order to attract tourism. One community activist highlighted the contradictions between the tourist image of Chinatown and the actual experiences of its residents.

> In Holiday Inn . . . there is a swimming pool on the roof and a grand
> view of the city . . . there is the plush of soft carpets, bright lights,
> and spacious quarters . . . there are bell boys in smart uniforms . . .
> there are hostesses in mini skirts and cheong sams . . . there is . . .
> Miss Holiday Inn, and now Miss San Francisco Chinatown . . . there
> are tourists and business men with their briefcases . . . it's all there,
> across from Portsmouth Square, where the poor, the old, and the very
> young while their time away before the sun goes down.[19]

The growing awareness about racial and class oppression also fostered critiques of the Miss Chinatown U.S.A. beauty pageant for objec-
tifying Chinese American women. Beginning in the late 1960s and
escalating throughout the decade, Chinese Americans criticized the
pageant for judging women based on physical standards and portraying them as "China dolls." Their criticisms were partly inspired by the
broader movement for women's equality. In 1968, women involved with
the budding feminist movement conducted a widely publicized protest
of the Miss America pageant in Atlantic City. They crowned "a live
sheep to symbolize the beauty pageant's objectification of female bodies,
and filled a 'freedom trashcan' with objects of female torture—girdles,
bras, curlers, issues of *Ladies' Home Journal*." Although no bras were
actually burned, the media referred to protesters as "bra-burners,"
which then became a simplistic derogatory term to refer to feminists.[20]

Chinese Americans concerned about women's issues echoed white
feminist criticisms of beauty pageants. Although Miss Chinatown contestants were supposedly judged according to their intelligence, "talent,
beauty, charm and knowledge of Chinese culture," critics argued that
physical appearance tended to be the main criterion. Pageant observers
pointed out that many "would-be queens" displayed a "sad lack of
'talent.'" Others commented that the interview session of the contest
did not really demonstrate the contestants' knowledge of Chinese culture or their intelligence. After attending her first Miss Chinatown
U.S.A. beauty pageant, Judy Yung criticized the candidates for obviously memorizing their responses to the Chinese portion of the interview session: "But even with preparation, their answers don't always
make sense, since they speak Chinese with a heavy American accent."

Because of these problems, the Chinese portion of the interview eventually became optional in 1980. Yung further complained that the English portion of the interview did not challenge the intelligence of the contestants, for judges asked questions such as

> (1) If you saw your best friend cheating, what would you do? or (2) If you dressed informally to a formal party, what would you do? or (3) If you found your hem falling during a public appearance, what would you do? Evidently, the judges are more interested in finding out how you can get out of difficult situations than what your knowledge and opinions are on current events and social problems.

Other critics of the pageant pointed out that the main purpose of the event was to display a "parade of flesh." One documentary filmmaker portrayed the 1973 Miss Chinatown beauty pageant, which took place during the year of the Ox, as a "Livestock Show."[21]

Chinese American feminists expanded beyond mainstream criticisms that beauty pageants objectified women by pointing out the racial implications of certain female images. Critics argued that despite the flowery language used to describe Chinese standards of beauty, the Miss Chinatown U.S.A. beauty pageant actually used white standards to judge Chinese American women. One community member stated her belief that the contest "shows that the closer you look like the Whites, the prettier you are." Another critic agreed that Asian Americans internalized "white standards" of beauty promoted by mass media. These images emphasized that "a beautiful woman has a high-bridged, narrow nose, a large bosom, and long legs." She pointed out that while "these and many other physical traits are not inherent in most Asian women," beauty pageants like the Miss Chinatown U.S.A. contest encouraged women to achieve that ideal. Asian women "can compensate by setting our hair, curling our eyelashes, or wearing false ones, applying gobs of eye make-up, and going to great lengths to be the most 'feminine' women in the world." In attempting to achieve this feminine image, Chinese American women perpetuated the stereotype of Asian women as the "exotic-erotic-Susie Wong-Geisha girl dream of white American males." As white women became active in demanding social equality, Asian women became associated with the sexuality and the submissiveness of the "ideal" woman.[22]

Contestant statements and articles on the beauty pageant support this notion that white standards of physical beauty were used to judge the competition. Some candidates, organizers, and observers believed that judges preferred taller contestants. One entrant, who was 5 foot 2, complained that "it was obvious those girls with height had it." Other evidence suggests that "Caucasian" eyes represented a standard of beauty for Chinese American contestants. When one 1973 entrant was asked if she had any special attributes that might make her stand out, she said that her eyes might be an advantage, because they were "larger than [those of] some of the girls." Larger eyes with double eyelids and longer eye lashes have traditionally been associated with a "western look," as opposed to smaller eyes with single eyelids. During the late 1960s, the double-eyelid look gained increasing popularity among Asians in Asia and the U.S. To achieve that look, women resorted to various methods. While teenagers "place[d] scotch tape or a gluey substance over their eyelids overnight," those with more resources paid for plastic surgery to westernize Oriental eyes." One pageant souvenir book even carried an advertisement for cosmetic surgery to convert "'oriental eyes' with single eyelids into 'Caucasian eyes' (with double-eyelids)."[23]

This emphasis on physical appearance placed psychological and emotional burdens on the contestants. In preparing for the competition, entrants experienced subtle and overt pressures to alter their physical appearance through cosmetics, dieting, and even plastic surgery. This emphasis on viewing women as sexual objects may have led to more abusive forms of behavior, such as sexual harassment. Celeste Wong remembered that "a lot of the people who directed the activities in Chinatown were older men who took advantage of the situation. You'd be in a taxi or car with somebody and all of a sudden you'd feel a hand slipping under your dress." Her sponsor, the Holiday Inn hotel, provided her with a white male escort and required her to attend various functions to promote their business projects. Once, when the Holiday Inn flew her to Memphis for the opening of a hotel, her escort reserved only one room for both of them. Only sixteen years old at the time, Wong responded to these advances by ignoring them or escaping from the situations. However, she did not have the words or confidence to expose the treatment she received. Wong later interpreted these incidents as a result of the beauty pageant, which encouraged young women to present themselves as physically desirable. The sexual harassment "had to do with the contest and had to do with being a young woman who's supposed [to] just win based on what you looked like." The men who harassed her translated the accessibility of her body image for commercial and cultural purposes as an accessibility of her body for their sexual purposes.[24]

In addition to exposing the personal and psychological effects of beauty pageants, community activists also criticized the pageant for promoting an elite image of Chinese American women. Because the competition sought to highlight educated, accomplished, poised, and beautiful Chinese American women, critics considered the image of contestants "bourgeois." They argued that "most of the contestants come from wealthy and influential backgrounds and know very little about Chinatown, the ghetto." Because the competition sought to present "the most 'beautiful' Chinese women in their fine clothes and just perfect make-up, pranc[ing] around the stage," critics did not consider this image as representative of Chinese American women. They pointed out that "the majority of Chinese women are hard-working, either with jobs or full-time family responsibilities, and in most cases it's both. They are not women of leisure and their 'beauty' is not in their 'made-up, worked on for hours' physical outward appearance." Instead of promoting exceptional women as representative of Chinese American womanhood, critics sought further recognition of the problems facing women as workers and family members.[25]

Activists preferred to promote an image of Chinese American women as protesters of injustice. Challenging the CCC's portrayal of Chinese culture as passive and non-revolutionary, the critics pointed to the growing militancy of women in Chinatown and throughout the third world. Just as some Chinatown publications regularly featured women from beauty contests, papers with more liberal and radical agendas emphasized women's activism in movements for social justice. For example, articles in the latter papers frequently covered the struggles of garment workers, striking for better working conditions and wages. The photographs of middle-aged women holding picket signs represented a dramatic departure from the images of young women in cheongsams and make-up. Community members concerned about working women's issues also began celebrating International Women's Day in Chinatown during this time period. Occurring in early March, this annual event could be interpreted as a symbolic alternative to the Miss Chinatown U.S.A. beauty pageant, which usually took place in late January or February.

These images of women as protesters rather than beauty queens were directly inspired by third-world female revolutionaries. Radicals criticized the CCC's emphasis on Confucian values as representative of Chinese culture. Instead, they sought inspiration from the new socialist societies forming throughout Asia. *Getting Together*, the newspaper for an Asian American Marxist-Leninist organization, regularly featured images of female cadre and revolutionaries transforming patriarchal family structures and building new societies in the People's Republic of China (PRC), Vietnam, the Philippines, and North Korea. Community radicals sought inspiration from the image of China's "Iron Girls," a group of women "who took on the most difficult and demanding tasks at work" and who developed legendary reputations for exerting superhuman energy. Community activists who promoted the third-world revolutionary women as role models for Chinese American women criticized the involvement of the ROC in the Chinese New Year Festival. As an alternative, pro-PRC supporters organized a noncommercial celebration of Chinese New Year. Rather than emphasizing China's Confucian tradition, their Spring Festival highlighted "the creative and innovative aspects of Chinese culture," as represented by developments in the PRC.[26]

The criticisms leveled against the Chinese New Year Festival and the Miss Chinatown U.S.A. pageant during the late 1960s and 1970s represented a contest over the definition of ethnic and gender identity. Influenced by radical social movements, a new generation of Chinese Americans began advocating new forms of interracial, gender, and class relationships. Instead of promoting a commercial image of Chinatown to attract tourists, the activists demanded support from city officials and community leaders to address social issues. Instead of encouraging women to achieve certain standards of beauty or personal advancement, they advocated community responsibility and political activism. Instead of seeking cultural inspiration from a Confucian past and political legitimation from nationalist Taiwan, they turned to Communist China. The vociferousness of community debates regarding gender and ethnic identity reflected the high degree of conflict within San Francisco Chinatown during the late 1960s and 1970s.

The Reform Tradition of Radicalism

The responses of pageant supporters to their critics demonstrate the diverse and often contradictory strategies available to advance racial and gender equality. On the one hand, pageant organizers and contestants expressed fundamental disagreement with the agenda of community reformers, radicals, and feminists. They questioned the cultural authenticity of their critics and disagreed with their views on tourism, the class bias of the pageant, and the gender roles portrayed through the image of Miss Chinatown. At the same time, pageant and New Year festival supporters also proclaimed their commitment to community service, accurate portrayals of Chinese culture, and women's achievements. While their critics sought to expose the contradictions involved in the Miss Chinatown U.S.A. beauty contest, pageant supporters revealed the contradictions embedded within the social movements that advocated racial and gender equality.

Reacting to criticisms of the pageant and the Chinese New Year festival, supporters questioned the ability of their critics to speak on behalf of Chinatown. One observer of the Holiday Inn rally suggested that the young radicals protesting for the good of the "community" did not necessarily understand the community. He pointed out that when one journalist asked the protesters what some older female residents were talking about in Chinese, "all the youths could respond was, 'I don't understand Chinese.'" Just as pageant critics questioned the ability of the CCC and other establishment leaders to represent the community, the ability of the liberals and radicals to speak on behalf of Chinatown also came into question.[27]

Claiming that they had the interest of the community at heart, pageant and festival supporters argued for the benefits of tourism. They suggested that "there's nothing wrong in bringing in large crowds" to Chinatown. Tourism provided an economic lifeline by supporting the restaurants and stores that in turn employed Chinatown residents. Furthermore, the public exposure gained through the Miss Chinatown U.S.A. beauty pageant and Chinese New Year festival helped Chinese Americans gain national and international attention. Some community members agreed that "in spite of the commercialization of Chinese New Year, it does help remind us that we belong to a unique culture." New Year festival supporters further suggested that those who wanted a less commercial version of Chinese New Year should turn to private celebrations. One organizer explained that "you have to understand the private and public celebrations are two very different things. . . . People will go on having the traditional New Year family reunions, feasts and gift-giving regardless of the parade." Pageant supporters thus downplayed their power to define ethnic identity by emphasizing the community's ability to celebrate cultural events in diverse ways.[28]

Pageant supporters also argued that the beauty competition transcended class divisions and helped promote upward mobility. They pointed to the enormous popularity of the pageant among the working class in Chinatown and the opportunities that the contest provided for women. Cynthia Chin-Lee, a 1977 contestant from Harvard University, agreed with this argument. She remembered that the pageant was more of a casual, fun experience for her, because "I was going to Harvard and I knew I had a different type of career ahead of me." However, other contestants who "didn't have real high power careers" approached the competition more seriously, because it offered an opportunity for social recognition and career advancement. The experiences of Rose Chung, Miss Chinatown 1981, illustrates the argument that beauty pageants provided opportunities for working-class women. Growing up in a single-parent household, Chung remembered that she stayed home to take care of her four siblings while her mother worked as a seamstress. The pageant offered an opportunity to gain public exposure and participate in a glamorous event. After winning the Miss Chinatown title, she received a $2000 scholarship and free trips to locations in the U.S., Canada, and Asia. Chung also became an instant celebrity, receiving recognition from the Chinatown community. She recalled that because of her sheltered childhood, she "always wanted to participate in community activities." After she won the Miss Chinatown title, Chung served as the president of the women's auxiliary group of her family association, as president of the San Francisco General Hospital Chinese Employee Association, and as a member of the Republican County Central Committee. She traces these accomplishments to her victory in the Miss Chinatown U.S.A. pageant.[29]

Pageant defenders also countered their critics by challenging the goals and methods of the women's movement. They disagreed with feminist critics on issues concerning the importance of beauty, marriage, and radical protest. Although supporters acknowledged that beauty pageants objectified women and fostered their feelings of insecurity, they believed that the competition provided overriding benefits. Because of the racial discrimination against minorities in mainstream pageants such as the Miss America contests, the Miss Chinatown U.S.A. and other ethnic pageants gave women of those backgrounds the opportunity to achieve recognition. The experiences of Sandra Wong, Miss 1973 Chinatown U.S.A., demonstrated this function of ethnic beauty pageants. Prior to entering the Miss Chinatown pageant, Wong competed twice in the local Miss San Leandro contest. Had she won, she would have been the first Asian American to be represented in the Miss California contest, a preliminary for the Miss America pageant. Although Wong won both the talent and swimsuit contests during her first attempt, she did not win the competition. During both years, she placed as first runner-up. She did not publicly protest these results as racially motivated, but others did. Journalist John Lum's exposé of Wong's experiences concluded that "discrimination doesn't only extend to housing, education, and jobs, it extends to beauty 'contests,' too." Because of racial discrimination in mainstream beauty pageants, as well as in careers involving modeling, acting, and performance, pageant defenders argued that the Miss Chinatown U.S.A. competition was important for promoting positive images of Chinese Americans. These supporters disagreed with feminist critics who argued that emphasis on external appearances necessarily degraded women.[30]

Pageant backers also explained their disregard for feminist criticisms by proclaiming their support for more traditional female roles. When questioned about their thoughts on "women's lib" and on their future plans, many contestants discussed their dual commitments to career and marriage. Contestants during the late 1960s tended to view the two goals in conflict and prioritized marriage over careers. For example, 1967 contestant Irene Ung acknowledged gender discrimination against women in her field of international marketing when she remarked that "being a woman can be a handicap when you're looking for a man's job in a man's world." However, Ung did not necessarily aspire to "a career of working." "Like any other girl," Ung explained, "someday I'll want to get married and have children," goals which presumably set her apart from the feminist movement. Other contestants also voiced their preference for more "gentlemen-like" behavior from their male companions. One contestant explained that she "still enjoys

having her cigarette lit and having somebody hold the door for her."
She interpreted these desires as antagonistic to the feminist agenda. Still
other contestants expressed their dissatisfaction with critiques of beauty
pageants by emphasizing the radical image of feminists. Sandra Wong
explained that she did not believe the women's liberation movement's
members "protesting and burning their bras." By explaining that feminists and beauty contestants operated in separate worlds and held different values, pageant supporters could partly explain their disregard of
feminist criticisms.[31]

Even as they questioned their critics' authority and disagreed with
the radical agenda, pageant defenders also professed similar goals of
racial and gender equality. In response to criticisms raised during the
1960s and 1970s, organizers and participants altered the pageant and
the New Year festival to assist community service projects and to project a less "plastic" version of Chinese culture. They also argued that the
pageant promoted the goal of gender equality by emphasizing the
importance of female bonding, women's achievements in the public
realm, and sexual liberation. Pageant defenders argued that they, like
their critics, shared the goals of advancing the Chinese American community and Chinese American women.

These reform efforts were often initiated by a new generation of
pageant supporters who had activist credentials. Gordon Yaw provides
one example. Yaw's family moved out of San Francisco when he was a
young boy, but he returned to attend Chinese school. Because he grew
up in an Oakland neighborhood where the Black Panthers had a positive
influence, Yaw became involved with the Berkeley Third World Strike
during the late 1960s. Through his protest activities, he met many Asian
American students who criticized the CCC and other Chinatown
establishment leaders for ignoring the needs of the community. They
also condemned the Miss Chinatown U.S.A. beauty pageant as a symbol
of the status quo. Rather than just criticize the event, however, Yaw
became involved and encouraged others to volunteer in order to change
the pageant and the Chinese New Year festival. *East West* editors
applauded these efforts, pointing out that "as presently arranged, most
of the New Year activities are organized by and for only a small segment
of the community. Changes are needed to involve the young and those
in the middle years, as well as the elderly, with meaningful activities."[32]

The involvement of younger people altered some of the content of the New Year festival. Through the lobbying efforts of Chinatown youth organizations, the CCC consented to include a community-sponsored Street Fair as part of the celebration in 1969. Rather than having a "traditional carnival organized by professional concessionaires," members of thirty youth organizations came together to create a street fair to raise funds for community services. The events, which included a run through Chinatown, ping-pong tournaments, cooking and shadow boxing demonstrations, were intended to "inform the public about Chinese culture, history and tradition" as well as to involve community members in recreational social activities. The organizers of the Street Fair wanted to use Chinese New Year to benefit the community directly. Beauty pageant contestants also demonstrated a growing consciousness about the need for social service. While pageant queens previously helped to raise funds and generate publicity about community projects, such as playgrounds for children, contestants in the 1970s also expressed career ambitions to serve the community. As one 1974 entrant explained, her life goal was "to be a social worker."[33]

In addition to emphasizing community service in the New Year festivities, the new generation of organizers and participants also sought to alter the cultural content of the events. Sensitive to charges that the festival projected an artificial tourist-oriented version of Chinese culture, organizers sought to revitalize the image of the celebration. For example, David Lei, one of the younger generation of organizers, traveled to Taiwan to research Chinese culture and purchase artifacts. To encourage tourists to look beyond "the old 'chop suey image' where people have a very superficial idea of what's Chinese culture," he "included a block-long bridal procession of the Han period" in the 1977 parade. Organizers of the beauty pageant also sought to incorporate Chinese culture into the event. One year, pageant organizer Louella Leon scripted the pageant in the form of a Chinese opera. The demographic changes in the Chinese American population also helped revitalize cultural aspects of the pageant. As immigrants from Hong Kong and Taiwan entered the pageant, contestants demonstrated greater knowledge and familiarity with Chinese language and culture.[34]

In addition to promoting community service and cultural education, younger pageant supporters also expressed their commitment to women's accomplishments. Like contemporary women's rights activists, they emphasized the importance of "sisterhood," women's achievements in the public realm, and sexual liberation. Almost all the contestants explained that their desire to meet other Chinese women constituted an important motivation for their decisions to enter the pageant. Jennifer Chung, a 1967 contestant, expressed her hope for "everlasting friends[hip]" with the other contestants. In their parting statements, Miss Chinatowns frequently invoked the rhetoric of female friendships. These expressions of "sisterhood" may not have reflected real experiences. When asked if she had developed any close friendships with other contestants, Chung admitted that her busy schedule preparing for the pageant did not allow her time to do so. Competition among contestants and the unequal treament of winners and losers after the pageant presented obstacles as well. Despite the unevenness of women's relationships with one another, the use of rhetoric emphasizing female bonding suggests that pageant supporters viewed sisterhood as an important value that helped to justify the competition.[35]

Whatever the obstacles to female friendships, the beauty competition promoted female achievements according to organizers. Participating in the Miss Chinatown U.S.A. beauty pageant provided contestants with an opportunity to acquire poise, grace, confidence, and public-speaking experience. These skills provided an important foundation for activities in the public realm. As one community member remarked, the pageant "gives Chinese girls an opportunity to meet people and get into things. Too many of them sit at home and don't do anything." In fact, many contestants viewed the pageant as a steppingstone to other challenges. In contrast to late 1960s' contestants, who prioritized marriage over their careers, the 1970s' contestants mainly discussed their future work plans or else emphasized the compatibility of marriage with careers. Jeannie Fung, Miss Chinatown U.S.A. 1975, expressed her desire to "be a medical technician and eventually to teach in junior college." Arleen Chow, a 1972 contestant, discussed the complementary roles of worker and mother. She believed that "a girl can do a man's job, mentally and physically, if trained properly. . . . The wife should be both a parent and a supporter." For these contestants, participation in the pageant did not conflict with goals for women's social equality. Many contestants explained that they supported women's liberation to the extent that they believed in equal access to jobs and in "equal pay for equal jobs." In fact, the description of pageant contestants as "intelligent, ambitious, and mature women" matched the image of "modern" career women.[36]

Perhaps in response to feminist criticisms, the Chinese Chamber of Commerce also began to promote female leadership among pageant organizers. Although women had always participated in organizing the pageant, the leadership positions had previously been male-dominated. In 1974, the CCC selected Carolyn Gan as the first female editor-in-chief for the annual souvenir book. In 1979, a woman was elected to the CCC board of directors. The all-female fashion show committee also made some adjustments in 1976 that appeared to respond to feminist critiques. In the midst of community debates about the exploitation of women, the fashion committee decided to include male models and men's fashions in the traditionally all-female fashion show. While these changes could be interpreted as responses to the growing criticisms of the pageant, their limited nature also demonstrate the difficulty of fundamentally changing the pageant or the CCC. The numbers of women in recognized leadership roles remained small, while the inclusion of male models and fashions occurred for only one year.

In addition to these attempts to integrate the leadership and content of the pageant, some proponents further claimed that their support for sexual liberation demonstrated their commitment to women's equality. In 1974, the fashion show committee included a "feminist fashion" selection that emphasized revealing clothing. One of the "Women's Lib" outfits was described as "a black full-length evening gown with neckline in back swooping to the waist." Others associated female activists with wearing mini-skirts. These interpretations of "feminism" emphasized women's willingness to express their sexual desirability in shocking ways. Ironically, this emphasis on physical exposure reinforced the objectification of female bodies that feminists criticized. For example, 1972 contestant Patricia Moy decided to give a speech on free love as her talent presentation. She argued that:

a) No one objects to free love, love meaning everything excluding the physical act of sex, which can be considered love. . . .

b) Virginity shouldn't be a prerequisite for marriage.

c) Homosexuality is not necessarily "bad" as society has always labeled it.

The main points of her speech coincided with developing feminist critiques of socially constructed heterosexual ideals and represented a radical departure from more conservative Chinese notions of sexuality. However, the manner of her presentation during the pageant suggests that she may have reinforced traditional sexual roles for women rather than transcended them. She began her act "by stripping off the top half of her pantsuit to reveal a bikini top, and the proceeded to deliver her original speech on free love, virginity, and homosexuality." Moy's decision to expose her body expressed her sexual freedom but also encouraged audience "gawkers" to view her as a sexual object.[37]

This relationship between increased sexual freedom and sexual exposure offers one explanation for the introduction of the swimsuit component to the Miss Chinatown U.S.A. beauty pageant. When the competition first began in 1958, organizers prided themselves for not having their contestants parade around in bathing suits. However, organizers introduced a "playsuit" portion in 1962, in which contestants displayed themselves in short-skirt outfits. In 1967, the bathing suit replaced the playsuit. One organizer claimed that the new requirement responded to the contestants' interest in displaying their beauty through wearing swimsuits. Although this explanation is not confirmed by other sources, his comment suggests that arguments for sexual liberation may have been used to justify sexual exploitation.[38]

During the 1960s and 1970s, pageant participants and supporters responded to critics both by disagreeing with them and by expressing their own commitments to gender and racial equality. The ability of pageant organizers to use the same concepts to refer to different strategies demonstrates the tensions within movements promoting social equality. By emphasizing the importance of individual role models to inspire Chinese Americans, women, and members of the working class, pageant supporters negated arguments calling for systemic structural changes. By stressing the importance of promoting beautiful images for Chinese Americans because of racial discrimination, pageant defenders downplayed the danger of encouraging women to use their physical appearance to gain social acceptance. Their arguments reveal the multiple and often contradictory strategies that could be used to advance racial and gender equality.

The Modern Chinese and Chinese American Woman

The debates surrounding the Miss Chinatown U.S.A. and Chinese New Year festival demonstrate the complex struggles to define Chinese American identity through gender images. The intensity of criticisms against the pageant coincided with the degree of community conflict surrounding issues of ethnic representation and gender roles, as well as class divisions and international allegiances. During the cold war, organizers of the Miss Chinatown U.S.A. beauty pageant successfully balanced tensions within the Chinese American community. By representing the Chinese community as a blend of the East and West, sponsors were able to address growing generational and cultural conflicts at a time when Chinese Americans sought to integrate into the broader community while also maintaining their cultural values. This conception of Chinese American identity as embodied by Miss Chinatown also served cultural, economic, and political purposes in the community's relationship with the broader society. However, as social movements of the 1960s raised fundamental critiques of the existing racial, sexual, and economic hierarchies, the Miss Chinatown pageant also came under attack. Pageant and festival supporters disagreed fundamentally with their critics on the importance of tourism, the evaluation of women based on physical standards, and the role of the ROC in the pageant. However, a new generation of organizers did reform certain aspects of the pageant in response to the criticisms. By emphasizing the importance of individual role models, pageant organizers justified the pageant as a means to promote gender and ethnic equality.

While the overt conflict surrounding the pageant decreased in the 1980s with the decline of radical social movements, the process of negotiating gender and ethnic identity continues both internationally and domestically. Both the PRC's changing attitudes toward commercial images of women and the motivations of Miss Chinatown U.S.A. contestants in the 1980s demonstrate the ambiguous benefits of beauty pageants.

With the normalization of relations between Communist China and the U.S. in 1979, political pressure was placed on CCC leaders to lessen its pro-Taiwan stance and extend a hand of welcome to the PRC. Pageant and festival supporters did so reluctantly. In the 1979 Chinese

New Year Parade, Chinese school marching bands and an airline sponsor of the Miss Chinatown U.S.A. beauty pageant displayed the Nationalist flag, even after Mayor Dianne Feinstein asked for assurances from organizers that this would not occur. In 1980, after Feinstein applied political pressure, the CCC reluctantly issued a last-minute invitation to the envoy of the PRC and then quickly withdrew the invitation to both the communist and the nationalist representatives. Pageant organizers chose to distance themselves from both countries rather than be forced to extend friendship to Communist China.

Despite the reluctance of the CCC to establish relations with the PRC, China was shifting its public image to accommodate the political, economic, and social changes that occurred following the Cultural Revolution. Ironically, even as Chinatown radicals promoted third-world socialist role models of working and revolutionary women, the PRC was commercializing the image of women to promote economic development and trade with the West. According to historians Emily Honig and Gail Hershatter, "adornment and sexuality, topics that had been off-limits to the generation of the Cultural Revolution, dominated publications for young women in the 1980s. Attention to beauty and fashion was part of a growing concern with the quality of personal life, and clearly captured the public fancy." Some state-owned businesses in China began instituting beauty requirements to hire women for service jobs. Beauty pageants reportedly have become very popular throughout China. Ironically, the living Chinese culture that community radicals promoted was evolving to adopt Western practices of commodifying women's beauty.[39]

Just as Communist China recognized the commercial uses of women's bodies in promoting their national economy, Chinese American women in the 1980s and 1990s continued to use the pageant as a means for personal and community advancement. According to filmmaker Valerie Soe, Miss Chinatown 1984 Cynthia Gouw first entered the Los Angeles pageant as part of an undercover reporting assignment for a school newspaper. Gouw was supposed to "expose the contest from a feminist leftist, socialist point of view . . . [and uncover] the oppression of Asian American women." However, after Gouw won the Miss L.A. and then the Miss Chinatown U.S.A. titles, she decided not to criticize the event. Gouw argued that here was no contradiction between the pageant and her feminist and political beliefs:

I didn't feel exploited at all. . . . I want to show people that I can be very articulate and assertive as opposed to a stereotypical beauty pageant winner. . . . What I want to represent to the Asian population is that I am very concerned about the community.

Gouw suggests that her personal advancement reflected upon the entire community, because groups who have traditionally been disadvantaged, women as well as racial minorities, need role models and spokespersons. After she won Miss Chinatown U.S.A., Gouw entered and won the Spokesmodel competition for Star Search. Since then she has appeared in films and TV commercials and worked as a news reporter. For her, the pageant opened up numerous opportunities, allowing her to achieve, in the words of Valerie Soe, the "American Dream." The question of whether Gouw in fact transcended stereotypes of Chinese American women, or merely benefited from perpetuating them, remains unanswered.[40]

The history of the Miss Chinatown U.S.A. pageant, from the early years of success through the years of controversy, demonstrates how idealized roles of womanhood represent broader concerns about power. Activists of the late 1960s and 1970s, like commercial leaders of the late 1950s, recognized the significance of gender roles in defining the identity of a community: The intensity of their debates about the pageant reflected a contest over ethnic and gender identity as well as international politics and class relations. The persistent success of the Miss Chinatown U.S.A. beauty pageant into the 1980s and 1990s suggests its unique ability to reconcile conflicting impulses within the Chinese American community. The competition continues to provide a means for exceptional Chinese American women to use their physical appearance and personality skills to achieve recognition within the existing commercialized society. The cultural event promotes recognition of disadvantaged groups without threatening the fundamental American values of individualism and meritocracy. The continued popularity of the pageant combined with the decrease in vocal opposition suggests the decline of alternative strategies that advocate structural change and group-based solutions to achieve gender and racial equality.

Judy Tzu-Chun Wu is a professor in the Department of History at Ohio State University in Columbus. She is co-editor with Philip Scranton of *Beauty and Business: Commerce, Gender and Culture in Modern America* (New York: Routledge, 2001).

NOTES

My thanks to those who shared their experiences with the Miss Chinatown U.S.A. Beauty Pageant and to the many who offered helpful criticisms of this essay. In particular, I want to mention Gordon Chang for recommending this research topic, Estelle Freedman for fostering a supportive intellectual community, the members of the 1993–1994 seminar on "Women, Family, and Sexuality" for "co-authoring" this paper, and Shawn Lahr for his willingness to read drafts, no matter how rough the quality. Earlier versions of this essay were presented at the Stanford History Gender and Sexuality Workshop (1995), the Association for Asian American Studies National Conference (1996), and the American Historical Association, Pacific Coast Branch Conference (1996).

1. *Miss Chinatown U.S.A. Pageant Program*, 21–22–23 February 1958; "June Chin," *California Living Magazine*, 17 February 1985, p. 9; The overall Chinese American population in 1960 was 237,292. Of the 29,000 Chinese living in San Francisco in 1960, 18,000 lived in Chinatown.
2. Although the pageant held symbolic value for Chinese American communities throughout the country, I focus on San Francisco and Bay Area responses to the competition as a part of the annual Chinese New Year celebration. On the one hand, San Francisco's Chinatown could be considered unique because of its large Chinese population, its historical relationship with the Nationalist Republic of China, and its exposure to local social movements. On the other hand, the tensions in San Francisco's community, the unofficial capital of American Chinatowns, were often representative of the conflicts in other Chinese American communities.

3. The main newspapers used for research include: *East West, San Francisco Journal,* and *Getting Together,* all bilingual Chinese American publications based in San Francisco's Chinatown; *Chinatown News,* a Chinese Canadian publication based in Vancouver, B.C.; *Asian Week,* an Asian American publication based in San Francisco; and the *San Francisco Chronicle.* Because of my limited Chinese reading skills, I was not able to access systematically Chinese language materials. Consequently, the experiences and perspectives of Chinese Americans who felt more comfortable expressing themselves in Chinese will not be represented as well as those who wrote in English. The perspectives of the former are not less valuable, but are nevertheless not accessible to me at this point. Fortunately, the staff of the bilingual newspapers did publish translations of some Chinese articles on the Miss Chinatown U.S.A. beauty pageant.

4. Colleen Ballerino Cohen, Richard Wilk, Beverly Stoeltje, eds., *Beauty Queens on the Global Stage: Gender, Contests, and Power* (New York: Routledge, 1996), 2. This collection examines a variety of beauty contests throughout the world for their significance concerning not only gender roles but also ethnic, class, and national identity formation. Prior to the publication of this collection, most scholars of beauty contests tended to focus on the Miss America pageant, which involves predominantly white contestants. See Frank Deford, *There She Is; The Life and Times of Miss America* (New York: Viking Press, 1971), A. R. Riverol, *Live From Atlantic City: The History of the Miss America Pageant Before, After, and in Spite of Television* (Bowling Green, Ohio: Bowling Green State University Popular Press, 1992), and Lois W. Banner, *American Beauty* (New York: Knopf, 1983). A few scholars have analyzed state or local beauty pageants and their significance in terms of community representation. See Frank Deford, "Beauty and Everlasting Faith at the Local Level," *Audience 1971* 1:5; p. 56–72; Geoffrey Dunn and Mark Schwartz, directors, *Miss . . . or Myth?* (Distributors: Cinema Guild, 1986), film; Robert Lavenda, "Minnesota Queen Pageants: Play, Fun, and Dead Seriousness in a Festive Mood," *Journal of American Folklore* 101:400 (1988): 68–175.

   For the most part, scholars of Chinese American women have not analyzed the Miss Chinatown U.S.A. beauty pageant. Their studies tend to focus on the emergence of women from the private realm of family concerns to the public realm of political organizing and work. See Huping Ling, "Surviving on the Gold Mountain: Chinese American Women and Their Lives," (Ph.D. dissertation, Miami University, 1991); Stacey G. H. Yap, *Gather Your Strength, Sisters: The Emerging Role of Chinese Women Community Workers* (New York: AMS Press, 1989); and Judy Yung, *Unbound Feet: A Social History of Chinese Women in San Francisco* (Berkeley: University of California Press, 1995). One exception is Judy Yung's paper entitled, "Miss Chinatown USA and the Representation of Beauty." She presented it at the 1992 Association for Asian American Studies National Conference in San Jose, but it is not available to the public at this time.

5. The title for this section is quoted from James H. Loo, "Who are the Chinese?" *San Francisco Chinatown On Parade in Picture and Story,* ed. H. K. Wong (San Francisco, 1961), 6–7.

   Beginning in the 1910s, San Francisco's Chinatown organizations sporadically sponsored community pageants as fundraisers for social services, such as the Chinese Hospital. In 1948, various merchant, family, and civic organizations initiated an annual Miss Chinatown pageant. Inspired by the earlier tradition of fundraising, the winners were determined by the contestants' ability to sell raffle tickets to benefit a social cause. H. K. Wong is credited with proposing the joint sponsorship of the beauty contest and the public celebration of the Chinese New Year festival in 1953. In the late 1950s, the CCC altered the format of the pageant so that a panel of judges selected winners based on such criteria as beauty, personality, and poise. Lim P. Lee, "The Chinese New Year Festival," *Asian Week*, 5 February 1981, p. 4, and "The Chinese New Year Festival II," *Asian Week*, 12 February 1981, [p. 2]; H. K. Wong, "Miss Chinatown USA Pageant," *San Francisco Chinese New Year Festival*, Souvenir Program, 4–7 February 1960; Alice Lowe, "Concealing-Yet Revealing," *San Francisco Chinatown On Parade*, 26–27.

6. Julie Smith, "A Little Tiff At the Chinese New Year," *San Francisco Chronicle*, 18 February 1977, p. 2; the proportions of Chinese American in the labor force exceeded those for white women during the decade of the 1940s. Whereas 39.5 percent of white women worked for pay compared to 22.3 percent of Chinese women in 1940, 30.8 percent of Chinese women compared to 28.1 percent of white women worked in 1950. In 1960, 44.2 percent of Chinese women worked in the labor force compared to only 36.0 percent of white women. The gap in labor participation between the two groups continued to increase. Huping Ling, "Surviving on the Gold Mountain," 134–135.

Following the war, the Miss America pageant increasingly gained popularity, culminating in its first national televised broadcast in 1954. Whereas previous pageants held significance mainly for the local audience of Atlantic City, television made the event a truly national one so that by 1959, every state was finally represented at the "Miss America" pageant. A. R. Riverol, *Live From Atlantic City*, 56.

7. "June Chin," *California Living Magazine*; Donald Canter, "In New Year of the Boar: Chinatown 'Moves West,'" 9 February 1959, clipping from Chinese Historical Society, San Francisco, Box 3, folder 16. The collection is located at the Asian American Studies Library of the University of California, Berkeley. Hereafter cited as CHS-SF.

8. Lim P. Lee, "The Chinese New Year Festival," *Asian Week*, 5 February 1981, p. 4.

9. Pageant souvenir booklets regularly included informational pieces explaining Chinese culture to audiences unfamiliar with the community.

Victor and Brett de Bary Nee use the terms "bachelor society" and "family society" to characterize the evolution of San Francisco's Chinatown community; see *Longtime Californ': A Documentary Study of an American Chinatown* (Stanford, Calif.: Stanford University Press, 1986). The development of the beauty pageant coincided with the balancing of sex ratios among Chinese Americans. In 1890, when the Chinese population reached a nineteenth-century peak of 107,488 in the U.S., men outnumbered women 26.8 to 1. Due to the combined influence of natural birth rates and immigration, the sex ratio became 1.3 to 1 by 1960. (Huping Ling, "Surviving on the Gold Mountain," 127.) For further discussions of Chinese American family and community life in the late nineteenth and early twentieth centuries, see Peggy Pascoe, "Gender Systems in Conflict: The Marriages of Mission-Educated Chinese American Women, 1874–1939," in *Unequal Sisters: A Multicultural Reader in U.S. Women's History*, ed. by Ellen Carol DuBois and Vicki L. Ruiz (New York: Routledge, 1990) and Sucheng Chan, "The Exclusion of Chinese Women, 1870–1943," in *Entry Denied: Exclusion and the Chinese Community in America, 1882–1943* (Philadelphia: Temple University Press, 1991).

Lyrics to "Miss Chinatown" by Charles L. Leong and Kenneth Lee, 1964, published in *Miss Chinatown U.S.A.: Chinese New Year Festival Souvenir Program*, 1975.

Robert H. Lavenda makes a similar argument that contestants of community pageants tend to represent "the community's daughters." Lavenda, "Minnesota Queen Pageants: Play, Fun, and Dead Seriousness in a Festive Mode," *Journal of American Folklore* 101 (1988): 169. Daisy Chinn, "Women of Initiative," *San Francisco Chinatown On Parade*, 64.

10. For an examination of how international relations influence portrayals of Asian Americans in popular culture, see *Slaying the Dragon*, directed by Deborah Gee (San Francisco: NAATA/Cross Current Media, 1987). In the late 1950s, C. Y. Lee's *Flower Drum Song* (New York: Farrar, Straus and Cudahy, 1957) a love story about intergenerational and cultural tensions set in San Francisco's Chinatown, became a best-seller. Rodgers and Hammerstein subsequently turned the book first into a Broadway musical hit and then into a motion picture, leading Hollywood and Broadway to declare 1959 the "year of the Oriental." Chinatown organizers cashed in on the publicity by honoring and promoting the author of the book during the New Year festivals in the late 1950s and early 1960s.

   As part of the city's efforts to promote the Miss Chinatown U.S.A. beauty pageant and the Chinese New Year Festival, mayors, police commissioners, and supervisors regularly appeared in the annual parade. Politicians and their wives served as judges for the pageant, and in 1963 the San Francisco Convention and Visitors Bureau became a co-sponsor of the festival. "To Rival Mardi Gras? Mayor Urges Big Chinatown Festival," 24 January 1957, CHS-SF, Box 3, folder 16; Arthur Hoppe, "Festival Overture, Opus I: Montgomery St. Hails Chinese New Year," clipping from CHS-SSF, Box 3, folder 15.

11. Donald Canter, "Speech," Chinese Historical Society of America, 1965, CHS-SF, box 3, folder 27.

12. T. Kong Lee, President, Chinese Chamber of Commerce, "Welcome to Chinatown," *San Francisco Chinatown On Parade*, 2.

13. James H. Loo, "Who are the Chinese?" *San Francisco Chinatown On Parade*, 6–7; W. K. Wong, "Interview," *Longtime Californ'*, 244–45.

14. *San Francisco Chinatown Souvenir Annual*, 1962.

15. H. K. Wong, "Concept of Beauty," *San Francisco Chinatown On Parade*, 79; Evelyn S. Rawski, "Ch'ing Imperial Marriage and Problems of Rulership," in *Marriage and Inequality in Chinese Society*, ed. by Rubie S. Watson and Patricia Buckley Ebrey (Berkeley: University of California Press, 1991), 180; Although pageant organizers argued that the beauty pageant drew inspiration from Chinese as well as American cultural practice, scholars attribute the growing popularity of beauty pageants in Asian countries following World War II to the commercialization and Westernization of those countries. Corporations in Taiwan, Hong Kong, Japan, the Philippines, and Southeast Asia increasingly sponsored pageants as a way to help advertise their products and to promote tourism. Some scholars further suggest that businesses "actively promote[d] Western-style sexual objectification as a means of insuring employee loyalty" by channeling the energy of female workers toward self-beautification through purchasing commodities. Barbara Ehrenreich and Annette Fuentes, "Life on the Global Assembly Line," *Feminist Frameworks: Alternative Theoretical Accounts of the Relations between Women and Men*, ed. by Alison M. Jaggar and Paula S. Rothenberg (New York: McGraw-Hill, 1984), 285.

16. David Lei, telephone interview, San Francisco, 23 November 1993; Shirley Sun, "Jumbo Banana Split Proves Too Much for Beautiful May Chiang," *East-West*, 21 February 1967, p. 5.

17. In 1971, 41 percent of Chinatown's population fell below the federally defined poverty level partly because of the low wages paid to immigrant workers. Immigrant men commonly found service jobs, such as waiters, and tended to work "ten hours a day, six days a week, for wages that average from $350 to an occasional high of $700 a month." Immigrant women usually worked as garment workers, receiving pay not by the hour but by the piece. These low wages as well as the lack of cultural familiarity made it unlikely that immigrant families would move out of Chinatown, despite the fact that 77 percent of the housing was considered substandard by city codes. In 1970, the population density of the community was the second highest in the country with 120 to 180 persons per acre. These crowded conditions created enormous health risks as demonstrated by the fact that Chinatown had the highest tuberculosis and suicide rates in the nation. To serve its population of over 40,000 people, Chinatown had only one hospital with sixty beds. Nee, *Longtime Californ'*, xxi–xxv.

18. "The Most Visible Event," *East West*, 14 February 1973, p. 2; George Chu, "A Wild Night in Old Chinatown," *San Francisco Chronicle*, 9 March 1969, pp. 18, 21. The racial tensions between Chinatown residents and white tourists and police officers were not necessarily new. However, the growing numbers of Chinese American youth as a result of immigration and the increased awareness of racial injustice during the 1960s raised the volatility of intergroup contact.

19. "Liberate Holiday Inn," *Getting Together*, February 1971, p. 2; Jade Fong, "The CHI-am Corner," *East West*, 3 February 1971, p. 3.

20. Sara Evans, *Personal Politics: The Roots of Women's Liberation in the Civil Rights Movement and the New Left* (New York: Knopf, 1979), 214, and "No More Miss America! August 1968," in *Sisterhood Is Powerful; An Anthology of Writings from the Women's Liberation Movement*, ed. by Robin Morgan (New York: Random House, 1970), 521–24.

21. "A Queen for the Year of the Canine," *East West*, 10 December 1969, p. 1; Ben Wong-Torres, "Miss Chinatown—a Few Immodest Proposals," *East West*, 11 March 1967, p. 3; Judy Yung wrote under the pen name, Jade Fong, "The CHI-am Corner," *East West*, 1 March 1972, p. 3; Mabel Ng, "The Chinatown Pageant ... A Miscarriage of Grace," *East West*, 30 January 1974, p. 10; Wei Chih, "Queen Contestants," translated from the *Chinese Pacific Weekly*, 16 January 1975, printed in *East West*, 22 January 1975, p. 2; Curtis Choy, *The Year of the Ox: The 1973 Livestock Show* (Oakland, 1985).

22. Lisa Fangonilo, quoted in "What Do You Think about the Miss Chinatown USA Beauty Contest?" *East West*, 27 January 1971, p. 9; Pam Lee, "Letter to the Editor," *East West*, 15 April 1970, p. 2.

23. Louella Leon, conversation with author. As of 1987, "the average height of Miss Chinatown U.S.A. winners is 5 feet 5.3 inches." *Miss Chinatown U.S.A. Pageant Souvenir Program*, 1987; Paul Hui, "Alice Kong Also Ran . . . ," *East West*, 20 February 1974, p. 5; Curtis Choy, *The Year of the Ox*; "Oriental Eyes Get Western Look," *Chinatown News*, 3 December 1969, p. 4.

The 1970 Miss Chinatown U.S.A. beauty pageant souvenir book carried an advertisement for cosmetic surgery by a Dr. David Wang, who invented a special technique for converting "'oriental eyes' with single eyelids into 'Caucasian eyes' (with double-eyelids)." Wang developed this technique through experiments done on volunteers who tended to be female "movie actresses, singing stars and participants in beauty contests." "Dr. David Wang—Face-Lifting Surgeon," *Chinatown News*, 18 December 1969, pp. 10–15.

24. The experiences of Nathele Sue Dong, reported in a promotion piece for the pageant, demonstrate the importance of cosmetics for helping contestants compete successfully. When Dong decided to run for the Miss Chinatown U.S.A. pageant in 1961, one of her supporters encouraged her to seek the advice of Helen Lew, the director of the Patricia Stevens modeling agency. Lew taught Dong the importance of cosmetics, clothing, jewelry, and hair-styling for creating the image of a beauty pageant contestant:

> Helen told the girl the only reason her face was shiny was because she'd never worn make-up, corrected it with a color that blends with Nathele's skin. Two pencil strokes and Nathele's eyebrows were intriguingly accentuated and slightly higher; a green Chinese dress (because green is very becoming with the Oriental skin) brought out the red pigment in her face. Nathele's first pair of earrings (rhinestone drops) a visit to the hairdresser (her hair shaped in closer) and you can see for yourself how Nathele has acquired the poise, personality and good looks required of a candidate for Miss Chinatown USA. ("They Look Twice Now," *San Francisco News-Call Bulletin*, 17 February 1961 CHS-SF, box 3, folder 20.)

> One Miss Chinatown contestant reportedly had a face-lift operation prior to the pageant. (Manchester Fu, "Manny and the Celestial 5," *East West*, 21 January 1970, p. 3); Many observers noted the disappointment of candidates who did not win a title in the pageant. Ronda Wei Jeyn-Ching, Miss Chinatown 1980, commented that "many young girls develop a poor self-image after failing to win a pageant title" ("A Parting Queen's Reflections," *Asian Week*, 26 February 1981). This feeling of inferiority partly arose from their failure to fulfill the expectations of parents and sponsors. Pageant organizer Louella "Lulu" Leon recalled that one contestant who did not win a title began crying backstage. She became even more traumatized when her mother yelled at her for making mistakes and not presenting herself in the best light during the competition. Because of what occurred, organizers decided to ban family members from backstage areas of the pageant. (Louella Leon communicated this incident regarding the contestant who lost in a conversation with me.)

> Celeste Wong (pseudonym), interview, San Francisco, 8 December, 1993; Wong had lied about her age to enter the Miss Chinatown U.S.A. beauty pageant, which required contestants to be between the ages of seventeen and twenty-six.

25. Pamela Tau, *East West*, 3 February 1971, p. 5; Pam Lee, "Letter to the Editor," *East West*, 15 April 1970, p. 2; "Reflections on Chinese New Year—2 Views," *Getting Together*, 3–16 February 1973, p. 3.

26. Emily Honig and Gail Hershatter, *Personal Voices: Chinese Women in the 1980s* (Stanford, Calif.: Stanford University Press, 1988), 24; "Public Invited to Spring Festival Celebration," *San Francisco Journal*, 9 February 1977.

27. Stan Yee, "Notes of a Chinese Bum on Holiday Inn," *East West*, 20 January 1971, p. 2.

28. Ann F. Nakao, "A Hard Look: The Fires behind Chinatown's Parade," *San Francisco Examiner*, 15 February 1977, p. 8; Carole Jan Lee, "Carole's Barrel," *East West*, 18 February 1970.

29. Cynthia Denise Chin-Lee, telephone interview, Palo Alto, 20 February 1994; Rose Chung, telephone interview, San Francisco, 2 December 1993.

30. John Lum, "The Miss San Leandro Contest: There's No Point to It," *East West,* 17 May 1972, p. 6; Y. C. Hong, a judge for the 1965 competition, explained that if he had a daughter, he would not wish her to enter the contest because he sympathized "with the heartaches of many beautiful girls who failed to get within the 'magic circle' and the disappointments of their parents and sponsors." Despite these reservations, he applauded the contestants for entering the competition and demonstrating the positive aspects of Chinese American culture. He believed that "it is a good thing for our Chinese in showing the peoples of the world that we do have many beautiful and talented Chinese girls from all parts of the country." Y. C. Hong, "Letter to the Editor," *East West,* 21 March 1967, p. 2.

31. Irene Ung, "Irene Ung Satisfied with Simple Things in Life," *East West,* 21 February 1967, p. 7; "Interviews with Two Bay Area Beauty Pageant Contestants," *East West,* 4 February 1976, p. 11; Doris G. Worsham, "There is a 'There' for Her," *Oakland Tribune,* 17 February 1973; clipping found in "Beauty Contests-CA" folder at UC Berkeley's Asian American Studies Library.

32. Gordon Yaw, telephone interview, Oakland, 7 February 1994; "Consider the Alternatives," *East West,* 30 January 1974, p. 2.

33. "Only a 'Fair' Fair," *East West,* 19 March 1969, p. 2; Katie Choy, "E-W interviews 'Miss Chinatown' Contestants," *East West,* 23 January 1974, p. 6.

34. Nakao, "A Hard Look," 1, 6.

35. Shirley Sun, "Tall & Lissome Jennifer Chung Fulfills Her Childhood Dream," *East West,* 21 February 1967, p. 6. Thanking the other contestants, Miss Chinatown U.S.A. 1976 Linda Chun wrote that we "are all dear friends and I shall cherish our moments together always." Linda Sue Kwai En Chun, "Reflections," *Chinatown San Francisco.* Souvenir Program, 1977, p. 42; Celeste Wong recalled that after she won the title of Miss San Francisco Chinatown, her fellow contestants were not as friendly toward her. Celeste Wong, interview.

36. Melanie Feng, "What Do You Think about the Miss Chinatown USA Beauty Contest?" *East West,* 27 January 1971, p. 4; Katie Choy and Paul K. Hui, "3 Beauties Interviewed," *East West,* 22 January 1975, p. 5; Judy Quan, "Three Queen Contestants: the Person Behind the Face," *East West,* 16 February 1972, p. 7; Worsham, "There is a 'There' for Her"; Fang Wei Lyan, "Under Those Plastic Smiles," *East West,* 21 January 1967, pp. 1–2.

In some cases, the pageant provided more opportunities for women to gain exposure to certain public sectors. Women interested in modeling, movie, or public relations careers viewed the pageant as a good way to gain recognition. After winning the Miss Chinatown U.S.A. title, Sandra Wong auditioned for a movie role opposite Clint Eastwood. Contestants who won trips to Asia gained some exposure to international politics by meeting such dignitaries as ROC President Chiang Kai-shek. Contestants might also learn about international finance, for the Chinese Chamber of Commerce used these "goodwill tours" to build trade relations with Taiwan, Hong Kong, and other Asian countries. The participation of recognizable national and state politicians, such as Anne Chennault and March K. Wong, as pageant judges also provided models of successful Chinese American women who transcended traditional female roles. In other words, pageant supporters argued that they, like their feminist critics, sought to promote female achievements in the public realm.

37. Mary Jew, "Fantastic Turnout at Fashion Show," *East West*, 13 February 1974, p. 5; "Come Alive," editorial, *East West*, 28 August 1968, p. 2; Judy Quan, "Three Queen Contestants: The Person Behind the Face," *East West*, 16 February 1972, p. 7. Moy did not win the pageant; Wally Lee, "Wahine Stewardess Miss Chinatown USA," *East West*, 23 February 1972, pp. 1–10.
38. Hing C. Tse, interview, San Francisco, 12 November 1993.
39. Honig and Hershatter, *Personal Voices: Chinese Women in the 1980s*, 335; "China Wants Good-Looking Stewardesses," *Chinatown News*, 18 January 1980, reprint from *New York Times*.
40. Cynsin: *An American Princess*, video by Valerie Soe, 1991; Lorena Tong, "Miss Chinatown Cynthia Gouw Insists She Is Not the 'Beauty Pageant' Type," *East West*, 5 December 1984, p. 8.

SELECTED BIBLIOGRAPHY

Books

Allison, Charlene J., Sue-Ellen Jacobs, and Mary A. Porter, eds. *Winds of Change: Women in Northwest Commercial Fishing.* Seattle: University of Washington Press, 1989.

Anderson, E. Frederick. *The Development of Leadership and Organization Building in the Black Community of Los Angeles from 1900 through World War II* (Saratoga, Calif.: Century Twenty One Publishing, 1980).

Anderson, Karen Tucker. *Wartime Women: Sex Roles, Family Relations, and the Status of Women During World War II.* Westport, Conn.: Greenwood Press, 1981.

Anzaldúa, Gloria. *Borderlands/La Frontera.* 2d ed. San Francisco: Aunt Lute Books, 1999.

Babcock, Barbara A., and Nancy J. Parezo. *Daughters of the Desert: Women Anthropologists and the Native American Southwest, 1880–1980.* Albuquerque: University of New Mexico Press, 1988.

Bass, Charlotta. *Forty Years: Memoirs from the Pages of a Newspaper* (Los Angeles, Calif.: *California Eagle,* 1960).

Blair, Karen J., ed. *Women in Pacific Northwest History: An Anthology.* Seattle: University of Washington Press, 1988.

Brave Bird, Mary, and Richard Erdoes. *Ohitika Woman.* New York: Grove Press, 1993.

Brunsman, Laura, and Ruth Askey, eds. *Modernism and Beyond: Women Artists of the Pacific Northwest.* New York: Midmarch Arts, 1993.

Bry, Doris, and Nicholas Calloway, eds. *Georgia O'Keefe in the West.* New York: Alfred A. Knopf, 1989.

Cochran, Jo, T. T. Stewart, and Mayumi Tsutakawa, eds. *Gathering Ground: New Writing and Art by Northwest Women of Color.* Seattle: Seal Press, 1984.

Comer, Krista. *Landscapes of the New West: Gender and Geography in Contemporary Women's Writing.* Chapel Hill: University of North Carolina Press, 1999.

Davidson, Sue. *A Heart in Politics: Jeanette Rankin and Patsy T. Mink.* Seattle: Seal Press, 1994.

Davis, Ronald L. *Hollywood Beauty: Linda Darnell and the American Dream.* Norman: University of Oklahoma Press, 1991.

Englander, Susan. *Class Conflict and Coalition in the California Woman Suffrage Movement, 1907–1912: The San Francisco Wage Earners' Suffrage League.* San Francisco: Edwin Mellen Press, 1992.

Etulain, Richard W., and Glenda Riley. *The Hollywood West: Lives of Film Legends Who Shaped It.* Golden, Colo.: Fulcrum Publishing, 2001.

Field, Connie. "The Life and Times of Rosie the Riveter" (Emeryville, Calif.: Rosie the Riveter Film Project, 1980).

Fink, Deborah. *Agrarian Women: Wives and Mothers in Rural Nebraska, 1880–1940.* Chapel Hill: University of North Carolina Press, 1992.

Fisher, Ellen Kingman. *Junior League of Denver: Leaders in Community Service, 1918–1993.* Denver: Colorado Historical Society, 1993.

Frank, Dana. *Purchasing Power: Consumer Organizing, Gender, and the Seattle Labor Movement, 1919–1929.* Cambridge, Mass.: Cambridge University Press, 1994.

Gaede, Marnie, Barton Wright, and Marc Gaede. *The Hopi Photographs: Kate Cary, 1905–1912.* Albuquerque: University of New Mexico Press, 1988.

Gerber, Philip L., ed. *Bachelor Bess: The Homesteading Letters of Elizabeth Corey, 1909–1919.* Iowa City: University of Iowa Press, 1990.

Glenn, Evelyn Nakano. *Issei, Nisei, War Bride: Three Generations Of Japanese American Women in Domestic Service.* Philadelphia: Temple University Press, 1986.

Gluck, Sherna Berger. *Rosie the Riveter Revisited: Women, the War, and Social Change.* Boston: Twayne Publishers, 1987; New York: New American Library, 1988).

————. *Rosie the Riveter Revisited: Women and the World War II Work Experience.* 45 vols. Long Beach: California State University Long Beach Foundation, 1983.

Grattan, Virginia L. *Mary Colter: Builder Upon the Red Earth.* Flagstaff, Ariz.: Northland Press, 1980; Grand Canyon, Ariz.: Grand Canyon Natural History Association, 1992.

Greenwood, Annie Pike. *We Sagebrush Folks.* New York: D. Appleton-Century Co., 1934; Moscow: University of Idaho Press, 1988.

Haarsager, Sandra. *Bertha Knight Landes of Seattle: Big-City Mayor.* Norman: University of Oklahoma Press, 1994.

Hanks, Maxine, ed. *Women and Authority: Re-emerging Mormon Feminism.* Salt Lake City: Signature Books, 1992.

Hansen, Arthur A. *Japanese American World War II Evacuation Oral History Project, Part I: Internees* (Westport, Conn.: Meckler Publishing, 1949).

Hendricks, Cecilia Hennel. *Letters from Honeyhill: A Woman's View of Homesteading, 1924–1931.* Boulder, Colo.: Pruett, 1986. 1990.

Hill, Anita. *Speaking Truth to Power.* Norman: University of Oklahoma Press, 2000.

Hine, Darlene Clark. *Black Women in White: Racial Conflict and Cooperation in the Nursing Profession, 1890–1950.* Bloomington: Indiana University Press, 1989.

Holt, Marilyn Irvin. *Linoleum, Better Babies, and the Modern Farm Woman, 1890–1930.* Albuquerque: University of New Mexico Press, 1995.

Honey, Maureen, ed. *Bitter Fruit: African American Women in World War II.* Columbia: University of Missouri Press, 1999.

Houston, Jeanne Wakatsuki, and James D. Houston. *Farewell to Manzanar: A True Story of Japanese American Experience during and after the World War II Internment.* New York: Bantam Books, 1973.

Ishigo, Estelle. *Lone Heart Mountain.* Los Angeles: Anderson, Ritchie & Simon, 1972.

Jacobs, Margaret D. *Engendered Encounters: Feminism and Pueblo Cultures 1879–1934.* Lincoln: University of Nebraska Press, 1999.

Jellison, Katherine. *Entitled to Power: Farm Women and Technology, 1913–1963.* Chapel Hill: University of North Carolina Press, 1993.

Jensen, Joan. *One Foot on the Rockies: Women and Creativity in the Modern American West.* Albuquerque: University of New Mexico Press, 1995.

Jones-Eddy, Julie. *Homesteading Women: An Oral History of Colorado, 1890–1950.* New York: Twayne Publishers, 1992.

Jordan, Teresa. *Cowgirls: Women of the American West.* Garden City, N.Y.: Anchor Press/Doubleday and Company, 1982.

———. *Graining the Mare: The Poetry of Ranch Women.* Salt Lake City: Gibbs Smith, 1994.

———. and James R. Hepworth, eds. *The Stories That Shape Us: Contemporary Women Write About the West.* New York: W. W. Norton, 1995.

Kim, Elaine H., Lilia V. Villanueva, and Asian Women United of California. *Making More Waves: New Writing by Asian American Women.* Boston: Beacon Press, 1997.

Knowles, Karen, ed. *Celebrating the Land: Women's Nature Writings, 1850–1991.* Flagstaff, Ariz.: Northland Publishing Co., 1992.

Lamphere, Louise, Patricia Zavella, and Felipe Gonzales, with Peter Evans. *Sunbelt Working Mothers: Reconciling Family and Factory.* Ithaca, N.Y.: Cornell University Press, 1993.

Lee, Hermione. *Willa Cather: A Life Saved Up.* New York: Pantheon, 1990.

Luhan, Mabel Dodge. *Intimate Memories: The Autobiography of Mabel Dodge Luhan,* ed. Lois Palken Rudnick. Albuquerque: University of New Mexico Press, 1999.

Martin, Patricia Preciado. *Songs My Mother Sang to Me: An Oral History of Mexican American Women.* Tucson: University of Arizona Press, 1992.

Murphy, Mary. *Mining Cultures: Men, Women, and Leisure in Butte, 1914–41.* Urbana: University of Illinois Press, 1997.

Myers, Gloria E. *A Municipal Mother: Portland's Lola Greene Baldwin, America's First Policewoman.* Corvallis: Oregon State University Press, 1995.

Osburn, Katherine Marie Birmingham. *Southern Ute Women: Autonomy and Assimilation on the Reservation, 1887–1934.* Albuquerque: University of New Mexico Press, 1998.

Pardo, Mary S. *Mexican American Women Activists: Identity and Resistance in Two Los Angeles Communities.* Philadelphia: Temple University Press, 1998.

Passett, Joanne E. *Cultural Crusaders: Women Librarians in the American West, 1900–1917.* Albuquerque: University of New Mexico Press, 1994.

Perrone, Bobette, H. Henrietta Stockel, and Victoria Krueger. *Medicine Women, Curanderas, and Women Doctors.* Norman: University of Oklahoma Press, 1989.

Peterson, Susan C., and Courtney Ann Vaughn-Roberson. *Women with Vision: The Presentation Sisters of South Dakota, 1880–1985.* Urbana: University of Illinois Press, 1988.

Rebolledo, Tey Diana, and Eliana S. Rivera, eds. *Infinite Divisions: An Anthology of Chicana Literature.* Tucson: University of Arizona Press, 1993.

Robinson, Roxana. *Georgia O'Keefe: A Life.* Reprint. Hanover: University Press of New England, 1999.

Rudnick, Lois Palken. *Mabel Dodge Luhan: New Woman, New Worlds.* Albuquerque: University of New Mexico Press, 1994.

Ruiz, Vicki L. *Cannery Women, Cannery Lives: Mexican Women, Unionization, and the California Food Processing Industry, 1930–1950.* Albuquerque: University of New Mexico Press, 1987.

Ruiz, Vicki L. and Ellen Carol DuBois, eds. *Unequal Sisters: A Multicultural Reader in U.S. Women's History.* 3d ed. New York: Routledge, 1999.

Sachs, Caroly E. *Gendered Fields: Rural Women, Agriculture, and Environment.* Boulder, Colo.: Westview Press, 1996.

Schackel, Sandra. *Social Housekeepers: Women Shaping Public Policy in New Mexico, 1920–1940.* Albuquerque: University of New Mexico Press, 1992.

Schlissel, Lillian, and Catherine Lavender. *The Western Women's Reader: The Remarkable Writings of Women Who Shaped the American West, Spanning 300 Years.* New York: Harper Collins, 2000.

Sharpless, Rebecca. *Fertile Ground, Narrow Choices: Women on Texas Cotton Farms, 1900–1940.* Chapel Hill: University of North Carolina, 1999.

Sone, Monica. *Nisei Daughter.* Seattle: University of Washington Press, 1979.

Stephens, Donna M. *One-Room School: Teaching in 1930s Western Oklahoma.* Norman: University of Oklahoma Press, 1990.

Stewart, Elinore Pruitt. *Letters of a Woman Homesteader.* Boston: Houghton Mifflin Company, 1914, 1982.

Stineman, Esther. *Mary Austin: Song of a Maverick.* New Haven, Conn.: Yale University Press, 1989.

Taylor, A. Elizabeth. *Citizens at Last: The Woman Suffrage Movement in Texas, Essays.* Austin, Tex.: Ellen C. Temple Publisher, 1987.

Tucker, Cynthia Grant. *Prophetic Sisterhood: Liberal Women Ministers of the Frontier, 1880–1930.* Boston: Beacon Press, 1990; Bloomington: Indiana University Press, 1994.

Tywoniak, Frances Esquibel, and Mario T. Garcia. *Migrant Daughter: Coming of Age as a Mexican American Woman.* Berkeley: University of California Press, 2000.

Woloch, Nancy. *Women and the American Experience.* Boston: McGraw-Hill Companies, 2000.

Yates, Norris. *Gender and Genre: An Introduction to Women Writers of Formula Westerns, 1900–1950.* Albuquerque: University of New Mexico Press, 1995.

Zanjani, Sally. *A Mine of Her Own: Women Prospectors in the American West, 1850–1950.* Lincoln: University of Nebraska Press, 2000.

Zavella, Patricia. *Women's Work and Chicano Families: Cannery Workers of the Santa Clara Valley.* Ithaca, N.Y.: Cornell University Press, 1987.

Articles

Aiken, Katherine G. "When I realized How Close Communism Was to Kellogg, I Was Willing to Devote Day and Night': Anti-Communism, Women, Community Values, and the Bunker Hill Strike of 1960." *Labor History* 36 (spring 1995): 165–87.

Anderson, Karen. "Work, Gender and Power in the American West." *Pacific Historical Review* 61 (November 1992): 481–99.

Anderson, Kathryn. "Steps to Political Equality: Woman Suffrage and Electoral Politics in the Lives of Emily Newell Blair, Anne Henrietta Martin, and Jeannette Rankin." *Frontiers* 18 (1997): 101–21.

Armitage, Susan and Sherna Berger Gluck. "Reflections on Women's Oral History: An Exchange." *Frontiers* XIX, no. 3 (1998): 1–11.

Bauman, Paula. "Single Women Homesteaders in Wyoming, 1880–1930." *Annals of Wyoming* 58 (spring 1986): 39–53.

Bernal, Dolores Delgado. "Grassroots Leadership Reconceptualized: Chicana Oral Histories and the 1968 East Los Angeles School Blowouts." *Frontiers* 19, no. 2 (1998): 113–42.

Bernstein, Alison. "A Mixed Record: The Political Enfranchisement of American Indian Women during the Indian New Deal." *Journal of the West* 23 (July 1984): 13–20.

Blackwelder, Julia Kirk. "Women in the Work Force: Atlanta, New Orleans, and San Antonio, 1930–1940." *Journal of Urban History* 4 (May 1978): 331–58.

Broyles-Gonzalez, Yolanda. "The Living Legacy of Chicana Performers: Preserving History through Oral Testimony." *Frontiers* 11 (1990): 46–52.

Bunker, Gary L., and Carol B. Bunker. "Woman Suffrage, Popular Art, and Utah." *Utah Historical Quarterly* 59 (winter 1991): 32–51.

Cantarow, Ellen. "Jessie Lopez de la Cruz." In *Moving the Mountain: Women Working for Social Change*, ed. Ellen Cantarow. Old Westbury, N.Y.: Feminist Press, 1980.

Carpenter, Stephanie Ann. "'Regular Farm Girl': The Women's Land Army in World War II." *Agricultural History* 71 (spring 1997): 162–86.

Castañeda, Antonio. "Women of Color and the Rewriting of Western History: The Discourse, Politics, and Decolonization of History." *Pacific Historical Review* 61 (November 1992): 481–99.

Castillo, Debra A., María Gudelia Rangel Gómez, and Bonnie Delgado. "Border Lives: Prostitute Women in Tijuana." *Signs: The Journal of Women in Culture and Society* 24 (winter 1999): 387–422.

Chato, Genevieve and Christine Conte. "The Legal Rights of American Indian Women." In *Western Women: Their Land, Their Lives*, ed. Lillian Schlissel, Vicki L. Ruiz, and Janice Monk. Albuquerque: University of New Mexico Press, 229–46.

Chinchilla, Norma and Nora Hamilton. "Latina Workers in Domestic Work and Street Vending in Los Angeles." *Humboldt Journal of Social Relations* 22, no. 1 (1996): 25–35.

Conte, Christine. "Ladies, Livestock, Land and Lucre: Women's Networks and Social Status on the Western Navajo Reservation." *American Indian Quarterly* 6 (spring/summer 1982): 105–24.

Cota-Cardena, Margarita. "The Faith of Activists: Barrios, Cities, and the Chicana Feminist Response." *Frontiers* 14 (1993): 51–80.

Dawson, Jan D. "'Lady Lookouts' in a 'Man's World' During World War II: A Reconsideration of American Women and Nature." *Journal of Women's History* 8 (fall 1996): 99–114.

Deutsch, Sarah. "Gender, Labor History, and Chicano/a Ethnic Identity." *Frontiers* 14 (1993): 1–22.

Dickson, Lynda F. "Lifting as We Climb: African American Women's Clubs of Denver, 1880–1925." In *Writing the Range: Race, Class, and Culture in the Women's West*, ed. Elizabeth Jameson and Susan Armitage. Norman: University of Oklahoma Press, 1997, 372–92.

Duron, Clementina. "Mexican Women and Labor Conflict in Los Angeles: The ILGWU Dressmakers' Strike of 1933." *Aztlán* 15 (spring 1984): 145–61.

Fagan, Michele L. "Nebraska Nursing Education during World War II." *Nebraska History* 73 (fall 1992): 126–37.

Franzen, Trisha. "Differences and Identities: Feminism and the Albuquerque Lesbian Community." *Signs* 18 (summer 1993): 891–906.

Garcia, Richard A. "Dolores Huerta: Woman Organizer, and Symbol." *California History* 72 (spring 1993): 56–71.

George, Susanne K. "Elinore Pruitt Stewart: The Adventurous Woman Homesteader." In *By Grit & Grace: Eleven Women Who Shaped the American West*, ed. Glenda Riley and Richard W. Etulain. Golden, Colo.: Fulcrum Publishing, 1997.

Gonzales, Gilbert G. "Women, Work, and Community in the Mexican *Colonias* of the Southern California Citrus Belt." *California History* 74 (spring 1995): 58–67.

Greenwald, Maurine Weiner. "Working Class Feminism and the Family Wage Ideal: The Seattle Debate on Married Women's Right to Work, 1914–1920." *Journal of American History* 76 (June 1989): 118–49.

Gullet, Gayle. "Women Progressives and the Politics of Americanization in California, 1915–1920." *Pacific Historical Review* 64 (February 1995): 71–94.

Hall, Kimberly A. "Women in Wartime: The San Diego Experience, 1941–1945." *Journal of San Diego History* 39 (fall 1993): 261–79.

Hefner, Loretta L. "The National Women's Relief Society and the U.S. Sheppard-Towner Act." *Utah Historical Quarterly* 50 (summer 1982): 255–67.

Hield, Melissa. "'Union-Minded': Women in the Texas ILGWU, 1933–1950." *Frontiers* 4 (summer 1979): 59–70.

Hill, Patricia Everidge. "Women's Groups and the Extension of City Services in Early Twentieth-Century Dallas." *East Texas Historical Journal* 30 (spring 1992): 3–10.

Hirshfield, Deborah Scott. "Women Shipyard Workers in the Second World War." *International History Review* 11 (August 1989): 478–85.

Hodges, Eva, and Cle Cervi. "Founded by Accident: The Denver Women's Press Club." *Colorado Heritage* (autumn 1997): 23–43.

Honig, Emily. "Striking Lives: Oral History and the Politics of Memory." *Journal of Women's History* 9 (spring 1997): 140–57.

———. "Women at Farah Revisited: Political Mobilization and Its Aftermath Among Chicana Workers in El Paso, Texas, 1972–1992." *Feminist Studies* 22 (summer 1996): 425–52.

Jacobs, Margaret D. "Shaping a New Way: White Women and the Movement to Promote Pueblo Indian Arts and Crafts, 1900–1935." *Journal of the Southwest* 40 (summer 1998): 187–215.

Jameson, Elizabeth and Susan Armitage, eds. *Writing the Range: Race, Class, and Culture in the Women's West.* Norman: University of Oklahoma Press, 1997.

Jensen, Billie Barnes. "'In the Weird and Wooly West': Anti-Suffrage Women, Gender Issues, and Woman Suffrage in the West." *Journal of the West* 32 (July 1993): 41–51.

Jensen, Joan M. "The Campaign for Women's Community Property Rights in New Mexico, 1940–1960." In *New Mexico Women: Intercultural Perspectives,* eds. Joan M. Jensen and Darlis A. Miller. Albuquerque: University of New Mexico Press, 1986, 333–55.

———. "Crossing Ethnic Barriers in the Southwest: Women's Agricultural Extension Education, 1914–1940." *Agricultural History* 60 (spring 1986): 169–81.

———. "'Disfranchisement Is a Disgrace': Women and Politics in New Mexico, 1900–1914." *New Mexico Historical Review* 56 (January 1981): 5–35.

———. "'I've Worked, I'm Not Afraid of Work': Farm Women in New Mexico, 1920–1940." *New Mexico Historical Review* 61 (January 1986): 27–52.

Kessler, Lauren. "The Fight for Woman Suffrage and the Oregon Press." In *Women in Pacific Northwest History: An Anthology,* ed. Karen J. Blair. Seattle: Washington University Press, 1988, 43–58.

Konek, Carol Wolfe. "Farm Wife: Goldie Keltner Ford (1890–1962)." *Frontiers* 12, no. 1 (1991): 126–40.

Landsman, Gail H. "The 'Other' as Political Symbol: Images of Indians in the Woman Suffrage Movement." *Ethnohistory* 39 (summer 1991): 247–84.

Ledesma, Irene. "Texas Newspapers and Chicana Workers' Activism, 1919–1974." *Western Historical Quarterly* 26 (autumn 1995): 309–31.

Ling, Susie. "The Mountain Movers: Asian American Women's Movement in Los Angeles." *Amerasia Journal* 15 (spring 1989): 51–67.

Lothrop, Gloria Ricci. "A Trio of Mermaids—Their Impact Upon the Southern California Sportswear Industry." *Journal of the West* 25 (January 1986): 73–82.

McCormick, John S. "Red Lights in Zion: Salt Lake City's Stockade, 1908–11." *Utah Historical Quarterly* 50 (spring 1982): 168–81.

Matsumoto, Valerie. "Desperately Seeking 'Deirdre': Gender Roles, Multicultural Relations, and Nisei Women Writers of the 1930s." In *Writing the Range: Race, Class, and Culture in the Women's West*, eds. Elizabeth Jameson and Susan Armitage. Norman: University of Oklahoma Press, 1997.

———. "Redefining Expectations: Nisei Women in the 1930s." *California History* 73 (spring 1994): 44–53.

Matthews, Glenna. "The Fruit Workers of the Santa Clara Valley: Alternative Paths to Union Organization during the 1930s." *Pacific Historical Review* 54 (February 1985): 51–70.

Mead, Rebecca J. "'Let the Women Get Their Wages as Men Do': Trade Union Women and the Legislated Minimum Wage in California." *Pacific Historical Review* 67 (August 1998): 317–47.

Melcher, Mary. "Tending Children, Chickens, and Cattle: Southern Arizona Ranch and Farm Women, 1910–1940." Ph.D. dissertation, Arizona State University, 1994.

———"'This is not Right': Rural Arizona Women Challenge Segregation and Ethnic Division, 1925–1950." *Frontiers* 10 (1999): 190–215.

———. "Times of Crisis and Joy: Pregnancy, Childbirth, and Mothering in Rural Arizona, 1910–1940." *Journal of Arizona History* 40 (summer 1999): 181–200.

Mercier, Laurie K. "'We Are Women Irish': Gender, Class, Religious, and Ethnic Identity in Anaconda, Montana." *Montana: The Magazine of Western History* 44 (winter 1994): 28–41.

Metcalf, Ann. "Navajo Women in the City: Lessons From a Quarter-Century of Relocation." *American Indian Quarterly* 6 (spring/summer 1982): 71–89.

Murphy, Mary. "A Place of Greater Opportunity: Irish Women's Search for Home, Family, and Leisure in Butte, Montana." *Journal of the West* 31 (1992): 73–78.

———. "Bootlegging Mothers and Drinking Daughters: Gender and Prohibition in Butte, Montana." *American Quarterly* 46 (June 1994): 174–94.

Noble, Antonette Chambers. "Utah's Rosies: Women in the Utah War Industries during World War II." *Utah Historical Quarterly* 59 (spring 1991): 123–45.

Norwood, Vera. "The Photographer and the Naturalist: Laura Gilpin and Mary Austin in the Southwest." *Journal of American Culture* 5 (summer 1982): 1–28.

Ochoa, Gilda Laura. "Everyday Ways of Resistance and Cooperation: Mexican American Women Building *Puentes* with Immigrants." *Frontiers* 20 (1999): 1–20.

Odem, Mary. "Single Mothers, Delinquent Daughters, and the Juvenile Court in Early 20th Century Los Angeles." *Journal of Social History* 25 (fall 1991): 227–44.

Orozco, Cynthia E. "Alice Dickerson Montemayor: Feminism and Mexican American Politics in the 1930s." In *Writing the Range: Race, Class, and Culture in the Women's West*, ed. Elizabeth Jameson and Susan Armitage. Norman: University of Oklahoma Press, 1997, 435–56.

———. "Regionalism, Politics, and Gender in Southwest History: The League of United Latin American Citizens' Expansion into New Mexico from Texas, 1929–1945." *Western Historical Quarterly* 29 (winter 1998): 459–83.

Pardo, Mary S. "Mexican American Women Grassroots Community Activists: 'Mothers of East Los Angeles.'" In *Writing the Range: Race, Class, and Culture in the Women's West*, ed. Elizabeth Jameson and Susan Armitage. Norman: University of Oklahoma Press, 1997, 553–68.

Patterson, Victoria D. "Indian Life in the City: A Glimpse of Pomo Women in the 1930s." *California History* 71 (fall 1992): 402–11.

Peterson, Susan C. "Adapting to Fill a Need: The Presentation Sisters and Health Care, 1901–61." *South Dakota History* 17 (spring 1987): 1–22.

Platt, Kamala. "Chicana Strategies for Success and Survival: Cultural Poetics of Environmental Justice from the Mothers of East Los Angeles." *Frontiers* 18 (1977): 48–57.

Pollard, Clarice F. "WAACS in Texas During the Second World War." *Southwestern Historical Quarterly* 93 (July 1989): 61–74.

Rathge, Richard W. "Women's Contribution to the Family Farm." *Great Plains Quarterly* 9 (winter 1989): 36–47.

Rodgers, B. Ann and Linda Schott. "'My Mother Was a Mover': African American Seminole Women in Brackettville, Texas, 1914–1964." In *Writing the Range: Race, Class, and Culture in the Women's West*, ed. Elizabeth Jameson and Susan Armitage. Norman: University of Oklahoma Press, 1997, 585–99.

Rodriguez-Estrada, Alicia I. "Dolores Del Rio and Lupe Velez: Images on and off the Screen, 1925–1944." In *Writing the Range: Race, Class, and Culture in the Women's West,* ed. Elizabeth Jameson and Susan Armitage. Norman: University of Oklahoma Press, 1997, 475–92.

Ross, Amy Elisa. "Every Home A Laboratory: Arizona Farm Women, the Extension Service, and Rural Modernization, 1932–1952." Ph.D. dissertation, Arizona State University, 1998.

Rozek, Barbara J. "The Entry of Mexican Women into Urban Based Industries: Experiences in Texas during the Twentieth Century." In *Women and Texas History: Selected Essays,* ed. Fane Downs and Nancy Baker Jones. Austin: Texas State Historical Association, 1993, 15–33.

Ruiz, Vicki L. "'Star Struck': Acculturation, Adolescence and Mexican American Women, 1920–1950." In *Small Worlds: Children and Adolescents in America, 1850–1950,* ed. Elliott West and Paula Petrick. Lawrence: University Press of Kansas, 1992.

Salas, Elizabeth. "Ethnicity, Gender, and Divorce: Issues in the 1922 Campaign by Adelina Otero-Warren for the U.S. House of Representatives." *New Mexico Historical Review* 70 (October 1995): 367–82.

Sallee, Shelley. "'The Woman of It': Governor Miriam Ferguson's 1924 Election." *Southwestern Historical Quarterly* 100 (July 1996): 1–16.

Sandweiss, Martha A. "The Historical Landscape: Laura Gilpin and the Tradition of American Landscape Photography." In *The Desert Is No Lady: Southwestern Landscapes in Women's Writing and Art,* ed. Vera Norwood and Janice Monk. New Haven, Conn.: Yale University Press, 1987; Tucson: University of Arizona Press, 1997, 62–73.

Schackel, Sandra. "Barbara Stanwyck: Uncommon Heroine." *California History* 72 (spring 1993): 441–55.

———. "Ranch and Farm Women in the Contemporary American West." In *The Rural West Since World War II,* ed. R. Douglas Hurt. Lawrence: University Press of Kansas, 1998.

———. "'The Tales Those Nurses Told!': Public Health Nurses Among the Pueblo and Navajo Indians." *New Mexico Historical Review* 65 (April 1990): 225–49.

Schaffer, Ruth C. "The Health and Social Functions of Black Midwives on the Texas Brazos Bottom, 1920–1985." *Rural Sociology* 56 (spring 1991): 89–105.

Scharff, Virginia. "'Else Surely We Shall All Hang Separately': The Politics of Western Women's History." *Pacific Historical Review* 61 (November 1992): 535–56.

———. "Feminism, Femininity, and Power: Nellie Tayloe Ross and the Woman Politician's Dilemma." *Frontiers* 15 (1995): 87–106.

Schwieder, Dorothy and Deborah Fink. "U.S. Prairie and Plains Women in the 1920s: A Comparison of Women, Family, and Environment." *Agricultural History* 73 (spring 1999): 183–200.

Segura, Denise. "Chicanas in White-Collar Jobs: 'You Have to Prove Yourself More.'" *Sociological Perspectives* 35 (1992): 163–82.

Sermon, Suzanne. "Early Women's Organizations in Boise." *Idaho Yesterdays* 41 (fall 1997): 20–26.

Sheehan, Nancy. "'Women Helping Women': The WCTU and the Foreign Population in the West, 1905–1930." *International Journal of Women's Studies* 6 (November/December 1983): 395–441.

Sillito, John R. "Women and the Socialist Party in Utah, 1900–1920." *Utah Historical Quarterly* 49 (summer 1981): 220–38.

Simpson, Caroline Chung. "'Out of an Obscure Place': Japanese War Brides and Cultural Pluralism in the 1950s." *Differences: A Journal of Feminist Cultural Studies* 10 (fall 1998): 47–81.

Simpson, Lee M. A. "Women, Real Estate, and Urban Growth: A Case Study of Two Generations of Women Property Owners in Redlands, California, 1880–1940." *California History* 76 (spring 1997): 24–43.

Skold, Karen Beck. "The Job He Left Behind: Women in the Shipyards During World War II." In *Women in Pacific Northwest History: An Anthology*, ed. Karen J. Blair. Seattle: University of Washington Press, 1988, 107–29.

Smith, Caron. "The Women's Land Army During World War II." *Kansas History* 14 (summer 1991): 82–88.

Spickard, Paul R. "Work and Hope: African American Women in Southern California during World War II." *Journal of the West* 32 (July 1993): 70–79.

Sturgis, Cynthia. "'How're You Gonna Keep 'Em Down on the Farm?': Rural Women and the Urban Model in Utah." *Agricultural History* 60 (spring 1986): 182–99.

Taylor, Sandra C. "Leaving the Concentration Camps: Japanese Americans and Resettlement in the Intermountain West." *Pacific Historical Review* 60 (May 1991): 169–94.

Trennert, Robert A. "Victorian Morality and the Supervision of Indian Women Working in Phoenix, 1906–1930." *Journal of Social History* 22 (fall 1988): 113–28.

Tzu-Chun Wu, Judy. "'Loveliest Daughter of Our Ancient Cathay!':
Presentations of Ethnic and Gender Identity in the Miss
Chinatown U.S.A. Beauty Pageant." *Journal of Social History* (fall
1997): 5–11.

Vargas, Zaragoa. "Tejana Radical: Emma Tenayuca and the San Antonio
Labor Movement During the Great Depression." *Pacific Historical
Review* 66 (November 1997): 553–80.

Vaughn-Roberson, Courtney Ann. "Having a Purpose in Life: Western
Women Teachers in the Twentieth Century." *Great Plains
Quarterly* 5 (spring 1985): 107–24.

———. "Sometimes Independent But Never Equal—Women Teachers,
1900–1950: The Oklahoma Example." *Pacific Historical Review* 53
(February 1984): 39–58.

Ward, Karen. "From Executive to Feminist: The Business Women's
Legislative Council of Los Angeles, 1927–1932." *Essays in
Economic and Business History* 74 (1989): 60–75.

Webb, George E. "A Woman's Place is in the Lab: Arizona's Women
Research Scientists, 1910–1950." *Journal of Arizona History* 34
(spring 1993): 45–64.

Weber, Devra Anne. "Raiz Fuerte: Oral History and Mexicana
Farmworkers." *Oral History Review* 17 (fall 1989): 47–62.

Weiler, Kathleen. "Women and Rural School Reform: California,
1900–1940." *History of Education Quarterly* 34 (spring 1991):
25–48.

Williams, Jean Calterone. "Domestic Violence and Poverty: The
Narratives of Homeless Women." *Frontiers* 19 (1998): 143–65.

Wimberly, Rosemary. "'The Ballot in the Hands of a Good Woman':
Margaret S. Roberts, Municipal Housekeeping, and Idaho
Partisan Politics, 1890–1952." *Idaho Yesterdays* 41 (fall 1997):
10–19.

———. "'Menaces to Society': Sex, Adultery, and Abortion Crimes of
Idaho Women Prisoners, 1900–1960." *Idaho Yesterdays* 41 (fall
1997): 27–36.

———. "Steps in a Subtle Revolution: Feminism, Politics and Social
Change in Idaho, 1967–1977." *Idaho Yesterdays* 41 (fall 1997):
27–36.

Zhao, Xiaojian, "Chinese American Women Defense Workers in World
War II," *California History* (summer 1996): 130–53.

DATE DUE
